BRITISH DIPLOMACY
1813-1815

BRITISH DIPLOMACY

1813-1815

SELECT DOCUMENTS DEALING WITH THE RECONSTRUCTION OF EUROPE

EDITED BY

C. K. WEBSTER, M.A.

PROFESSOR OF MODERN HISTORY IN THE UNIVERSITY OF LIVERPOOL
AUTHOR OF "THE CONGRESS OF VIENNA, 1814-1815," ETC.

LONDON
G. BELL AND SONS LTD.
1921

A

TO

M. le COMMANDANT M. H. WEIL

IN TOKEN OF

FRIENDSHIP AND ADMIRATION

PREFACE.

This book has been produced in response to requests from those interested in the subject with which it is concerned, and in particular from the Board of Studies in Modern History of Cambridge University. Present events have induced many to take a lively interest in the only European settlement which can at all compare in extent and importance with that of our own day. The period is, however, not one which is easily studied. The *Castlereagh Correspondence* and the *Wellington Supplementary Dispatches* contain a large quantity of information, but these works are often inaccessible to students. Moreover, much of their contents is unintelligible without reference to the unpublished material in the Record Office, while the absence of editing makes it difficult to understand their meaning. In many cases, for example, dispatches are wrongly dated, and thus the whole of their intention rendered obscure.

I have attempted, therefore, to make a selection of the most important dispatches and Memoranda of the period from the published or unpublished material available. Perhaps fifty or sixty thousand documents have been consulted for this purpose, and it is obvious that the task of selection was no easy one. My choice was governed mainly by the desire to confine attention to the main picture, and thus I have had rigorously to exclude correspondence on the details of the subordinate questions. There is little in this work, therefore, about the Spanish, Italian, Swedish, or Dutch affairs, except in so far as they influence the broad lines of the settlement. For the same reason I have had to exclude the negotiations with the United States at Ghent, interesting and important as they are, as being outside the principle events of the time.

In order to facilitate reference, each document has been given a number in Roman figures ; its source has also been stated. With a view to economising space I have abbreviated many of the documents, where necessary, enclosing in square brackets a short précis of the portion left out. The same process has been applied to the long Memoranda, a knowledge of whose

contents is necessary for the understanding of the diplomacy, but
which are often terribly prolix and involved. In this portion of
the work I was much assisted by my secretary, Miss E. Kidwell.
The dispatches have also been modernised in spelling and
punctuation in the manner of those previously printed.

I have endeavoured to confine the notes to the explanation of
facts and references which might assist the student to understand
the content of the dispatches, but, as about half the book is selected
from unpublished documents, I have occasionally allowed myself
the luxury of making observations, which I hope may be of some
use to scholars who may be interested in the new material which
is here printed. Some of it has been known in extract, and, in
particular, part of that concerned with the Congress of Vienna
was published as an appendix to an article in the Transactions
of the Royal Historical Society. I have not thought it necessary
to indicate where such well-known writers as Oncken, Fyffe, and
Professor Alison Phillips have referred to dispatches here published *in extenso*. My obligations to their works is, of course,
immense.

The *Introduction* is intended rather to suggest ideas to the
student than to provide him with information. The general
history of the period can be studied in the works of the writers
mentioned above, while I have myself attempted a survey of
the diplomacy of the time in my *Congress of Vienna*, and more
particularly with reference to Great Britain, in the forthcoming
Cambridge History of British Foreign Policy. It seemed, therefore, superfluous to include a narrative of events in this book.

I have to thank Professor H. W. C. Davis, Professor Holland
Rose, Mr. C. R. Cruttwell, and Mr. H. W. V. Temperley for
advice on various points, for which I am deeply grateful, and I
should like once more to record my appreciation of the kindness
of all at the Record Office, particularly Mr. Hall and Mr. Headlam.

I have throughout studiously avoided comparison with the
events of our own day. The period does, indeed, contain
lessons of the greatest importance to this generation, but it is
not the province of the historian, as such, to make the necessary
deductions.

LIVERPOOL,   C. K. W.
    August, 1921.

CONTENTS

CONTENTS

PART II. THE MAKING OF THE ALLIANCE AND THE FIRST PEACE OF PARIS, 1814.

CONTENTS

CONTENTS

PART III. THE CONGRESS OF VIENNA, 1814-15.

CONTENTS

CONTENTS

CONTENTS xxiii

NUMBER   PAGE

CCIX. CASTLEREAGH TO LIVERPOOL, July 29th, 1815   353
   Forwards a Russian Memorandum prepared
   in conjunction with the British Ministers.

CCX. CASTLEREAGH TO LIVERPOOL, Aug. 3rd, 1815   354
   Criticises the Austrian and Prussian Memoranda and forwards Wellington's views on the
   extent of the occupation.

CCXI. LIVERPOOL TO CASTLEREAGH, Aug. 3rd, 1815   355
   Encloses : *Observations on a Russian Paper
   mentioned by Lord Castlereagh.*

CCXII. WELLINGTON TO CASTLEREAGH, Aug. 11th, 1815   357
   States his views on the obligations and
   interests of the Allies and advocates temporary
   occupation.

CCXIII. LIVERPOOL TO CASTLEREAGH, Aug. 11th, 1815   359
   Doubts the wisdom of forbearance towards
   France.

CCXIV. CASTLEREAGH TO LIVERPOOL, Aug. 12th, 1815   360
   Reports his endeavours to convince the
   Allies of the necessity of reducing France to
   the limits of 1790, and of the policy of tem-
   porary occupation.
   Encloses : *Memorandum of Lord Castlereagh.*

CCXV. CASTLEREAGH TO LIVERPOOL, Aug. 17th, 1815   362
   Sums up the discussions and urges the wisdom
   of the policy of temporary occupation and
   reasonable indemnities.

CCXVI. LIVERPOOL TO CASTLEREAGH, Aug. 18th, 1815   367
   Criticises the Prussian demands but advises
   the acceptance of those of Austria.

CCXVII. LIVERPOOL TO CASTLEREAGH, Aug. 23rd, 1815   368
   Intimates the acquiescence of the Cabinet in
   his policy.

CCXVIII. CASTLEREAGH TO LIVERPOOL, Aug. 24th, 1815   370
   Urges the necessity of not asking the Allies
   to contribute to the expenses of Napoleon's
   captivity.

CCXIX. CASTLEREAGH TO LIVERPOOL, Aug. 24th, 1815   370
   Demands the consent of the Cabinet to his
   proposals.

CCXX. BATHURST TO CASTLEREAGH, Aug. 25th, 1815   371
   Points out that the new fortresses must be
   paid for by France and not by Great Britain.

CCXXI. LIVERPOOL TO CASTLEREAGH, Aug. 28th, 1815   372
   Promises the full support of the Cabinet for
   his policy.

CCXXII. WELLINGTON TO CASTLEREAGH, Aug. 31st, 1815   374
   Memorandum on the question of temporary
   occupation.

CCXXIII. CASTLEREAGH TO LIVERPOOL, Sept. 4th, 1815   375
   Comments on the extravagant demands of
   some of the Powers, and analyses their
   motives.

LIST OF ABBREVIATIONS
USED IN IDENTIFYING THE DOCUMENTS

The abbreviations in Italics in square brackets immediately after the number in Roman figures are as follows:

FOR THE FOREIGN OFFICE RECORDS AT THE RECORD OFFICE:

The letters *F.O.* followed by the Country or Series in question, e.g. *F.O. Russia* 83.

F.O. Cont. and *F.O. Cont. Arch.* refer to the two series of papers connected with the special missions of Castlereagh, Wellington, etc. The first contains the papers received in London and the drafts of those sent to the Continent, the second the papers received on the Continent and the drafts of those sent to London. The two series are largely, but by no means entirely, duplicate of one another.

FOR THE PUBLISHED WORKS:

C.C.—The Correspondence, Despatches and other Papers of the 2nd Marquess of Londonderry (Castlereagh) edited by his brother (Lord Stewart) Vols. VIII., IX., X., XI., London, 1851-3.

Gurwood—The Despatches of Field Marshal the Duke of Wellington, edited by Lieut.-Colonel Gurwood, London 1838.

W.S.D.—Supplementary Despatches, Correspondence and Memoranda of the Duke of Wellington edited by his son, Vols. VIII., IX., X., XI. London 1861-4.

INTRODUCTION

The period covered by the Documents brought together in this book extends for only 31 months, but it is one of the most important and dramatic in Modern History. The downfall of Napoleon and the reconstruction of Europe which followed the destruction of his Empire has deservedly attracted the attention of posterity, and never more so than to-day at the close of a conflict even more terrible and portentous. Round Napoleon himself a literature has grown which has analysed in the minutest detail every scrap of information which could throw light on his immense and versatile genius. Though not so much attention has been paid to the processes by which he was overthrown, yet in all countries the great upheaval of 1812–1815 has been much studied. No continental victory is more famous in this country than Waterloo, and the British, like the Germans, the Russians or the Spaniards, are apt to claim a special share in bringing about the downfall of the most successful soldier and statesman of modern Europe. History can only make very rough quantitative estimates, and to attempt to apportion the exact share of any one nation in a result that was due to the union of so many different forces is both ludicrous and unsatisfying. Nevertheless it should be both a duty and a pleasure to know something of events by which succeeding generations have been intimately affected, while the principles and methods which were used by British statesmen of a hundred years ago still have much to teach us to-day.

The study of foreign policy is never easy, and it becomes increasingly difficult in a period like that of 1813–15. The history of the Great Alliance of rulers and peoples which finally overthrew the Napoleonic Empire has not yet been fully written. A number of circumstances made it specially difficult to find out exactly what happened. Not only were a large number of different people directly concerned, but during most of this period the Sovereigns and their principal ministers were assembled together in one spot. At a time, therefore, when events were moving with unexampled rapidity, the most important decisions were often made after hurried interviews between the parties concerned and embodied in mere verbal agreements or promises. No one has a better claim to generalise on the diplomacy of this epoch than Metternich, who has laid down very clearly the special difficulties of the historian in the records which he compiled of his own share in these events :—

" By a coincidence which was not only singular at the time, but without example in the annals of history, the chief personages in the great drama found themselves together in the very same place. The Emperors of Austria and of Russia, the King of Prussia, and their three cabinets, were really never separated. The leader of the English cabinet had also generally been with his colleagues of Austria, Russia, and Prussia. At the Congress of Vienna most of the Princes who now form the German Confederation were also present at the negotiations. Since, therefore, the European potentates and their ministers were in the same place, the forms of diplomatic business had to adapt themselves to circumstances. The most difficult affairs, and the arrangements most complicated in their nature, were, so to speak, negotiated from one room to another ; no sending of couriers, no written negotiations, no medium between the Courts : all these things, so necessary in ordinary times, had disappeared. Many a business which under any other circumstances would have required a long time for arrangement was concluded in the course of a forenoon. This state of things had two results : the first and the happiest was the success of the vast undertakings ; the second, and it may be lamented, was this, that now the courts concerned are without any written accounts of the course of the most important negotiations." [1]

But Metternich had to confess that these conditions did not apply to all the countries concerned. " While asserting the fact," he added, " that the diplomatic archives of the courts most concerned contain no documents relating to some of the most important negotiations of the years 1813, 1814, and 1815, we must except those of England and France at the time of the Vienna Congress. Lord Castlereagh and the Plenipotentiaries of England and France constantly corresponded with their Governments." This is true, and, as Castlereagh was also with the Allied Sovereigns during the winter campaign of 1814 and the negotiation of the two peaces of Paris in 1814 and 1815, the remarks apply especially to the British Archives. Castlereagh also, unlike Talleyrand, was a member of the Alliance, indeed in a sense its founder, and the accounts which he forwarded to England are the most important record of these events that exists. Unlike those of Talleyrand and Metternich they are composed exclusively of letters, dispatches, and memoranda written at the time, and not of memoirs composed at leisure when causes and motives could be

[1] Metternich Memoirs. English Edition, I., 172.

adduced to suit the historical events. Both Metternich and Talleyrand were concerned to preserve the good opinion of posterity : there is no record that Castlereagh ever worried very much about the verdict of History on his own personality. The documents which he left behind him were intended to serve the purpose of the moment, and there was no attempt to do more than to give to his colleagues an account (sometimes, unfortunately, of a very general character) of the negotiations with which he was concerned, or to transmit to his subordinates the information and instructions which events rendered necessary. Not all his letters and dispatches have come down to us, but in the four or five hundred volumes at the Record Office and in the private collections of the Londonderry and Wellington papers there is a fairly complete account of these momentous years. Wellington himself played a large part in diplomacy, as well as in strategy. His Embassy at Paris was of great importance ; he succeeded Castlereagh at the Congress of Vienna and by the time of Napoleon's return from Elba he held a unique position in the council of the Alliance which the events of the Hundred Days were to make even more important. For the years 1814–15, therefore, the dispatches quoted in this book are mainly the correspondence of Castlereagh and Wellington with the British Cabinet and one another.

In the year 1813 British Diplomacy played a less important part. Until the end of the year the dispatches took nearly a month to reach their destination, and it was thus impossible for Castlereagh to keep pace with the rapidly changing situation on the Continent. Nevertheless, the foundation of the Quadruple Alliance was laid in this year and the policy of the subsequent period can scarcely be fully understood without some knowledge of its origin. In the correspondence of Castlereagh with Cathcart, Stewart and Aberdeen, the British Ambassadors to the Russian, Prussian, and Austrian Courts, there is a fairly complete record of the hopes and fears of the British policy, though they were only partially informed of the transactions between the three Continental Powers.

The first necessity in the study of a collection of documents such as is contained in this book is to know the relations that exist between the writers. The position which the Foreign

Minister held in the Cabinet, and especially his relations with the Prime Minister, are of fundamental importance, whatever period of Modern History is being studied. It is also necessary to know how far the Foreign Minister was inclined to trust his subordinates and the character and achievements of each of these are factors in determining the value of the reports for which they are responsible. The student may determine many of these points for himself by an intelligent study of the documents themselves. The commanding position which Castlereagh held in the Cabinet, the very tentative way in which the Prime Minister attempted to influence his work, the enormous responsibility he was prepared to take upon himself at moments of crisis, are clearly indicated on every page of his dispatches. His trust in Wellington and the latter's confidence in him are also easily discerned. The relations of Castlereagh to Alexander, Metternich, Hardenberg, and Talleyrand are also defined by Castlereagh himself in the course of his correspondence. Nevertheless it may be of some assistance to point out some of the circumstances which determine the scope and value of the records from which this selection is made and to indicate the principles and methods on which Castlereagh's policy appears to have been founded.

Castlereagh had been brought into the Perceval Cabinet in March, 1812. He succeeded Wellesley, whose wayward genius had proved to be peculiarly unsuited to the difficulties of the post of Foreign Secretary, and whose energy and ability had both failed him. Liverpool, on his accession to the Premiership in June, 1812, after the assassination of Perceval, undoubtedly preferred Canning, and indeed made a great effort to get him into the Ministry as Foreign Secretary. Castlereagh was prepared to surrender this post, if he kept the lead of the House. But Canning's own vanity and the ill-advised flattery of his friends prevented this combination, and Castlereagh was therefore left with the conduct of Foreign Affairs as well as the lead of the House of Commons. Only two other of his colleagues were commoners and these had neither ability nor reputation. As a result, therefore, Castlereagh almost immediately became the leading member of the Government ; and, down to his death in 1822, he was more responsible for its decisions than any other member of it. His influence was consolidated by the energy and success with which he conducted his own special department and managed the general policy of the Government in the Commons. He was a first-class party manager, and his dignity, good manners, and debating skill gave him an almost complete ascendency over the House. The scurrility of writers like Creevey and the jealousy of rivals like Brougham have perpetuated a tradition that Castlereagh was an almost unintelligible speaker and that his position rested entirely on a corrupt and subservient House of Commons. Nothing could be further from the truth. Though he had none of Canning's power of oratory, yet Castlereagh was a clear and effective speaker, and, as Canning himself has confessed, he was far the abler at an impromptu, however inferior in a set speech. This power of argumentative debate was to serve him in good stead in his round table conferences in these years. He had, moreover, a considerable experience of Foreign Affairs, and Pitt regarded him as one of his most promising pupils. As a member of the Cabinet and Secretary of State for War in 1804-6 he had played an important part in determining Pitt's attitude and, above all, made himself thoroughly conversant with Pitt's ideas on the reconstruction of Europe. His later career as Secretary of State for War had been a chequered one, and marred by the failure of the Walcheren expedition. Nevertheless, he had learnt something of the limitations that strategy lays down for politics, and in that period began his association with Wellington which was to prove of such enormous importance in the succeeding years.

British Foreign policy at this period was determined mainly by Castlereagh himself. He had, indeed, to carry with him a Cabinet which contained, besides the Prime Minister himself, such stalwarts as Eldon and Harrowby, and an energetic War Minister in Bathurst. Foreign Affairs were, however, but little known to most of them and they never obtained a real comprehension of the events and problems of their time. The acquisition of Colonies, the protection of the Sea Power and the " Maritime rights " of their own country were objects which they could understand and had at heart. They had, too, a passionate hatred of Napoleon, which they shared with most of their countrymen. But they were not much concerned with the construction of a new Europe. Foreign policy was therefore left to Liverpool and Bathurst, who had both held the office of Foreign Minister, and it is to these two that Castlereagh mainly addresses himself. His instructions in 1814 were indeed debated with a full Cabinet, and in the question of the first Restoration of the Bourbons and the policy to be pursued after Waterloo the whole Cabinet appears to have shewn a lively interest. But even so important a point as the ratification of the Treaty of January 3rd, 1815, was decided without a full Cabinet being summoned, and, if Liverpool was in agreement, Castlereagh seems to have been quite sure of his ground. Nor did the Prime Minister generally do more than give advice, leaving for the most part the final decisions to Castlereagh himself. Such a policy was, indeed, almost a necessity. When Parliament was not sitting the Prime Minister was generally at Bath and his colleagues scattered about in their country seats. The exigencies of their offices kept Bathurst and Melville in London, but the others could transact necessary business at a distance ; and even Castlereagh himself wrote many of his dispatches from Cray Farm or other country seats following the practice of his time, when a Minister and his private secretaries made their office the place that best suited their personal predilections. When the House was sitting, matters were rather different ; but even then, when Castlereagh was on the Continent, the safest course was to profess ignorance or the necessity of delay until the Foreign Minister returned. Only on points like the Slave Trade on which there was an organised body of public opinion of which the Whigs could take advantage, did the Ministry find it necessary to insist on something being done.

The Opposition was, indeed, like all oppositions when the Ministry is conducting, or has just concluded a successful war, pitifully weak. Apart from the hostility of the Prince Regent and the corruption of the Commons, the Whigs were suffering from the fact that the Tories had brought to a triumphant conclusion the most deadly conflict in which the country had ever been engaged. The Opposition had sometimes been unable to resist the temptation of making party capital out of the misfortunes of the previous years, and their ill-omened prophecies could now be used with deadly effect against them. In the final crisis in 1814 they behaved with commendable restraint and the first peace of Paris was welcomed and approved by them. But during the Congress of Vienna and the Hundred Days, they made an attempt to advocate principles which had been forgotten under the stress of the conflict, with as much success as such efforts usually attain. The people of this country were wildly delighted with a period of victory after twenty years of warfare. They knew little of the details of Foreign policy. Their fierce hatred of the French and especially of " Boney " was now given full play, and their only complaint was that the terms inflicted on France were not half hard enough. To a few educated people the questions of Poland, Saxony or Italy appealed, but information was hard to obtain and matters were decided before they knew much about them. Only on the question of the Slave Trade, which the abundant energy and skilful propaganda of Clarkson, Wilberforce, Macaulay, and others had made a really popular subject, was there any considerable feeling.

Neither his colleagues, the Opposition, nor public opinion, were therefore likely to affect Castlereagh very much. Over almost all his subordinates, also, he had complete control, and, with the all-important exception of Wellington, they had little influence on his policy. Several of the most important of them were not professional diplomatists but relations or friends of the Tory Ministers. Others were soldiers who had the virtues and defects of their profession. In this collection it is three especially whose personalities are of importance since they were accredited to the three other members of the Great Alliance, and in the critical year 1813 Castlereagh could only attempt to put his plans into action with their aid. These three, the Earl of Cathcart, Sir Charles Stewart, and the Earl of Aberdeen, were none of them diplomatists by profession. Cathcart was an eminent soldier who had commanded the British forces at Copenhagen in 1807. He had been attached to the Russian headquarters during the year 1812, and he remained as Ambassador throughout this period. He was a rather stupid man who lacked both insight and energy and never grasped the problems with which he was confronted. Alexander and his ministers found him complacent and ignored him or used him as they chose. Nevertheless his military profession and a decorous exterior made him a favourite of the Tsar and he could sometimes get concessions from Alexander when no one else could approach him. Sir Robert Wilson, a wonderfully brave and foolish soldier, was also attached to Russian headquarters in 1812 and 1813 in an unofficial position, but Cathcart never trusted him, and with reason, for he was constantly opposing the policy of his Government.

Stewart, Castlereagh's half-brother, was much more energetic and much less discreet than Cathcart. He had been a dashing cavalry leader, but Wellington distrusted his capacity for the more extended command which he desired. Castlereagh therefore gave him the Mission to the Prussian Court in 1813, and he played a big part in all the events of these years, being subsequently Ambassador at Vienna and a Plenipotentiary at the Congress, where his vanity and pomp were a bye-word. Nevertheless, he was generally at the right place at the critical moment, and his zeal and energy, as well as his intimate connection with the Foreign Minister, who had a great affection for him, made him a conspicuous figure in these years. George Jackson, who accompanied him as his principal subordinate, had acted in the same capacity to his brother, F. J. Jackson, in 1806. He was a zealous and well-intentioned official, but had not much influence.

Aberdeen was a man of quite a different stamp and consorted ill with his colleagues. The future Foreign Minister and Premier was then only 29 years of age and had rather reluctantly accepted his diplomatic mission which had been earnestly pressed by Liverpool and Castlereagh on the ward of Pitt. He was a shy and inexperienced man, and it must be confessed fell a victim to Metternich's wiles. His honesty and desire for peace made him an awkward colleague in that age, and perhaps all were as relieved as he certainly was himself when he refused to continue after the first Peace of Paris. The mistakes and rivalries of these three Ambassadors and their laborious and utterly inadequate attempts to carry out Castlereagh's instructions in 1813 furnish the theme of Part I. of this collection. After that they drop out of the picture, for in 1814 and 1815 Castlereagh was himself with the Alliance during most of the time and in his presence his subordinates played no independent part.

More useful to Castlereagh than any of these three was the Earl of Clancarty, Minister at the Hague in 1813–1814 and Castlereagh's principal subordinate at the Congress of Vienna, where he was left as First Plenipotentiary after the departure of Wellington. Clancarty was a subordinate member of the Ministry and a devoted admirer of Castlereagh. His outlook was a very limited one, but he had industry, self-confidence, and administrative capacity, and played a really important part at the Vienna Congress. He enjoyed the full confidence of his chief and worked throughout this period with unexampled diligence and on the whole with success.

Another personage of very considerable importance in these years was Count Münster, who represented the Prince Regent as ruler of Hanover in all the conferences of the time. His influence on Castlereagh was considerable, since he had a great knowledge of men and events and possessed the full confidence of the Prince Regent. In purely German affairs he determined to a large extent the course of British policy, and his advice undoubtedly carried weight in other matters. But though Castlereagh had to take Hanoverian interests into account, he kept them completely subordinate to British policy and sacrificed them ruthlessly to larger issues. Münster's chief role, indeed, appears to have been to supply information, of which he had always an ample supply, for he was a member of the inner circle of European diplomatists.

Castlereagh had other important subordinates, but as they were stationed at minor Courts their correspondence is not included in this collection. Of these, Sir Henry Wellesley managed with a fine restraint and immense prestige the complicated relations between the British and the Spanish Junta and subsequently the restored Spanish King. Lord William Bentinck, a violent Whig, combined a military and diplomatic command in Sicily, which island he really governed. He was a man of ideas, and these bore little relation to the policy of the Ministry which he was serving. They included the freeing of Italy from the foreigner and the erection of Sicily, where in 1812 a Constitution had been established, into a British protectorate, which was to be a model for the peoples of Europe. Castlereagh had perforce to tolerate these extravagances in 1813 and 1814, but he prevented them from interfering in his own policy which he had inherited from Pitt, namely, to exclude French influence from the Peninsula by substituting Austrian in its stead. Edward Thornton had the difficult task of looking after the ambitious and untrustworthy

B

Bernadotte, who had hopes of succeeding Napoleon on the throne of France. He was a man of but moderate parts and was fooled by the intriguing Charles Jean in 1814, but it is doubtful whether any one else could have done better. Amongst other Ministers may be mentioned Stratford Canning, British representative in Switzerland, whose affairs he helped to arrange at the Vienna Congress, just then at the threshold of his great career, though he had already concluded the Peace of Bucharest in 1812 ; his successor at Constantinople, Sir Robert Liston, a weak and feeble minister ; Lord Beresford, who practically controlled Portuguese policy, and Sir Charles Stuart, an energetic and capable man who succeeded Wellington at Paris, but whom Castlereagh did not trust very far.

Mention should also be made of Castlereagh's permanent staff, William Hamilton and Edward Cooke, the Under Secretaries of State, the latter accompanying Castlereagh to Vienna and corresponding directly with Liverpool, and the discreet and able private secretary, Joseph Planta, who accompanied his master in most of his journeys.

These were Castlereagh's principal instruments, not a very brilliant, but on the whole a zealous and trustworthy set of men. With the exception of Bentinck and Sir Robert Wilson, Castlereagh could rely on their loyalty, and most of them were Tories like himself. If they threw an immense burden on him personally, his method of work was to rely on himself rather than to delegate affairs to others. Only Wellington, whose services as a diplomatist were invaluable to him, had in any way a policy of his own, and even with him Castlereagh was the dominating mind. The Foreign policy of Great Britain was therefore imagined, inspired, and largely carried out by the Foreign Minister himself.

This almost complete control of Foreign policy was essential to Castlereagh, if he was to meet on anything like equal terms the Sovereigns and statesmen of the Alliance. Of these he had naturally but little knowledge when he took over his charge and his policy in 1813 betrays the fact that he knew little of the men who were controlling events on the Continent. England had been in a sense isolated for many years, and personalities like Metternich and Hardenberg were quite unknown to most of her statesmen. Alexander had, indeed, been the principal founder to the Third

Coalition, but since then the peace of Tilsit had intervened and the suspicions which Pitt had always felt concerning Russia—the main inspiration of the Armed Neutrality—had been inherited by his disciples and especially by Castlereagh. The Austrian Mediation was also viewed with deep distrust in England, and Metternich was regarded as the founder of the Hapsburg connection with Napoleon. The resentment felt at Prussia's policy towards Hanover in 1805-6 was still alive and entered into the relations of these years. Throughout the year 1813, therefore, Castlereagh was dealing at a distance with men whom he had some reason to distrust, and it must be admitted that his Ambassadors were none of them sufficiently able to fathom the motives by which the three great Powers were animated or to prevent agreements being made by which British interests might possibly be gravely compromised. Yet on the whole Castlereagh's policy was one of trust and confidence. He had, as is seen in the dispatches, a plan of welding the Alliance more closely together and constantly urged closer co-operation, more courage in the face of the enemy, and greater exertions on the part of all.

The Armistice, the Conference at Prague, and above all, the " Frankfort Proposals," were none of them relished in London, and British statesmen thought that they had a legitimate grievance in the fact that their Allies neglected to give British commitments to the Spaniards a due place in the propositions which were made to Napoleon at various times. The methods by which Metternich procured Aberdeen's adherence to the Frankfort proposals not only caused grave misgivings to the British Cabinet but also brought the three British Ambassadors to the verge of an open quarrel. Castlereagh found it impossible to obtain a due influence over these events from London, and it was this fact that made the Cabinet send the Foreign Minister himself to the Allied headquarters. During 1814-1815, therefore, Castlereagh carried out his own policy and negotiated in person.

The personal intervention of the Foreign Secretary was of profound importance in Continental politics. By months of close and constant intercourse Castlereagh came to know intimately all the principal Continental personalities and to obtain a knowledge of men and affairs which no correspondence, however skilfully conducted, could have produced. It gave him a point of view which his colleagues never shared—a wider outlook and a less rigorous insistence on a national policy. The idea of an Alliance (the Alliance which subsequently developed into the " Congress System ") had been adumbrated in the State Paper of 1805 and put forward by Castlereagh in 1813, yet his zeal for some new form of Continental diplomacy and his conviction that only by round table conferences could Continental problems be adequately solved, are undoubtedly mainly a result of his experiences in 1814-15.

It was in this period also that the close personal relations between Castlereagh and Metternich were begun. Metternich's temperament was undoubtedly the most congenial to Castlereagh of all those with whom he had to deal. The Austrian minister stood out as a cool and practical statesman, especially when compared with the vacillating and mysterious Alexander and the sluggish and rapidly ageing Hardenberg. " He is charged with more faults than belong to him," wrote Castlereagh after his first interviews in 1814, " but he has his full share, mixed up, however, with considerable means for carrying forward the machine, more than any other person I have met with at headquarters."[1] The dispatches of 1814, on the other hand, shew how antipathetic to Castlereagh were Alexander's emotional outbursts, and though he was from the first allowed by the Tsar a frankness of statement of which he availed himself on many occasions, yet there was always the difficulty of dealing with a Sovereign in person. Until the visit of the Sovereigns to London in June, 1814, Alexander was, however, far more popular with the Prime Minister (who always disliked Metternich) and the Cabinet than the Austrians. But his mistaken and even ridiculous behaviour during this visit mortally offended the Prince Regent, while his attempts to establish close relations with the Whigs alienated the sympathies of the Tory cabinet. Henceforth Alexander was distrusted, and his attitude at the Congress of Vienna increased these suspicions. This was one reason why Castlereagh found it so hard to win his Cabinet over to his policy in the autumn of 1815, when events made it necessary for him to work with Alexander rather than with Metternich.

In spite of all the inevitable friction between the Allies during

[1] *Infra* p. 160.

the progress of the reconstruction of Europe, there can be no doubt, however, as to the commanding influence which Castlereagh obtained on the councils of the Alliance. There were, indeed, factors in the situation which gave him an irresistible authority if he cared to exercise it. He was the paymaster of the coalition and the Continental Powers were all of them almost bankrupt. They relied, too, on Great Britain for much *materiel* of war, as well as for the manufactured goods of which they had been deprived so long. In spite of the American War the colonial and maritime supremacy of the British Empire was overwhelming. In the year 1813, moreover, by the victory of Vittoria, Wellington had at last enabled Great Britain to assume a position as a military as well as a naval Power.

These were great advantages. Nevertheless, in 1814, Castlereagh was at the headquarters of a vast army in which were no British troops. The political decisions had to be enforced at the expense of the armies of his Allies, who, in spite of their immense preponderance in numbers, were still daunted by the prestige of Napoleon and the heroism of his handful of young conscripts. Moreover, when Castlereagh arrived on the Continent the Allies were hopelessly at variance. Sovereigns, statesmen, and soldiers were full of suspicion, and though a great and elaborate campaign had been planned, its ends were not defined, and its principles had not been accepted by all the Allied armies. It was Castlereagh who infused energy and purpose into the halting counsels of the Alliance and at last succeeded in obtaining the signature of a common instrument which bound them together to resist French aggression for twenty years. Even as it was, Castlereagh failed to settle the future disposition of the conquered territories before the peace with France was signed, as his instructions and dispatches clearly shew was his intention. At the Congress of Vienna he had therefore once more to take up the rôle of conciliator, and it was his energy and initiative that finally produced the compromises accepted by the Great Powers. After Napoleon's defeat in 1815 Castlereagh had the prestige of Waterloo and the authority of Wellington to aid him, but it was the Foreign Minister's diplomacy that induced the Germans and Austrians, as well as his own Cabinet, to shew moderation at the moment of victory. In spite of many checks and failures the settlement of 1814-15 was, on the whole, the work of Castlereagh more than of any other single person, not only as regards the principles to be applied but in the choice of expedients by which the principles were translated into political acts.

Castlereagh did not invent, but inherited from Pitt, the principles upon which his actions were based. In the first place he had to insist upon the special interests of Great Britain, her maritime and colonial rights. The maritime rights were naturally regarded with almost as much hostility by the Allies and especially by Russia, as by France. The unyielding nature of British statesmen on this point had, however, been demonstrated by the fact that even at the height of the struggle with Napoleon Great Britain had not shrunk from a war with the United States in order to preserve them in their most vigorous and brutal form. It is probable, indeed, that if Castlereagh had entered into office a little earlier he might have avoided this futile and unnecessary struggle, but once engaged, he found it impossible to surrender any of the rights which Britain claimed to exercise as a belligerent Power. Still less, therefore, could the subject be admitted as one liable to be discussed by the European Powers, and, in spite of an ingenious attempt on the part of Napoleon, Castlereagh easily succeeded in maintaining this point of view intact throughout all his negotiations.

On colonial questions Castlereagh was able to shew more moderation. All the French, Dutch, and Danish colonies were in British hands. The power of the British Empire had grown so much during the course of the struggle that there was no great desire to retain these conquests in order to increase possession. But it was claimed that some were necessary to the strategic safety of the British Empire and especially of the route to India. These, among which were included not only Malta, but the Cape, the Cabinet insisted on retaining. The rest were placed at Castlereagh's disposal, and were one of the means by which he exercised his influence in the negotiations between the Allies and France. He endeavoured in fact to use them to obtain the kind of reconstruction which he thought best. Nevertheless, the renunciation of the rich Dutch colonial Empire in the East Indies was a piece of disinterested statesmanship which astounded some contemporaries.

Lastly, as a special British interest Castlereagh had to advocate at every opportunity the abolition of the Slave Trade. This duty gave him more trouble than almost any other, since he had to try and impose it on unwilling and suspicious Allies, as well as on France. It cannot be doubted that it was only the strong and persistent pressure of public opinion in England that made him devote so much time and energy to this subject in the midst of other urgent and pressing claims. Nevertheless he showed a practical wisdom in endeavouring to set up machinery by which abolition might be made into a reality when the principle was obtained, and though Spain and Portugal were not won over completely during this period, the total abolition of the Slave Trade was practically secured.

In all these matters Castlereagh was merely expressing the views of his Cabinet and countrymen. It was in his general attitude towards European problems that he showed his difference from his colleagues. He had himself as deep an interest in the reconstruction of Europe as he had in purely British interests, but it was only with difficulty that he persuaded his ill-informed and insular colleagues to agree with him on these former questions. He did indeed share with them an almost complete unconsciousness of the strength of the national forces which had been called into new life by the French Revolution and the Napoleonic system. The aspirations of Poles, Italians, or Germans left him unmoved. He thought, as almost all the men of action of his time thought, in the terms of the Eighteenth Century. He was, indeed, not unaware that the last struggle against Napoleon was something different from all those that had preceded it. The importance of awakening " national sentiment " was continually stressed by him in his dispatches during the year 1813. But he never encouraged the expression of these sentiments in the new Europe, or he was content at least to subordinate them to strategic exigencies or the claims of Allied dynasties.

His main object was to establish a Balance of Power, or, as he generally phrases it, " a just equilibrium " in Europe. This he announced to his Allies, was his fixed purpose, and to it he was prepared to subordinate all minor points. It was France who had overthrown the Balance of Power, and therefore it was against France that a balance must first be constructed, though Castlereagh was also concerned with the growth of the power of Russia. The system which he desired for this purpose he inherited from his master, Pitt. As he confesses, it was on the State Paper of 1805, which he had himself helped to prepare, that he founded his policy. To build up Austria and Prussia once more into powerful States and thus create a strong central Europe was the essence of his statesmanship, as it had been of Pitt's. The dominance of Prussia in North Germany and on the Rhine, and the supremacy of Austria in Italy may be traced to the same source, and it will be seen from the dispatches how much these solutions owed to Castlereagh's consistent and powerful advocacy. There were, of course, differences in detail owing to lapse of years, but it is surprising how many of Pitt's schemes Castlereagh was able to put into practice. Even the creation of the Netherlands can be seen in Pitt's " Barrier," and the placing of the line of fortresses along the Rhine in the hands of the two great German Powers, was partially carried out. The dangers and disadvantages of such a policy are stated in their most convincing form in the speech of Mackintosh, which is given in the Appendix. Nevertheless it may be doubted if any other solution was possible at the time, especially as it combined with security a means of rewarding those Powers to whose exertions the fall of Napoleon was ultimately due. The speech in which Castlereagh defends his policy, if not so eloquent nor idealistic as his opponent's, yet is convincing in its sincerity and common sense.

Nor did Castlereagh's wish to safeguard the peace of Europe stop at the Balance of Power. In Pitt's paper appears the device of a special guarantee of the reconstructed Europe which he adopted from a suggestion made to him by Alexander through Novossiltzov. This also Castlereagh attempted to put into practical shape in these years. The expedient of the special Treaty, by which the Powers guaranteed for twenty years the new order of things against French attack, appears also to have come to him from this source, and it was certainly the basis of the abortive attempt to obtain a special guarantee by all the Powers of the Vienna settlement. If the main result was the Quadruple Alliance which merely guarded against the special dangers from France, that was in itself a great achievement, and the dispatches show how difficult it was to obtain until Castlereagh conducted the negotiation in person.

But even more important was the new system of diplomacy which arose in these years, and of which to the end of his life Castlereagh was the ardent and consistent defender. The period was an especially important one in the development of new diplomatic forms. Many of the old absurdities of diplomatic intercourse had been overthrown by the French Revolution and Napoleon. The statesmen of the Congress of Vienna were no longer hampered by absurd disputes as to precedence and form. The frankness of Alexander and the common sense of Metternich and Castlereagh produced an atmosphere of practical business relations in which new expedients were easily adopted. They developed, for example, a new system of attaching Memoranda to the Protocols or records of their formal conferences which has persisted ever since. But most important of all was the fact that for almost two years the Sovereigns and leading statesmen of the Great Powers were in close personal contact with one another. The coalition only obtained some sort of political and strategic direction by the institution at headquarters of a Supreme Council by which the great questions at issue could be decided. There affairs were discussed in intimate and confidential interviews before they were brought to a formal conference. The same policy was pursued at the Congress of Vienna and thus grew up a system of Diplomacy by Conference, which Castlereagh, who firmly believed in it, desired to make permanent. How different his position was in 1814 and 1815, when he was a member of such a Conference, from that which he held in 1813, when he vainly tried to get his views adopted through the medium of a number of Ambassadors ! It was his experience which converted Castlereagh to what has since been called the Congress System. " If the Councils of the Sovereigns had not been brought together," he said in the House in 1816, " if they had been forced to look at their special interests through that cloud of prejudice and uncertainty which must always intervene when events are viewed at a distance . . . he was sure the councils of Europe would have been disturbed to such an extent by doubts and misapprehensions that those great exertions whose successful issue was now before the world, would never have been made." While Alexander's unstable and emotional nature was busy with schemes like the Holy Alliance, Castlereagh was anxious that some permanent system of round table conferences should be established, and it was, in fact, due to him that in the revision of the Treaty of Alliance in 1815 such special conferences were made part of the European system. It was thus that the " Congress System " grew up, the precursor of the so-called " Concert of Europe," and in a sense Castlereagh may be considered its founder. The prejudices and ignorance of his countrymen, and the ill-advised attempts in later years of Metternich and Alexander to distort its purpose, prevented him doing more than adumbrate such a scheme. So long, indeed, as it depended on the personalities of one or two statesmen who had special experience and remained without support of public opinion, it was foredoomed to failure. Nevertheless Castlereagh is entitled to the credit of being the first statesman to devise a practical expedient by which international affairs might be regulated by a European Council.

Closely connected with this development is the evolution of the special rights and privileges of the Great Powers which began at this time. The institution of a European Conference made it necessary to determine who should compose it, and as a result it was found that the four Great Powers of the Alliance could alone conveniently share the responsibility, since they alone had the resources necessary to enforce its decisions. The development of European armies as a result of wars of the Revolution and the new methods of conscription and *levées en masse* had, indeed, made so great a difference in power between large and small countries that no other result was possible. But it was only gradually and partially that the fact was recognised, and there was at the outset of 1814 no general consent as to who exactly the Great Powers were. In Castlereagh's Treaty of Alliance, Sweden and possibly Spain were originally intended to have the same rights as the other Powers. It was only when the obligations to be incurred were examined that it became apparent that they could only be assumed by the Four. Thus inevitably these obtained a position which was strengthened by the trend of affairs at the Congress of Vienna. The smaller Powers naturally protested against the privileged position of the great, but their protests were unavailing, since they had no means of enforcing them. Castlereagh's attitude throughout was one of conciliation. He recognised that efficiency could only be obtained by confining the direction of the European Conference to the Great Powers.

At the same time he was anxious that they should aim at influence rather than authority over their smaller neighbours. The subject was, of course, to be one of great importance during the next few years, when the question of the exact rights of the Great Powers in Europe became one of the main causes of the failure of the " Congress System."

Specially interesting is it also to trace Castlereagh's attitude towards the evolution of constitutional liberty in Europe. In this matter he showed himself the most unbending of Tories and did not scruple to use his influence against any concession of popular rights when he could do so without risk of exposure in Parliament. His attitude towards the restoration of the Bourbons in 1814 follows very closely that laid down in Pitt's paper of 1805. He desired the complete overthrow of Napoleon as much as any of his colleagues, but he was doubtful of its expediency. At any rate, he wished most scrupulously to avoid any appearance of forcing the old dynasty on an unwilling France. It must be confessed that he managed that thorny question which threatened to wreck the Alliance in 1814 with much address. The *Charte* was, however, the work of Alexander and Talleyrand, and Castlereagh was as little pleased with it as Metternich himself. Towards the other constitutional experiments in Europe he shewed himself uniformly hostile. Bentinck's wild and doctrinaire policy in Italy did indeed need restraint to prevent it from endangering the Alliance at a critical moment. But Castlereagh, in his zeal for Austrian interests in Italy, did not scruple to support Metternich's policy of preventing liberal ideas from obtaining any recognition at all. His attitude towards the Spanish Cortes betrayed the same dislike of constitutional experiments. Neither this policy nor his very dubious conduct in the negotiations with Murat could be avowed, and he was forced at times into statements which lacked both candour and truth. The new constitutions were admittedly ill adapted to the conditions of the countries in which they had been established, but Castlereagh's hostility appears to have gone beyond the form to the principle. At any rate he was prepared to sacrifice them completely to the diplomatic advantages of the Austrian connection.

Such principles Castlereagh advocated consistently and on the whole with remarkable success during these years. As a British minister he was, of course, in a very strong position diplomatically, for Great Britain was less exhausted than any continental country. Moreover his Allies for the most part were not directly interested in the special objects of British policy and were perfectly ready to concede them in return for British support. But Castlereagh also obtained an influence over Continental problems which few British statesmen have possessed. His personality was indeed peculiarly suited to the position which he wished to occupy. He had great dignity, charm of manner, and, above all, moral courage. Moreover, his mind was sufficiently agile to adapt his schemes to the shifting circumstances of the moment. He was not an able writer and his dispatches, as this volume reveals, were full of long and involved sentences. Nevertheless, their purpose is generally abundantly clear, and, if they lack grace and point, they marshall the arguments with force and sometimes with very skilful dialectic. Nor was Castlereagh unable to employ irony and sarcasm when the occasion merited it. But on the whole he avoided all such methods. He was as expert at disarming his opponents as moderating the pretensions of his friends, and his aim was always conciliation and compromise. He undoubtedly possessed to a marked degree that indefinable quality of power which is called " personality," which gave his words more weight than they intrinsically possessed. It was thus at the council table and especially at the informal conferences that he excelled rather than in the exchange of notes and memoranda. His manner was sufficiently intimidating without being provocative, and he was able to adapt it to the various personages with whom he came in contact. That he was perhaps too tortuous on occasion, too anxious to obtain a result, whatever the means, sometimes deliberately deceptive in order to accommodate his secret designs to his avowed and actual policy, must be allowed. But it must be remembered that he had to deal with diplomatists as skilful and supple-minded as Metternich and Talleyrand, and he may claim that at any rate they rarely deceived him. Alexander's emotional and vague idealism was also especially repugnant to Castlereagh since it retarded rather than assisted the success of the expedients which his own cautious and intensely practical mind devised for the needs of the time.

It must be remembered also that Castlereagh never obtained the support of an enlightened public opinion for the wisest parts of his policy. His countrymen were not interested in these

problems on which he rightly saw that the peace of the world,
and thus their own interests, ultimately depended. The Whigs
who championed the principles of nationality and constitutional liberty were unwise and doctrinaire critics when their
practical application came to be discussed. As Lord Salisbury
pointed out in his essay sixty years ago, if they had had
their way, the union of Italy and Germany would have
been made harder to attain in subsequent years. Even more did
Castlereagh stand alone in his attempt to substitute discussion
and agreement for force in International affairs. In this matter
he remained in practical isolation in his own country. The liberals
and idealists refused to associate themselves with the reactionary
statesmen of the restored monarchies. The Tories were content
to consider merely the selfish interests of the moment. It was
Castlereagh alone who secured a trial of the system of Conferences.
In such circumstances he could only lay down the vaguest of
formulæ and he had no appeal to any body of public opinion in
this country. The system depended merely on his own personal
position in the councils of his country and his Allies, and was
bound to die with him. His diplomatic skill and ceaseless energy
therefore merely availed to construct a new Europe which bore
within itself the seeds of its own dissolution.

PART I

THE PREPARATION OF THE ALLIANCE, 1813

PART I.

THE PREPARATION OF THE ALLIANCE 1813.

(i.)—*Correspondence of Viscount Cathcart, April to December,* 1813.

I. [*C. C. VIII.* 355.]

CASTLEREAGH TO CATHCART.

Foreign Office, April 8th, 1813.

I hope my official despatches will furnish you and my Brother with the means of coming to a satisfactory arrangement with the two Allied Courts ; and that they will be disposed to do justice to our exertions in their support. The few additional observations which occur, I shall throw into a private letter, which you will consider as addressed to you both. . . .

The political arrangement of Europe, in a larger sense, is more difficult at this early moment to decide on. So much depends on events, that it is perhaps better not to be too prompt in encountering litigated questions. The main features we are agreed upon—that, to keep France in order, we require great masses— that Prussia, Austria, and Russia ought to be as great and powerful as they have ever been—and that the inferior States must be summoned to assist, or pay the forfeit of resistance. I see many inconveniences in premature conclusions, but we ought not to be unprepared.

As an outline to reason from, I send you, as a private communication, a despatch [1] on which the confederacy in 1805 was founded ; the Emperor of Russia probably has not this interesting document at head-quarters : (interesting it is to my recollection, as I well remember having more than one conversation with Mr. Pitt on its details, *before he wrote it*) some of the suggestions may now be inapplicable, but it is so masterly an outline for the restoration of Europe, that I should be glad your lordship would reduce it into distinct propositions, and learn the bearings of his Imperial Majesty's mind upon its contents. An unofficial communication of this nature between two Powers that have no partialities to indulge may prepare them the better to fulfil their duties at a future moment. . . .

[1] See Appendix I. The Reader should at once refer to this dispatch of the 19th January, 1805, which is the text of all the British diplomacy of the period.

II.   [*F. O. Russia* 83[1]]
CASTLEREAGH TO CATHCART (No. 12).
Foreign Office, [9th] April, 1813.

Your Lordship will receive enclosed a representation with an explanatory map, which has been presented by Count Münster,[2] relative to the interests of His Majesty's Hanoverian dominions.

The obvious inconvenience to which the Electoral Government must be exposed from the intervention of the bishoprick of Hildesheim, and the small territories of Minden and Ravensburg in the midst of the Hanoverian territory, makes the incorporation of these inconsiderable possessions of essential importance to the free and tranquil enjoyment of the ancient dominions of His Majesty in Germany. Your Lordship will represent these considerations without delay to the Emperor of Russia, and you will acquaint His Imperial Majesty that the British Government, as well from a sense of duty to His Majesty as from a grateful recollection both of the sufferings and services of his Hanoverian subjects in the common cause, cannot but feel the most lively interest that, in any general arrangement of the North of Germany, these claims should be attended to.

The Prince Regent, disclaiming all views of mere aggrandizement on the part of the Electorate, and limiting his pretensions solely to the territories above specified which are essential to the more convenient enjoyment of the antient patrimony of his family, relies with confidence on the friendly interposition of His Imperial Majesty for giving effect to these his limited and moderate views. His Royal Highness trusts that His Prussian Majesty will not feel less disposed to gratify his wishes with respect to an arrangement which is calculated to remove all future jealousies and misunderstandings between their respective states. With a view of giving effect to this object, your Lordship will propose in any treaty you may conclude with the Courts of St. Petersburgh and Berlin, that it should be stipulated in a secret article that these concessions shall be secured upon a peace to His Majesty in His Electoral character. You will also take care that the territories of Brunswick shall be understood and declared to be comprehended in what is referred to in the secret article of the Treaty of Kalisch as the " antient possessions of the House of Hanover."

[1] Printed in Oncken.   *Oesterreich und Preussen im Befreiungskriege* II. 691. The date is not given in the original, but it was sent in with another dated April 9th.
    [2] The representative of the Prince Regent as ruler of Hanover. Throughout this period he acts as the Prince Regent's representative in all matters affecting the internal affairs of Germany, but his actions were in the last resort subject to control by the British ministers.

With this reserve and a due attention to the indemnities to be provided for Denmark in the North of Germany under the late treaties, in case that power should join the Confederacy, the Prince Regent will be disposed most cordially to concur in re-establishing His Prussian Majesty in his former extent of power and authority in the North of Germany.

A copy of this despatch will be transmitted to Sir Charles Stewart with instructions to make a communication to His Prussian Majesty of these His Royal Highness's sentiments. Sir Charles Stewart will be directed to concert with your Lordship as to the execution of his instructions on this subject.

III. [C. C. VIII. 374.]
CASTLEREAGH TO CATHCART.
April 20th, 1813.

. . . The great question is how the control within the Germanic body is hereafter to subsist. In latter times, the rivalship between Austria and Prussia weakened the confederacy, and gave the ascendency to France. To render Austria, in fact as well as in name, predominant, many intelligent persons, of which Count Münster was one, would have preferred to see the power of Prussia somewhat reduced. Perhaps in theory they were right in that sentiment ; but it appeared to me from the first, as your lordship knows, that the great objec twas to embark Prussia in the war ; that, without her aid, Russia could do nothing offensively ; and that the declaration of Prussia was an indispensable preliminary to any change in the system of Austria. My opinion was, therefore, in full coincidence with the Treaty of Breslau,[1] that Prussia must be secured, and to be secured and embarked with effect, she must be reintegrated. It is impossible not to perceive that this indispensable act of policy revives the question of ascendancy between the courts of Vienna and Berlin, which it may be difficult hereafter to arrange ; but this is a secondary evil, and must be managed in subordination to the great object of their present union against France.

Count Münster adverts to a letter of Gneisenau's[2] to the Chancellor Hardenberg, in which he quotes my opinion as countenancing a divided confederacy in Germany, under the separate

[1] A convention signed between Prussia and Russia on the 19th March 1813, arranging for the provisional administration of such parts of Germany as were freed from French domination. It reflected Stein's wishes for a Federal Germany.
[2] The Prussian General whose views on the form of the Federal State differed from those of Stein.

protection of the two great military Powers. He certainly must have misunderstood me. I may and probably did speak of the importance of both being restored to their former station and authority, as the natural and necessary barriers to secure the North and the South of Germany against France ; but, as to their internal relations, I never had sufficiently considered the subject to have formed a conclusive opinion, more particularly as to the expediency of dissolving the ancient constitution of the Germanic body.

I observe a right is reserved to the *Powers* not named in the Convention of Breslau to send a Minister to the Council, as soon as their armies take the field, the *Princes* having only a common representative. I presume in the former class not only Sweden, but Saxony, Bavaria, and the more considerable Germanic States of the second order, are meant to be included : to confine their influence within the limits of a joint representative would be to exclude them from the confederacy.

I should be glad your lordship would send me any ideas that may occur on these subjects. It is, however, desirable to encourage the Allied Powers not to waste their deliberations at present upon these subjects ; it is time enough, when the enemy is overcome, to provide for the future ; at present, controversy ought to be discountenanced.

IV. [*F. O. Supplementary* 343.]
CATHCART TO CASTLEREAGH (Private and Confidential).
Imperial Head Quarters, Ob. Grodwitz,
Near Schweidnitz,
June 1st, 1813.

Count Stadion having received no later communications than those I stated in my despatches from Goldberg, the Emperor yesterday sent Count Nesselrode to Vienna. Being well assured that no endeavour will be spared by B.P.[1] to draw the councils of Austria to his interest [continues in cipher] I advised His Imperial Majesty to have recourse to every expedient ; and knowing the absolute want of means in the department of Secret Service, I thought it right in giving this advice to offer to make good any engagement in that way by which a determination to act in concert might be obtained and Count Nesselrode is authorised and instructed accordingly [cipher ends]. I trust argument in support of this measure would be superfluous ; if it were required I am

[1] Bonaparte.

sufficiently in possession of your Lordship's indulgence to find a powerful advocate.

V. [*F. O. Russia* 83.]
CASTLEREAGH TO CATHCART (No. 37.)
Foreign Office, June 30th, 1813.

The importance of the existing crisis and the uncertainty that yet appears to prevail as to the actual view and intentions of the Austrian Cabinet, renders it necessary, in the judgment of His Majesty's Government, to take a direct step for the purpose of calling upon that Power for an explicit avowal of its sentiments and determination. I should have authorized your Lordship to take measures for this purpose before the present moment, had not the confidential communications received through Count Hardenberg [1] encouraged an expectation, that the Court of Vienna only awaited the period necessary for the assembly of the army, to make a specific proposition to France, on the refusal of which her troops would join the Allies.

The period assigned for a decision having now been repeatedly postponed, and the Baron de Wessenberg [2] not having received any intimation of the views of his Court ; I am to signify to your Lordship the Prince Regent's pleasure, that, in such manner as may be deemed most eligible, your Lordship should open a direct communication with Count Metternich, for the purpose of inviting him to make an unreserved and confidential communication of the sentiments of his Court to the British Government. With this view I enclose under a flying seal a letter [3] addressed to Count Metternich, to be delivered either by your lordship or such person as you may think fit to charge with this confidential mission, requesting that Minister to open himself without reserve to the British Cabinet.

In the event of the Austrian army being actually engaged in hostilities against the enemy ; as an aid to assist their first efforts, your Lordship is authorized to place at the disposal of that Govern-

[1] Hanoverian representative at Vienna, brother to the Prussian Chancellor.
[2] The Austrian Ambassador at London.
[3] The letter to Metternich runs as follows :—"Sir, the importance of the present crisis rendering it of the most essential consequence that the Prince Regent should without loss of time be informed in the most authentic and confidential manner of the views and intentions of the Austrian Cabinet, I have by His Royal Highness' command charged Lord Cathcart to open a direct communication with your Excellency for this purpose. Your Excellency will be pleased to submit this request on the part of the Prince Regent to H.I.M. and I have further to beg that your Excellency will give credit to such communications as your Excellency may receive from Lord Cathcart in execution of his instructions. (Signed) Castlereagh."

ment the £500,000 which was entrusted to your Lordship on leaving England for extraordinary purposes. You will concert as to the best mode of rendering this credit available, without interfering with the pecuniary operations of the other Allied Powers : with this view it ought to be drawn for gradually, and ostensibly on commercial account.

Your Lordship was authorized by my private letter of the (——) to deny that any actual refusal of aid had been experienced by the Austrian Government. It may also be represented that, if the resources of Great Britain have been preferably directed to other Powers, it has alone arisen from those Powers being already committed in exertions on the success of which Austria had repeatedly declared her own ability to interfere must mainly depend. Under these circumstances it was for Austria first to open herself to Great Britain ; whose disposition could not be doubted, to push her exertions to the utmost, and to distribute her means as might best serve the common cause.

The object being to obtain an unreserved communication of the views of the Austrian Cabinet, your Lordship will feel the advantage of executing the present instruction by personal communication rather than in writing. You will use your own discretion in concerting with the Emperor of Russia as to the steps you may think fit to adopt, and you will either take measures for having a personal interview with Count Metternich, or, if it should appear that your being absent from the Head Quarters might be prejudicial to the public service, or be calculated too much to attract the enemy's observation, your Lordship will send a confidential person, on whose ability you can depend, to execute your instructions.

VI.   [F. O. Russia 83.]

CASTLEREAGH TO CATHCART (No. 42).

Foreign Office, July 5th, 1813.

Your Lordship's Dispatch No. [53] transmitting the basis on which the Emperor of Russia had signified to the Court of Vienna his disposition to negotiate for a general peace has been received and laid before the Prince Regent.[1] I have delayed

[1] On the 16th May, at Wurschen, Nesselrode gave to Stadion the conditions on which Russia was prepared to treat. These insisted not only on the restoration of Austria and Prussia to their position in 1805, the dissolution of the Confederation of the Rhine and the Duchy of Warsaw, but also on the freedom of Holland, the restoration of the Bourbons in Spain and even the exclusion of the French from Italy. These points were not accepted by Austria in the subsequent negotiations at Gitschin, but were reduced to an ultimatum of the four points only which were all that were made absolute in the secret Treaty of Reichenbach of the 27th June, 1813. These four points were : (1) The dissolution of the Duchy of Warsaw and its partition between the three Eastern Powers ; (2) The aggrandisement of Prussia ; (3) The restitution of the Illinau Provinces to Austria ; (4) The re-establishment of Hamburg, Lubeck, and the part of North Germany annexed to France in 1810.

conveying to your Lordship His Royal Highness's sentiments upon this important communication, your Lordship's letter of the 7th having acquainted me that Count Nesselrode had proceeded to meet the Emperor of Austria at Gitschin, and that you expected in a few days to be enabled to apprise me, as well of the reception given to these propositions, as of the final intentions of the Austrian Government. It was the less necessary to accelerate my answer, as it appeared, that no satisfactory opinion could well be given from hence, unless either upon an actual proposition made to this Government, or upon a more precise knowledge of the sentiments of the several Powers engaged in these discussions.

Any immediate declaration on the part of the British Cabinet appeared the less pressing, as the point of Spain, on which France had repeatedly declared she would not give way, and on which Great Britain could under no possible circumstances relax, seemed to oppose an insuperable obstacle to accommodation. So long as the French army continued to occupy a considerable proportion of Spain, and Joseph to remain in the exercise of authority within that kingdom, there seemed no probable solution of this difficulty. As, however, the rapid and victorious progress of the Allied armies, under the command of Field Marshal the Marquess of Wellington, may at no distant period, by the expulsion of the enemy from the Peninsula, give a new shape to this question, I have received the Prince Regent's commands to convey to your Lordship His Royal Highness's sentiments for your information and guidance.

In the first place your Lordship will inform the Emperor, that, in conformity to the wish some time since expressed by His Imperial Majesty to that effect, it is the intention of the British Government (in the event of the enemy being expelled from Spain) actively to employ the Allied armies on that side of France, in such manner as may best serve to occupy the attention and military resources of the enemy, and thereby to favour the exertions of the Allies in other parts of Europe.

With respect to negotiations for peace, it is the determination of the Prince Regent not to separate his interests from those of the Allies ; and as His Royal Highness persuaded himself that a peace in any degree calculated to provide for the common safety can only be secured by a cordial union, both of councils and arms, he is disposed to regulate his views, as to the Continental objects in which the good faith and honour of his own Government are not immediately involved, by what the great Continental Powers shall, under all the circumstances, consider best calculated to provide for their general security and independence.

That your Lordship may be the better enabled to open the Prince Regent's views explicitly to the Emperor of Russia on this subject, I am commanded to state to you, 1st. The points upon which His Royal Highness can under no circumstances relax, the faith of his Government being formally pledged to their inviolable maintenance. 2nd. The points upon which, either on account of engagements subsisting, or implied, or from considerations of paramount policy His Royal Highness feels it necessary to insist in conjunction with his Allies. 3rd. The points which appear to His Royal Highness of the highest moment to be attended to in any general arrangements ; but on which, not deeming that Great Britain has the same necessity or duty to insist, His Royal Highness would incline in a great measure to regulate his conduct by the sentiments of those Powers through whose exertions these objects can alone successfully be pursued ; and to whose protection their being secured is of greater moment than to that of Great Britain.

Under the first head of engagements under Treaty, and without which Great Britain cannot be party to any peace, your Lordship may enumerate : 1st, Spain ; 2ndly, Portugal ; 3rdly, Sicily, to be respectively secured under their legitimate sovereigns, in strict conformity with the subsisting treaties, and 4thly, the fulfilment of our existing engagements with Sweden.

Your Lordship will, under the second head, inform His Imperial Majesty, that, in order to lay the foundation of some counterpoise in the centre of Europe to the power of France, His Royal Highness deems it indispensably necessary to require, and is prepared in conjunction with his Allies peremptorily to insist upon, the restoration of the Austrian and Prussian Monarchies to such an extent of power and consequence as may enable them to maintain such a counterpoise. The importance of Holland to the freedom and security of Europe, will make His Royal Highness not less ready to co-operate with his Allies in requiring its liberation from the French Empire, and its recognition and re-establishment as an independent Power. His Royal Highness must also expect the complete and absolute restoration of His Majesty's Hanoverian dominions.

Under the 3rd head, your Lordship will bring forward the restoration of the rest of Germany, including Switzerland and Italy, to an order of things more consonant to the common safety. It is unnecessary to press upon your Lordship's attention the extent to which these objects may, in their several degrees, be essentially connected with the freedom and repose of Europe. What may be the means of the Allies, or their determination to contend for them, can alone be judged of when the views of the great Continental Powers are more fully disclosed to us. If Austria comes forward, the attainment of a solid peace, founded on a basis on which these great objects may all be reasonably provided for, seems upon every military calculation within our reach. What may be accomplished without the aid of that Power, may be more difficult to pronounce ; but your Lordship may assure the Emperor of Russia, that, so long as His Imperial Majesty and the Allies with whom we are at present acting, will stand by each other, and by the cause of the Continent against France, they may rely with confidence upon receiving from His Royal Highness the most liberal and decided support.

The expression of the Prince Regent's sentiments at the present moment, must necessarily be general. Your Lordship need not, however, hesitate to assure His Imperial Majesty that Great Britain was never better prepared, or more determined cordially to co-operate with the Continental Powers. The exertions in the course of the present year in all quarters will best attest the reliance that may be placed on her firm and zealous support. His Royal Highness is nevertheless ready, in conjunction with his Allies, to meet a desire of peace, whenever it shall really disclose itself on the part of the enemy ; and as His Royal Highness has contended for the common safety, so he will be prepared, as far as his separate interests are concerned, to negotiate in the same spirit.

But whilst His Royal Highness does not decline to concur in negociation, he trusts that it may not be made an instrument in the hands of the enemy to gain time, and your Lordship will urge His Imperial Majesty that the season for active exertion may not be unnecessarily sacrificed by a prolongation of the Armistice.

There is only one other point on which I feel it necessary to caution your Lordship, and it is the more necessary you should lose no time in coming to an explicit understanding with His Imperial Majesty on this important subject, as I understand two American Commissioners have arrived in the Baltick, in the hope of being received at the Emperor's Head Quarters. I am afraid this tender of mediation, which, on a question of maritime right, can not be listened to by Great Britain, however kindly and liberally intended, will have had the unfortunate effect of protracting the war with the United States. It is to be lamented, that the formal offer was made to America before the disposition of the British Government was previously sounded as to its acceptance of a mediation. It has enabled the President to hold out to the people of America a vague expectation of peace, under which he may reconcile them, with less repugnance to submit to the measures of the Government :—This evil, however, cannot now be avoided, and it only remains to prevent this question from producing any embarrassment between Great Britain and Russia.

Your Lordship will be enabled to satisfy the Emperor that, if this is a subject on which the mediation of an Ally cannot be accepted, it is still less a question that we could consent to discuss in a general Congress, however ready the Prince Regent will be at all times to treat for peace with America, and for a settlement of all differences. Your Lordship will, under all these circumstances, press the Emperor of Russia, in the strongest manner, not to push his personal interference on this point further. And as the maritime question is one which Buonaparte will endeavour to bring before a Congress, principally in the hope of creating disunion between Great Britain and her Allies, you will use your utmost endeavour to persuade His Imperial Majesty, that every consideration of policy should determine him pointedly to discountenance a design so mischievously calculated to promote the views of France.

VII.   [*C. C. IX.* 30.]
CASTLEREAGH TO CATHCART.
Foreign Office, July 6th, 1813.

.   .   .   Not having yet had time to bring the subject regularly under the consideration of my colleagues, I can only now state that your Lordship's and Sir Charles Stewart's conduct in concluding the Treaties at the period they were signed is fully approved.[1]   I must leave to your joint discretion what use it may be advisable to make of the instruction herewith sent[2] ;   much must depend upon the circumstances of the moment. If negotiation is not at an end, and hostilities renewed (which if determined on in the spirit of concert and exertion, and especially with Austria, would, I am satisfied, prove the wisest as well as the safest policy for Europe in the long run), you must guard against a Continental peace being made to our exclusion. Impracticability on our part might hazard this, notwithstanding our Treaties, which might not have the force to resist the menace both of French and Austrian hostility ;   for this purpose, our readiness to treat with our Allies must be avowed, that they may have no reproach to make against us. The four points on which we must

---

[1] The Treaties of Reichenbach signed with Prussia and Russia on June 14th and 15th.
[2] VI.

separately insist as *sine qua nons* must be distinctly put forward, nor can they complain of any one of these ; they were notorious from the first both to Russia and Prussia ; and, in good faith and fairness, all their assurances as well as their engagements not to make a separate peace must have been made in full contemplation that we had no possible option as to the points in question. With respect to others, which, in truth, involve the whole question of Continental policy, we must contend for as much as the Allies can be brought to stand to with firmness and spirit. But it is in vain to suppose that we can inspire the determination, if it does not exist. We may animate by our counsels as well as by our example, but we must avoid the appearance of idly pressing them against the grain. Such a line might weaken our influence, and would incur the responsibility of whatever disunion or failure followed.

The great practical question is a renewal of hostilities or a prolongation of armistice. When our Allies know what is indispensable on our part, and have made up their minds on what is essential to themselves, they must then consider what is the prospect of France agreeing to these demands, and, if agreed to, of observing her engagements. If the accomplishment of a reasonably solid peace, through negotiation, is not clear, *hesitation* in recurring to hostilities will damp and disunite the confederacy, and the resources of the Allies will be wasted in inactivity ; better in that case try the fate of war for the remainder of the campaign, and let future policy be governed by the result.

The recent successes in Spain [1] have put us on strong ground. We can now with honour evince a disposition to concur with our Continental Allies in negotiations ; having done so, we shall act our own part with more effect, if fortune or our friends should forsake us. Lord Wellington's successes may now give us the title to treat for our Allies, the Spaniards, with the possession of the Peninsula on our side ; to hazard such an advantage by showing a reluctance to negotiate, whilst Russia and Prussia are negotiating under the Austrian mediation, could not be borne out as a line of separate policy. The risk of treating with France is great, but the risk of losing our Continental Allies and the confidence of our own nation is greater. We must preserve our own faith inviolate to Spain, Portugal, Sicily, and Sweden. We must maintain our most important conquests, employing others to improve the general arrangements on points which are not likely to be carried by other means ; and with respect to the Continent, we must sustain and animate those Powers through whose exertions we can alone hope to improve it, taking care, in aiming at too much, not to destroy our future means of connexion and resistance. . . .

[1] The battle of Vittoria, June 21st, 1813.

VIII.   [*F. O. Russia* 83.]
CASTLEREAGH TO CATHCART (No. 45).
Foreign Office, July 13th, 1813.
[The Russian and Prussian Ambassadors have urged Great Britain to accept the Austrian mediation.]

You will express to the Emperor of Russia the Prince Regent's sense of the delicacy and candour which has, on the late as well as on all former occasions, distinguished His Imperial Majesty's conduct :—You may assure His Imperial Majesty of His Royal Highness's entire confidence in His Imperial Majesty's magnanimity and firmness, not doubting that the same wise and provident spirit which has characterized His Imperial Majesty's councils throughout the late most glorious contest, will continue to guide his counsels in any discussions that may be had with a view to peace.   Confiding implicitly in these sentiments, the Prince Regent authorizes your Lordship to acquaint the Emeror of Russia that His Royal Highness is now ready to accept the mediation of the Emperor of Austria.   It being understood that he does so, at the instance, and in conjunction with his Allies, and upon an express understanding as to those conditions from which, as laid down in my Dispatch No. 42 [1] and in conformity to the faith of treaties, Great Britain can under no circumstances recede.   As it is the Prince Regent's desire to act in the most entire concert with his Allies, your Lordship will be governed by the sentiments of Their Imperial and Prussian Majesties, and by the state of affairs at the moment as to the steps to be taken in pursuance of this Dispatch.   With their concurrence your Lordship is authorized to notify to the Austrian Government that the mediation of the Emperor of Austria has, in conjunction with his Allies, been accepted by the Prince Regent, and that your Lordship is authorized to explain the general principles upon which His Royal Highness would be prepared to assist in a general pacification.

Your Lordship will assure the Emperor of Austria that if this step has been delayed on the part of Great Britain, the delay has not arisen from any want of confidence in His Imperial Majesty's intentions :—but from considerations which have since to a certain degree ceased to operate.   The ruler of France, by indicating a disposition to treat with respect to the affairs of Spain, has afforded some prospects at least that the indispensable claims of good faith which bind Great Britain to that nation may be acceded to, and His Royal Highness has now also the satisfaction of knowing that His Imperial Majesty has, as a mediator, assumed that character which belongs to him as an independent and powerful sovereign.

[1] VI.

Under these circumstances, relying on His Imperial Majesty's enlightened views for the repose and independence of Europe, the Prince Regent accepts the mediation of the Emperor of Austria, and is ready to concur, so far as his existing engagements to other powers, and a just consideration of what is due as well to Continental arrangements, as to the immediate interests of Great Britain will allow in negotiating for a general peace.

IX. [*F. O. Russia* 83.]
CASTLEREAGH TO CATHCART. (No. 46.)
Foreign Office, July 13th, 1813.

In the present state of the discussions between the principal powers, it does not appear to His Majesty's Government possible to furnish your Lordship with instructions more precise, for the direction of your conduct, than those contained in my Dispatch No. 45,[1] with the single exception of the language which your Lordship is to hold with respect to the immediate conquests of Great Britain.

Your Lordship may declare, that the Prince Regent will not insist upon retaining all his conquests, however the acquisitions of France, of which it may not be deemed expedient, under present circumstances of Europe, to require the surrender, might entitle him to do so, provided His Royal Highness can hope by their partial restitution the better to provide for the general security of Europe. Your Lordship must always, however, declare, that there are certain conquests made by this country, of which under no circumstances, the Prince Regent can consent to divest himself. With this reserve, your Lordship may admit the principle, that there are others which His Royal Highness may be induced to relinquish for equivalents calculated to provide additional safeguards for the security of the Continent.

As the extent to which sacrifices of the part of Great Britain can be expected, must depend on the nature of the proposed general arrangement, I do not feel myself enabled at present to furnish your Lordship with any instructions founded upon the application of this principle. It may be sufficient to remark that, as any Colonial concessions are rather in their nature and value calculated to improve in the detail an outline of pacification previously understood, it may not be possible to give your Lordship more precise directions upon this subject, till I am in possession of the actual basis (if such should be agreed on) upon which the Continental Powers propose to negotiate.

It is, however, necessary to observe, with respect to the Dutch
[1] VIII.

Colonies, that, as any claim even to their partial restoration can only arise out of the complete separation of Holland from France, so the degree in which their restoration could be acceded to must mainly depend upon the apparent adequacy or inadequacy of the arrangements thus made for securing the independence of Holland. The Danish Colonies His Royal Highness is ready to consider as exclusively applicable to secure for Sweden those arrangements for which the Allied Powers have entered into engagements. The possessions immediately conquered from France must remain with certain exceptions, as the principal resource from which His Royal Highness would be willing to provide the means of improving in other respects the Continental peace ; but your Lordship will represent that this is not a fund that can be applied to obtain those arrangements, which the great Powers are entitled to insist upon as indispensable features in their own peace, but that it should be kept rather in reserve to procure other concessions, which may improve the general arrangements. . . .

X. [*C. C. IX.* 34.]
CASTLEREAGH TO CATHCART.
St. James's Square, July 14th, 1813.

I cannot omit again impressing upon your Lordship the importance of awakening the Emperor's mind to the necessity, for his own interests as well as ours, of peremptorily excluding from the general negotiations every maritime question. If he does not, he will risk a similar misunderstanding between those Powers on whose union the safety of Europe now rests. Great Britain may be driven out of a Congress, but not out of her maritime rights, and, if the Continental Powers know their own interests, they will not hazard this.

It is of great importance to strip any negotiation between America and us even of the *appearance* of foreign intervention. The Emperor, if he knows anything of England, must be convinced that no Government dare surrender the right of search for enemy's property, or British subjects : that the only question is, whether it can be so regulated by municipal laws, and regulations, as to the mode of conducting the search, and accounting for the person so withdrawn from the ship searched, as to guard against abuse, so far as this may be found practicable : there is every disposition to meet the question fairly, but the mere fact of an arrangement being made through the intervention of a third Power would probably decide the nation against it. You must, therefore, press London [1]; and, if that cannot be managed, you will consider Gottenburgh as a *sine qua non*. Any place near the Russian Court, or the seat of other negotiations, would give to our refusal of the mediation the air of a shabby pretence.

XI. [*C. C. IX.* 36.]

CASTLEREAGH TO CATHCART.

Foreign Office, July 14th, 1813.

I send by the present messenger authority to accept the Austrian mediation, if the state of affairs should continue, in the judgment of our Allies, to render it expedient. I consider the official letter before addressed to Count Metternich as a sufficient authority to accredit your Lordship for this purpose, coupled with the subsequent instructions, explanatory of our views with respect to a general pacification. In the present stage of the discussions, it is impossible to give full powers to treat and to conclude. We must know more of the basis on which the Continental Powers are prepared to negociate before we can finally instruct a Minister to act for us. At present, I conceive more is not required than that some accredited person should be prepared to enter into explanations on the part of the British Government, in like manner as Count Nesselrode and the Chancellor Hardenberg have hitherto done on the part of their respective Courts.

Your Lordship will feel the importance of ascertaining clearly the Continental basis before we can say a word as to particular cessions ; beyond the mere admission of the principle, we cannot advance till this is known. I trust that such will not be the case ; but we are justified in supposing it *possible, at least* that the basis agreed to by the Continental Powers under the Austrian mediation might be so defective as to afford no temptation to Great Britain to make a sacrifice of *any* of her conquests for the purpose of giving effect to such an arrangement. We must, therefore, know the nature of the object aimed at before we can judge what it becomes us to do ; and this course is the most likely to render our support useful to our Allies. You must make the Emperor feel that we cannot advance money for armistices, and that it is, therefore, of more importance to bring matters to a short issue. . . .

XII. [*F. O. Russia* 86.]

CATHCART TO CASTLEREAGH. (No. 79.)

Reichenbach, August 5th, 1813.

[Castlereagh's despatch No. 42,[2] of July 5th, read to the Emperor Alexander, who expressed his entire approval of its contents, especially the instructions to Wellington to advance into

[1] As a place of negotiation between Great Britain and America.
[2] VI.

the South of France, which the Emperor had himself already suggested.] The adherence to our positive engagements to Spain, Portugal, and Sicily he had all along expected as a matter of course on our part, and the question of Sweden was equally before him. He had always in like manner, considered all questions concerning Hanover to be indispensable to Great Britain and he fully concurred in the policy of the other propositions stated.

In regard to the American Commissioners, His Imperial Majesty begged that it might be fully understood that his object in offering mediation was simply this, that, foreseeing that the peace of Europe could not be obtained without a general struggle, he thought it was desirable as much as possible to make up all separate differences in which any of the powers likely to beconfederated might be engaged, and that he thought relieving Great Britain from this disturbance might increase her resources dis poseable for the general object, but that the mediation having been declined for the reason stated, that business was at an end. As to the Commissioners, they had made good their voyage to St. Petersburgh, but would have no passports to come to his head quarters.

The Emperor concluded that he could have no partiality and no personal knowledge of the ministers who at present form the Cabinet of His Royal Highness the Prince Regent, or of those persons who frequently differ from them in Parliament upon political questions, and that certainly some pains had been taken [1] to give to him an unfavourable view of the talents and energy of the former, but that it was only a justice due to them to declare, that in every transaction which had taken place within his knowledge and observation, he had remarked in their councils, great wisdom, ability, firmness, and moderation and in no instance more than in the statement which had now been presented to his consideration.

XIII. [*C. C. IX.* 39.]
Castlereagh to Cathcart.
Cray Farm, August 7th, 1813.

We have just received your account of the Trachenberg [2] Conferences, which, with the letter from the Emperor of Austria to

---

[1] Sir Robert Wilson, who had been with the Russians throughout the campaigns, was a vehement Whig.

[2] At this conference the Allied plan of ccmpaign was decided by the Prussian and Russian soldiers and Bernadotte, and co-operation with the Austrian army arranged.

the Crown Prince, renders the whole of that proceeding a most important and, I trust, auspicious incident in the Continental drama. The *dénouement* of the plot is yet a matter of anxiety. I trust, however, the impulse which has been given will not yield to nominal concessions.

I should hope, if the Austrian terms were not opened by Metternich at Dresden, that the Emperor is yet free to insist upon an arrangement more consonant to the general interests. The events in Spain not only justify, but require his Imperial Majesty, as a mediator, to alter his terms. He must see how fatal it would be to all were he to separate his cause from that of the other Powers. Neutrality must exhaust his resources as much as war, and, if Buonaparte should triumph over the others, his own fate is sealed. My despatches of the 6th and 14th[1] of July must have arrived in full time to enable your Lordship to bring our claims forward. It is impossible that Russia and Prussia can hesitate in standing by the four points that we have made *sine qua non*. I can as little conceive that Austria, assuming the task of mediating *a general peace*, can reject demands so just and moderate in themselves. This will in itself so largely extend the preliminary base, as materially to diminish the chance of Bonaparte yielding. Besides, if he could bring himself to stoop so low, the Allies would, of course, not take this upon trust, upon a mere paper engagement. They must, in common sense, before they sacrifice the whole season for acting, require some substantial securities, such as the retreat of the French armies, and the restoration of the Prussian fortresses. Here will be a new stumbling-block. I can hardly conceive it possible that the Conferences at Prague can, under present circumstances, end in peace, if the Allies are true to themselves and to each other. Bonaparte has had a severe lesson, but, whilst he has such a force under arms, he will not *submit* to any arrangement which even Count Metternich could have the face to sign his name to, as providing " on solid principles for the repose of Europe."

Lord Aberdeen leaves town to-day for Yarmouth, and will lose no time in joining your Lordship. I have acquainted Baron Wessenberg in general terms of his being charged with a mission to the Emperor.

. . . Before Lord Wellington forms his future plans, he must know what is to happen in Germany ; his whole policy must be governed upon that of the Allies. He writes in great spirits, and the Continental Powers may rely upon his doing his best for

---

[1] VIII. and IX.

E

them. Fatal would it be for them, and for the world, if they could
for a moment think of seeking their safety in what is called a
Continental peace. We have done wonders in the Peninsula,
but don't let the experiment be tried of a single combat again in
that quarter. We *may* sink before the undivided power of France,
and if we do Germany, and even Russia, will soon resume their
fetters. We are protected against this evil by the obligations of
good faith, but we are also protected against it by the plainest
dictates of common interest. We have now the bull close pinioned
between us, and if either of us let go our hold till we render him
harmless we shall deserve to suffer for it.

XIV. [*C. C. IX.*, 45.]
CASTLEREAGH TO CATHCART.
Foreign Office, September 1st, 1813.
Your letters of the 12th[1] were most acceptable. However
sanguine you had taught us to be on the issue, we were nevertheless, deeply anxious. I approve entirely of your holding your
hand on the mediation when my despatch reached : the authority
to do so was given *en prévoyance* of the case, as the acceptance was
acceded by Great Britain to the formal request of the Allies.

I wish you to ascertain clearly whether any and what basis of
Alliance between the three great Powers has been laid at Prague
—I should be glad to know *how and when* your lordship was first
informed of the interview with Murat. I have the greatest confidence and admiration of the Emperor, but I do not like his
concealing anything which is in progress from your Lordship, of
which there has been a striking instance recently,[2] although I am
sure from no bad motive. When it can be done without unnecessarily retarding business, if the sentiments of the British
Cabinet cannot be consulted, the opinion of their Minister on the
spot should be taken previous to decision. Engagements of
secrecy against us are of bad precedent, and must not be. I
advert to this the rather because I believe both the Treaties with
Prussia were signed before your lordship saw them.

As the fact of our being prepared to accept the Austrian
mediation is now known to all the Allies, I presume your lordship
did not attempt to conceal it from Austria when at Prague. I am

---

[1] Narrating Alexander's reception of Nos. VIII. and IX. and his wish that
the acceptance by Great Britain of Austria's mediation should not be announced
as war was inevitable.

[2] The Treaty of Reichenbach of the 27th June. See XLII.

not aware of any objection to a full disclosure in that quarter. Our line was friendly and respectful to that Court, and I am sure Metternich will not complain that your lordship saved him from the embarrassments of the disclosure at the eve of the rupture.

I rather expect Bonaparte, notwithstanding the resumption of hostilities, will have sent a *contre-projet* to Austria, if possible, to embarrass. Metternich seems to have outmanœuvred him. It was said a certain not very popular Minister in Russia saved his country by tempting the enemy to speculate upon his weakness and his influence : perhaps a speculation of the same nature may have produced another false calculation—would that it may lead to as signal a result ! .   .   .

XV. [*F. O. Russia* 83¹.]
        CASTLEREAGH TO CATHCART.   (No. 65.)
                Foreign Office, September 18th, 1813.
Hostilities having recommenced, and the Emperor of Austria having joined his arms to those of the Allies, it has become necessary to reconsider the foreign relations of the country with a view of seeing whether a greater degree of union and consistency may not be given to the Confederacy against France than results from the several Treaties which have been successively signed between the respective Powers.

The present Confederacy may be considered as the union of nearly the whole of Europe against the unbounded and faithless ambition of an individual. It comprehends not only all the great monarchies, but a great proportion of the secondary Powers. It is not more distinguished from former Confederacies against France by the number and magnitude of the Powers engaged than by the national character which the war has assumed throughout the respective states. On former occasions it was a contest of sovereigns, in some instances perhaps, against the prevailing sentiment of their subjects ; it is now a struggle dictated by the feelings of the people of all ranks as well as by the necessity of the case. The sovereigns of the Europe have at last confederated together for their common safety, having in vain sought that safety in detached and insulated compromises with the enemy. They have successively found that no extent of submission could procure for them either safety or repose, and that they no sooner ceased to be objects of hostility themselves, than they were com-

¹ This important despatch is the first attempt to construct the Alliance which Castlereagh finally secured at Chaumont in March, 1814.

pelled to become instruments in the hands of France for effectuating the conquest of other unoffending states. The present Confederacy may therefore be pronounced to originate in higher motives and to rest upon more solid principles than any of those that have preceded it, and the several Powers to be bound together for the first time by one paramount consideration of an imminent and common danger.

It is this common danger which ought always to be kept in view as the true basis of the alliance, and which ought to preclude defection from the common cause. It must be represented to the Allies that having determined to deliver themselves from the vengeance of the conqueror by their collective strength, if collectively they fail, they are separately lost. He never will again trust any one of them with the means of self-defence—their only rational policy then is inseparable union—to make the contest that of their respective nations, to persevere under ever' disaster, and to be satisfied that to end the contest safely the enemy must be compelled to treat with them collectively, whilst the best chance of an early peace is at once to satisfy the enemy that a separate negotiation is unattainable.

As opposed to France, a peace concluded in concert, though less advantageous in its terms, would be preferable to the largest concessions received from the enemy as the price of disunion. The great object of the Allies, whether in war or negotiation, should be to keep together, and to drive back and confine the armies of France within the circle of their own immediate resources. This alone can bring down the military force of the enemy to its natural level, and save Europe from being progressively conquered with its own spoils.

To suppose that the Powers on the side of Germany might be induced to sign a peace, leaving Great Britain and the nations of the Peninsula to carry on the war, or that the enemy being expelled from the Peninsula, Spain might sheath the sword, leaving the Continental Powers to sustain the undivided shock of French power, is to impute to them all a total blindness to their common safety. Were either of these interests to attempt to shelter themselves in a separate peace, it must leave France master of the fate of the other, and ultimately of both. It is by the war in Spain that Russia has been preserved, and that Germany may be delivered ; it is by the war in Germany that Spain may look to escape the subjugation that otherwise ultimately await her. So long as both manfully contend in the field against France, neither can be absolutely overwhelmed, and both, upon every sound principle of military calculation, must by perseverance triumph. To determine to stand or fall together is their only safety, and to effect this the confederates must be brought to agree to certain fixed principles of common interest. It is to be hoped that this has in a great measure been already effected, but the bond of union is to be collected rather by inference than to be found embodied in any one ostensible instrument common to all the powers.

In calling your Lordship's attention to the measures which remain to be adopted, it may be expedient to explain shortly the extent and nature of the engagements which exist, and to explain in what respect the general understanding requires to be rendered more explicit. The inclosed extracts from the Treaties concluded between Great Britain, Russia, Prussia, and Sweden,[1] leave no doubt as to these Powers being embarked (as far as Treaties can bind them) in a common cause, and although the integrity and independence of Spain is not in terms stipulated in these conventions, yet this obligation must nevertheless be considered as included in the engagements which these several Powers have formed with Great Britain—the stipulation not to make a separate peace being entered into by them all in full contemplation of the latter Power having previously bound itself not to terminate the war with France without providing for the interests of Spain. The independence of Spain having been distinctly brought forward by Russia and Prussia, in the note of the 16th of May,[2] as one of the necessary bases of a peace with France, and it being understood by the declarations of Austria that, although she would only be driven into war by the refusal of France to accede to the more restricted terms which she proposed, yet that when the sword was once drawn, in consequence of that refusal, she adopted as her own the basis proposed by the Allies, Austria may now be considered as substantially pledged with Russia and Prussia to insist upon the independence of the Peninsula. As yet no treaty to this effect exists between Great Britain and Austria. Instructions, however, have been given to Lord Aberdeen to make the signature of an engagement similar to those contracted with Russia and Prussia the condition of the subsidiary aid which his Lordship has been authorized to afford to that Government, and there is no reason to presume that the Court of Vienna will feel any reluctance to a stipulation of this nature.

[1] The Treaties of Subsidy and Alliance.
[2] See VI. Note 1.

It may then be asserted that all the great principles upon which the Confederacy should rest have already been recognized, and are now binding upon the principal Powers. It is, however, desirable that they should be brought together in a common Treaty, and your Lordship will lose no time in submitting to the Emperor the expediency of forming an Alliance, offensive and defensive, against France, providing adequately and comprehensively for the interests of all the Confederates. I transmit for consideration a sketch of a Treaty[1] for this purpose, which to save time might be negotiated and signed by the Ministers of Great Britain, Russia, Austria, Prussia, and Sweden, now assembled on the Continent, and an invitation be inserted in the Treaty to Spain, Portugal, and Sicily afterwards to accede. In submitting this project to the Emperor, your Lordship will represent that the object aimed at in framing the Treaty has been to select certain leading objects in which all the Confederates must fee a common, if not an equal, interest, and to the accomplishment ot which all may be bound as terms *sine qua non* of peace, without incurring in the eyes of each other or of the world the imputation of having bound themselves to demand conditions either extravagant or hopeless. Reserving the further reduction of the power of France, especially on the side of Holland and Italy to be pursued as the fortune of war may admit, there can be but one sentiment, that a peace which does not provide for the independence both of Germany and of the Peninsula would be wholly inadequate to afford the smallest protection to any one of the Powers engaged in the war, and to accept of less would be to treat upon a principle of submission, and not of security. This line is drawn, not only as the best in itself, but as indispensable to unite the extremities of Europe in one common cause. The nations of the Peninsula have now a right to be assured that the great Powers of the Continent are contending for *their* liberties as well as for their own. Great Britain has also a right to be assured of it, for, pledged as she is to Spain, it is essential in the management of her resources that she should know the nature of the struggle she may have to maintain. It may be found necessary, to satisfy particular States, to specify in more detail the various objects to which the efforts of the Confederacy are to be directed, but this had better be done in a secret article. The Russian and Prussian conditions of the 16th of May, to which the Court of Vienna has since acceded, may, with some additions, form a suitable basis for such an article; but His Imperial

---

[1] Appended to this dispatch.

Majesty will, I have no doubt, feel the advantage of confining the public treaty to broad and general principles.

The other articles of the Projet are such as have usually been agreed to in all Confederacies, to preserve an unity of action and a common interest. In laying them before the Emperor, you will state to His Imperial Majesty that the Prince Regent is in no degree tenacious of the form of the instrument—it is the substance concerning which he alone feels solicitous, and which he trusts, through the powerful intervention of His Imperial Majesty may be reduced into a suitable form without delay. Your Lordship, should you find it necessary, may urge the importance of such a direct pledge and avowal between all the Powers engaged in the war, from the distrust which the late negotiations for what was termed " Preliminaries of a Continental Peace to serve as a basis of a general peace " were calculated to   ire. No doubt exists in the Councils of Great Britain that   Russia and Prussia, in the qualified acquiescence which they gave to the Austrian conditions, faithfully and fully intended that the whole arrangement should be eventually subject to the just demands of Great Britain to be subsequently brought forward, and that the Allies never thought for a moment of signing an engagement in separation from the Prince Regent. But these distinct and successive negotiations, not comprehending the general interests, are calculated in an extended Confederacy to embarrass and disunite, and ought hereafter to be avoided, if it were only to guard against the evils of a protracted armistice. The latter inconvenience is particularly deserving of attention, for had France accepted the Austrian basis, whilst Great Britain was employed in bringing forward her demands with reference to such preliminaries, the French armies in Spain might have been reinforced, and the relative claims of the parties varied, possibly without hazard to the French armies in Germany, and without France being irrevocably committed to any arrangement which could afford a pledge of her disposition to accede to a general peace. Your Lordship will therefore press the necessity not only of mutual engagements, but that any preliminaries to be hereafter listened to must be general, and not partial. They must explicitly provide for the main interests of all the Powers, and not leave it open to the enemy, first to satisfy certain claims in the hope of sowing jealousy and disunion, and thereby of depriving the just pretensions of other Powers of their due support.

Your Lordship will take this occasion of renewing in the strongest terms to the Emperor of Russia the assurance of the deep and imperishable impression which His Imperial Majesty's conduct throughout the whole of their intercourse has implanted in the mind of the Prince Regent; this sentiment has, if possible, been augmented by His Imperial Majesty's late reception of His Royal Highness's sentiments on the great concerns that are now at issue. The Prince Regent has on this, as on all former occasions, imparted without reserve to His Imperial Majesty his views for the general welfare. He has done so in the confidence that they will be followed by His Imperial Majesty with that enlightened adherence to the cause of Europe which has characterised His Imperial Majesty's conduct throughout the war, and His Royal Highness will rejoice to find that a Confederacy which has owed its origin so largely to the councils as well as to the arms of Russia has been at length successfully matured and consolidated under the auspices of His Imperial Majesty.

I shall send copies of this Despatch to His Majesty's Ministers at the Courts of Vienna, Berlin, and Stockholm, with directions to act in concert with your Lordship in carrying the same into effect, but not to make any communication of the same to their respective Courts till they have conferred with your Lordship as to the mode in which the subject may be most advantageously brought forward.

PROJET OF A TREATY OF ALLIANCE OFFENSIVE AND DEFENSIVE AGAINST FRANCE.

Preamble.

(1)
The High Contracting Parties solemnly bind themselves to each other to call forth the utmost energies of their respective States in the vigorous prosecution of the present contest against France and to employ them in perfect concert, and in the most intimate confidence for the purpose of procuring for themselves and for Europe a general Peace, under the protection of which their rights and liberties may be secured, and their States and subjects at length delivered from the rapacity and oppression of France.

(2)
That it shall not be lawful for any one of the High Contracting Parties to withdraw himself from the war, or to enter separately with the enemy into any convention, Treaty of Peace, or truce, without the common consent and concurrence of the Allies.

(3)
That, in case of negociations for peace or truce being entered into with common consent, all things that are transacted shall be mutually communicated, nor shall any one State conclude any Treaty or convention but with common consent.

(4)
That after peace shall be concluded by common consent, there shall continue between the said High Contracting Parties a perpetual defensive Alliance for the maintenance of such peace, and for the mutual protection of their respective States.

(5)

That in case of attack hereafter by France on any one of the said High Contracting Parties, the several Powers will support the party so attacked with all their forces if necessary, and see justice done.

(6)

That the several Treaties and engagements already contracted between the respective High Contracting Parties in the course of the war shall remain good and valid.

(7)

That the Sovereign Cortes now administering the Government of Spain in the name of Ferdinand the 7th, His Sicilian Majesty, and the Prince Regent of Portugal, be forthwith invited to accede to the present Treaty.

(8)

That the present treaty shall be ratified, and the ratifications exchanged within [   ] weeks.

XVI. [*F. O. Russia* 83.]
CASTLEREAGH TO CATHCART. (No. 66.)
Foreign Office, September 18th, 1813.

Referring to that part of my Dispatch No. 65,[1] which relates to a secret article, your Lordship will receive enclosed a Projet for carrying this suggestion into effect. In presenting the same for His Imperial Majesty's consideration you will represent that it has been formed upon the basis of the Russian and Prussian conditions of the 16th of May.

The seven first objects[2] to which the efforts of the Confederacy are to be directed are taken from the documents in question, with a slight alteration in the 5th, extending the principle of restitution to the Germanic Provinces absorbed in the newly created Kingdom of Westphalia, as well as to those actually annexed to France. In the 5th it has been deemed advisable to point to the necessity of an adequate barrier for Holland. The 8th, 9th, and 10th are additions which it has appeared to the Prince Regent advisable to introduce, in order to obviate misconceptions, and to satisfy the different Powers engaged that the Confederacy has been founded in a just and liberal determination to support their several interests.

With respect to the introduction of an engagement as to Norway, your Lordship will state that its being included in the proposed secret article does not necessarily imply that it shall upon a general peace become a matter of direct negotiation or stipulation with France. Should the same considerations of treating this as a point purely Northern continue to operate, it may be left for

---

[1] See XV., p. 22.

[2] See the draft of the articles enclosed in this dispatch which are appended on p. 26.

separate discussion—its introduction into the Treaty will have no other effect than satisfying Sweden that, in addition to the specific engagements which particular states have entered into with her in regard to Norway, and which by Article 6th of the proposed treaty are to continue in full force, the Confederacy generally bind themselves to support her in that object as one not only important to her immediate security, but connected with the independence of the North.

I trust His Imperial Majesty will feel the indispensable necessity, after enumerating the general objects to which the efforts of the Confederacy are to be directed, of fixing the minimum of security upon which peace can be agreed to. Without a *sine qua non*, the Treaty will be either considered as extravagant in its pretensions, or loose in its obligations, and my persuasion is that the spirit of the Confederacy will stand more firmly to the whole purpose, when they boldly decide the principles which admit of no compromise.

Projet of Secret Articles.

In order more fully and clearly to define the views of the several Powers in concluding the said Alliance the said High Contracting Parties hereby agree faithfully and diligently to unite their councils as well as their arms, and to employ their utmost exertions to procure a general peace, which shall effectually provide for the following objects, viz. :—

1. The re-establishment of Austria in the degree of power and extent of territory which she possessed previous to 1805, as well in Italy as in Germany.

2. The reconstruction of the Prussian Monarchy in the same extent of population and territory in which it existed previous to 1806.

3. The dissolution of the Confederation of the Rhine—Germany to be rendered independent, and the provinces thereof in the north, either united to France or subjected to the family of Napoleon, to be restored.

4. The Duchy of Warsaw to cease to exist, as at present, and its future to be regulated without the intervention of France.

5. The separation, with an adequate barrier, of Holland from France.

6. The re-establishment of the ancient and lawful dynasty of Spain.

7. The liberation of Italy from the rule and influence of France.

8. The restoration of the House of Brunswick-Luneburgh (both Electoral and Ducal) to their dominions and rights.

9. The exclusion of French power and influence from the northern side of the Baltic by the annexation of Norway to the Crown of Sweden.

10. The restoration of the Kingdom of Naples or a suitable equivalent to His Sicilian Majesty.

And the said High Contracting Parties agree and bind themselves solemnly to each other not to lay down their arms till the independence of Germany, and especially the re-establishment of the strength and power of the Austrian and Prussian Monarchies, as essential to the permanence and conservation thereof, and likewise till the independence of the nations of the Peninsula under their lawful sovereigns shall have been fully secured and provided for, as barriers without which no equilibrium can be established in Europe, or any security afforded for the due fulfilment or permanence of a Treaty of peace with France.

This Secret Article to make a part of the said Treaty of Alliance, and to be as valid and binding as if inserted in the Treaty itself.

XVII. [*F. O. Supplementary* 343.]
CASTLEREAGH TO CATHCART. (Private.)
Foreign Office, September 18th, 1813.

I shall hope that the motives which have dictated the important instructions which I now transmit to your Lordship are sufficiently developed in my two public dispatches[1] with their enclosures.

With respect to the management of the negotiation, I deem it expedient that the overture should be made in the first instance to Russia, and that the subsequent steps to be taken at the other Courts, should be in concert with His Imperial Majesty, and upon a previous communication with your Lordship. In order that they may be fully apprized of the views of their Government, I shall send copies of these instructions to the Earl of Aberdeen, Sir Charles Stewart, and Mr. Thornton, but with instructions not to stir the question with their respective Courts till they know from your Lordship the reception it has met with from the Emperor, and especially till His Imperial Majesty's sentiments as to the best mode of giving it effect have been ascertained.

Austria, it is to be presumed, is the Court which may be expected to hesitate most as to a decisive measure of this nature, yet, committed as she now is, I conceive she ought above all others to desire that the Confederacy should be effectually and irrevocably

[1] XV. and XVI.

consolidated, and with this view she could not in prudence herself propose conditions less comprehensive than those suggested. Your Lordship will feel the value of time on this subject in two points of view.   1st. As with relation to our own Parliament (which meets the first week in November) it is very desirable, if asked whether the Powers of the Continent and those of the Peninsula are avowedly engaged in a common cause, that our answer should be direct and not constructive.   2nd. As the Cabinet will have occasion probably before Christmas to frame their system for the ensuing campaign, it is essential they should be assured on this main fact before they decide largely to anticipate resources, which, in the contingency of being abandoned by the Continental Powers, would be required to sustain a protracted contest in the Peninsula, from which neither the honour nor the interest of Great Britain will permit them to withdraw.

It will be necessary to press this topic strongly, and our Allies must be made to feel that we cannot go to Parliament to ask for the aids we are desirous of affording them unless they give us a clear, manly, and vigorous line of policy to stand on.

As soon as you have conferred with the Emperor, I think Lord Aberdeen should lose no time in opening the measure to Austria, and in point of attention the communication to Russia ought not to be postponed. That there may be no unnecessary delay in carrying the measure into effect, if the principal Powers are agreed, I shall forward a full power by the first messenger enabling your Lordship and your two colleagues at Head Quarters to sign at once on the part of Great Britain.

You will perceive Sweden is included as a principal in the treaty, and as one of the Continental Powers now prominently engaged ; if the time admits of it, I consider it desirable she should be invited to take a direct part in the negotiations ; but if the reference to Stockholm for full powers would impede the early conclusion of an alliance, in which she must feel so strong an interest, I am not aware (the point of Norway being enumerated amongst the general objects of the Confederacy) that there could be any objection, under a suitable explanation, to class Sweden amongst the Powers who are to be invited to accede, of which number Spain being one the dignity of His Swedish Majesty could not suffer, where the motive in both cases was the same, namely, to avoid delay.

The only practical objection which it occurs to me may be felt to the proposed Treaty is the difficulty of procuring the consents required in cases of emergency, but this difficulty appears more imaginary than real, and at all events to be far outweighed by the advantages, I should say by the necessity, of the measure. Once agreed upon main principles, and there will be little difficulty in the rest. The more distant Powers will be prepared in a great measure to confide their interests to their Allies, and it will not be difficult to give an adequate authority to the respective ministers at Head Quarters to act upon circumstances as they arise in the few cases that can require so prompt a decision.

Your communication to Mr. Thornton, I conceive, cannot satisfactorily be made till you have come to an understanding, at least to a certain extent, both with Russia, Prussia, and especially with Austria, and I shall prepare him to expect some short delay on this account. It will afford me great pleasure should the disposition of the Allies and the nature of the instructions be such as to admit of the signature of the Treaty without reference home.

XVIII. [*F. O. Supplementary 343.*]
CASTLEREAGH TO CATHCART. (Private.)
Foreign Office, September 21st, 1813.

Your last dispatches are of the 12th of August. We have letters from my brother, Count Hardenburgh [*sic*], Metternich, etc., to the 30th.

You will see by the Gazette that we meet Parliament the 4th of November. Finance and other motives connected with the vigorous prosecution of the war have rendered this necessary. I trust you will secure the Alliance against distrust by conclusion of the Treaty before that time. The only hope either of a *short* or *successful* war is to put an end to all hope on the part of the enemy of playing for a separate peace. When this hope is altogether at an end the Allies will be united, and Napoleon[1] may be subdued. Are you clear that this concealment of the politics of Great Britain from Austria is judicious, when they are known to Prussia, Sweden, and Spain, and most probably must be avowed in outline at least in debate ? I do not wish to press any idea peremptorily from hence, imperfectly informed as I am, but my own feelings would have suggested the expediency of the Emperor of Russia explaining to his brother Emperor the whole with as little delay as possible, with his own very wise reasons for keeping back the communication at the moment it arrived ; and

[1] A slip, and again later in this dispatch. *Bonaparte* is almost invariably used.

I am strongly inclined to think that the best, if not the only, way to make a cautious Court *bold* is to convince them that they have to act with temperate but decided Allies, but that to succeed themselves they must be true to those Allies. Flattering myself that we have proved our views not only to be temperate, but disinterested, I am not afraid of Austria knowing the principles upon which we act. She cannot suppose they are calculated to countenance the principle of a separate peace in any quarter—so far from it, that the very object of our moderation and deference to the sentiments of the Continent as to the conditions of the general arrangement in which they have the primary interest, I mean the Continental arrangements on the side of Germany, is to keep the whole together, and whilst we bring forward no conditions which are not indispensable, we are reluctant to urge them to contend for more than we think necessary, their means and prospects being fairly considered. But it must be one cause and one effort or it is nothing.

I know M. de Metternich is fond of negotiating, but the best remedy for this is to convince him that England is as tired of the war as he can be, and as ready to negotiate at a proper moment. The British Government only deprecates ineffectual negotiations, as relaxing the tone and spirit of the Allies, and as enabling the enemy to call forth new resources in the expectation of their facilitating his peace. I have heard of a suggestion of Napoleon, that whilst the war is going on, there should be a sort of concurrent negotiation on neutral ground. I am sure this idea cannot have received any countenance; it would be fatal to all military exertion. How could M. de Metternich hope to invigorate his own nation, to rouse them to exertion, or to animate them to great pecuniary sacrifices whilst the white flag was flying? Can he suppose that any oppressed nation will join him, that the Tyrol will rise, that Holland or Italy will attempt to emancipate themselves, or the Confederacy of the Rhine throw off its allegiance if they suppose that a peace may surprise and sacrifice them at the very outset. The Austrian Minister has, through a course of negotiations, the merit of which I need not now examine, embarked his sovereign in a common cause with nearly the whole of Europe; let him perfect this work by a Treaty of Alliance before he gives facilities to the enemy to repair his own blunders. When the Confederacy is placed beyond the reach of Bonaparte's cunning, as I flatter myself it is of his arms, they may receive a proposition for peace, or they may make one at a suitable moment, but don't let them countenance proceedings which are calculated to create a doubt whether they are fighting or negotiating. This doubt would be the necessary result to anything like pending discussions for peace. The only invigorating remedy is a common alliance. As Allies let us be temperate in our councils, but let us avow to each other, and to the world, that we are not to be seduced from our allegiance to the common safety. . . .

XIX.   [*F. O. Supplementary* 343.]
CASTLEREAGH TO CATHCART.   (Private.)
Foreign Office, September 27th, 1813.

Having confidentially communicated the Projet of the Treaty of Alliance offensive and defensive against France, as enclosed in my letter No. 65[1] to the Count de Lieven, I deem it proper to advert to some remarks he made upon it, and to furnish your Lordship with instructions upon these points for the guidance of your conduct in case similar observations should be brought forward in the course of the discussions.

The first relates to what was certainly understood, if not expressed in the Treaty, when the Alliance was proposed, viz., that the several Powers engaged in the common cause should continue to receive as heretofore such pecuniary aid from Great Britain as circumstances may permit. It is, however, a principle to the express recording of which on the face of the Treaty there can be no objection, and it perhaps may most conveniently be done by the insertion of words to this effect at the end of Article 1, in which the Allies bind themselves to call forth their utmost resources, and to employ them in concert against the common enemy.

The next case adverted to by the Russian Ambassador was that of France in the negotiation for a general peace insisting upon the introduction of the maritime question [in which case the Continental Powers, although the terms of peace might otherwise be arranged, would be obliged to continue to make war upon France on this account alone, the engagement not to sign a separate peace being unqualified].[2] The observation [to this observation][2] is that the maritime code never yet was made a matter of general discussion in any European Congress. At the Peace of Utrecht France and England negotiated separately on certain points of this nature, but it is not a code which the Powers of Europe have

---

[1] See XV. Lieven was Russian Ambassador at London.
[2] So in the draft, but the words in brackets were to be cut out before dispatch.

ever undertaken[1] to settle by a general convention, and France has no right to bring forward such a demand.

Such an attempt on the part of France can only be made for sinister purposes, and that the Emperor of Russia will not countenance such a claim the accompanying dispatch from Count Nesselrode affords the most complete assurance. Supposing that there did exist between Great Britain and France any reasonable difference of opinion upon the maritime question, which we deny, why would either State press their views on this subject, upon a Congress, to the obstruction of a general peace, when that peace at once puts an end to the exercise of any of the litigated rights. Surely if a real desire of peace exists, and if all other differences can be accommodated, it cannot be necessary now to continue the war, in the vain hope of regulating the exercise of maritime rights in some future, and we may hope, distant war.

If France prefers her views upon this question upon a Congress, we have an equal right to press ours, and the object of France may thus be accomplished of creating a new war upon new principles. Great Britain, on the contrary, is willing to waive wholly the discussion of the subject ; she desires no concession whatever to be made to her on this point, and only insists that no concession shall be demanded of her by those who are disposed to maintain opposite principles. Her maritime rights no British Minister could dare to compromise, and France did not attempt to question them at the peace of Amiens ; and if the Powers of Europe are resolved to establish a counterpoise against the power of France, they must not hazard discussion among themselves by suffering this subject for the first time to be introduced into a general Congress.

The only other point mentioned was the American War, which did not seem to have any practical bearing on the question. The Emperor of Russia has already explicitly stated the only ground on which he thought of interfering, even to the extent of offering his mediation, namely, from a laudable desire of reconciling two States, with both of whom he was in friendly relations. But this interference has been most explicitly and liberally abandoned, and there does not appear any pretence for mixing a question purely domestic between Great Britain and America with the settlement of Europe. There is no misunderstanding with Russia or any other European Power on the subject of the maritime code. With Russia we came to a clear understanding

---

[1] Originally "can pretend." The whole of these paragraphs dealing with the maritime rights were drafted with extreme care.

in the Treaty of [   ]¹ on all the main principles of maritime law, on blockades, on contraband of war, on the right of search, and the non-protection of enemy's property by the British or Russian flags when neutral.

The discrimination and impressment of our own subjects on board Russian merchant ships can never be a subject of grievance ; first, because they are not in the practice of resorting to that service in any numbers; second, because they are at once distinguishable when there. The whole question with America (except so far as it has been complicated by their Acts of Naturalization) is one not of principle, but of practice, the oppressions alleged to be committed in impressing Americans, as British subjects, [arising] from the impossibility of discrimination. To this the British Government has always professed their willingness to apply a remedy so far as they could do so without essential prejudice to their naval service and to the right itself, but this cannot by possibility be a point of difficulty with any other nation, and it is one which Great Britain and America are alone competent to settle.

I have been induced to say thus much on this point, as there prevails much misconception and prejudice on this subject, from which I think the Count de Lieven is himself not altogether exempt. I am confident he has no wish to revive any of those questions which have been happily settled with the Northern Powers. It is only an impatience of the war going on with America to the inconvenience of general commerce which weighs with him ; but if this should be the case, let America, who chooses to stir these questions, answer for the consequences. We stand on our long-established practice, from which we never deviated till the Decrees of France led to the adoption of the retaliatory Orders in Council, and by which ancient practice we profess to consider ourselves at all times implicitly bound, except towards a Power that renounces all principles of law for the purpose of attempting our destruction.

I should hope your Lordship will have no occasion to enter into these subjects even cursorily. I thought, however, it could do no harm to furnish you with some general ideas in this informal manner, in case the Count de Lieven should have thrown such suggestions before his Government, or in case the same ideas should present themselves to the Russian Ministers.

¹ Left blank in the original. The Convention concluded at St. Petersburg of the 17th June, 1801, appears to be meant.

XX. [*F. O. Supplementary* 343.]

CASTLEREAGH TO CATHCART. (Private).

Dover Castle, October 14th, 1813.

[News prevented by heavy gales ; nothing received from the armies since September 14th except what is got through Paris. On the 29th Bonaparte was on the Elbe with Augerau marching to Erfurt to protect his rear, which he seems to be able to do.] I have been most impatiently expecting your friends in the Tyrol to shew themselves. It will be a great disappointment if the Austrians and all the popular indignation of the South can be held in check by *Bavarians* and *Italians*, without the substraction of a single French Corps from the enemy's main operation.

[News from France of the new conscription etc.] leaves no doubt that a great effort is to be made, and that there is nothing further from Bonaparte's intentions than to subscribe to any peace which shall rescue Germany and the Peninsula from hi military dominion—an army in Germany and an army in Spain i what his system requires, and M. Metternich may rest assured he will not *negotiate* him out of it.   It really appears to me quite impossible to mistake the true issue, and the sooner the Austrian minister makes up his own mind to it, and makes the Austrian monarchy feel it to the very extremities, the less risk he runs of a serious impression being made by the armed multitudes that France will pour forth if she can send them to feed and plunder beyond her own borders.   It is become a contest of nations to all intents and purposes and not a game of statesmen, and he will play into Bonaparte's hands if he deals with it upon any other principle.   The three great military Powers of the Continent start with immense advantages—armies, the most magnificent in numbers, spirit, and discipline, conscious of their own superiority gloriously re-established—but this may perish before numbers unremittingly poured forth, if the whole is not sustained by a national sentiment and by that impulse, which is alone to be communicated by calling the mass of the people into action.   If this is done in Austria with the spirit it was done last year in Russia, and with which it has recently been done in Prussia, and if the councils of the Allies can be once inseparably united in the common cause, and all determined at whatever sacrifices to maintain the contest in that spirit of steady, patient, and determined perseverance, by which originally with small means we have progressively rescued the Peninsula from the enemy's arms, we shall beyond all question triumph, but don't let us deceive ourselves as to the nature of the struggle or the efforts Bonaparte will yet make.

One advantage at least must follow from the Duke of Bassano's report[1] that he will have furnished your Lordship with unanswerable arguments in support of the system of unqualified union amongst the Powers contending against France which you are directed to improve, and of the futility of looking to any other relief against the hazards of war but persevering exertion, whilst a rational hope cannot exist that the individual against whom we have to contend will brook the notion of a compromise. I am confident the Emperor of Russia will look at the crisis with the mind of a statesman, and animate all around him to the performance of their duties.

XXI. [*F. O. Supplementary* 343.]
CATHCART TO CASTLEREAGH. (Private.)
Meiningen, October 30th, 1813.

I cannot delay the important news this messenger is to convey for the sake of adding a detailed report of the proceedings in the negotiation of the Treaty of Alliance.[2] It was not till the 26th that I had an opportunity of going fully into that business with His Imperial Majesty. Several appointments were made for that purpose at Leipzig and at Weimar, but they were always interrupted by military concerns. On arriving at Ansbatt the Emperor was pleased to invite me to dine in private, and after dinner to go with the greatest attention into every part of that subject.

His Imperial Majesty did not seem in any shape averse to what is proposed, and which is throughout analagous to his declared opinions, approved entirely of my removing any restraint upon the communications which Lord Aberdeen and Sir Charles Stewart are ready to make to their respective Courts, and requested me to discuss the matter also with Count Nesselrode, and seemed impressed with a due sense of the convenience which would in all respects ensue, with reference to the British arrangements of supply from next year's subsidies, from finishing the Treaty at least with the Powers present as soon as possible.

His Imperial Majesty touched slightly the three observations which had occurred to Count de Lieven, and it was therefore extremely advantageous to me to have received since the date of my first communication on this subject at Leipzig your Lord-

[1] As to the position and preparations of France.

[2] Cathcart received Castlereagh's instructions (XV. and XVI.), at Leipzig just after the battle had been fought. (See XLIX.)

ship's private letter,[1] which enables me to answer satisfactorily the point concerning a continuance of such supply as may be expedient, and furnished in all such able and irresistible arguments on the remaining two points. There is some apprehension on these subjects, which are not fully understood but upon which I have already discovered that great pains have been taken long ere now to impart prejudice. Prince Metternich is, I hear, more free from jealousy or apprehension upon either of those subjects which do not in any way concern his Court : and therefore, as Lord Aberdeen will probably convince him, I expect great aid from him in surmounting all apprehensions of engaging in an offensive and defensive alliance to maintain doubtful questions, if I should not succeed in removing them myself.

It is not wished to make the communication in the first instance to Sweden, but rather to propose to that Power to accede. Indeed it is not probable that the Prince will be so much within reach treating as the others. But even to reassemble these Powers wi require some time, as the King and his minister are absent, and it looks as if the Emperors also are within a short distance at present of each other will now proceed to Frankfort, or to some other city by different routes. I am extremely mortified that this is the case, and I have spared no endeavour to accelerate what depended upon me. But I flatter myself Lord Aberdeen's treaty with Austria and the general course of proceeding in the field and in the closet here will supply the want of a general treaty in the present moment. Every exertion shall, however, be made to get it ready as soon as circumstances will permit. . . .

XXII. [F. O. Russia 87.]
CATHCART TO CASTLEREAGH. (No. 109.)
Frankfort on the Maine, November 10th, 1813.
[Interview this morning with the Emperor of Russia.]

The Emperor, after stating what I had learned from Count Nesselrode, said that considering all that had passed last winter concerning the invasion of Russia, he confessed it was more agreeable to his feelings that any communication which became necessary with the enemy should be conducted through other hands than his, and that he was therefore extremely satisfied that Prince Metternich should undertake the instructing and dispatching Mr. de St. Aignan,[2] the person employed to sound the disposition of

---

[1] XIX.
[2] See LXI. and LXII. as to the negotiations with St. Aignan.

the French Cabinet ; that he had desired nothing should be held forth but what was in strict conformity with the policy of the British Cabinet, as the same had been stated in the dispatches addressed to me, and that Prince Metternich should invite the British Ambassador to be present ; that Lord Aberdeen had accordingly been present, and was privy to all the instructions which had been given to M. de St. Aignan ;   that his Imperial Majesty was not only desirous of giving to me the fullest informa- tion of every particular himself or through Count Nesselrode, but wished me to call upon Lord Aberdeen for his statement, and to compare it with what I learned from him, and rather to rely on the accuracy of his Lordship's statement than any other. I accordingly went to Lord Aberdeen, and learned from His Excellency the proceedings which took place at a late hour last night in his presence.   For the particulars of this conference I must, of course, refer your Lordship to Lord Aberdeen, who will by this messenger send a full report.   I flatter myself what has been said and explained to M. St. Aignan will not prove incon- sistent with the views of His Royal Highness the Prince Regent's Government.

XXIII. [*F. O. Russia* 87.]
CATHCART TO CASTLEREAGH. (Secret. No. 112.)
Frankfort on the Maine, November 11th, 1813.
. . .   The Emperor had ordered a paper to be drawn up on the subject of your Lordship's dispatches, Nos. 65 and 66,[1] and their inclosures : from the military and political business which has daily arisen that paper could not be taken into consideration till late last night, and it was communicated to me this morning. It came in the form of a draft of a dispatch to Count Lieven, setting forth the grounds of confidence to which Russia is entitled from her conduct, and the want of necessity of forming a more precise engagement to induce her to persevere, and that Austria, the Power considered most averse to positive engagements when your Lordship's dispatch was framed, is now the one among the Allies who has gone the furthest in engagements concerning Spain ; that the Emperor does not object to the principle of increasing his connection with Great Britain by an Alliance offensive and defensive, but thinks such a Treaty should be framed according to existing circumstances, and not as matters stood two months ago ; for this reason, that it would be useful at this junc-

[1] XV. and XVI.

ture that Great Britain should make an engagement relative to the aid Russia and the Allies might depend upon in the event of the continuance of the war, and in case of negotiation that Great Britain should particularize in any such Treaty the cessions she is disposed to make for the common cause.

I objected entirely to the mode of negotiation thus proposed, stating that I had opened the business in the most expeditious and simple manner, by reading parts of the dispatches, but that I was not the less ready to put the negotiation or any part of it into the form of note, or minute of conference, and that it was more than probable that my powers and instructions would enable me to remove any difficulties without resorting to the tedious course of reference to London either through Count Lieven or myself. That I could introduce a general stipulation for the continuance of such pecuniary aid from Great Britain as circum stances may permit, but that it might not be convenient o practicable in a general treaty to fix the precise amount of the whole aid, or to detail the distribution. That in regard to restitution of conquests nothing could be more liberal or more explicit than what England had already declared in your Lordship's dispatch (No. 46)[1] to me, of which they had full notice, *viz.*, the use Great Britain proposed to make of the acquisitions from Holland and Denmark, and the objects to which such restitutions as it might be found expedient to make of conquests made from France would be applied.

That a general engagement to make restitutions to obtain peace on conditions advantageous to the general interest and to procure such cessions from France necessary to justice, and to secure the repose of Europe, as had not been gained by force of arms, might be made, but that it was too much to desire that particular conquests should be named as stipulated to be restored before the objects for which they were to be exchanged came under discussion.

I had in former conversations got rid of the objections grounded on maritime questions and American discussions. But I clearly see that there is a strong objection to a general Treaty such as is proposed, from the difficulties which it is supposed will arise, in regard to other Powers who will consider themselves as much entitled to be included as any Power of the second order already named, and therefore it would be preferred to confine the Treaty of Alliance to Great Britain, Russia, Austria, and Prussia. There would be no objection to consider Spain as a Power of the first

[1] See IX.

order, were it not for the dependant state in which the weakness of her Government must for some time place her, and it is therefore conceived that an engagement not to lay down arms till Ferdinand the VII. is replaced, and his dynasty and the independence of Spain are insured, might amply suffice without making Spain a party to the proposed alliance.

This conversation is to be resumed before any dispatch is made up to Count Lieven, but I think this Government will not be inclined to enter into the Projet until it shall be tried whether Great Britain will not prefer renewing the Treaty of concert and subsidy for the next year, Russia at the same time contracting a solemn engagement in regard to Spain. I said Holland with a barrier, Switzerland, and Italy, including perhaps the consideration of Sardinia, and Sicily should be included. The answer was there could be no doubt of the Emperor's inclination, and of the desire of His Imperial Majesty, in common with all the Allies, to accomplish these objects, but that perhaps it was better to avoid binding more than was necessary by Treaty, lest in striving to do too much we should lose the opportunity of doing anything. I have, however, no doubt but that Holland in particular might be included as well as the Peninsula, and I see no difficulty in regard to Italy.

I will do what I can to carry through the Projet, but I doubt its being concluded without reference, for the reasons I have stated.

XXIV. [F. O. Russia 87.]
      CATHCART TO CASTLEREAGH. (Secret. No. 114.)
            Frankfort on the Maine, November 17th, 1813.
[Cathcart took the earliest opportunity of delivering to the Emperor the Prince Regent's message on the subject of the defensive treaty of the 9th of September between Austria and Russia.[1] He urged the expediency of adopting the proposal of Alliance, which would provide a document on the faith of which the British Government might contradict any argument drawn from the omission of essential points in the defensive Treaties between Russia and Austria, and between Russia and Prussia, particularly in regard to the Peninsula.]

His Imperial Majesty was pleased to attend to this subject with the greatest interest, and to state that the observations which

[1] The British Government protested against the omission of Spain from the objects of the war specified in the Secret Articles of the Treaty signed at Tooplitz between Austria, Russia, and Prussia.

had been made on the Projet had occurred to the Ministers of other Powers as well as to his own, and that he was happy to find in the present conversation additional proof that what was proposed in the Projet and secret article did not arise from any mistrust of his perseverance, and His Imperial Majesty charged me to repeat to the Prince Regent how much he was gratified by every mark of His Royal Highness's confidence ; that whatever difficulties might be found in a Projet which was to embrace so many parties, he had none in taking any engagement we might deem useful to the cause, in regard to the Peninsula, and that I was at full liberty to adjust with Count Nesselrode any mode of framing an article that should make as strong an engagement for the maintenance of the dynasty of Ferdinand VII. and the Braganza family in Spain and Portugal, and for the independence of those realms, as had been contracted with Austria. His Imperial Majesty professed the greatest desire to meet the ideas of the Prince Regent's Government in regard to the Projet, but seemed impressed with the apprehension of the difficulties and inconvenience which have been alluded to in a former dispatch.

In talking over this matter with Count Nesselrode, it was proposed to add an article similar to the secret article in the Treaty signed with Austria by Lord Aberdeen, Article 5, §4[1], to the Treaty of concert and subsidy signed at Reichenbach between Great Britain and Russia, and that the same measure should also be proposed to Prussia, and Count Nesselrode declared his readiness to propose to the Emperor that he should be authorised to sign such a secret article with me immediately or to send full powers to Count Lieven to sign an article to that effect at London.

I have had the great advantage of conferring with Lord Aberdeen on this subject, and of reading over together your Lordship's dispatches bearing on this point. It seems clear to us that of the points named, the one concerning which His Majesty's Government is most anxious is to obtain an engagement relative to the Peninsula, and that it should be contracted with the three principal Powers. Now both these objects are gained by the mode proposed, and all jealousies and future difficulties in regard to other Powers are obviated, as it is only the addition of an article to existing Treaties ; but, if this proposal were accepted here, it would amount to an abandonment by us of the measure proposed by the Prince Regent's Government, and therefore as there seems no ground for anxiety on the subject to warrant a decision on the spot to follow a course so different from the one your Lordship

[1] The subsidy treaty with Austria signed at Toeplitz on October 3rd, 1813.

wished to be carried through, without a reference home, it has been judged by both of us to be most expedient to state the matter to your Lordship, and to obtain instructions and powers to be sent without any delay to Count Lieven and Baron Jacobi-Kleist. I have accordingly been again this day with the Emperor and with Count Nesselrode, and the latter intends by this conveyance to write to Count Lieven, and will immediately prepare instructions to be submitted to His Imperial Majesty, which will be shown to me in the draft, and will be forwarded with the powers together with the ratifications of the Convention of 30th September by a Russian messenger.

It is understood that this course is resorted to, lest His Royal Highness's Government should not be satisfied to take this additional article in lieu of the Projet.   I went over all the secret articles in No. 66.[1]

There is no disinclination to adopt any proposition here, except 5, 7, and 10 ; the importance of the objects in the first instance and for establishing future balance is admitted, but the expediency of binding the hands of the Allies by express stipulations which might not suit when the time of using them shall arrive is considered doubtful.   With regard to 9, Great Britain and certain other Powers are bound to the same object by separate Treaty and by accession, and it is not judged necessary that they should become bound to each other to perform what they have already engaged to do.   The last paragraph of the secret article is much approved and admired, but, upon the whole, there is a leaning in favour of the words of the Austrian Treaty, which also comprehends Sicily.

It is further in contemplation to make a communication to relieve His Royal Highness's Government from the engagement of secrecy in regard to so much of the secret article of the Austrian Treaty signed by Lord Aberdeen and of those now proposed to be added to the Treaties of Reichenbach as may be desirable for the satisfaction of the British Parliament, and may be fit to be now declared as principles on which the Allies are pledged to act, without, however, publishing other parts which for the present had best remain secret.

XXV. [F. O. Supplementary 343.]

CATHCART TO CASTLEREAGH. (Private.)

Frankfort on the Maine, November 24th, 1813.

A report was this morning received that a French General

[1] See XVI.

Officer with a Flag of Truce had presented himself at the advanced posts on the side of Mayence. He was stopped there, and he sent a letter to Field Marshal Prince Schwarzenberg to state that he was charged with communications of importance. I am not sure of his name, but I think it is Clausell. The Field Marshal at first thought of going to meet him, but that intention was changed, and a General Officer of each nation was sent, General Neipperg, Count Schouvaloff, and Knesebeck. They are returned, but I cannot give the result by Sir Charles's messenger because I have not seen the Emperor, and Count Nesselrode, whom I have been with at the last moment, is not yet in possession of it. A Russian courier will be dispatched to-morrow with the ratification of the Convention of 30th September and the other documents I mentioned, and I have no doubt but that by him I shall be enabled to report all that may have taken place up to the moment of his departure.[1]

That Napoleon will wish to enter into negotiation I have no doubt, but it will be for the purpose of gaining time of paralyzing exertions, and, if possible, of exciting disunion somewhere, even in the British Parliament. But I cannot believe that he will seriously negotiate with a view to make peace until he shall have advanced his preparation and put himself in a better attitude. This is the opinion of those here on whose judgment and knowledge I am most inclined to rely, and there is every determination here to give him no time. All the decisions now to be acted upon are critical and important, and I trust they will be coolly and disinterestedly weighed. . . .

There are some communications not easily made at a distance, and especially when secrets are not thought necessary and even creep into public orders, and there was a considerable feeling in regard to silence on the subject of M. de St. Aignan.[2] . . . I have done all that I could to put this matter to rest, and I trust I have been successful. The Emperor has done everything on his part in the very best manner. But he will not depart from the principle on which I have had occasion lately to enlarge in treating of the Projet and will not be bound to make disclosures to *all* his Allies at the same moment and to the same extent on all subjects.

I do not yet give up the hope of carrying through the Projet in the great quarters in most points as you desire it, and I think

---

[1] This officer brought Napoleon's evasive answer to the Frankfort proposals, dated 16th November, the last note under Maret's signature.

[2] See LII.

Prince Metternich will assist : but I still fear it will not do in regard to accession for the reasons I have stated, and therefore I think it so much clear gain to send the powers and instructions for the additional article similar to that with Austria, which will be forwarded to-morrow, without prejudice to the Projet or so much of it as can be carried. Looking back to the proceedings which have taken place since this period of last year, it is impossible not to do justice to the perseverance of the Emperor and to the firmness with which he has carried on all the business of negotiation and in the field, in spite of real difficulties and disappointments, and in spite of all the obstacles of party and of difference of honest opinion as well of more interested ones among his own confidential servants. The present is a moment of at least as great trial as any, and I am sure, my dear Lord, you will feel that he deserves every encouragement and support, in order that the great work which has arrived at a state of so much promise and even maturity may be brought to completion, and I believe all are aware how much depends upon him.

Every credit is due to P. Metternich for his conduct : he has been roughly handled by them who did not know or trust his sentiments. I think some public applause would be well bestowed, and I am quite sure it would be gratifying. The obloquy was much felt. . . .

XXVI. [F. O. Supplementary.]
CATHCART TO CASTLEREAGH. (Private and Confidential.)
Frankfort on the Maine, November 28th, 1813.

. . . I have already had occasion to state that Prince Metternich's great abilities as a statesman found their due level at the United Head Quarters of those Courts.

The Emperor Alexander is his own minister. His regular ministers are at St. Petersburgh, and the few confidential servants he employs here cannot assume the authority of ministers without special instructions in the cases which present themselves. H.I.M. is fully aware to the talent and ability of the Austrian minister, he is satisfied with the advice he has given and with the energy and activity he has shown since the Courts have been united. Prince Metternich has ready access to him, and H.I.M. certainly listens to his suggestions with confidence as suggestions or points, but on those points only on which the interests of the two empires run parallel. There are, indeed, few cases at present where they do not. But no man is more able to discriminate.

Prince Metternich, of course, cultivates this advantage by every observance, and his frank and apparently most open and unreserved manner is in the highest degree prepossessing. The Prince is not solicitous to conceal his influence in the general counsels, and, on the contrary, most anxious to stand acquitted in the eyes of Europe, and particularly of England, of the charge of having ever been in his heart attached to French politics. He is on the best terms with Count Nesselrode and the Chancellor Hardenberg. He is extremely attentive to Lord Aberdeen, who lives with him apparently in habits of great intimacy and confidence. I have always found the same disposition. But since Lord Aberdeen's arrival I have left him to his own Ambassador, although when there is opportunity I keep up an intimate acquaintance. I think it right to make this statement, as it is explanatory of our transactions here.

I hinted to your Lordship at less leisure that we were to put this influence to the proof for a beneficial purpose, and to endeavour to bring about the Projet at least with the three Powers here at present. Lord Aberdeen has made great progress in so far as to have got Prince Metternich to recommend it, and he states that the Emperor would accede to a proposition to sign in England ; but this would only be to revert to the answer first given to me, which was to include the Projet in a new Treaty of concert and subsidy, it being supposed that a negotiation for an object devised by the British Government carried on in London might lead to increase the portion of supply for the Continent, and I have hopes that on the Emperor's return the Prince will join in endeavouring to obtain a consent to sign here if the scruples which have prevented it hitherto can be removed. . . . Your brother will not be satisfied if we do not obtain to the full extent of your instructions everything wished by His Majesty's Government. You know his zeal, and I promise you his practice proves it as much as his letters. We fully agree with him, and use our best endeavours, but if we cannot by any exertion get everything we at least endeavour to obtain and to secure as much as we can.

The note[1] Lord Aberdeen acquaints me he has given to P. Metternich (I have not read it) appears to be very proper to secure him from being misrepresented, and Metternich has promised to give him an answer attesting its accuracy. I read over with him the portion of one of your Lordship's private letters in answer to an observation of Count Lieven's, which is the only document

[1] Protesting against St. Aignan's misrepresentations of the conversation at Frankfort on the subject of the maritime rights.   See LXIV. p 113.

which treats of the principle of not discussing maritime points between England and France, if any such shall occur in a general negotiation.[1] . . .

XXVII. [*F. O. Russia* 83.]
CASTLEREAGH TO CATHCART. (No. 87.)
Foreign Office, November 30th, 1813.
I have received your Lordship's report of your discussions with the Emperor on the subject of the Treaty.[2] I am surprised and not a little disappointed to find difficulties made in the quarter from whence aid was expected.

I shall abstain from sending your Lordship further instructions on this subject till I hear again, flattering myself that the difficulties put forward will be overcome.   I cannot suppose that His Imperial Majesty can seriously expect us to propose to Parliament now to vote a scale of subsidy for an indefinite period of war, still less that we should disqualify ourselves from treating at all by stipulating by anticipation the surrender of our conquests these suggestions would be inadmissible on the part of any Power, and are, to say the least, not very appropriate to a nation that has acted the part we have done.   If this species of negotiation is persisted in, better at once decline the measure altogether.   And I am yet to learn why Great Britain is more interested in cementing the Confederacy than Russia.

The multiplication of contracting parties, by extending the treaty to the secondary Powers, is an objection fairly open to discussion.   And it may deserve consideration whether, upon the whole, it might not be better that the Powers of the first order should stipulate for their interests than contract with them—but the main question is : shall the confederates by a common Treaty now identify their cause, and lay the foundation of a defensive alliance for mutual protection against France hereafter ?   If Russia is prepared for this, I cannot persuade myself that the shape to be given to the Treaty can be of difficult arrangement. As a bond of union I still consider it to be of the utmost importance.

XXVIII. [*F. O. Supplementary* 343.]
CATHCART TO CASTLEREAGH. (Private.)
Frankfort on the Maine, December 4th, 1813.
. . . I have had one conference with H.I.M. since his

[1] See XIX.
[2] See XXIII.

return from his excursion to visit the relations of his Empress. On this occasion I mentioned the unqualified declaration which the Chancellor Hardenberg has given to Sir Charles Stewart of the disposition of the Court of Prussia to enter into an Alliance to the full extent of the Projet and secret article and to consult with the ministers of Austria, Russia, Prussia, and *Sweden*, or separately with him, and that I had officially requested Sir Charles to represent to Baron Hardenberg the expediency of not naming this business to the Swedish minister until the concurrence of Russia and Austria should be obtained ; that I understand from Lord Aberdeen that Austria was ready to declare her concurrence in writing though to a more limited extent in regard to the Swedish business, and probably to the measure only of a Quadruple Alliance between Great Britain, Austria, Russia, and Prussia, and that Prince Metternich would speak to him on the subject. H.I.M. immediately said that he would be most ready to concur with his other Allies in any measure which was desired by the Government of H.R.H. the Prince Regent. So that if Prince Metternich will really go as far as Lord Aberdeen has reason to expect, I think that a Quadruple Alliance may be brought about concluding most of the points stated in the secret article and perhaps reserving the question of inviting other Powers to accede.

There is some intention of sending Pozzo di Borgo[1] to England to explain the ideas of this Court in regard to some important arrangements which, it is thought, it would be most desirable to settle to the satisfaction of those concerned before the negotiations of a general peace come on, if it were possible. I have always declared that Great Britain will neither recede in principle nor practice from any engagement she has taken, and as Russia makes the same declaration no such question will, I trust, arise, but it would, I think, be advantageous if it could be done to settle the business between Sweden and Denmark as soon as possible, and to ensure the successes of the Northern Army in Holland and Brabant, so as to proceed without delay to the Scheldt. . . .

There is certainly no communication whatsoever that I have kept back from either Lord Aberdeen or Sir Charles on points not exclusively belonging to Russia. But although the former has always communicated everything I have asked for, such communications have not always been early or spontaneous, and scarcely in a single instance in the way of consultation, and what is singular is that this reserve, which perhaps is constitutional, is more remarkable in regard to military matters. Your Lordship

[1] He was sent. See XXX.

has not answered a letter I wrote on the subject of Sir R. Wilson.[1]
That officer has exerted himself in every way and not very prudently to obtain the appointment of which Lord Burghersh is in
possession at the Head Quarters of the Austrian Army, and in
this view has gained completely the confidence of Lord Aberdeen,
having persuaded him that he can govern the Commander-in-
Chief and the Head Quarters at least of the other Allies. Lord
A. informs me that your Lordship has written to him that if I
do not object Sir R. may be sent to Marshal Bellegarde's army
in Italy. I have answered that Sir R. is placed on the Staff
under my command and that whenever I am authorized to send
him to the Austrian Army there will be no sort of objection on
my part to his going to the army in Italy. But I see no use in
his being at the Head Quarters where I am with several officers,
and I must repeat that I have the strongest objection to it, although,
as I have said before, he may be usefully employed on a detached
service. I have not detached him because I expect your Lordship's decision. His intrigues in a lower rank would be ridiculous
because they are very little disguised, but in his rank and with
reference to mine they are highly indecent. His distinguished
gallantry in the field and his good qualities gain him the affection
of everybody and mine in particular, but when his inclination
to intrigue and party leads him to interfere with the service I
am compelled to check it, because it may go to dangerous lengths,
and in the meanwhile certainly impedes the means I might have
of doing more for the public service. It is very well known that
he would readily carry an order to the mouths of the guns of the
enemy's batteries. But it will as easily be believed that he will
guide Prince Metternich in conducting the administration of the
Austrian Government as that he will influence the military plans
of the Austrian generals. I have some reason to think it more
than probable he has asked a great person to apply to the Prince
Regent to have him kept at this Head Quarter—there are also
certain reasons for thinking such a request would not be wholly
disregarded. I have said all this with reluctance, and I add
no more. . . .
   I hope your Lordship will understand that, notwithstanding

---

[1] Lord Aberdeen and Metternich had eagerly supported Sir R. Wilson's
urgent request to be British Military Representative at the Austrian Headquarters of the Grand Army. Castlereagh was, however, adamant, and in view of
the candidate's Whiggism and the fact that he was urging the conclusion of
peace, the decision is not surprising. Cathcart, who was himself a soldier,
had always refused to allow Wilson to have any official position. The other
side of the case is seen in Lord Stanmore's *Life of Aberdeen*, p. 42, and Sir
Robert Wilson's *Private Diary*, II., p. 267.

what I have said of communications, which I think you may by
a hint put on the best footing.   I am highly delighted with both
my colleagues, and give them every possible praise for their great,
able, and successful exertions.   .   .   .

XXIX.   [*F. O. Russia* 87.]
CATHCART TO CASTLEREAGH.   (No. 126.)
Frankfort, December 5th, 1813.

[A further opportunity given by Sir Charles Stewart's messenger
of stating the progress made in negotiating the Treaty of Alliance.]
The Emperor had doubts of the utility or expediency of the
measure as proposed, under the change of circumstances which
has taken place, even though the powers given to the plenipotentiaries should enable them to remove doubts and objections which
presented themselves on perusing the draft.   Various objection
occurred to inviting Powers of the second order either to join
in this Alliance as principals, or to accede to it, and therefore
it was considered more eligible that the Alliance if concluded
should be quadruple, and limited to Great Britain, Russia, Austria
and Prussia.

In the next place, as the Powers last-named are now united
in the same cause by common interest and by separate Treaties,
it was conceived that any new Alliance should not only give
additional force to the engagements separately contracted, but
that it should also be made to contain some new principles
applicable to the further progress of the war and its termination ;
that, in this view, it might be expedient to look to the next
campaign, and to ascertain what would be the amount of force,
arms, and equipment or subsidy the several Powers might undertake to furnish.   And, in the third place, in reference to the state
of the parties engaged in war.   They are divided into three
classes : France, who has overrun, injured or oppressed all Europe ;
Great Britain, who has conquered all the islands and the
dominion of the sea ; and, thirdly, all the other Powers of Europe,
who being been overrun, injured, or oppressed by France, are now
united to place her in her proper limits.

Two of these classes are therefore joined against one, and it is
more than probable that they will succeed.   But, as England
alone has conquests to restore, and has declared that to improve
and secure a peace she will make restitution, under certain
reservations, it is interesting to the Allies to invite England to
declare in a secret article not only that she will make restitutions

generally, but to name the conquests which she will retain, which conquests so to be retained the Allies might on their part guarantee to Great Britain. Now, as neither the amount of subsidy to be furnished by Great Britain, nor the specification of the conquests which she may choose to retain seem to fall within the scope of the full powers given to the plenipotentiaries of His Britannic Majesty, it was proposed to send a counter-project to be negotiated at London.

The Emperor of Russia having considered this question, and having consulted his Allies, or those within his reach, ordered a statement of these arguments to be drawn up, which was done in the form of a draft of a dispatch to Count Lieven, which was read to me.

I objected strongly to this mode as calculated to defeat its object by delay, offering to stipulate generally for the continuance of such subsidy as Great Britain could afford and for the application of such conquests made from France as Great Britain might be disposed to give up for the improvement and for the better securing the duration of a peace, conquests from Denmark and Holland being reserved for purposes connected with those States, and I requested that the draft should be reconsidered before any further use should be made of it.

Your Lordship's dispatch, No. 76,[1] upon the defensive alliances concluded at Toeplitz afforded me a very early opportunity of again bringing forward the Prince Regent's sentiments on the general interests of the Confederacy as connected with the Treaty of Alliance now proposed. The Emperor said that whatever doubts or difficulties might arise in framing a Treaty of Alliance, there could be no hesitation on his part in taking an engagement to stipulate in the general peace for the independance of the Peninsula, as well as of Germany, and His Imperial Majesty was pleased to authorize me to go immediately to the Secretary of State to consider with him the most expedient mode of making this engagement. It was proposed to do it by adding a separate article to the Treaty of Reichenbach, and then a question arose whether this should be done in London or here. I agreed to its being done in London, if your Lordship should approve of it, lest my signing it here should be considered as an acceptance on my part of this additional article as an equivalent for the treaty proposed.

On the 25th or 26th of Nov. the instructions were dispatched for Count Lieven, with powers to sign a separate article. On the 29th

[1] Of the 15th October, instructing Cathcart to draw attention to the omission of any mention of Spain.

Sir Charles Stewart communicated to me a copy of a letter from the Chancellor Hardenberg, declaring the concurrence of the King of Prussia in the Projet of Alliance which had been submitted to him, and stating his readiness to meet the ministers of Russia, Austria, and Sweden, to concert with them the proceedings, or to treat with Sir Charles. I deprecated the mentioning the Projet to the Swedish Government in the present stage of the business. The Earl of Aberdeen also acquainted me that any scruples which Prince Metternich had entertained were removed, that the Emperor of Austria was prepared to concur in the proposal of alliance, and that Prince Metternich was ready either to speak to the Emperor of Russia upon the business, or to give to His Excellency a declaration in writing.

I lost not a moment in stating these circumstances to the Emperor, who was pleased to say that it was a matter in which he was not inclined to act contrary to the opinion of his Allies, but that he would speak to Prince Metternich, and if he found no objection, there certainly should be none on His Imperial Majesty's part to a measure which was recommended and desired by the British Government. This morning (Dec. 5th) the Emperor told me that he had seen Prince Metternich, and that he believed an Alliance might be concluded here, and that therefore I was at full liberty to take such measures as I might judge most expedient to bring it forward. I went from the Emperor to the Earl of Aberdeen, and with his Excellency to Prince Metternich, who undertook to speak again to the Emperor with a view to receive from him authority to proceed with the ministers of Russia and Prussia and the British plenipotentiaries.

The proposal of adding an article fixing the amount of subsidy for the next campaign was discussed with Prince Metternich, and it was in great measure given up by him as belonging at least as properly to a separate Treaty. This minister seemed much more tenacious of the argument in favour of a secret article concerning retrocessions, distinguishing the conquests Great Britain is determined to retain. He was decidedly of opinion that the Alliance should be quadruple, but that all the Allies might be invited to accede, and agreed that as Spain, a Power certainly of the first order, could not be a principal, Sweden would have no cause to complain. In regard to the question of Norway, he saw no reason why the Powers who had separately come under engagements on that subject should not do so collectively, but that as negotiations are on foot between Austria and Denmark, his Court must be excepted for the present from any article relating to that question.

I have communicated all that has passed to Count Nesselrode, whom I could not see in the morning, and I learned from him that he has by the Emperor's command written to Count Lieven to desire His Excellency to move your Lordship to send to us further instructions in regard to subsidy and retrocession.

If no new impediment occurs, I will to-morrow press the nomination of plenipotentiaries and an appointment of a time and place for the first conference.

XXX. [*F. O. Supplementary* 343.]
CATHCART TO CASTLEREAGH. (Private.)
Frankfort on the Maine, December 9th, 1813.

My last letters to your Lordship were sent by General Pozzo de Borgo, whose intended mission to London I had announced in former correspondence. The General left me about eight in the evening of the 6th, after which I wrote my letters and sent them to his quarter at a late hour during the same night or at one or two the following morning. I mentioned to your Lordship that he was to receive the Emperor's orders at some period of that night, and that it was very possible he might thereby become the bearer of some information which had not reached me. Accordingly he received a copy of the Duke of Vicence's letter,[1] with instructions to Count Lieven relative to the communication of that letter and the probable answer. The next morning I went as usual to the parade, at which time I generally call at the office after coming from the Emperor, and I there received a copy of the Duke of Vicence's letter, which was prepared for me. I asked at what hour it had been received, and I was answered the preceding evening. I asked whether General Pozzo had carried a copy to London, and was answered in the affirmative, and that it was considered that this letter went so far, and so much farther than Napoleon had ever gone before, that there seemed to be no doubt but that some proceeding must take place upon it. That it was probable a negotiation between plenipotentiaries of Great Britain, Russia, Austria, and Prussia, with one for France, would be preferred to a congress of a more extended description, at least to define the basis, and that the answer would be that England was invited to send a plenipotentiary to this negotiation, and that the Courts here would wait the concurrence of their Ally before a final answer could be given to France. I am also assured that

[1] Letter of the Duc de Vicence (Caulaincourt) to Metternich, Dec. 2nd, 1813. Caulaincourt, who desired peace, had replaced Maret as Foreign Minister, and this communication accepted the terms offered to St. Aignan.

the answer was not drawn up *rédigé*, and that it should be sent to me as soon as it was settled. The original letter was sent by Prince Metternich to Lord Aberdeen ; I do not know at what hour a communication was made to Sir Charles Stewart by the Prussian Chancellor.

Sir Charles contrived to have intelligence of the arrival of the Duke of Vicence's letter in the night, and obtained a copy of it and of the instructions or probable instructions to be given to Count Lieven and the other ministers at London. He conceived the mission of General Pozzo to be for this purpose, and was extremely indignant. Whether Lord Aberdeen and I were objects of any part of the indignation at that moment I know not, but he sent off two messengers, one by Holland the other by the Weser, with this intelligence in the night between the 6th and 7th, without giving any notice to either of us, or inquiring whether we had any information on this subject of this letter, nor did I know that h had sent till late in the following evening when I happened to call upon him.

This place is so full of political agents and there is such universal expectation of great events that, as may naturally be expected, everything that is done or said by the ministers of the three Courts or by the foreign ministers is watched and recorded, and the very strong language which he had not been very studious to conceal in speaking of the conduct of the ministers, and the circumstance of the concealment of his dispatching messengers, has made a very great sensation here, and has caused a great deal of irritation. We know that it proceeds from excessive zeal and a little exaltation in obtaining and in sending home the earliest intelligence, and therefore though we have not spared our animadversions, it has not interrupted the harmony in which we live together, but we have not, as far as I can judge, at all convinced him that he is in the wrong, and as the public service must suffer if this continues, it is quite necessary that your Lordship should learn from us what will, I apprehend, come from several quarters, and give such advice as you may think expedient. He did mention his intention of sending Mr. Jackson to Lord Clancarty to put his Lordship in full possession of the state of affairs here, but it was not till the day after his departure that he communicated to me his having added a destination to Downing Street. The points in the conduct of the Ministers of State which have so much offended Sir Charles are, as I understand them, the following :—

The sending important communications to the ministers at

London for the information of the Prince Regent's Government instead of sending such information through the ministers accredited to those Courts, which he considers a very great indignity ; secondly, the concealment of this important letter, or rather, as it has proved, the attempt to conceal it till after it was dispatched by a messenger of their own ; and thirdly, the frequent practice of communicating measures after they are completed and not while under deliberation.

These are all proceedings which it is our business to discourage and to prevent by all the means we can devise, and to remonstrate against or complain of in the manner we may judge most effectual, and we have all done so. I do not, however, know that Governments have, otherwise than by express stipulation in particular cases, considered themselves as bound to make their communications to each other through the Ambassador or Envoy of the Court which is to receive the communication. It is usual for a Court which makes a communication to another through its own Ambassador to give notice to the Ambassador of the Court which receives it that such communication has been made, but not always in time to enable the latter to anticipate the communication already sent off. And in regard to consulting the Ambassadors of foreign Powers upon measures under deliberation, I have always understood that, unless regulated by express stipulation, it is a matter of discretion generally depending upon personal confidence.

Upon these grounds I did not feel it necessary to express very violent indignation at the preference which has been given to the mode of communicating this information through Gen. Pozzo in addition to the other parts of his instructions which have been opened to me. Lord Aberdeen and myself have, however, not failed to make our representations, and the answers we have received are nearly the same.

It was very well known that there was a difference of opinion in regard to Sir Charles upon some of the things that have taken place, and therefore it occurred that what is now proposed would have a chance of being more impartially considered as stated by Pozzo or by their own ministers than if it came accompanied by our animadversions, all of which might differ with each other as expressed by us, and thereby lose the effect which any single opinion might have ; in the next place that, although each Court might be disposed to communicate with one foreign minister, it did not follow that each or the three Courts together would choose to debate their measures with any three. The publicity of the discovery of the letter and of the obtaining a copy has also excited great suspicion and investigation, in so much that Prince Metternich told me in conversation this evening that he had dismissed six persons from his office because he had reason to suppose that one or more of them was concerned in giving this information.

The Courts will now probably be at some distance from each other, as the Emperor of Austria goes in the first instance to Wurtzburgh, and the King of Prussia has not declared where he will go when the movement takes place, so that, with a little caution, we may gain the character of more unanimity and obtain more confidence as a collective body, if we all meet again to reside for any length of time in the same town.

After all, I am not aware of any very material difference of opinion that has existed between us, although the General[1] supposes that he differs from Lord Aberdeen and me, and it is only in regard to what is likely to be the view or decision of the Prince Regent's Government and the mode of proceeding. He has invited me to read all his dispatches, which I really have not had time to do ; but I must do away one error which I understand exists in one of them. I had told him that the Emperor Alexander was extremely glad that the communication through M. de St. Aignan was made through the Austrian minister, and that he did not make the communication. Some days afterwards, in reading with Sir Charles a copy of a minute of the conversation with M. de St. Aignan which he had, I observed that Count Nesselrode's name was mentioned in it, and I said that I believed H.I.M. would have been better pleased with that minute if his Secretary of State had not been named. But nothing was further from my intention than to say that there was anything else in that paper of which the Emperor disapproved or that I had any authority to say that the Emperor had expressed disapprobation of Count Nesselrode's having been named.

I received your Lordship's dispatches, circular, and private letter of the 29th and 30th ult.[2] by the messenger Johnston last night. I cannot have an audience for business with the Emperor till to-morrow evening, and I must therefore defer my official letters till after that audience ; I trust I shall by the same conveyance be then enabled to send a copy of the answer to the Duke of Vicence. Prince Metternich, whom I met this evening, told me it was drawn up but had not yet been circulated. I understand it is to say that a communication is to be made to the *Allies* instead of to *Great*

[1] *i.e.*, Sir Charles Stewart.
[2] See XXVII.

Britain, as at first proposed, in order to avoid giving offence. But Lord Aberdeen, who has seen the draft, has probably given a more detailed account.

I have had a great deal of conversation this day about the Alliance proposed, and Lord Aberdeen has met with P. Metternich and Count Nesselrode together and had a long debate ; I fear they will persist on the subject, insisting upon Great Britain naming the conquests she *will not* bring into negotiation if any general Treaty of Alliance is made. . . .[1] Still, Russia and Prussia must either have Alliances with Great Britain by separate Treaty or must have particular articles in a general Treaty. Therefore Austria might consent to sign the Alliance proposed as it stands, but Russia and Prussia must have separate articles, unless they are put on a footing with Austria by having each a Treaty of Alliance. I could not discover why these separate articles, or new Treaties were to contain a specification of British conquests to be retained. . . .

XXXI. [*F. O. Russia* 87.]
CATHCART TO CASTLEREAGH. (No. 128.)
Frankfort, December 12th, 1813.

I have now the honour to enclose herewith a copy of the reply which has been given to Prince Metternich by the Duke of Vicence, as Minister of France for Foreign Affairs, and of the answer[2] which has been sent to this reply, together with Count Nesselrode's note communicating the latter. The Emperor was pleased to signify his intention of speaking to me of this business, but various circumstances prevented it until late last night. His Imperial Majesty desired me, in forwarding these documents, to state, that there was much reason to apprehend that the readiness with which the ruler of France now consented to negotiate upon a basis so different from what he would have listened to at any former period did not arise from any real pacific intention, but to make it impossible for the Allies not to negotiate, expecting thereby to relax their military exertions, and, if possible, to find some question which might produce disunion and dissolve the Confederacy ; that, to counteract this object, His Imperial Majesty

---

[1] Two sentences of the letter are omitted here, as several words are illegible. They refer to the wish of Prussia and Russia, whose relations with Great Britain are on a different basis to that of Austria, to have Subsidy Treaties separate from the Treaty of Alliance.

[2] Metternich to Caulaincourt, Dec. 10th, 1813. A vague and non-committal reply.

had formed an opinion, in which he was supported by Prince Metternich, that the most expedient course is to confine the basis to questions on which there can be no difference of opinion and which lead to the least discussion, leaving out all questions which can be decided by the Allies among themselves.

The regulation of the frontier to be assigned to France seemed therefore to embrace the whole question, taking for a general description the Pyrenees, Alps, and Rhine, and negotiating further only for the portion of Piedmont and of the Netherlands to be comprehended within this frontier. The matter of the cession of Norway and all questions of frontier among the Allies, and even those for the preservation of a future Balance of Power, are considered unnecessary to be brought into this discussion with France, as they are at the disposal of the Allies.

I have neither on this nor on any former occasion found the Emperor so much averse to a general Treaty of Alliance offensive and defensive, as proposed by your Lordship, as the ministers are. The language of Prince Metternich on the subject of specifying in a treaty of this sort the conquests, which Great Britain would keep or bring into negotiation, has been stated. I do not see the object of calling for this declaration unless it be to take out of the hands of Great Britain the preponderance in the negotiations which must arise from the important circumstance of being the only Power which has conquests to restore. But His Imperial Majesty will not decide without the Allies to agree to this Treaty, and although Prince Metternich attributes the opposition to Russia, he is the only person who is eloquent in supporting that opposition, and it neither occurred to the Emperor nor to Count Nesselrode till after consultation with him. Admitting the principle of this basis of negotiation with France, it seems to me that a general alliance offensive and defensive between all the Powers now at war against France would be particularly desirable.

I am not sanguine that peace will be made at the present moment, but if all attempts to weaken or dissolve the Confederacy shall prove abortive, and if the operations and preparation of war are continued on the present scale, I do not see anything but the unfortunate event of several battles that can prevent a general pacification. . . .

XXXII. [*F. O. Russia* 83.]
CASTLEREAGH TO CATHCART. (No. 93.)
Foreign Office, December 18th, 1813.
I have to acquaint you that the Count de Lieven has read to me

confidentially a dispatch addressed to him by Count Nesselrode on the subject of the Projet of General Alliance which your Excellency was authorized to propose. I forbear enumerating the topics contained in this dispatch. It brings forward the same view of the question which has been reported by your Excellency to have been urged by the Russian Minister in your discussions at Head Quarters, and the dispatch has probably been seen in extenso by your Lordship.

This instruction does not authorize Count Lieven to decline the proposal, it only expresses a desire, in consequence of the great change that has taken place in the state of affairs since the Projet was sent from hence, that it should be reconsidered with a view of rendering its provisions more conformable to existing circumstances ; I took occasion, in regretting the delay which had already occurred, to ask the Russian Ambassador whether he had received full powers and instructions from his Court to treat on any modifications which they were inclined to propose. Not finding that the Count de Lieven had received any such powers or authority, I informed him that the subject having already been so fully opened and discussed, it appeared to me unavailing that any further official negotiation should take place in the abscence of any regular authority to come to an arrangement.

Having on these grounds declined for the present any official proceeding, I told the Count de Lieven that I could not conceal from him, in that personal confidence with which we were in the habit of conversing, my individual surprise at the tone of misconception which appeared to me to pervade the greater proportion of the dispatch which he had read to me. That it was happily true that a great change had taken place in the face of affairs since the end of September when this measure originated, but not, as I conceived, to impede, but, on the contrary, greatly to facilitate its execution. That whilst the successes of the Allies rendered the stipulations contained in the secret article of the proposed Treaty more attainable, and consequently less onerous, they in no degree impaired the considerations which dictated to the Allies the necessity of union and concert, not only throughout the course but after the termination of the contest ;

That I was unable to conceive how any Power could be supposed to insinuate distrust towards its Allies, which has suggested, as Great Britain had done, the expediency of collecting their scattered and separate engagements into one common Treaty; to which, if all the Confederates should not be actual parties, the nature of the Treaty should serve to inspire all with confidence in the principles of common interest upon which the leading Powers had agreed and were known to act ;

That if he supposed distrust as a general proposition was without foundation it was obviously inapplicable in a peculiar degree to that Power, namely, Russia, which Great Britain had selected for its earliest confidence, and on whose enlarged views and known influence it had avowedly rested its chief reliance for the success of the measure.

If Great Britain was the first Power to move in this transaction, it was not from any sense that *her* particular interests most required its adoption. Perhaps, without arrogance, it might be asserted that, from her insular situation and known resources, Great Britain was the last Power to whom any engagement of this nature could be deemed necessary with a view to her own immediate security. Such a proposition for the general welfare might be regarded therefore as coming from her with a better grace. Russia, from her peculiar circumstances, might be considered as standing nearly in a similar predicament, which certainly was amongst the principal motives, in addition to the unbounded confidence with which the two Governments were than acting, which induced the Prince Regent's ministers preferably and in the first instance to open their views to the Court of St. Petersburgh on the subject.

If any assurance had existed, that with the war was to terminate the military despotism of France. If the existence of a Government in France likely to found its dominion upon a revival upon the ancient pacific relations of Europe could have been calculated upon, the British Government would have then been of opinion, that the objects of the Alliance being attained, the Confederacy might safely be dissolved, and the various Powers be permitted to fall back into the ordinary course of their accustomed politics. But whilst Bonaparte shall continue to rule France, perhaps even while the system itself, which he has matured, shall continue to give impulse to the military resources of that great Empire, the only safety for the other Powers of Europe is to impose upon the ambitious propensities of France that constraint in time of peace, to which alone they will owe the concessions, which may by war be extracted from the enemy.

It is the persuasion that the strength and power of the Alliance will be great in proportion as common engagements are known to bind at least the Powers of the first order, that first induced the British Government to bring forward this Projet of a General Treaty for the purpose of embodying the Confederacy not only to procure, but to preserve peace. The terms of peace are, no doubt, of essential moment, and the arrangement of limits indispensable to the common safety. Nothing, however, but a defensive League is likely to deter France from returning to the old system of progressive encroachment. The proposition for such a League, it was conceived, would come with most propriety from Great Britain and from Russia, as the Powers least exposed to suffer in the first instance from French encroachments. It appeared that the example of two such leading Powers, ready to lend themselves to a system of common protection, would give confidence to the more exposed States, and encourage them to lean on such alliance for security, rather than attempt to fall back within the circle of French influence. That whatever might be the hazards of a system of this nature upon every enlarged view of policy, it became both Great Britain and Russia, even with a view to their own separate interests, not to shrink from bearing their share in it.

I stated to the Count de Lieven that I was happy to find that to such an Alliance neither Prussia nor Austria felt any reluctance. That it was a question fairly open to consideration, whether it should be limited to the Powers of the first, or be extended to those of the second and third order. That the Treaty, if made upon a comprehensive view of the general interests, could not fail to give general satisfaction to the other states, although they should not be invited expressly to concur in it as signing parties. That it was extremely desirable, however, that Spain should not be omitted; her rank and station in Europe, and more especially her military position with relation to France, rendered it a measure of indispensable policy that as the principal Power in the Peninsula she should be included.

That perhaps it might be expedient to follow the course lately adopted in the defensive Treaties between Austria, Russia, and Prussia, and to confine the defensive obligation in the first instance to a certain extent of stipulated succour. That in taking the engagements in question as the standard, a line would be drawn which, without offence to any State, would confine the measure to the five greater Powers, viz., Great Britain, Austria, Russia, Prussia, and Spain, each of which might form corresponding engagements with the several Allies, thus binding up the whole into one interest, at the same time narrowing the councils of the Confederacy within more convenient limits. By this means one of the principal objections stated on the part of Russia might be obviated, which, it must be admitted, has gained additional weight from the great augmentation that has latterly taken place in the number of the Allies.

Count Nesselrode's dispatch having adverted to the question of the armistice, with a view of justifying that to which the Emperor had given his consent in June, I observed that the Projet in question did not in point of fact touch the point of armistice, that it only required treaties, conventions, or truces to be made with common consent. That whilst it was a reciprocal duty in agreeing to any armistice to consider how it might affect all the Allied Armies in the field, those on the side of the Pyrenees, as well as of the Rhine and the Alps, it never had occurred to place under undue restraint the power of concluding an armistice, which must be considered as a discretion incident to, and inseparable from, the command of troops, and that as to the particular armistice, namely, that concluded by the Allies in June last, it was well-known that both the British Government and its Ministers abroad did complete justice at the moment to the considerations under which that act was concluded. The dispatch towards the close stated the augmented exertions which the Allies were making, and urged corresponding efforts on the part of Great Britain. It also particularly relied on the claim the Continental Powers had that Great Britain should now stipulate as to the conquests which she was prepared to yield for the interest of the Continent.

For the extent of the exertions the British Government was disposed to make, I stated that I could only refer to our uniform policy throughout the war, and more particularly the measures which had recently received the sanction of Parliament. That with respect to stipulating as to our *conquests*, I was not aware upon what principle such a demand could justly be urged. That the British Government had voluntarily in August last avowed this friendly principle in behalf of her Allies, naturally reserving to itself the right to apply the same according to the Continental arrangements intended, and upon a fair consideration of equivalents to be conceded by the enemy, but the British Government never once conceived that it could be expected that Great Britain would by Treaty pass this discretion into other hands, and confide to its Allies the trust of negotiating for her at a general peace. I further stated that I could not understand why Great Britain should stipulate as to her conquests, whilst Russia and the other Continental Powers were to remain free as to the ultimate destination of the territories occupied by their arms. That it was very true that the question of peace, and consequently the interests of the whole Alliance, might be materially affected by the manner in which Great Britain acted upon the principle in question. But that it was not less true that the same, or at least an equal, evil might result from the Continental Powers pursuing unreasonable views as to their conquests. A too tenacious spirit in any particular State as to their distribution might embroil the whole Confederacy, and render the peace, though otherwise good, of less value to Great Britain. That I must therefore decline till some better ground was urged than mere distrust (a sentiment which I was confident the Emperor could not feel either towards the Prince Regent or ministers) to acquiesce in the justice of such an exclusive stipulation when even in its more general form, but to expect Great Britain to stipulate as to particular conquests was obviously inadmissible. That I trusted, however, no unfavourable inference could be drawn from this reasoning to the prejudice of the liberal intentions professed towards the Continent, intentions which had been spontaneously announced at an early period on the part of this country, and which had been again recorded in an official act within these few days.

I concluded by disavowing that any sentiment of distrust was to be inferred towards any of the Allied Powers, and especially towards the Emperor of Russia, whose magnanimous and persevering zeal was above all praise, from the measure which Great Britain had proposed for their adoption. That, on the other hand, I must protest against the notion that the projected Alliance was an arrangement of such peculiar interest to Great Britain that it was for her to purchase it as a boon from her Allies. That the British Government were from principle disposed to pursue their own interests through the general interests of the Continent, if they found a suitable disposition in the Allies adequately to sustain the common cause ; but, if not, that England was not the State likely first to suffer from an insulated policy.

I only further added that, amidst the fluctuating policy of States, which too frequently varied with the predominance of particular statesmen, it appeared to me, not less an act of wisdom, than of duty to the world, that Great Britain and Russia should take this occasion of solemnly binding themselves, in conjunction with the more exposed States of the Continent, to oppose a Barrier hereafter to the oppression of France. The determination to take upon themselves this generous and provident task would afford to Europe the best, perhaps the only prospect of a durable peace, and when the experience of latter times was examined with respect to the policy of indifference to the fate of neighbouring States, the most anxious and interested politician would find little to give countenance to an abstracted and selfish line of policy.

I transmit this report of my conversation with the Count de Lieven in order that your Lordship's language may be regulated by the reasoning to which it gave occasion, and I am to instruct your Lordship, if the Treaty has not been already signed, to request that powers may be sent to the Russian, Austrian, and Prussian Ministers in London to bring these long-pending discussions to some precise decision.

P.S.—I ought to have noticed that, in the course of our conversation, the Count de Lieven stated that his Court, considering Spain to be the prominent and immediate object of solicitude to the British Government, had authorized him to sign an engagement on this point similar to that taken by Austria, and that he was ready immediately to do so, in the form of an additional article, to the Treaty of Concert and Subsidy. I suggested the expediency of at least delaying such a measure, in the hope that it might make a part of a more extended arrangement, which I was persuaded would give much more satisfaction to Spain and to the Allies generally than an insulated engagement of this nature. That, in offering this suggestion, I trusted His Excellency would perceive that I did not act in distrust of Russia, or call in question the validity of those engagements which that great Power had already, in spirit at least, taken with Great Britain upon this subject; that, as my real and only object was to create a permanent counterpoise to the powers of France, in peace as well as in war, His Excellency must be aware that for this purpose the necessity for the measure on a larger scale would, according to my judgment, continue to exist, even though the Allies should be upon the eve of concluding a general peace; and I ventured to represent to His Excellency that the defensive policy of the Treaty appeared to me of not less importance in the view of its operation upon peace than the offensive branch of the arrangement was calculated to lead to a vigorous prosecution of the war.

P.S. 21st Dec.

Circumstances[1] having occurred since the above dispatch was closed, which render the removal of the negotiation to London inexpedient, your Lordship will abstain for the present from taking any steps in execution of that part of my dispatch.

XXXIII. [*F. O. Supplementary* 343.]
CASTLEREAGH TO CATHCART. (Private.)
St. James' Square, December 22nd, 1813.
The great interests at stake and the difficulty of deciding upon them at a distance has induced the Prince Regent to lay his

---

[1] *i.e.*, the decision to send Castlereagh to the Continent.

commands upon me to proceed without delay to Head Quarters, then in my capacity of Secretary of State to issue such directions in pursuance of His Majesty's pleasure as the state of public affairs may require. I have called upon the respective missions here to furnish me with memoranda on all the points on which they may deem it of importance that I should go prepared to decide. This will facilitate my progress on my arrival, but I have declined any discussion here on the various subjects which formed the object of General Pozzo di Borgo's mission. You have passed from operations so rapidly to negotiations that my arrangements have not kept pace with you. Had I foreseen that you were likely to open an intercourse with Paris, I should have deemed some central authority indispensable, and should have at least required the three ministers at Head Quarters to deliberate and decide on matters of general interest collectively. As it is, I hope no real mischief has occurred, and I rely upon finding all drawing cordially together.

(ii.)—*Correspondence of Sir Charles Stewart,
June to December,* 1813.

XXXIV. [*F. O. Prussia* 87.]
STEWART TO CASTLEREAGH. (No. 32.)
Reichenbach, June 6th, 1813.
In reference to my Dispatch, No. 31 of this date, acquainting your Lordship with the Armistice[1] that has been signed between the Allies and the enemy it may not be superfluous on my part to detail to your Lordship, as well as I am able, the sentiments prevalent here relative to the measure, and above all to impress upon your Lordship's mind my firm conviction that the august sovereigns who have agreed to the suspension of hostilities have been actuated by no gloomy contemplation of the state of their affairs or military interests, but principally, if not solely, by a desire to conciliate the Austrian Cabinet, which certainly has strenuously favoured and anxiously supported the negotiations which have been brought to a conclusion. [Military considerations,]
. . .
It may then be justly stated that the inferiority of our numbers, the immense importance of holding Schweidnitz, the immediate security of the Prussian Provinces not yet armed, the effectual organization of the Landwehr, the want of supplies of ammunition, and, above all, the wishes of Austria, are the weighty reasons that

---

[1] The Armistice of Pläswitz signed on the 4th June, 1813.

operated in acceding to the present Armistice, which, it must be admitted, brings with it considerable advantages. The proved position in which the Allies stand must not be lost sight of : in a few short weeks they have given two decided battles to infinitely superior numbers ; no day has passed without trophies of victory arriving at the Head Quarters of the army ; no day has gone by without affairs or skirmishes in which they have uniformly had the advantage ; committed to a desperate battle at Lützen, where they triumphantly stood and conquered, and from which the difficulty of getting up ammunition alone obliged them to retire, they executed the passage of the Elbe, than which no more difficult operation can be conceived, in the presence of a superior enemy, and traversed an extent of country of near 300 miles retiring, contending position after position, and carrying with them between 600 and 700 pieces of cannon, without losing a gun or sacrificing any of their baggage. That these are most triumphant efforts no one, under any circumstances, will be disposed to deny. But taking the enemy's advantages of his fortresses on the rivers, and his facilities of operation, the retreat of the Allies is not surpassed by any other ever known in history. To husband the advantages derived in the late campaign, to forbear to hazard them where the chance was doubtful, to act, as many officers here have argued, upon the great example of Lord Wellington, has been the object of the Allies in concluding the suspension of hostilities, thus gaining time for renewed and increased efforts, and thus expecting to bring Austria forward as a belligerent in the common cause.

Too plainly has it been denoted during the course of this protracted war that nothing but force will ever compel Bonaparte to make such a peace as would satisfy Europe. It is evident under the present circumstances that the Allied Armies are not in a situation to conquer the peace desired. The period of the cession of hostilities may produce much from Austria ; at all events it will enable the Allies to wield new and most powerful means, and they will have the opportunity of re-establishing an order of system, which, from various untoward circumstances, not necessary now to go into, has been completely relaxed.

In looking to the details of this Armistice, it is a subject worthy of remark that it is perhaps the only one ever entered into by Bonaparte in which he has yielded territory, in arranging the line of demarcation, and the evacuation of Breslau and other points clearly demonstrate that the enemy were much more eager for the accomplishment of this measure than the Allies ; this may be interpreted equally to the cause of Austria [*sic*], who has evidently placed herself in a situation in which she can dictate to all parties.

It occurs naturally to calculate what effect this proceeding will have on the operations in the Peninsula. I can well imagine the Armistice will give a great stimulus and spirit of enterprise to the French forces acting in Spain. This, however, Lord Wellington most probably may profit by, as it is to be hoped the duration of the term is not long enough nor the prospect of peace in any degree so inviting as to enable Bonaparte to accumulate suddenly in the Peninsula ; he will require all he can muster between the Elbe and the Oder.

The affairs in the North, and the difficulties that have existed between Sweden and Denmark, have drawn on so long that an additional period of time to meet their development may not be attended with evil, provided the Prince Royal is secure from attack, which it is to be presumed he is, under the Armistice, and if Hamburgh remains in the hands of the Allies there is reason to hope a good system of operations in this interval may be decided on in that quarter.

With respect to the relative situation the armies may be in as to numbers at the expiration of the Armistice, one must be guided a good deal by reports in forming an opinion, having no certain data. Russia affects upwards of 100,000 men now on their march. These, I am assured, will positively join. The declarations of Prussia leave no doubt to believe her Landwehr will be increased at least to 60,000, so that her force may be brought to near 200,000 men. That the enemy may do much in the meantime also, I am not disposed to controvert, but with the universal spirit and sentiment that still reigns throughout every part of these armies (and I should not do justice, especially to the King of Prussia, if I did not enforce in the strongest terms the firmness and determination with which he contemplates the future) there is every reason to hope for most successful and brilliant successes, and a glorious termination to the contest.

XXXV. [*C. C. IX.* 22.]
STEWART TO CASTLEREAGH.
Imperial Head-quarters, Reichenbach.
June 6th, 1813.

The news we sent home is not the best, and, from what I see, I fear political treachery and the machinations that are in the wind more than any evils from Bonaparte's myrmidons. We must keep a sharp look-out, especially since our refusal of Austrian mediation. We are not considered (from all I see going on) in the Cabinet. The accounts from Hamburgh and Stralsund are bad. I fear the Swedes will go, and Bonaparte gets 20,000 Danes in the North. However, we shall trim him yet, if we can confine him to fair fighting.

The Prince Royal has not been managed as he should have been by Russia, and if the Emperor does not lower his tone, Bernadotte will yet seize Finland. The disorder in the Russian army is great ; Prussians are infinitely better. They have everywhere greatly distinguished themselves, and will do much more in a little time. You cannot send them too much ammunition and arms. Russia rides the bear over them, but they are obedient and patient, and I will pledge my faith for theirs ; although the Germans will not burn *their Moscow*, and lay waste their country, still they will be true ; and Prussia will not be the first Power that will withdraw from English Alliance. I trust Parliament will be up before the bright hopes in England are the least over-clouded. At all events, Wellington must send you a victory to bruit forth with the armistice.

I cannot help thinking the great personages of the drama here will meet, and Metternich will attempt some *family* alliances to aid the object of peace. If things turn to a Congress, and if you acquiesce in sending a negotiator, pray select a very able man. Depend upon it, he will be required. I fear military diplomatists will not be quite satisfactory to you. Mr. Disbrowe says he is going to Vienna. You will want a devilish clever fellow there, and I am afraid he is too inexperienced. I have seen enough in a little time of the windings and turnings of diplomatic chicane to fear. I do your business very imperfectly, and therefore I may be allowed to express my doubts of others. . . .

XXXVI. [*F. O. Prussia* 87.]
STEWART TO CASTLEREAGH. (No. 37.)
Reichenbach, June 16th, 1813.

On considering the nature and purport of the communications carrying on through Austria,[1] and the share Prussia takes in the same, it is essential to see how far she lends herself to any act

---

[1] Russia and Prussia had accepted the mediation of Austria, and this last Power was now engaged in obtaining from the two first their conditions of peace.

that can militate against the fair, true, and literal interpretation of the Treaty[1] just signed.

After the most careful consideration of the enclosure it appears to me that Prussia does not depart from her engagements with Great Britain in receiving the communications of a Power whose mediation we know she had accepted previous to our making this Treaty ; on those communications she has commented, and annexed other conditions ; she is desirous England should go along with her in establishing preliminary conferences on which the great work of a General Peace may be founded. At the same time Prussia has declared the object of the war distinctly in her treaty ; she has bound herself not to negotiate or conclude either truce or peace with the enemy but in concert with her Allies. But she has not bound herself not to communicate with a neutral on the grounds on which she would wish for peace, and she is anxious to bring Great Britain to preliminary measures with a view to final adjustment, or rather, by the display of Great Britain, to give Austria no possible ground of complaint that all the Allies have not gone along with her to the utmost extent in endeavouring in her own way to accomplish a peace upon a solid basis. It is that Austria may not have the power to urge that a single point in the conduct of the Allies has differed from her dictation, that she may not have a shadow of ground to refuse them her support, and that she may be finally forced forward, that every measure now adopted has been framed to make her confident in the warlike dispositions of the Allies; to uphold her by showing we look to war even without her, to convince her that England and Sweden are firmly united to Russia and Prussia, and finally to make her adhere to propositions, which Bonaparte (it is declared) will not accept, is the surest mode of gaining her as a belligerent.

I expressed to the Chancellor Hardenberg my incompetence to answer him as to the sanction of England to the late proceedings ; I had accepted and signed his Treaty in the literal sense ; the most important points appeared to me to have been neglected in the propositions alluded to, and those most interesting to England; without reference or instructions, I had no reason to believe Great Britain would take any part in what had occurred, but upon the complete fulfilment of the late Treaty I relied. His assurances in answer were cordial and satisfactory.

I understand from Lord Cathcart that Count Nesselrode called on him yesterday evening and communicated to His Excellency

[1] The Treaty of Reichenbach between Great Britain and Prussia signed June 14th, 1813.

the Austrian propositions and Russia's line of proceeding on
the result of the various conferences hitherto carried on, laying
much stress on the candour and openness of His Imperial
Majesty in not wishing Lord Cathcart to sign the Treaty (which
in fact had been signed two days before in Brouillon), and he
left it for His Excellency's consideration if, after these communications, he thought proper under his instructions to sign *this day*.
From a conversation which I have had with him this morning I
understand that he intends to sign.[1]

The explanation given by Russia previous to signing the
Treaty may be argued as rendering nugatory on her part the
clause binding her not to treat separately. If the Austrian
propositions now under consideration are agreed to, Russia has
also completely lost sight of Spain, a point so interesting to Great
Britain.[2] It is a curious distinction that is made between a
Preliminary Peace and a General Peace, which is not very easy
to comprehend. I confess that I am alarmed at these late
proceedings. When I saw Count Nesselrode sign the draught
of all the articles of the Treaty the preceding evening without
an alluson to the propositions that are now unfolded, I had little
idea of what has since occurred, and I could not imagine I was
precipitate in signing the following day with Prussia. I know
not the excuse Russia will urge for abandoning Spain and Holland
in her view of a Preliminary Peace, but these are parts of present
transactions that are not satisfactory. I have thought it necessary
your Lordship should be acquainted with the whole progress of
these affairs, and therefore have detailed them at some length.
It remains to be seen what will be the result of the Austrian
propositions as a preliminary to general negotiations. I am
assured no direct communications between the Allies and France
are to take place, and no Congress is to be held, but that individuals
are to be instructed and sent to some particular place, to render
the communications more expeditious. I certainly have not
augured favourably of Austria from the beginning (as Your
Lordship knows) ; she is not improved in my good graces from any
one transaction that has come to my knowledge. Russia and
Prussia both feel that they are dependent upon her, and if she
fails them I will not answer for their firmness. I hope the
Treaties are the best pledges to Great Britain, and viewing her

---

[1] The Treaty between Great Britain and Russia was dated June 15th,
1813.

[2] Russia and Prussia eventually agreed to the Austrian mediation on a basis
of six points. See VI. Note 2.

interests in every quarter I entertain an ardent hope that in any event I shall not be reprehensible for having furthered to the utmost of my power and concluded the Convention with Prussia.

. . .

XXXVII. [*Alison.*[1]]
STEWART TO CASTLEREAGH (most private and secret).
Reichenbach, June 16th, 1813.

Count Hardenberg[2] has arrived from Vienna, and Mr. Humboldt[3]. I have had many conversations with both. Both have hopes, but I will not vouch for the solidity of the basis on which they are rested. It seems now that Metternich is valiant, and that the Emperor Francis is the timid person. To wind him up to a proper key, to pat him on the back and to commit him, decidedly is the present aim. To accomplish this it is necessary to hold the stoutest language : to declare that even without him the war will be carried on ; to clench treaties for succour more binding with England ; and, in short, to look only to war. Upon this policy they are now acting. How it will answer is in the womb of time. His Imperial Majesty, Francis, does not see things so advantageously as is desirable, and when it is pointed out to him that a movement in Bonaparte's rear with the Austrian force would annihilate his son-in-law, he rather looks to his reigning in those limits which peaceable arrangements may bring about.

Count Stadion declared yesterday that the Emperor Francis had positively refused a meeting with Bonaparte, which the latter had urged. If this is the case the visits of the Russian Emperor and the King of Prussia will be equally declined. . . . The arrival of the news of the armistice at Leipsic was very *mal apropos*. A great victory would have been gained then by Woronzoff. When it was received the Prussian officers were so indignant that they tore off their pelisses and trampled them under foot. Count Stadion received reports yesterday from Count Bubna at Dresden which positively assert that the loss of the French army since the opening of the campaign amounts at least to 60,000 men. Bonaparte is anxious to have it believed that it only depends on him to negotiate separately with Russia. In my official despatches you will see the progress and conclusion

---

[1] Lives of Castlereagh and Stewart. I., 667.
[2] The Hanoverian Minister, brother to the Prussian Chancellor.
[3] The Prussian Minister and the Chancellor Hardenberg's principal colleague.

of our treaties. I shall always lament the dilatory proceedings
attending their completion. They should have been finished
at Dresden or Grossberg, and we could then have done it without
difficulty, and should have been then free from the accompanying
explanations. But this I could not rectify. Although you may
not now carry us through our signatures, still, if we had not concluded, the alternative would have been an incapacity in Prussia
to continue her preparations, the direct loss of Austria, and
Russia looking to her own frontier. As it is, we have the hope
Bonaparte will spurn the propositions made. We could not
wait for orders from home. We give our game the last chance,
and if the worst happen we need never be a party to the pacific
negotiations ; and if we are left in the lurch, it is not without
having done our utmost. The loss of a part of our subsidy need
not signify.

With regard to the numbers to be kept up by the Allies, Prussia
to the last would have inserted 100,000, and Russia alone prevented
this. It may be said that Prussia was engaged by her former
treaty with Russia to furnish 80,000 men, and that we get no more
by our subsidy. But the fact is that it would be quite impossible
for Prussia to make good the losses she has sustained since the
commencement of hostilities, and to bring up her effective in the
field to 80,000 men without England's aid. But with what has
been given I am sure she will be brought up to the very utmost
mark. I cannot conceal from you that Lord C.'s [Cathcart]
extraordinary partiality to Russia will never let him see a greater
exertion in another quarter than he can accomplish, therefore
the lower number was inserted in the treaty even after the higher
had been three times inserted. I was obliged to be obedient as
to 80,000, as Russia would not go higher. I fear you will be much
disappointed, but I act under orders. I hope my Hussar
proceedings as to an advance will not electrify you. The fact is
Prussia cannot go on just now without a lift ; the machine is really
at a stand for want of oil.

It may be right to put you in possession of the arguments
that are used by those who do not press Austria so much forward
as we would desire. It is said the positive refusal of England to
give any subsidy has created in Metternich great dissatisfaction ;
that even the name of a small subsidy, in the event of their acting,
would be of immense importance. The non-interference also
of Sweden, up to the present time, upon whom they say we have

expended our millions, and her suffering Hamburg to fall, is urged as a reason for Austria keeping back, she having originally stipulated, as one of the conditions that would induce her to take a part, the employment of a large Swedish army on the lower Elbe.

XXXVIII. [*F. O. Prussia* 87].
STEWART TO CASTLEREAGH. (No. 40.)
Reichenbach, June 22nd, 1813.

[Hardenberg returned yesterday from an interview with Metternich at Gitschin concerning the conference. Russia or Prussia having previously refused to send *Plenipotentiaries* with full Powers to communicate direct with the French authorities, it was arranged that *Negotiators* should be appointed. The distinction appears to be a nice one.]

It appears next that the propositions made by Austria and modified by the Allies (as explained in the letter to Jacobi) have not yet been communicated to Bonaparte. Count Metternich's policy seems to be to draw from Bonaparte the basis on which he will make peace before he communicates to him the ultimatum of Austria and the Allies. The Chancellor Hardenberg pressed Count Metternich to open to Bonaparte the original conditions of the 16th of May [1] as proposed by the Allies ; Count Metternich begged to use his discretion on this subject ; he stated his knowledge of Bonaparte's anxiety to receive them, but he believed his object was only to publish them to the French nation as the grounds of the absolute necessity of continuing the war. Count Metternich also seemed of opinion that it was advisable to protect the issue of the negotiations and the important subject under discussion until a very short period before the rupture of the armistice in order to give Bonaparte as little time for exercising his talents of throwing difficulties in the way as possible. Count Metternich insinuated his conviction of Bonaparte's desire for the general Congress, and this object he had reason to apprehend would be very much pressed (if only to gain more time by a prolongation of the armistice). It is to be hoped, however, this will be stoutly resisted. Count Metternich expressed his opinion decidedly that war would be ultimately the issue of these events, which is an exhilarating circumstance. He was to proceed imme-

- See VI. Note 1.

diately to Dresden to see Bonaparte, after which interview more
important circumstances will be known. . . .

Having received the intimation above detailed previous to
seeing the Chancellor Hardenberg, I deemed it my duty to have
an immediate conference with him, in which I begged to know
what had passed with Count Metternich, and strongly observed
on our Treaty, which pledges Prussia not to act separately from
Great Britain. I put to him the question how he justified the
proceedings going to the length they are doing without England's
participation, and I also urged him to explain the difference he
understood between negotiators and plenipotentiaries with full
powers.

The Chancellor Hardenberg, in reply, gave me the fullest
assurances that Prussia was regulated in her proceedings solely
with the anxious hope of carrying Austria forwards by acting
according to her ideas in the scene that is now passing. His
Excellency did not conceive Prussia was departing from her
Treaty in sending negotiators to communicate with Count Metternich, and he pledged himself to me, in the presence of two wit-
nesses, that the Prussian negotiator should on no account have
any communication direct with the French authorities. His
Excellency repeated pretty much the substance of what I have
above written, and declared his confidence in Count Metternich's
good intentions to make any modification of the Articles she had
proposed, which, however, he thought the French Emperor would
never consent to.

XXXIX. [F. O. Prussia 88.]
JACKSON[1] TO STEWART.
Reichenbach, July 27th, 1813.
[. . . War now considered certain between Austria and
France.]
I have further to inform you that the Russian and Prussian
Plenipotentiaries (in contemplation of Bonaparte's suddenly
breaking the armistice under pretext of the differences which had
occurred at Newmarck) received from the Austrian minister a
written assurance that the Emperor, his master, would consider

---

[1] Stewart having gone to the North of Germany to inspect the Prussian
and Swedish forces there, Jackson was left to report proceedings at Head-
quarters. His dispatches, nominally addressed to his superior, Stewart, were
intended for the information of the Home Government.

such a measure as a declaration of *general* war, and that the Allies might in such a case not only rely upon the full aid and resources of his Empire, but also, in case of necessity, march their troops into his provinces.

I have the greatest satisfaction in reporting to you, Sir, the above intelligence, so much more favourable than circumstances had hitherto allowed us to hope for.   In looking for the cause of this change, and apparently sudden maturity of the Austrian Councils, it is impossible not to feel that the late brilliant and glorious successes[1] of Field Marshal Wellington have had a very great share in producing them.   Bonaparte's own conduct has happily come in aid of this ; it would have been difficult for his most mortal enemy to have dictated a line of conduct better calculated to bring this about than that which his own blind passions have led him to pursue for these last three or four weeks.

His obstinate silence ; his delay in sending a plenipotentiary ; the chicane which, on his part, marked the discussions relative to the prolongation of the Armistice ; the indecent and insulting tone of Marshal Berthier's letter to the Commissioners at New-marck, in a word, everything he has done, or, rather, everything he has not done, has, at last, forced Austria to open her eyes to his real designs, and, I hope and trust, finally convinced her that it is in vain to hope to bring him to reason but by force of arms.

It is, however, still possible, perhaps probable, that Bonaparte may wish, now that he sees the decided tone that Austria is disposed to take, to retrace his steps, and may affect at the opening of the negotiations a considerable degree of pliancy and a disposition to yield on some of the points proposed to him, with the reserve, however, that it would be impossible to conclude anything definitely without knowing the sentiments of Great Britain, and whether any sacrifices he might make would be the means of obtaining a Maritime peace.   Fallacious as such language would be, especially should the circumstance I had the honour to mention to you in my letter of yesterday prove correct, it is not the less certain that, a short time since, it might have had the effect of *spinning out* the negotiations, and, by prolonging a consequent state of uncertainty, might have eventually paralysed and weakened the Concert and efforts of the Allies ; but there is reason to hope that the moment is passed when he might have played this part with success, and that Austria, no longer the dupe of such an artifice, would consider it only as equivalent of war.

[1] The Battle of Vittoria, June 21st, 1813.

XL.   [*F. O. Prussia* 88.]

JACKSON TO STEWART.

Reichenbach, August 2nd, 1813.

[Retails the negotiations between Metternich and Caulaincourt at Prague.]

I have thus, Sir, had the honour of detailing to you the state of affairs as they stood when the last accounts left Prague. They are certainly more favourable than a very short time ago we could have ventured to expect, and are alone attributable to the constancy with which our policy relative to the Peninsula has been followed up, and to the ability and success which have marked its execution.

I should not, however, be justifying the trust and confidence which the Prince Regent's Government have done me the honour to repose in me if I did not (in contemplation of the possibility of a Continental peace) call your attention to the situation in which such an event, however advantageous the conditions of it might in the first instance appear, would place Great Britain. Our Allies give us the most solemn assurances, and have sealed them with positive engagements ; still, however, without intending to call in question their sincerity, I cannot but observe that a " *brilliant* " Continental peace, as the preliminary and necessary forerunner of a Maritime one, is a very favourite idea, and one which, supposing Bonaparte finally to take the part of concession, they would with difficulty reject.

I need not expose to you, Sir, the inconveniences which would result from such a proceeding, even if accompanied by a formal and solemn engagement, on the part of our Allies, to recommence hostilities in the event of their failing to effect a Maritime peace ; but, without such a pledge, is it not evident that, so far from facilitating that object, it would only render its accomplishment more remote ? And would not Great Britain—the Power to whom those of the Continent would be chiefly indebted for the advantages which had relieved them from the burden of war—be left to bear the whole weight of it alone ? How much more forcibly would this apply if the complete freedom of the Peninsula from French dominion did not form a part of such a Treaty !

I should, perhaps, apologise, Sir, for troubling you with these observations, but the necessity of being prepared for all events, and of insisting in case of the worst with our Allies upon some guarantee on the above subject, strikes my mind so forcibly that I cannot but mention it to you.

XLI. [*F. O. Prussia* 88.]
JACKSON TO STEWART.
Reichenbach, August 7th, 1813.

[Confirms account of situation at Prague.]   The conduct of the French Minister since his arrival is reported to have been beyond anything perfidious and insulting.   It is now quite clear that he brought with him no instructions whatever respecting either the form or the substance of the negotiation : this appears as well from the silence and uncertain course he has observed as from some private conversations which Count Metternich has had with him.   M. de Narbonne and himself still persist in their refusal to adopt the mode proposed by the Austrian Ministers for the conduct of the negotiations, alleging that, Bonaparte expecting direct and verbal conferences, they could not concede this point without further instructions.   They have equally objected to comply with the simple request renewed by M. de Metternich that they would deliver their full powers into his hands, repeating their determination not to exhibit them except in a full conference, a sufficient proof, if any were wanting, of the real dispositions by which they are actuated, and affording a strong presumption that the surmise of the mediation of Austria being disavowed in this instrument is not without foundation.

It is said still to be the determination of the Cabinet of Vienna to put an end to all negotiations on the 10th inst. unless—a thing next to impossible—Preliminaries of Peace should be signed before that period.   The expectation entertained at Prague I understand to be that Bonaparte immediately on his return to Dresden will address a solemn note to the Austrian Government, accusing them of all the delays that have taken place, and proclaiming an ultimatum, the answer to which it is confidently anticipated will be a Declaration of War.   I am the more inclined to give credit to this information, which I believe I may venture to assure you, Sir, rests upon very good authority, as the face of the Austrian Cabinet has undergone an entire change within the last fortnight. The Emperor and those about His Imperial Majesty's person who till very lately acquiesced most reluctantly in the idea of war have now unreservedly declared themselves in favour of it, as the only chance, the only alternative left them. . . .

XLII. [F. O. Prussia 89.]
JACKSON TO STEWART.
Reichenbach, August 12th, 1813.

With reference to a part of your Dispatch, No. 69,[1] of this day's date, which, however unintentional as I am convinced it was on your part, I cannot but consider as casting a degree of reflection upon me, I trust you will excuse me if I venture to request of you distinctly to state to His Majesty's Government that, upon his return from the Conference at Trachenberg, I acquainted His Majesty's Ambassador at the Court of Russia with my belief that a convention had been signed between the Allies and Austria.

Immediately before your return I took occasion pointedly to ask Baron de Hardenberg if any such existed, when His Excellency returned me the same answer I had before received from Lord Viscount Cathcart, namely, that my supposition was utterly unfounded.

I trust I need not assure you, Sir, that I have no wish to take the smallest shadow of credit to myself on this occasion, and that my sole object is simply to remove the imputation on my zeal and exertions in the execution of the trust reposed in me, which, had such a transaction taken place during the interval I had the honour of being charged with His Majesty's interests at this Court without my coming to a knowledge of it, could not but have attached to me.

I will only further trespass upon you, Sir, to explain to you that if I did not expressly mention the circumstance in my official correspondence it arose, first, from a conviction that the whole of the transactions between the Allies and the Court of Austria had been made known to you by Lord Viscount Cathcart, and through you to His Majesty's Government ; and, secondly, from the positive assurance given me officially in writing by the Chancellor Hardenberg that he had communicated them to you. . . .

[1] STEWART TO CASTLEREAGH. (No. 69). Reichenbach, August 12th, 1813. . . . " I have discovered since my return to this place that a Treaty was signed on the 27th of June between Austria, Russia, and Prussia, which has been kept concealed from Great Britain in consequence of Austria's requiring this as a stipulation. As things have turned out, this may be excuseable, but certainly after the signature of the Treaty of Reichenbach, good faith required nothing of this sort should have been adopted but with our concurrence. I have deemed my duty, however, to animadvert most strongly on this subject to the Chancellor Hardenberg. His Excellency has promised me in confidence a copy of the Treaty, and defended his not communicating it by throwing it on Russia." F. O. Prussia 89. For the Treaty of Reichenbach See VI. Note 1.

XLIII. [*F. O. Prussia* 89.]
STEWART TO CASTLEREAGH. (No. 73.)
Landeck, August 15th, 1813.
[Sends further documents of Prague Congress. Napoleon may reply to the Austrian declaration, but still war is inevitable.] It would be in vain to conceal, however, that one point, yielded by Bonaparte to Austria, would have arrested the fortunate event we now look to, and so nice and deep has been the political manœuvring that I believe one false step on the part of the Allies would have lost everything. The King of Prussia, as well as the Emperor, deserves the highest credit for his firmness throughout, and from accurate observation I am persuaded His Majesty only requires to be in good hands to take the high line in every subject. If his Majesty had more confidence in himself his interests would be better attended to ; sensible and aimiable to a degree, he is timid and reserved, and is too easy with those who surround him. The Chancellor Hardenberg, although a most excellent man, is arrived at an age when neither his powers nor faculties enable him to go through the weight of business that falls to his lot. Foreign affairs, finance and war, all are united in one person. Any change in the minister or dividing his labours would perhaps give an impression now of a change of politicians, so things are suffered to go on. But an observer cannot help lamenting that the administration and resources of this country are not better regulated. The assistance afforded by Great Britain and the delay occasioned by the armistice has enabled Prussia to bring into the field 183,000 men ; she is thus far superior in numbers to either of the other Powers. . . .

XLIV. [*F. O. Prussia* 89.]
STEWART TO CASTLEREAGH. (No. 78.)
Prague, August 20th, 1813.
In reference to my Dispatch, No. 69,[1] in which I had the honour to detail to your Lordship some circumstances that had come to my knowledge about a Treaty having been signed between Austria, Russia, and Prussia on the 27th June, which was purposely concealed from Great Britain, I have now the satisfaction of enclosing to your Lordship in strict confidence a copy of this Treaty ; I say strict confidence, because the Chancellor Hardenberg assured me that the communication of it to me was a mark of personal favour and partiality, which he would have shewn to no other

[1] See XLII.

person ; and your Lordship will easily imagine that if Russia has not made this communication through Lord Cathcart, or if Count Lieven has not mentioned it, the confidence from Prussia in the first instance might lead to unpleasant feelings between those two Courts.[1]

Sweden also has, probably, not been communicated with, and, above all, I am persuaded your Lordship will see the necessity (as affairs have turned out so prosperously) of not committing the Chancellor Hardenberg, as he has, although late, perhaps acted in a more confidential manner than the Russian Ministers, as far, at least, as I am informed. . . .

From this Treaty I think it is pretty evident, according to the impressions I have all along entertained, that if the Allies, before Lord Wellington's victory, could have got Bonaparte to yield even four of the six points, much more if he had conceded the six propositions, that a preliminary peace would have been arranged, and England, notwithstanding all her gigantic efforts and magnanimous exertions, would have been left alone to prosecute the war, or to take her own line. Experience has shewn us since that Bonaparte, if he had not hoped to bully Austria, would ultimately have yielded the four objects in question. Baron Hardenberg says the Treaty was entered into to secure the signature of Austria to some specific articles, as though the result has been as Baron Hardenberg states in his letter ; still, it has not arisen because Bonaparte would not yield the points mentioned, but that he held out from mistaken calculation too long.

This is all right as things are, but that upon the face of a new

---

[1] Hardenberg's letter of the 20th August ran as follows :—
" Mon cher General,

Je remplis ma promesse en vous communiquant sous le sceau de secret la convention du 27 Juin entre la Prusse la Russie et l'Autriche dont vous connoissiez l'éxistence, me fiant entièrement à la parole que vous m'avez donnée de n'en faire part à qui que ce soit, excepte à monsieur votre frère, My lord Castlereagh. Vous trouverez dans cette pièce, l'article par lequel l'Autriche a expressement stipulé que ce Traité ne seroit point communiqué aux Alliés. Nous avons dû nous soumettre à cette condition parcequ'il était essentiel avant toute chose, de s'assurer de la Cour de Vienne. Elle ne vouloit se prêter a établir comme conditions *sine qua non* que les 4 qui sont énoncées dans le Traité. Nous nous sommes bien gardés d'y accéder et nous avons déclaré positivement, que ces conditions ne pouvoient nous suffire, ni pour nous, ni pour nos Alliés, mais il valoit sans doute mieux avoir une base sûre pour la coopération de l'Autriche, que de n'en avoir aucune et nous pouvions prévoir avec certitude comme l'effêt l'a prouvé, que Napoleon n'accepteroit pas même ces quatre points. Nous croyons avoir rendu un très grand service à la cause conmmune, en ayant saisi le seul moyen de ranger décidément la Cour de Vienne de notre côté. Maintenant elle est astreinte à toutes les conditions contenues dans notre Note du 16 de Mai que vous connoissez et qui répond à tous les désires que votre Gouvernement peut former." . . .

Treaty an express article should be framed to keep it concealed from the Allies of the signing Powers, Prussia having a few days before concluded a Treaty with one of those Allies, in which there is a pledge to communicate everything relating to their political relations, and having received from her in faith of that pledge and the sincerity of her intentions a considerable pecuniary advance, is certainly a very strange proceeding, to say the least of it, and it is a plain proof that Great Britain can never be too much alive to her own situation in every Continental transaction. Had affairs turned out ill in Spain, or had Bonaparte been moderate, your Lordship may make your own conjectures as to what might have happened. I trust I shall stand excused with the Prince Regent's Government if I have taken, at various times, a more *suspicious* and more unfavourable view of affairs, especially with regard to the marche politique of Austria, than others have done ; the more I reflect on the past, the more I am satisfied I was not in error in being constantly on the *qui vive*. Events have turned out so gloriously that the former detailers of black tidings may be unpopular, but, from a careful review of my dispatches, I can conscientiously declare that there is no point or opinion I would not re-state under similar circumstances, and I again repeat that we owe everything to Lord Wellington's victories and Bonaparte's obstinacy and persuasion that Austria, in no event, would declare against him.

I have been honoured to-day by a long conversation with Count Metternich ; he began by detailing to me the course he had pursued since he had taken the reins of government ; he found the Austrian Monarchy in beggary, and at the lowest ebb. He arranged the marriage to give his country the first step upwards from the ruin into which she had fallen, never intending, when existence and power was secured again, that the marriage should influence or direct the politics of the Cabinet of Vienna. He persevered in his course, he added, deaf to the opinions and entreaties of all. He would not stir, notwithstanding the most urgent solicitations, when the Russians were on the Niemen. He told them to come to the Oder and to the Elbe, and, when Austria was ready, he would act. He was universally suspected, but he had but one view—to raise his country and give peace to the world.

He said he knew the British Cabinet had always doubted him ; he did not wonder at it, but that he hoped he should now stand justified in their eyes ; he wished for nothing so much as to establish the most cordial relations betwen the two countries, which he hoped would be effected without delay. I think it right to add, as your Lordship may wish for an opportunity of forestalling the wishes of the Court of Vienna, that His Excellency stated their extreme want of arms, and I am sure a supply from Great Britain, if it could be afforded, would be of the greatest importance.

Count Metternich is to be at the Emperor Francis's Head Quarters during military operations. Notwithstanding the extreme civility and kindness of Count Metternich to me, he did not go so far as to acquaint me, what I have since learnt, that, up to a very recent period, communications have been carried on with Bonaparte. He has been endeavouring, by yielding, to reopen negotiation, but the Allies have been quite firm, and will hear of nothing now but the proposals of the 16th May from Wurschen, and England being a principal in the negotiations. The spirit is so great now that there can be no rational doubt of the result if the present system of active offensive hostilities is persevered in.

The last letter which arrived from Bassano[1] to Metternich was received yesterday; it began in an offensive tone, stating that Austria *avoit prostitué* the character of a mediator, for that to their knowledge she had been long united to the Allies; that nevertheless the extreme and urgent desire of the Emperor, his master, prompted him to make another offer that some neutral point should be fixed for negotiators to assemble, even during the progress of hostilities.

The answer, which was to be sent this day, was that the Allies would never refuse to listen to negotiations for peace, provided England and Sweden consented and assisted at the negotiations, and that the propositions of the 16th May were to form the basis. Your Lordship will thus see, by these renewed offers of Bonaparte, how hardly pressed he must be, and how perfectly [sic][2] he must contemplate the difficulties he has to contend with.

XLV. [*F. O. Prussia* 89.]
STEWART TO CASTLEREAGH. (No. 86.)
Toeplitz, September 4th, 1813.

. . . . However great and formidable the alliance against France now appears, however zealous and cordial all the Powers are for the common cause, still it is impossible the great leaders of the different armies should not have their military opinions in some degree governed by the immediate interests of the power which they serve. It is Russia's interest to act in Saxony in as

[1] 18th August, 1813.
[2] " Seriously " is doubtless meant.

much as she may be looking to it.   It is Austria's to rouse the
Tyrolese to recover Italy ; the movements of Bavaria upon the
Danube are more congenial to her objects and make her feel more
secure.   It is Prussia's to drive the war from Silesia and regain
her strong places.   All these objects would be accomplished by
the overthrow of the enemy, but it ever has and will be the nature
of a great alliance that the powers concerned cannot divest themselves of their immediate interests, or forego their future objects
during the progress of military operations.   No Commander-in-
Chief ever had before two Emperors and a King superintending
and controlling not only movements in agitation but also operations
decided on.   .   .   .

XLVI.   [*F. O. Prussia* 89.]
JACKSON TO STEWART.
Toeplitz, September 17th, 1813.
In reading over the Treaty[1] which Baron Hardenberg put into
my hands, I could not but observe how much it fell short of the
former pretensions of the Allied Powers, as touching their own
immediate interests, and how utterly unsatisfactory it was with
regard to those of Great Britain, neither Spain, Sweden, or Holland
being mentioned in it, and even the Hanse Towns only indirectly
and by deduction.
The Prussian Minister replied to my observations by saying
that, with regard to the first of these points, the Treaty had
purposely been framed upon the principle of generalizing the
tenor of it as much as possible, and that, with respect to those
in which Great Britain was more immediately concerned, it had
been thought most advisable to leave them to her care alone,
adding, however, that this instrument, according to his interpretation of it, did extend to the independence of Holland.   I
acknowledge my inability to comprehend how the Prussian Minister
understands this.   The rest is but a poor subterfuge at best,
but if it is intended, as he took occasion to hint, to invite Great
Britain to accede to it as a basis upon which to open a negotiation
with Bonaparte, it assumes a very different and inadmissible
aspect.
P.S., September 18th, 1813.
Since writing the above I have had a very long and confidential
conversation with Baron de Humboldt on this subject, which,
though it has left some of the preceding objections in their full

[1] Treaty of Toeplitz between Austria, Russia, and Prussia.   Sept. 9th, 1813.

I

force, has at the same time, I am free to confess, considerably relieved my anxiety on others, the more so as we may consider M. de Humboldt as the organ on this occasion of the Chancellor's own sentiments and feelings, he having assisted the latter in the drawing up of the Treaty, and having been present at my interview with His Excellency yesterday. Upon my repeating to M. de Humboldt the same remarks, he replied that it was necessary carefully to distinguish the Treaty *Patent* from the secret articles accompanying it : that it was to the former only (applicable, as it was intended to be, to any future contingency) that the accession of Great Britain was desired, and that it would be open to her (as indeed to any other Power acceding to it, and who could come to an understanding upon the subject with Austria) to add any such claims thereto as she might think fit, claims to which he considered himself warranted in assuring me that there would be no objection on the part of Prussia, satisfied as he was that they would not fail to be marked by the same spirit of justice and moderation which had uniformly characterized His Majesty's Government ;

That, with regard to the vagueness of the expression " la plus rapprochée de celle où Elles se trouvaient en 1805,[1]" which, with reference to the first head, I particularly commented upon, it was specifically chosen for two reasons :—

1. From the embarrassment which must attend any final arrangement of the affairs of Germany, and the inconsistency of providing for the future settlement of countries not yet rescued from the hands of the enemy, and 2. From the disinclination of Austria (of which also this Government in some measure partook) to tie herself down to any distinct specification of territory, as both Austria and Prussia might very possibly, when the time came, be desirous of deviating, in some respects, from their ancient limits for the sake of a better arrondissement.   It was this consideration which had induced the selection of a middle line of expression between the detailed and particular mode adopted in their treaty with Russia and the vague and indefinite one made use of in the Treaty *Patent*.

The same want of precision is observable, and for the same cause, in the period specified as the data on which this proposed scale is to rest, but I perceive a disposition to represent the term " 1805 " as meaning the state of things prior, instead of subsequent to, the war of that year—a construction which, though I am far

_____
[1] Prussia and Austria were to be restored to a situation " la plus rapprochée, etc."

from believing such to have been the understanding of the framers of this Treaty, may, by extending, on the one hand, the Prussian States to the Rhine, and, on the other, including the Venetian Provinces in the Austrian Monarchy, explain the assertion attempted to be maintained that by it the questions of both Holland and Italy are in part, at least, provided for.

That I am right in this supposition, as well as in believing that the interpretation is not much relied on, appears, I think, from the further explanation which M. de Humboldt gave of the omission of any mention of Holland, namely, that, as it could not exist as an independent country without its colonies and commerce, delicacy towards Great Britain prevented any decision respecting it till such time as the Continental Powers should be made acquainted with her views and dispositions upon this particular point.

With respect to Spain, M. de Humboldt said that it was considered superfluous to introduce anything upon the subject, as the French were, in fact, no longer in possession of that country. and that, as to Sweden, though Prussia had guaranteed to her the possession of Norway, mention could not have been made of it in a Treaty with Austria, no engagements as yet existing between that Power and Sweden, or even with Great Britain.   I replied that a similar case, in part, existed when the Treaty between Russia and Prussia was signed, and yet care was taken to insert in it a clause on which to found an indemnity for Denmark, in case of her ceding Norway and joining the Coalition.

To this, as to every other observation relating to British objects, I received no other answer than that it was purposely left open to His Majesty's Government to make such proposals as might be found expedient, and the assurance that His Prussian Majesty would see with pleasure any such additions to the existing engagements, referring me, as a proof of this, to the 11th Article of the Treaty *Patent* and to the second of the secret Articles[1].

Having listened to these various Explanations of the Prussian Minister with the greatest attention, I observed that there was still one point on which I requested him to answer me with the same candour and openness which his preceding replies had manifested.

" *Le But de la Guerre* " is stated to be the four points contained in the first secret Article ; to obtain these would (as expressed in another part of the Treaty) secure " *son plein succes.*"   Was it meant, therefore, I asked, that, supposing Bonaparte to agree to those conditions to-morrow, peace might be immediately made ?

[1] These two articles safeguard Treaties previously contracted with other Powers.

His answer was : not without Great Britain ; this is only considered as the basis on which it might be practicable to treat *conjointly* with England, who would, of course, propose her own terms in addition.

I should not omit to inform you that, in the course of conversation, the Prussian Minister distinctly stated that the complete dissolution of the Kingdom of Westphalia was understood to be a positive stipulation of this Treaty, adding that it would be the wish of His Prussian Majesty that the countries composing it should, generally speaking, revert to their former possessors, naming specifically the Elector of Hesse Cassel. I should perhaps, apologize, Sir, for troubling you with this explanation which the *spirit* of the Treaty would seem to render superfluous, but it appears to me that the *letter* of it might be capable of a different interpretation.

XLVII. [*F. O. Prussia* 89.]
STEWART TO CASTLEREAGH. (No. 93.)
Prague, September 21st, 1813.

I have the honour to enclose Your Lordship a dispatch I have received from Mr. Jackson, containing an account of a conversation he has had with the Chancellor Hardenberg and M. de Humboldt on the late Treaty with Austria.[1]

I own the Treaty has appeared to my humble judgment as wise and judicious in all its parts (considering the various contending interests) as could have been devised. The grand *But de la Guerre* is laid down. No propositions now will be listened to but in concert with England. And although neither Spain, Holland, nor Italy are mentioned, still it may be argued, with regard to the two latter, that in the two paragraphs of Article II. of the Secret Articles the Independence of the greater part of both Holland and Italy may be secured. The words are " la disposition de la Conféderation d'u Rhin, et l'Indépendance entière et absolue des Etats intermediaires entre les Frontières des Monarchies autrichienne et prussienne reconstruites d'après l'échelle mentionnée ci-dessus d'un côté, *et le Rhin et les Alpes de l'autre.*" Now certainly if the course of the Rhine and Alps is taken, and all one side is restored to independence, the greater part of Holland and Italy would be included.

With regard to the restoration of the Austrian and Prussian

[1] See XLVI.

Monarchies, nearly to the state they were in 1805 ; Prussia will naturally urge and argue the State before 1805 to recover the possession of Anspach and Bayreuth ; nor do I think from what I can learn that Austria would throw much difficulty in the way of this—on the contrary, I am inclined to believe she would rather that Prussia occupied those territories than Bavaria. All the Powers, however, look to some transfers and amicable changes in the event of a General Peace and Settlement ; hence has it been thought desirable to make this Treaty very general, to establish a reciprocal guarantee of interests, and to unite the great features of the war [sic].

Article 9 of the Treaty declares that other Powers may found upon this general basis other Treaties, and if His Majesty's Government think proper to form more extended engagements with any of the contracting Parties, which probably may be thought necessary with Austria, the accession to this Treaty by the British Government would by no means fetter their future objects.

With regard to no mention being made of Sweden, from what I learn Austria will be cautious of committing anything to paper with respect to the guarantee of Norway ; but Lord Aberdeen will give your Lordship ample information on this subject. Russia could dictate to Prussia when their Treaty was signed—thus Sweden's objects were secured ; but Russia and Prussia cannot dictate to Austria, and she still has an eye to Denmark's being separated from France. *Au reste,* when one considers the position in which we were two months since, and then regard this Treaty, and remember also how long Austria was coming to the collar, I think we should be very difficult indeed if we were to pick holes in it. I should not have troubled your Lordship at all on this subject if it had not been for Mr. Jackson's letter, which, however, I could not enclose without these few observations, as otherwise it might appear I had not considered, as far as I was able, this important subject.

XLVIII. [*F. O. Prussia* 90.]
         STEWART TO CASTLEREAGH. (No. 104.)
                         Toeplitz, September 29th, 1813.
         . . . It is a glorious and exalted era for Great Britain to see herself rewarded for her unexampled perseverance, and by having the Continent of Europe looking up to the wisdom of her councils after they have been dazzled by the efforts of her arms

for her decision on the destinies of Europe.   Nobly are her labours repaid, gloriously are her efforts crowned.   With the bright and cheering view I cannot but observe from a general concurrence of circumstances that the Powers of the Continent would be best satisfied if they could obtain a peace upon solid grounds rather than protract the present contest.   The length of its duration, the little jealousies of individual commanders in the Allied Armies, the particular object of each Power (demonstrated at this moment unceasingly by the Prince Royal of Sweden), and lastly, the Family Alliance between the Emperor of Austria and Bonaparte, lead me to believe that the Austrian Minister, who, after all, being the Commander-in-Chief as well as Prime Minister here, will work rather to that object in a direct line rather than to active war with a view to obtaining it [sic].   It seems certainly difficult to point out now how the Congress proposed is to proceed, if assented to by all parties, but I cannot believe that Count Metternich so little sees his way before him as not to have imagined the cessions Bonaparte might make and how the general interest of Europe might be poised.   He is not so young in politics as when he looks to a particular measure not to imagine a result, and, whatever may be the language he holds, I think no person would be entirely guided by it.

XLIX.   [*F. O. Prussia* 90.]
STEWART TO CASTLEREAGH.   (No. 119.)
Leipzig, October 21st, 1813.
[Cathcart received yesterday Castlereagh's Projet of a Treaty[1] of Alliance. Aberdeen arrived.]   I was most anxious steps should be taken, as we were all united in this place to leave each at liberty to communicate with their respective Courts, but Lord Cathcart has found it impossible to get the Emperor to go into the question, and he marches to-morrow.   As we have thus lost a valuable day, I fear it may be some time before we can make progress, as Lord Cathcart will not permit us to broach the subject to Prussia or Austria until the Emperor's pleasure shall have been taken in detail.   The admirable wisdom of this Sheet Anchor Alliance strikes me so forcibly, even in the moment of exulting triumph, that, in my opinion, everything should have been sacrificed to bring the point immediately to bear.   I regret that it should have been impracticable at the present moment, especially considering the meeting of Parliament.

[1] See XV. and XVI.

L.   [*F. O. Prussia* 91.]
JACKSON TO STEWART.[1]
Frankfort, November 11th, 1813.

. . . Upon my questioning the Prussian Minister upon the nature of the proposals to be made by M. de St. Aignan,[2] he professed to attach little importance to them, and not at all to consider them as likely to lead to peace ; said that it was a mere *pour parler* in answer to that made through General Merfeldt,[3] that it was more an Austrian transaction than any other, and that he supposed Prince Metternich had communicated the whole to Lord Aberdeen, but that he could tell me that they were strictly conformable to the existing engagements between Great Britain and the Allies, and specifically to the Treaty with Austria. I observed that the stipulations of that Treaty concluded before our late successes were very limited, and did not embrace many of the objects broached in the conversation with the Austrian General.   He replied that is true but the propositions in question insist further on the independence of Holland and Italy, without which peace was impossible, and the demolition of all fortresses on the Rhine.   He then informed me, as a casual intimation, that it was determined to await the result of this overture before they concluded the offensive and defensive Alliance proposed by Lord Castlereagh's late instructions, assuring me, however, that in the meantime every effort will be made to prosecute the war with the utmost vigour.

I have thought it my duty, Sir, to detail to you this conversation, though on a topic as respecting which His Majesty's Ministers will be much more accurately informed, because I consider it to be not wholly without interest that you should possess the view taken by the Prussian Government of the present state of affairs. At the same time I am afraid we must regard the above language rather as that of the Chancellor personally than as the measure by which to judge of the dispositions of the Allied Powers ; their backwardness to adopt the admirable Projet of Lord Castlereagh is, to my mind, a proof of this.   The fact is their armies have suffered excessively ; there remains little beyond the reserve fit for active service, and both Austria and Russia will, I am satisfied, be too happy to conclude a peace, if anything like an honourable opportunity offers of giving up the contest.

[1] Stewart had gone from Frankfort to Hanover.   [2] See LXI. and LXII.
[3] The Austrian General who had had a long conversation with Napoleon at Leipzig on possible terms of peace.   See LXII. p. 110.

LI.   [*F. O. Prussia* 91.]
STEWART TO CASTLEREAGH.   (No. 146.]
Frankfort, November 24th, 1813.

[With regard to the proposed Treaty of Alliance.] Since my arrival here I have had frequent discussions with His Excellency respecting it, and I have great satisfaction in acquainting your Lordship that the Prussian Minister enters entirely into the views of His Majesty's Government on this head, and has repeatedly assured me that, being assured that the policy of Prussia is to cultivate the strictest union with Great Britain, and fully sensible both of the wisdom and justice of the proposed Treaty, the King, his master, will be ready to conclude such whenever he shall be called upon, whatever may be the intention of the Courts of Austria and Russia.   .   .   .

I am, however, not without hopes that an ulterior determination may yet be taken on this important subject. Your Lordship has so forcibly pointed out that the bond of union between the Great Powers is to be collected by inference rather than to be found embodied in any one ostensible instrument, and you have at the same time so far predicted the engagements which have happily taken place with Austria that I confess I see no grounds on this latter account nor on that of a proposition to insert additional articles in existing Treaties to depart from the great measure of consolidating the union of the Allies by one general instrument, which appears to me to be the spirit of your Lordship's instructions.

LII.   [*F. O. Prussia* 91.]
STEWART TO CASTLEREAGH.   (No. 149.)
Frankfort, November 28th, 1813.

[Forwards a letter from Hardenberg.[1]]

.   .   .   It is equally incumbent on me to declare that I have not had the advantage of stating through any official channel the ideas that would have occurred to my humble judgment on

___

[1] Hardenberg to Stewart, Nov. 28th, 1813.

.   .   .   J'ai encore relu avec la plus grande attention, la correspondence touchant l'envoy de M. de St. Aignan et je me suis persuadé de plus en plus, que vos appréhensions ne sont pas fondées. La pièce redigée par M. de St. Aignan *est* et *reste* une pièce *non officielle* et *sans aucune authenticité* car vous observerez que dans la réponse du Prince Metternich au Duc de Bassano il est dit : " Elles sont prêtes à entrer en negotiation, des qu'elles auront la certitude que S. M. l'Empéreur des francois admêt les bases générales et sommaires, que j'ai indiquées *dans mon entretien* avec le Baron de St. Aignan."
.   .   .

these proceedings, ideas which I have endeavoured to found upon the instructions received from your Lordship : it is very possible I may be in error, but I felt myself called upon to declare to the Prussian Minister that so long as I am honoured by his Majesty's credentials to this Court I cannot submit (without representation) to receive a proceeding, which, according to existing Treaties, should be adopted in complete concert, but which has been brought to a conclusion without the individual honoured by His Majesty's confidence at the court of Prussia having had it in his power to express even an opinion upon the various important points which these papers embrace. The Prussian Minister declared to me that his mouth had been sealed with regard to communication with me, until this affair was brought to a conclusion, by a promise exacted from His Excellency by Prince Metternich.

Had I had the good fortune to have been taken into the consultations which have preceded the documents I now transmit, I should not have presumed on an infallible judgment, nor should I have considered that on the Rhine the Prince Regent and his Government would depart from those great principles in opening negotiations to which the attention of His Majesty's Ministers at the Allied Courts were called when we were upon the Oder, and the armies of France still unbroken and unbeaten.

Your Lordship has distinctly pointed out " the points on which His Royal Highness's Government in negotiation can under *no* circumstances relax the faith of His Government being formally pledged to their inviolable maintenance—Spain, Portugal, Sicily—the fulfilment of our existing engagements with Sweden."

The conversation that took place with M. de St. Aignan, of which a minute has been made by him, shewn and approved, is either an official or an unofficial document : if the former, which I own I am led to conceive it is become from Prince Metternich's answer to the Duke of Bassano, I humbly think if it is stamped in any shape with the acquiescence of Great Britain, it completely loses sight of three out of the four *sine qua nons* to which our attention has been called : in this minute not a word of Sweden, not a word of Sicily, not a word of Portugal, and yet your Lordship reiterates " our four points must be *distinctly* put forward, and that Great Britain had no possible option as to the points in question." Again, in your Lordship's dispatches you state " that with regard to our maritime rights, if this is a subject on which the mediation of an Ally cannot be accepted, it is still less a question Great Britain could consent to discuss in a general Congress, and as the maritime question is one which Bonaparte will endeavour to bring before a Congress principally with the hope of creating disunion between Great Britain and her Allies, every consideration of policy should determine pointedly to discountenance a design so mischievously calculated to promote the views of France." In addition to this strong general instruction your Lordship's private letter to Lord Cathcart of 27th September[1] more forcibly and more in detail discants on this subject. Now it would almost seem that your Lordship had foretold the very proceeding of M. de St. Aignan, for whatever may have been the conversation that passed, M. de St. Aignan introduces a sentence in this minute which, to say the least of it, may form a very tolerable fund for discussion at a Congress, and whatever may have been the feelings and explanations of the British Ambassador present, unfortunately we have no written document or minute in any shape to be apprised of them. Here is an advantage in the outset of this proceeding on the part of France, which at least we shall have to explain away ; I admit we are as yet committed to nothing, but if Bonaparte accepts the basis talked over by Prince Metternich we go to a Congress (with all the advantages we *now* possess) hampered with a necessity of unsatisfactory explanation to Sweden, Sicily, etc., and loaded with the difference of the construction which the British Ambassador and the French Authorities may please to put on that part of the minute, which so unnecessarily touches upon the great sacrifices which England would make for a peace, and the question of commerce and navigation to which " la France a le droit de prétendre."[2]

With respect to the sacrifices Great Britain would make for a peace, if I understand your Lordship correctly, the sacrifices of surrendering conquests would be made by England to ameliorate a Continental peace after the general arrangements were made ; but this is the first time my attention has been called to Great Britain making sacrifices for a basis short of the great principles which she has laid down.

I come next to observe on the commencement of the Duke of Bassano's letter, which states that M. de St. Aignan had reported that England had assented to the proposition for the opening of a Congress for a general peace ; now I cannot discover in what manner Great Britain has expressed this consent, for the reasoning in your Lordship's Dispatch of the 28th September to the Earl of Aberdeen[3] is directly opposed to such a declaration. You

[1] XIX.
[2] See LXIV. p. 113.
[3] LVIII.

deprecate on the strongest ground the assembling of a Congress until some satisfactory basis is previously understood, and then you emphatically add that " What the nature of that basis should be has been defined with as much precision as an arrangement necessarily dependent to a certain degree on circumstances can well admit, both in the Russian and Prussian Notes of the 16th of May, and recently by the British Government in the Projet of a Secret Article enclosed in No. 11." How far the basis now alluded to approximates to your Lordship's ideas you will certainly be the best able to determine, and I shall be sincerely rejoiced if I have taken a wrong view of this important question.

I have foreborne to touch on what may have been the views with regard to Holland in the important conversation which is the origin of this negotiation, because whatever they may have been I fervently trust the late happy intelligence from thence will completely put that question on its legs.

If M. de St. Aignan's minute is considered entirely as an unofficial paper, I think it is a little singular that, in the Prince Metternich's answer to the Duke of Bassano, he declares the Allies will be ready to enter into negotiations whenever they are certain that Bonaparte will accept the basis, which he has announced in his conversation with M. de St. Aignan. Now if Prince Metternich conceived that M. de St. Aignan had mistated what passed would it not have been natural to accompany his official Note with an official statement of the basis ? and I have reason to believe the Prussian Minister proposed and urged that Commissioners should be sent for this purpose, which, however, Prince Metternich rejected. I beg here to remark in this second proceeding that the Minister of Russia is not specifically named, and I have some reason to know that there is a feeling that Russia would have been glad if her Minister had not in any manner been named in the concern. Prince Metternich, in his last letter, talks of the conversation he had with M. de St. Aignan as his own, and I have no doubt he sees his way very clearly before him, but, gifted with very moderate powers and wholly unacquainted with difficult diplomacy, I have presumed to give your Lordship my opinions. If the Allies go to Congress with this commencement I do not think it very difficult to predict the result ; above all, in my humble conviction according to the declared sentiments of the Prince Regent's Government, I do not contemplate that a Minister would be sent to a Congress under the circumstances above detailed.

LIII.   [*F. O. Prussia* 86.]
CASTLEREAGH TO STEWART.   (No. 82.)
Foreign Office, December 17th, 1813.

Your Dispatch, No. 149,[1] relative to the mission of M. de St.
Aignan has been received and laid before the Prince Regent.
His Royal Highness has been pleased very graciously to approve
of the zeal evinced by you on this, as upon all former occasions,
for the good of his service.

My dispatches to the Earl of Aberdeen of the 1st, 7th, and
10th[2] instant (copies of which have been transmitted to you)
will have fully explained the Prince Regent's sentiments upon the
substance of the overture in question, and I should not deem it
necessary now to recur to the subject did I not consider it material
to call your attention to one part of your very able dispatch, which
it is of the more importance to notice, lest upon similar grounds
of reasoning the Swedish Government should have drawn an
unfavourable inference from the silence of the basis as to the point
of Norway. Upon this subject Mr. Thornton will be directed
to give to the Swedish Government the most unequivocal assurances that the British Government never would have countenanced for a moment that basis had they conceived they were
thereby prejudicing, much less sacrificing, the just pretensions
of Sweden under her existing engagements. They conceive,
however, that no ground whatever exists for such a supposition.

In your reasoning upon this point you have not sufficiently
adverted to the distinction between a basis and a Treaty : the
former is necessarily general, the latter particular in its provisions. The use of the former is to ascertain whether the views
of the parties sufficiently approximate to afford some prospect
they may be reconciled upon discussion. Were all the *sine qua
nons* on both sides necessarily to be included in the basis it
would render the arrangement of a basis nearly as complex and
consequently as difficult to adjust as the Treaty itself, and thus
all the advantage of proceeding upon a previous agreement as to
basis would be lost.

In the particular case the Prince Regent's Government conceive
that the most appropriate principle on which a principle could have
been framed [*sic*] is one which should admit on the part of France,
as a preliminary, the reduction of her late limits, and should
endeavour in outline to describe the extent of that reduction.
In doing this nothing is conceded as to any interests upon which
the basis is silent.

[1] LII.
[2] LXV., LXVI., LXVII.

Considerable doubt may exist whether it would be for the advantage of Sweden that the Allies should be the first to move, especially in a basis, on the point of Norway. Committed, as France now is by treaty to Denmark, the affording to that Power, unnecessarily, an opportunity of proving her fixed adherence to those engagements might, at such a moment as the present, powerfully encourage Denmark to a more obstinate perseverance in the war. The policy, however, is not so material for our present view of the subject as to establish that the question of Norway is in no degree prejudiced by its remaining to be hereafter brought forward with a variety of other interests, viz., the Duchy of Warsaw, Hanover, the scale of Austria, of Prussia, Sicily and Portugal. All these points, with many others, the several Allied Powers will have to maintain in conformity either to their respective engagements or interests, whenever negotiation shall be actually entered upon, at which period Sweden will find Great Britain prepared, as hitherto, to discharge towards her the duty of a good and faithful Ally with firmness and zeal. The express recognition in the basis of the independence of Germany, Spain, Holland and Italy, was necessary in explanation of the basis itself, for without these essential characteristics the limits therein assigned would have had no intelligible meaning, but all other interests not specifically pronounced upon in the basis remain on both sides wholly unprejudiced and open to discussion.

It is true a much more detailed specification of objects is to be found in the instructions from home, especially in the Secret Article to the proposed Treaty of Alliance. These instructions were prepared with a view of establishing a complete and perfect concert with the Allies as to the objects for which we contend. They were also alluded to, as you justly observe, in my dispatch to the Earl of Aberdeen, as descriptive not only of the extent and nature of our views, but of the basis it might be proper to require. But it did not follow from such allusion that the basis should embrace the whole of the objects therein referred to, or even the points, *sine qua non*, of an actual peace, and it is considered that the basis in question is in no degree inconsistent with the spirit of these instructions, though it leaves much to be insisted upon in the ultimate negotiation.

I trust this view of the question, on which alone I consider your reasoning to have been incorrect, will prove satisfactory, and enable you to remove any impressions of an unfavourable nature which may have been received in any quarter.

(iii.)—*Correspondence of the Earl of Aberdeen,
August to December,* 1813.

LIV. [*F. O. Austria* 101.]
CASTLEREAGH TO ABERDEEN. (No. 2.)
August 6th, 1813.

[General instructions on Mission to Austria ; he is to re-establish relations with Austrian Court, whether hostilities renewed or negotiations continued, unless Austria had unexpectedly severed herself from the Allies.]   Your Lordship will collect from these instructions that the basis of a general peace, in order to provide adequately for the tranquility and independence of Europe, ought in the judgment of H.M.'s Government to confine France at least within the Pyrenees, the Alps and the Rhine, and if the other great Powers of Europe should feel themselves enabled to contend for such a peace, Great Britain is fully prepared to concur with them in such a line of policy.   If however the Powers most immediately interested should determine, rather than encounter the risks of a more protracted struggle, to trust for their security to a more imperfect arrangement, it never has been the practice of the British Government to attempt to dictate to other States a perserverance in war, which they did not themselves recognize to be essential to their own as well as to the common safety. . . .

LV. [*F. O. Austria* 101.]
CASTLEREAGH TO ABERDEEN. (No. 3.)
August 6th, 1813.

I have stated in a former dispatch that it is to be presumed in the recommencement of hostilities the attention of the Austrian Government will be immediately directed to the recovery of its ancient footing in the Tyrol and in the North of Italy, and, as a means to this end, to the exclusion of the French power beyond the Alps.   The large accumulation of force near Verona under Beauharnais, the magnitude of the lines in Bavaria, and the army assembled under Augerau upon Wurtzberg and Faldon will no doubt render it necessary for the Austrian Cabinet to have recourse to every expedient, which can enable them to assume the offensive in that quarter, to contend against the resources both of the Kingdom of Italy and of Bavaria with such aids as can be spared from France.   It will probably be found necessary both to encourage insurrection in the Tyrol and also to enter into an understanding with Murat.   Your Lordship is aware that overtures have already been received both by the British and Austrian Governments from that person. I transmit for your confidential information what has already passed on this subject, as also a variety of documents[1] which will put your Lordship in possession of the strong disposition which we have had reason to suppose exists in the Tyrol, the Vorarlberg, the Venetian States, and in Italy generally to throw off the French yoke.

Should the Austrian Government open itself to your Lordship on the subject of Murat you are authorized confidentially to explain to them the nature of the discussions which have taken place with Lord William Bentinck on this subject. You may apprize them of the authority which has been given to Lord William eventually to sign a convention with Murat upon the basis[2] settled between His Lordship and the Hereditary Prince of Sicily. And should Murat renew his overture to the Court of Vienna, as it may save time and accelerate his declaration against the enemy, Your Lordship is at liberty in concert with the Court of Vienna to conclude a convention upon the basis laid down by Lord William Bentinck.

In discussing the future system of Italy you may represent that the main object the Prince Regent has at heart is to create the most effectual barrier against France in that quarter, and that with such view H.R.H. is ready to concert his measures with the Emperor of Austria, as far as the concern he takes in the interest of his Ally, the King of the two Sicilies, will permit. Your Lordship may further state that the P.R. will see with the greatest satisfaction the House of Austria resumes its ancient preponderance in the North of Italy. H.R.H. is especially desirous of seeing the important position of Venice placed in His Imperial Majesty's hands. H.R.H. is also desirous of contributing as far as depends on him to the restoration of His Holiness the Pope to his former dominions, security and independence, and hopes that the success of the Allied arms may be such as eventually to re-establish the King of Sardinia.

Holding all these principal objects in view, the Prince Regent persuades himself that a liberal establishment may be found for Murat in the centre of Italy without prejudice to the rights of the Sicilian family to the Crown of Naples. On all these points Your Lordship will ascertain the sentiments of the Austrian Cabinet and transmit them for consideration.

[1] Dispatches to and from Lord William Bentinck as to the negotiations which were entered into at Ponza, and others concerning a British scheme for stirring up the Tyrol which had been preparing during the winter 1812–1813.

[2] viz., That " compensation " should be found for Murat in Italy if he surrendered Naples to the Bourbons and joined the Allies.

With respect to military co-operation on the part of the British Government, I can only at present authorize your Lordship to speak generally. Our means, both pecuniary and military, are at the present so deeply engaged in Spain that no effort of any magnitude can be directed to Italy. At what moment or to what extent Italy can be made the theatre of our future exertions must depend upon circumstances. Your Lordship will at present confine yourself to declaring that the deliverance of Italy is an object of which the British Government will not lose sight, and that their means will be directed to it as the course of events may allow.

Your Lordship will not fail, however, in all your discussions with the Austrian Government to impress upon their attention that in opening the views of the British Government on the subject of Italy it is not done from any desire to direct their efforts to that front in competition with the more pressing exigencies of the war in Germany. It will be for His Imperial Majesty to judge in what direction His military exertions can most advantageously be made. The object of this instruction is to enable Your Lordship to concert measures, if necessary, with respect to Italy without the unnecessary delay of a reference home.

LVI. [*F. O. Austria* 101.]
CASTLEREAGH TO ABERDEEN. (Most Secret and Separate.)
August 6th, 1813.

On referring to the enclosed dispatch[1] your Lordship will observe that, previous to Lord William Bentinck's negotiation at Ponza, the question was under discussion between his Lordship and the Hereditary Prince whether it might not be for the interest of his family, under possible circumstances, to cede the Kingdom of Naples for an equivalent, to which arrangement [*sic*], although considerable disinclination was expressed, His Royal Highness seemed prepared to admit that as the success of the common cause could alone accomplish anything for his family on the Continent, if the co-operation of Murat should be deemed essential and should depend upon their lending themselves to such an arrangement, it might be prudent for them to accept a fair equivalent rather than impede the general interest.

As the proposition may be again revived, in the event of its being countenanced by the Austrian Government and pressed by them as conducive to the common cause, your Lordship will

---

[1] A dispatch from Lord William Bentinck dated the 10th June, 1813.

not in that case discourage the idea. It may be pressed by
Murat as the *sine qua non* of his co-operation, in which case it
might be of the utmost importance that it should not be declined.
It is also to be remarked that Murat might feel a stronger inducement for exertion if his claim to the Throne of Naples depended
on an equivalent for the Sicilian Family being conquered elsewhere, than if the effect of such an acquisition would be his
transfer from thence.

Should your Lordship under all the circumstances of the case
deem it expedient to yield to the representations of the Court of
Vienna on this point you may take upon yourself jointly with
Austria to sign a convention to this effect *sub spe rati.*

LVII. [*F. O. Austria* 101.]
       CASTLEREAGH TO ABERDEEN. (Most Confidential.)
                       Foreign Office, September 21st, 1813.
   You will find from the dispatches I now send you that there
is yet something left to exercise your talents upon in Austria.
You will have the labouring oar in this negotiation, and, if you
succeed in placing the key-stone in the arch which is to sustain
us hereafter, you will not feel that your labour has been thrown
away.
   I am not conscious that I can give you any hints that are
material for your consideration. I rather hope that the point of
the mediation has been explained to Metternich—half-confidences
are often more hazardous than plain-dealing—but as the concealment was Russian, the Emperor ought to have the merit of the
explanation. My notion is that in proportion as Austria observes
the tone of our politics to be moderate and disinterested, she will
be the more disposed to embark with us in the deeper engagement
which is now proposed for her acceptance. I recur to this topic
in consequence of Jacobi having shown me this evening a letter
from the Chancellor Hardenberg, in which he says that it is not
proposed to say anything to Austria on the subject of the acceptance by England of her mediation. You will recollect, however,
that we can hardly disguise in discussion here so important a
feature in our own policy.
   I observe Metternich writes in great spirits and apparent
self-satisfaction. I am inclined to think it is best to make a hero
of him, and, by giving him a reputation, to excite him to sustain
it. He opened himself very much to my brother—detailed all
his difficulties and progress, knew that he was not confided in

                                                          K

by England, and did not wonder at it.   If you deem it useful
you may tell him from me I am perfectly ready to adopt him upon
his own avowal, and to meet vigorous exertion on his part with
perfect goodwill and confidence on mine, and that as long as he
will wield the great machine in his hands with determination and
spirit I will support him as zealously as I have done the Prince
Royal[1] against all his calumniators, and I hope not less successfully.

I shall send you a paper of Münster's on German politics
merely for information, and that you may send me your ideas
upon it.   I rather wish to keep clear of the German internal
politics as much as possible, and only to interfere in extraordinary
cases.   The secret article confirming the Hanoverian Arrondissement I should hope Austria will not object to.   The Prince will
consider it as a personal attention.

LVIII. [F. O. Austria 101.]
CASTLEREAGH TO ABERDEEN. (No. 14.)
Foreign Office, September 28th, 1813.

I have to enclose to your Lordship by the Prince Regent's
command copy of a note received from the Baron de Wessenberg,
with its enclosure, together with the reply which has been returned
to the same.[2] The language which your Lordship is to hold
with respect to the present overture must necessarily be founded
upon the principles laid down in my instructions as referred to
in the margin,[3] copies of which have been transmitted to your
Lordship, the substance of which I presume will ere this have
been communicated to His Imperial Majesty the Emperor of
Austria.

In considering what course it may be expedient for the Allies
to adopt upon the proposition contained in the Duke of Bassano's
letter, the Prince Regent proceeds upon the assumption that the
Powers now carrying on the war against France are engaged in
one common effort for their mutual security and independence,
that they are agreed upon the general principles upon which
negotiation when entered upon should be conducted, and are deter-

---

[1] Bernadotte.

[2] This brought to the notice of the British Government the Duc de Bassano's
note of the 18th August, sent immediately after the rupture of the negotiations
at Prague, proposing a Congress, and Metternich's reply of the 21st August,
which merely stated that he would bring the proposal to the notice of Austria's
Allies. See XLIV.

[3] Dispatches to Lord Cathcart. See VI., VIII., IX., XV., XVI., XVII.

mined not to treat except together. That being premised you
will acquaint the Emperor that the Prince Regent, in submitting
his sentiments, desires to be understood as not disposed to withdraw himself from any discussions for the restoration of peace
which His Imperial Majesty and the Allies may consider calculated
to lead to this much-desired event, and agreed with his Allies as
to the objects for which they contend ; they will always find His
Royal Highness disposed to defer in a considerable degree to their
wishes and judgment as to the time and mode of endeavouring
to give effect to the common desire for a solid, durable, and
honourable peace. But there are considerations in the present
state of Europe and of the war which His Royal Highness cannot
abstain from bringing under the Emperor's notice, more especially
with reference to the particular overture which His Imperial
Majesty has recently received from the French Government.

The first and most important consideration is the influence
which a Congress of the nature proposed, supposing it to meet
and make no effectual progress towards peace, would inevitably
have upon the relative interests of the belligerents. In considering
this, it is obvious that the entire advantage must belong to the
enemy—without the slighest intention of making any substantial
concession, it might enable him at once to tranquillize the public
mind in France by announcing a peace as at hand—it would thus
not only deliver him from all danger of internal convulsion, but
render fresh requisitions tolerable to the people of France under the
idea that in submitting to them they were contributing to put an
end to the war. It must also enable him to address himself to
his other Allies as he lately did to Murat, and to confirm their
allegiance as the only remaining hope of having their interests
protected in the general arrangements.

If the cause of the Allies is the cause of all nations, and if it
is through the efforts of national impulse they may expect that
the Saxons, the Bavarians, the Tyrolese, and even the people
of Holland and Italy, will yet successively assist them in confining
the power of France within reasonable bounds, are the Allies
prepared altogether to forego this hope, or do they conceive that
any Government or any people will embark with them in the war
with a negotiation pending of the result of which they may consider
themselves the presumptive sacrifices ?

If the success of the Allied arms had already operated its full
result, and there appeared no longer any rational hope that the
sphere of the Confederacy could be extended, a negotiation might
in that case be a less hazardous experiment on the part of the

Allies.   But even then it could not fail to enfeeble exertion and
to abate those impressions amongst their own subjects which are
to reconcile them to great sacrifice and to carry them forward
in the contest.   The very sitting of such a Congress for any time
would imply that it was become a war of terms instead of a war of
national independence, that it was a question of territory and
not a contest whether France should continue to oppress, invade,
and plunder the other States of Europe.   If such be the obvious
results of a blind compliance with the proposal of the enemy,
there seems little internal evidence either in the overture itself,
or in the transactions which preceded it, to induce a supposition
that it was made for any other purpose than the possible advantage
that might result to Bonaparte in France from having a proposition,
nominally pacific, refused, for he could hardly suppose that
without any preliminary understanding such a proposal could be
accepted.

The magnitude of the Confederacy may well make Napoleon
tremble for his own power, but it is not from the tenor of this
paper, which is quite unexampled in the tone of indignity it
assumes throughout towards Austria, it is not from his conduct
in the late negotiations that any settled purpose of terminating
the war can be inferred ; and, if so, why should the Allies, without
any such pledge of sincerity, concede to him an engine which
is to sustain his fortunes and to become a substitute for victories ?

He says, was there ever such an idea entertained as that of
dictating a peace in a limited number of days, montre en main—
was the Peace of Utrecht, of Nimeguen, of Ryswick, or Aix la
Chapelle settled in such a manner ?   The reasoning is correct as
applied to a definite arrangement, after the parties understand
each other upon preliminary principles ; but where is the instance
of the states of Europe assembling in Congress, not only without
any preliminary understanding, but with the strongest grounds
to presume that their differences, for the moment at least, are
fundamentally irreconcileable ?

Is, then, the war to be eternal, and is there no mode in which
by explanation the belligerents may approximate ?   The difficulty
is not in the form of proceeding, it is in the determined purpose
of the individual at the head of the French Government not to
compromise his authority as a conqueror, and the resolution he
appears to have taken to perish rather than descend from the
eminence of dominion on which he has at the sacrifice of every
principle so long laboured to place himself.   It is not necessary to
proceed to a Congress to ascertain whether the Allies and the

ruler of France understand each other upon the basis on which
an equilibrium in Europe can be revived. Until this is agreed
upon all proceedings in Congress must be at a stand, and a Congress is the last place where such an understanding is likely to
take place.

What, then, is to be done ?   To all appearances nothing according to the present pretensions of the parties towards accommodation.   The question is still at issue whether an individual
shall hold the rest of Europe in subjection, or whether after long
suffering and hopeless submission the great Powers shall now
deliver themselves from bondage, and resume their former
station in the Commonwealth of Europe. This is in its nature
an issue of arms, and not of diplomacy, and it seems as yet un-
decided in the temper of either parties.

When Bonaparte proposes a Congress let him state the principles on which he is ready to negotiate, and it will be then in the
power of the Allies, comparing them with the acknowledged
principles which bind them together, to judge whether discussion
can be advisable on such a basis.   It may also be open to the Allies
to propose, at a suitable moment, terms of their own, but in dealing
with such an enemy, and meaning to require an arrangement
which is to give peace to Europe, they ought not to hazard a premature proposition, which, if unsupported by corresponding successes,
would afford advantages in point of impression to their antagonist.

In thus explaining to your Lordship so much at large the mode
in which this overture has been viewed by His Majesty's Government, I have perhaps gone into unnecessary argument ; the proposition itself, as was natural, does not seem to have received any
countenance from the Austrian Government. It appears to have
been taken merely ad referendum by the Emperor of Austria for
communication to his Allies, and to have been since presented
for their consideration, but not pressed. The Baron de Wessenberg does not express any wish on the part of his Court that the
suggestion should be entertained, whilst the Russian and Prussian
Ministers in London have been wholly silent on the subject.

In submitting, so far as you may deem it expedient, the reasoning above stated to the consideration of the Cabinet of Vienna,
your Lordship will assure them that the Prince Regent will always
be ready to enter into negotiations for peace in conjunction with
the Allies ; he only deprecates illusory discussions, which must
damp the ardour of the Confederacy, and conceives that no steps
ought to be taken to assemble a Congress till some satisfactory
basis is previously understood. What the nature of that basis

should be has been defined with as much precision as an arrangement necessarily dependent to a certain degree on circumstances
can well admit, both in the Russian and Prussian Notes of the 16th
of May,[1] and recently by the British Government in the Projet
of a Secret Article enclosed in my Letter No. 11[2] to your Lordship ;
further than this it does not seem possible under present circumstances for this Government to explain itself, but you may assure
His Imperial Majesty that they will always be ready to consider
with the utmost deference and cordiality any suggestion coming
from their Allies on the subject of peace.   At the same time they
cannot disguise the persuasion they feel, that it is by a vigorous
and successful prosecution of the war that peace is most likely
to be attained, the enemy never having shown down to the
present moment the smallest disposition to recede from his
established system of conquest and dominion.

LIX. [*F. O. Austria* 101.]
      CASTLEREAGH TO ABERDEEN. (Private and Confidential.)
                        Dover Castle, October 15th, 1813.
      I lose no time in relieving you from all anxiety upon the point
of Murat![3] It is a strong measure but warranted by the state
of Italy, of which important portion of Europe, in a military sense,
I consider the soi-disant King of Naples to be completely master,
for with his army he can at once march uninterruptedly to the
Tagliamento, and unless the Viceroy evacuates the whole of what
is called the Illyrian Provinces his communications and his
Kingdom of Italy are in equal jeopardy.   I own, however, I am
not sanguine as to the result of the negotiation, because I assume
Murat to be a mere calculator, and there is a spirit of negotiation
about Metternich upon which such adventurers will always so far
speculate as to endeavour to gain time.
      I know how imperfectly one can judge at a distance of the true
shades of political management, and if my reasoning appears to
you wrong you will not attempt to act upon it in your discussions,
but I wish I could see the Austrian Minister rely more upon
exertion and less upon negotiation.   His game with Bavaria may
be right, but in playing it, if he mistakes the views of the Bavarian
Government, he sacrifices his entire prospects in the Tyrol, for
he must be prepared to expect that all his forbearance is ruin to
a popular cause, and therefore the utmost to which his policy in

    [1] See VI.
    [2] See XVI., p. 26.
    [3] Aberdeen had informed Metternich of his secret instructions as to Murat
(LVI.) and even given him a note to that effect.

that quarter, as I conceive, tends is to neutralize Bavaria for the present, possibly to swim with the stream, if the Allies are eminently successful, but as certainly to fight vigorously on the side of France, if they are not. Now I may have been misled, but I had hoped that the Tyrol might have constituted in itself a powerful diversion, and that, supported by the Austrians, the flame in that quarter would have blazed so strongly as to have required at least the presence of Augereau's Corps in addition to the Viceroy and General Wrede, instead of the former being at liberty to move upon the Saale to reopen and maintain the communications of the Grand Army.

The same sort of spirit of catching at everything that can be twisted into even the hope of a negotiation seems to pervade his policy towards the enemy. What could be more weak than to meet the Duke of Bassano's proposition for a Congress, which was nothing more than the old offer which had been rejected in June revived in language of peculiar offence to Austria, with a milk-and-water answer, considering this most insulting letter as still affording " un lueur d'espoir."[1] Whilst such propositions are entertained and sent to England for the purpose of gaining time, the misfortune is Bonaparte feels that his opponents cannot make up their mind *firmly* to the contest, and he speculates upon their irresolution, upon their disunion, and upon their pecuniary embarrassments. Can M. de Metternich suppose that, if Bonaparte had a serious intention of coming to a reasonable arrangement, that he would not find some more distinct mode of explaining himself ? In one only instance has this system of temporizing succeeded, and that is in deceiving the enemy as to the real intention of Austria with regard to war, but now that she is at war, let her think of war and not of negotiation, until it comes in some shape that justifies a hope that his policy is really pacific, and whenever that shall be presumeable we shall all be disposed to meet it.

When I admit that the Austrian minister overreached Bonaparte in the conduct of the mediation, I must, however, remark that he did so at no small sacrifice as to the means of resisting him. His negotiations lost Saxony beyond all question. Denmark would not probably have ventured to declare for France if the Allies had been supported by Austria on the Saale. The intermediate countries towards the Rhine were then in fermentation. This spirit has been allowed to evaporate, and the Tyrol has been paralysed whilst Beauharnais has been allowed time, as well as France, to appear in force. No doubt Austria and the Allies have

[1] See LVIII.

not been idle, but I don't know why they might not have called forth the same means, preserving a more advantageous theatre to produce them upon, had Austria not insisted upon the parade of a preliminary negotiation.

However, this is gone by, and the future is our concern. In this view I am most anxious to hear from you that the Austrian minister is resolute in considering a successful war as the surest road to peace, and that he is prepared not only to feel so himself but to avow it to the nation and to call forth all their energies upon this avowal. It is the golden opportunity for him to do so. Why not imitate Prussia and make the Austrians an armed people? In no other character can they be safe in the vicinity of France; so organised, with the defensive Alliance now happily in progress, they may.

If you ever mention to M. de Metternich my individual sentiments upon these subjects you can, from your own knowledge, assure him that I am not one of those who cannot reconcile themselves to contemplate the possibility of peace even with Bonaparte, but I am satisfied it must be a peace founded upon a principle of authority and not of submission. That to obtain, and still more to preserve it, we must rouse and arm the people we have to conduct, and it is in the earnest desire of peace that I wish to see him employed, rather in preparing the nation for sacrifices and exertions than in idly flattering them with the notion that peace is at hand. I am anxious to learn what the internal system of Austria is at the present moment as to armament and exertions of all kinds, and I beg you will procure for me not only the *state* and *distribution* of their army, but information as to their means of keeping up their force, and also what steps have been taken to call forth in case of emergency the Landwehr or Militia. Until a solid organization of the mass of the population is secured we shall always find them timid as to acquisitions to the southward, and avaricious of extension on their Eastern frontier.

The progress made by the three Powers in the consolidation of a defensive system is a new and happy era in the revival, I trust, of European independence. It is in itself a mighty change in the face of affairs, and if it is sustained by a national sentiment in each State it may carry us through, but it must be interwoven with the Peninsula if we mean to bring France to terms. How many years since would the war have been terminated if the expectation of dividing her opponents (a hope but too frequently realized) had not tempted France to persevere? The elements of resistance now abound, if they can only be successfully combined.

If I have done injustice in any of my observations to your friend, Metternich, I shall be most happy to be corrected.

P.S.—Since writing the above I have received the Moniteur with the Austrian and Swedish papers. I hope this manifesto will make its due impression at Vienna. It is decisive as to the character the war is likely to assume, and Austria cannot too soon call forth the mass of her people. Nothing but an animated and armed population can secure her against the fate that awaits her if the French deluge should again burst in that direction. I recollect when Caulaincourt took leave at Prague nothing was to be published that could widen the breach between the father-in-law and his dutiful son-in-law, and yet I fear such nonsense was not without its effect, else Metternich could not have written so tame an answer to Bassano's Philippic. It appears as if his ears could hardly yet bear the sound of war, and that he is disposed rather to whisper than to din it into the ears of the nation. This message will, I trust, make him feel that he has no time to lose in making every part of the monarchy ring with the note of preparation. I cannot I own but consider the present communication as a serious and awful summons to us all for renewed vigilance and exertion. It convinces me that Bonaparte has determined to be numerically powerful on all points. This, I think, he has the means of being for a limited period and upon the confines of France. Having men under arms in abundance, he can make this gigantic array, but he cannot sustain it. If confined, even for a time to the sphere within which he now moves, it must dissolve, but the whole military history of the Revolution has taught us to dread that the monster once engendered on French ground may break loose to seek its sustenance elsewhere. This is the true danger against which the Continent, and especially Austria, has to provide, and she ought not to lose an hour in appealing forcibly to the nation. The people are now the only barrier. They are against France, and this is the shield above all others that a State should determine to interpose for its protection, which is so wholly destitute as Austria of a defensible frontier. With respect to means, the same question existed in Russia, and with tenfold force in Prussia. The necessity of the case, the spirit of the people once roused, and the energy of a determined Government soon called them forth. It is for Austria, infinitely more wealthy than either, to imitate their exertions. And she may thereby lay the foundation for a long peace. I have been carried much beyond my purpose, but the subject is endless, and I cannot disguise the dread I feel that the Austrian Minister is trifling with an opponent who meditates nothing less than a *compromise* with his competitors for empire. If Europe is lost it will be on this rock the vessel will founder.

LX. [*F. O. Austria* 101.]
CASTLEREAGH TO ABERDEEN. (No. 26.)
Foreign Office, November 5th, 1813.
[Transmits the ratifications of the Treaty of Toeplitz.]

I have received the Prince Regent's commands to communicate in the most gracious terms to your Lordship H.R.H.'s full approbation of your conduct in having so far anticipated H.R.H.'s views by prevailing on the Court of Vienna to comprehend in the engagements contained in the present Treaty those points for which the faith of the British Government stood pledged, and the cordality with which these several engagements have been adopted by the Austrian Government is received by the Prince Regent not only as a proof of the enlightened policy which actuates the Councils of the Emperor of Austria, but of H.I.M.'s personal desire to renew with this Government a connection of the closest description. I shall address Your Excellency in a separate dispatch on the subject of our engagements with Sweden. I shall therefore only here observe that the grounds on which this point was in Treaty omitted as a matter of express stipulation are considered here as satisfactory, and H.R.H. doubts not they will be so regarded by the Swedish Government.

Your Lordship will have received ere this the instructions of the 28th September,[1] so long detained by contrary winds, relative to the shape which H.R.H.'S confidential servants are desirous of giving to their engagements with the Continental Powers. In comparing the arrangements therein suggested with the stipulations contained in the Treaty as signed, you will find the main distinction to be, that in the latter the several points stated in the secret Article are successively enumerated as objects of the Alliance, but no discrimination is made in the obligation contracted between those that are desirable and those that are essential. In the Projet, as transmitted from hence, the object was, after describing the leading arrangements to which the efforts of the Confederacy were to be directed, to take out of that general class such as were considered in their nature indispensable to the reconstruction of a counterpoise against the power of France, and to declare these to be terms *sine qua non* of a peace. It is

[1] XVII.

also to be observed that in the Secret Articles as signed no notice is taken of Italy in enumerating the objects of the Alliance, and the reference to Holland, by taking the Rhine throughout as the barrier, amounts to a dismemberment, leaving the most important division of the United Provinces in the hands of the enemy.

In adverting to this distinction, however important, Your Excellency will not suppose that the progress you have made towards consolidating the system of the Continent is not duly appreciated. The measure you have achieved is considered, on the contrary, as leaving comparatively little to be done, whilst all-accomplishment is essentially facilitated. I shall under these impressions abstain from giving any further directions of this subject till I am in possession of the measures adopted at the Head Quarters in consequence of the instructions already referred to. In the meantime no hesitation has been felt in at once ratifying what Your Excellency *has accomplished* with equal judgment and ability, leaving it to subsequent deliberation to decide what further measures it may be prudent to adopt for the complete consolidation of the Confederacy, after we are fully possessed of the sentiments of the several Allied Courts.

LXI. [*F. O. Austria* 102.]
ABERDEEN TO CASTLEREAGH.
(Most Secret. No. 27.)
Frankfort, November 8th, 1813.

M. de St. Aignan arrived here this day, and had an interview with Prince Metternich. Immediately after his departure I had a long conference with the Prince and Count Nesselrode. It is determined that he should return to-morrow morning to France and repair with all expedition to Paris, where it is said that Bonaparte now is. He is to bear the propositions which I mentioned to your Lordship in my dispatch No. 23.[1]

A question arose between us whether it would be proper to inform Bonaparte of any objects connected with the French frontier which might be open to negotiation. Count Nesselrode wished to state the terms of the Allies in the first instance as high as possible, and reduce them afterwards in the event of negotiation. I was of opinion that it would be the preferable course to

[1] Aberdeen to Castlereagh (No. 23), October 29th, 1813. " In consequence of the British answer having been received [No. LVIII.] it has been determined to open a communication with Bonaparte, but in such a manner as to give rise to as little speculation as possible, and indeed the whole affair is to be kept a profound secret." F. O. Austria 102.

state the terms as low as possible, and firmly to adhere to them. I told him that, if the propositions were made with the hope of being accepted, common sense dictated that they should be rendered as palatable to Bonaparte as was consistent with the fixed views of the Allies. If the propositions were made without any such hope, I deprecated the whole proceeding as being most erroneous in principle, and calculated to produce the greatest injury to the common cause. I observed that it would be much better to defer making any overture at all, if it was not thought that we were in a sufficiently commanding situation to make that which we were determined to press. In this reasoning Prince Metternich concurred, and it was at last agreed that the specific line of the French frontier towards Holland and Piedmont should be open to discussion, taking care to make the independence of Italy and Holland conditions of peace *sine quibus non*. Thus the matter stands at present; but I should inform your Lordship that M. de St. Aignan is not sanguine in his belief of Bonaparte being sufficiently reduced to accept our terms. I have urged the necessity of secrecy in the strongest manner, and have obtained a promise from Count Nesselrode and the Prince that M. de St. Aignan should not see either of the Emperors previous to his departure, as had been originally intended.

I took this opportunity of asking the Prince his intentions respecting the Proclamation,[1] which I also mentioned to your Lordship in my Dispatch No. 23. He told me that he meant to publish it forthwith. On this subject I had thought a good deal, and had come to the determination to dissuade him from adopting this measure at the present moment. I told him that a proclamation issued at the time of making propositions to Bonaparte could not possibly produce a good effect—that however moderate it might be it would certainly tend to irritate Bonaparte, at the same time that, from a decent regard to him, the Allies deprived themselves of the benefit of a vigorous and energetic appeal to the feelings of all those countries about to throw off his yoke. If he accepted our propositions, the proclamation was useless or injurious ; if he refused to treat, we might compose a much better than we could now venture to issue. Count Nesselrode appeared to assent to the propriety of my observations, and finally the Prince consented, at my entreaty, to delay the publication in order to give effect to the mission of M. de St. Aignan, and then to act as circumstances may require. The fact is that I am not sanguine

---

[1] The Proclamation to the French people subsequently issued on 1st December.

as to the effect of this or any other proclamation on the people of France, and if your Lordship will call to mind the evidence of history on these subjects, I think you will assent to the justice of this opinion.   If the inhabitants of an enemy's country be well disposed they will rise without proclamations, and I am not aware of any instance in which a people were ever moved by these means, who were not otherwise well inclined.   The possible effect of such a measure in France should be a secondary object, but there is no doubt that it might be of essential service in encouraging the perseverance and fortifying the zeal of those countries, who are struggling for independence.   It is to them that we should show the absolute necessity of continued exertion, and should prove that the blessings of peace are not withheld from them by any hopeless projects of ambition and unjustifiable views of foreign conquest.

I am happy to inform your Lordship that, notwithstanding the pacific overtures to which I have drawn your attention, the military preparations and movements continue with unabated activity, nor will any pause be produced in consequence of this or any other measure of the kind.   The present plan for the continuance of the campaign I shall have the honour of detailing to your Lordship in a separate dispatch.

LXII. [*F. O. Austria* 102.]
ABERDEEN TO CASTLEREAGH. (Most secret. No. 31.)
Frankfort, November 9th, 1813.
Prince Metternich and Count Nesselrode were to see M. de St. Aignan this evening previous to his departure in order to settle finally the propositions to be made to Bonaparte.   They requested me to join them, as if by accident, in the course of their meeting, which I accordingly did.

M. de St. Aignan reduced to writing, but in an informal manner, the utter impossibility of a Continental peace.   The notion of anything but a general pacification could never for an instant be admitted, and the Allied Powers were too closely united ever to swerve from this decision, or to abandon the basis on which only they were prepared to treat.   Among the conditions, *sine quibus non*, were stated the adoption by Bonaparte of the natural limits of France, meaning generally the Alps, the Rhine, and the Pyrenees.

The absolute independence of Germany and the renunciation of every species of constitutional influence on the part of France, not meaning thereby the natural and indispensable influence which every powerful state must exercise over its weaker neighbours.

The restoration of Ferdinand VII. and the ancient dynasty to the throne of Spain.

The existence of states, absolutely independent, between the Austrian and French frontier towards Italy.

The absolute independence of Holland, but the precise line of frontier as well as form of Government to be subject to negotiation.

These were the principal conditions which might be considered as a basis of negotiation ; if they were accepted, a place on the right bank of the Rhine might be rendered neutral and a Congress assembled. On no account whatever would any armistice or truce be concluded, nor would the progress of military operations be interrupted.

M. de St. Aignan noted also that England was ready to make great sacrifices in order to obtain peace for Europe, that she did not interfere with the freedom of commerce or with those maritime rights to which France could with justice pretend. I particularly cautioned him against supposing that any possible consideration could induce Great Britain to abandon a particle of what she felt to belong to her maritime code, from which in no case could she ever recede, but that, with this understanding, she had no wish to interfere with the reasonable pretensions of France. I took this opportunity to contradict the assertion which Bonaparte had made to General Merfeldt[1] of the intention of the British Government to limit him to thirty ships of the line, and declared that, so far as I knew, it was a prejudice without any foundation. Of course the whole transaction and interview were understood to be perfectly unofficial, and merely following up the conversation which Bonaparte had recently held with General Merfeldt. M. de St. Aignan seemed to be very doubtful of the probability of these terms being accepted, but he thought that, if the question could be placed with honour to the French nation, the magnitude of the sacrifices would not present any insurmountable obstacle to a general pacification.

I trust your Lordship will not disapprove of the part which I have taken in this affair. My great object, if any propositions were made, was to frame them so as to afford the greatest probability of success consistent with the fixed policy of the Allies. I hope the communication which has been made will be found to embrace the most essential points, and to demand as much as our actual situation entitles us to expect. My next object was that the whole transaction should be conducted with the utmost secrecy

[1] See L. Note 3.

and expedition. The return of M. de St. Aignan has not been attended with any remarkable circumstances, and instead of the shortest delay, the most energetic and vigorous measures will be continued for the purpose of carrying into effect the grand objects of the campaign.

LXIII. [*C. C. IX.* 73.]
CASTLEREAGH TO ABERDEEN.
Foreign Office, November 13th,[1] 1813.

Your dispatches from Frankfort of the 8th and 9th, with their accompanying private explanations, arrived by the Weser before those of an earlier date on the same subject were received. This was fortunate, else we should have felt some alarm at the notion of Louis being thought of for the Government of Holland.

I trust we may also feel assured, from the last accounts, that Metternich has no idea of a suspension of hostilities pending negotiations, even should a basis be agreed upon. Either of these expedients is deprecated here in the strongest manner. The former is now happily out of the question, by the act of the Dutch nation, to which we are parties ; and the offer made by France in August to negotiate without a suspension of arms, renders it easy to decline a proposition which would protract discussion till the armies of France were again prepared to take the field.

You will not be surprised to learn, after such a tide of success, that this nation is likely to view with disfavour any peace which does not confine France strictly within her ancient limits. Indeed, peace with Bonaparte on any terms will be far from popular, distrusting, as the people naturally do, his submitting to destiny for any length of time ; but you will perceive that these opinions have not turned us from our course. We still are ready to encounter, with our Allies, the hazards of peace, if peace can be made on the basis proposed, satisfactorily executed ; and we are not inclined to go out of our way to interfere in the internal government of France, however much we might desire to see it placed in more pacific hands. But I am satisfied we must not encourage our Allies to patch up an imperfect arrangement. If they will do so, we must submit ; but it should appear, in that case, to be their own act, and not ours.

I am aware that the internal difficulties of the Confederacy are great, but, once dispersed, to reassemble it will be impossible. We must, therefore, labour to render it effectual to its purpose

---

[1] So given, but it is obviously of a rather later date.

now, and your last reports encourage me to hope that such will be the result. The revolution in Holland is in itself a new feature in the war, and the fall of Dresden a great accession of strength.

I must particularly entreat you to keep your attention upon Antwerp. The destruction of that arsenal is essential to our safety. To leave it in the hands of France is little short of imposing upon Great Britain the charge of a perpetual war establishment. After all we have done for the Continent in this war they owe it to us and to themselves to extinguish this fruitful source of danger to both. Press this as a primary object of their operations, and, in order to render the value of the fleet, if taken or destroyed, more available for their present expenses, we shall be ready to pay them immediately in credit bills, which they can now realize as advantageously on the Continent as a bill upon the Treasury.

I hope my correspondence has latterly satisfied you that we do justice to your exertions and to the conduct of your Court. When we write we both naturally take our tone from the circumstances, not as then existing, but as known to us. Thus, when I was fretting about the Elbe and the apprehended indecision of Austria, the Allies were laying the solid foundation of all their subsequent glory, and Metternich was performing miracles, both in negotiations and in his armaments. You may assure him I shall not fail him in the long run, however I may complain when I am not satisfied the wheel is moving. There is no preference in any quarter which ought to give him umbrage, but some management which may keep the Russians more cordially at his back. He has behaved in the most loyal manner to us since we became friends, and he shall see, in our arrangements for the ensuing campaign, that we do him justice. . . .

LXIV. [*F. O. Austria* 103.]
ABERDEEN TO CASTLEREAGH. (Secret No. 47.)
Frankfort, November 28th, 1813.

I have the honour to enclose for your Lordship's information copies of a letter addressed by the Duke of Bassano to Prince Metternich, and of the Prince's answer.[1]

Your Lordship will understand that the first intimation which Bonaparte had received of the consent of Great Britain to the meeting of a Congress during the war was conveyed by M. de St. Aignan. I have already informed your Lordship that I com-

---

[1] Duke of Bassano to Metternich, November 16th, 1813 ; Metternich to the Duke of Bassano, November 25th, 1813.

municated the substance of your Lordship's Dispatch No. 14[1] to
Prince Metternich, and that in consequence of the reasoning contained in it the peculiar form of M. de St. Aignan's Mission was
adopted. It is from a conviction of the truth of this reasoning
that a private intercourse is still preferred to a public overture,
at least until the parties shall agree on some general basis. The
whole advantage of a public official intercourse would be on the
side of France. The hopes of peace would stimulate the French
nation to greater exertions and fresh sacrifices, while it would
only damp the spirit of the Allies and paralyse their energy. As
it is, Bonaparte may probably hold out these hopes to the people
of France, his success must be incomplete ; while our silence
and the activity of our military movements keep alive the warlike
ardour of our friends. Whatever may be the preferable course
respecting this question, I can assure your Lordship that both
the Imperial Courts have framed their conduct on their belief of
what would be most approved of by the British Government.

The answer of Prince Metternich to the Duke of Bassano
appears to be perfectly conformable to the reasoning employed
in your Lordship's dispatch, No. 14. No Congress will be thought
of or negotiations entered into without a previous agreement of
some general basis, and although the enemy seems to wish to
avoid coming to any specific statement, there are private accounts
from Paris worthy of credit which indicate the probability of his
pacific disposition being more sincere than it has hitherto been.

In consequence of the allusion of the Duke of Bassano to M.
de St. Aignan's report of what had been said by the British
Minister, I thought it right to address a note to Prince Metternich,
stating explicitly the share which I had taken in the conversation
and the circumstances in which I was placed. Your Lordship
is already informed from my dispatches Nos. 31 and 39[2] of the
particulars of the proceeding, but I thought this step necessary
to avoid the possibility of all error or misinterpretation. I have
the honour to enclose a copy of the note in question, as well as of
Prince Metternich's answer,[3] which I trust your Lordship will find
satisfactory in all its parts. It is probable that Bonaparte may
endeavour to entangle us in the question of maritime rights, and
in the event of the failure of any negotiation to throw the whole
odium of the prolongation of the war upon England. With this
prospect your Lordship cannot fail to consider the declaration
of the Austrian Minister as peculiarly gratifying ; I shall com-

[1] LVIII.   [2] See LXII.
[3] Protesting against St. Aignan's insinuation that Aberdeen had agreed to
    discuss the "maritime rights."

L

municate officially to the Courts of Russia, Prussia, and Sweden copies of these papers, in order that the passage of the Duke of Bassano's letter may be perfectly understood.

Your Lordship is not to understand that the unofficial communication made by M. de St. Aignan embraced the whole basis of negotiation, or contained a specification of every condition *sine qua non* on the part of the Allies, but it was thought right to confine the proposition in the first instance to those questions directly affecting the French frontier, and in which France was most immediately concerned. For this reason no mention was made of Poland, an object of the deepest interest to the three great Continental Powers ; for this reason also all mention of Norway was postponed. It is in this point of view that your Lordship is to consider the omission of Portugal, Sicily, and a variety of important objects in M. de St. Aignan's minute ; but it appears to me that if Bonaparte agrees to the summary conditions recited in that paper, we should not be justified in desisting from the endeavour to ascertain by negotiation whether he may be brought to accede to the whole of those conditions of peace, which are absolutely indispensable on the part of the Allies. . . .

LXV. [*F. O. Austria* 101.]
CASTLEREAGH TO ABERDEEN. (No. 38.)
Foreign Office, November 30th, 1813.

[Acknowledges Aberdeen's account of the overture to St. Aignan.]

With respect to the period which has been selected for this overture, His Royal Highness is disposed to defer to the judgment of his Allies, it being a question on which they must, for various reasons, be more competent to decide than himself. And your Lordship is authorized to acquaint the Emperor of Austria that His Royal Highness will be prepared to negotiate on the basis proposed, in the event of its being accepted by the enemy, understanding thereby the Alps and the Pyrenees to be admitted as the boundary of France and the Rhine, with such departure therefrom as may sufficiently provide for the independence and security of Holland and of Switzerland, although the latter is not specifically named in your dispatch.

The Prince Regent highly applauds the determination taken by the Allies upon no account to suffer active operations to be suspended in consequence of this overture or during any discussions that may grow out of it. Your Lordship must be aware that the protraction of the negotiation would not fail to prove most prejudicial to the common cause. His Royal Highness also trusts that any unnecessary delay or equivocation in accepting this basis will be at once considered tantamount to its rejection by the enemy, and that the Allies will in that case make such an early declaration of the measures adopted by them for terminating the war as may satisfy the world that the continuance of the war is not owing to the unreasonableness of the Allies, but to the ambition of the ruler of France, and that no hope can exist of obtaining a secure and honourable peace except from a vigorous prosecution of the contest.

The Prince Regent desires your Lordship will further declare his entire approbation of the omission in the proposed basis of any proposition on which the Allies were not prepared peremptorily to insist. And His Royal Highness persuades himself that his desire for peace will not be questioned, when he declares that in his judgment less could not have been demanded at the present moment from the enemy than what has been proposed, in justice to the great and progressive successes which have blessed the Allied arms, and, above all, to the future repose and security of Europe. In agreeing to negotiate in concert with his Allies upon this basis, moderate as it must be deemed to be in the present circumstances of the war, His Royal Highness trusts that its admission will be insisted upon as preliminary to any discussions.

His Royal Highness considers it highly material to the general interests that such sacrifices as Great Britain may be prepared to make for the welfare of the Continent shall be applied to the satisfactory arrangement of those limits which appear to be left indefinite in the basis, viz., the Frontier of France towards Piedmont and Holland, and more especially to such an arrangement for the latter as may place it in a competent state of strength and security. In adverting to the basis as affecting Holland, your Lordship will perceive that the form of the government of that State can no longer be matter of negotiation between the Allied Powers and France. His Royal Highness feels confident, after the glorious and successful effort recently made by the people of that country to assert their independence under the Government of the House of Orange, that there will be but one sentiment am:ngst the Allies as to the support they shall receive, a support which Great Britain has not hesitated to afford of the largest scale which circumstances would permit.

In contemplating the magnitude of the interests that are now at stake it is most gratifying to His Royal Highness to observe the gigantic means which the energies and attachment of their subjects have placed at the disposal of the Allied Sovereigns. His Royal Highness is satisfied that on their wisdom, firmness, and union, Europe may confidently rely for its future safety, and that they will not lay down their arms until this, the great object of the Confederacy, shall have been satisfactorily secured. In this persuasion I have only further to perform the grateful duty of signifying to your Lordship that the Prince Regent has been pleased most graciously to approve of the part your Lordship has borne in these delicate and momentous discussions.

LXVI. [*F. O. Austria* 101.]
CASTLEREAGH TO ABERDEEN. (No. 44.)
Foreign Office, December 7th, 1813.
[Further concerning the overture to St. Aignan.]

Your Lordship's letter of the 16th transmitting a memorandum as drawn up by that gentleman of what he chose to represent as having passed at the interview with the Austrian and Russian ministers in your Lordship's presence was only yesterday received. Your Lordship upon perusal of this memorandum very properly protested against the accuracy of this document, but as it does not appear that this protest was made in writing,[1] His Royal Highness's Government considers it highly expedient that your Lordship should make such a communication in the form of a note verbal to the Ministers of the Allied Powers who were present at that interview, as may record that your Lordship was not to be considered as a party, even unofficially, to the terms in which the memorandum was drawn up, and that this protest may include the sentiments of your Government upon the said minute I enclose the sketch of a note which appears to His Royal Highness's Ministers suitable to the occasion.

Your Lordship must be aware that the document in question is not merely objectionable in putting forward a very loose and equivocal description of the sentiments of this Government on what is called the freedom of commerce and navigation. The manner in which this subject is referred to is obviously calculated to encourage the enemy to attempt to introduce discussions upon maritime rights into the negotiations for peace. Against any such attempt your Excellency is directed to protest in the strongest manner on the part of your Court. And for the sentiments which determine His Royal Highness's Government to consider this point as a condition *sine qua non* of negotiation on their part, I beg leave to refer your Excellency to the enclosed extract of my dispatch to Lord Cathcart of the 27th of September last.[2]

---

[1] But see p. 113.   [2] XIX.

Your Excellency will also observe that in referring to the independence of Holland this memorandum is altogether silent on the important point of an adequate barrier for that State. It also very unjustifiably assumes the Pyrenees, the Alps, and the Rhine to be the *natural* boundaries of France, a concession which there can be no pretence on the part of the enemy for claiming, because the Allies may, on grounds of expediency, have acquiesced at the period this overture was made in negotiating on such a basis, subject, however, to certain important modifications. Neither will the enemy have any ground of claim hereafter to assume that basis as against the Allies, should he decline the proposition now made to him. The reference to the natural influence of France over the intermediate States is also capable of misconception, and ought to be protested against as far as it may be liable to be perverted into a disclaimer on the part of the Germanic body of any right to form a federal connection under a constitutional head to the exclusion of foreign influence.

Your Lordship's determination not to make yourself a party to the memorandum in question, by suggesting any alterations in the frame of it, was perfectly proper. But as misconception may hereafter exist upon this subject it is requisite that your dissent, and that of your Court from its accuracy, should be recorded in the manner above suggested, both for your own justification and that of your Government.

LXVII. [*C. C. IX.*, 89.]
CASTLEREAGH TO ABERDEEN.
Foreign Office, December 7th, 1813.

You know how acutely we feel upon all political subjects when our feelings have been long excited by animating events, but that, at all times, a maritime question touches us to the quick. I cannot conceal from you the uneasiness of the Government upon the perusal of St. Aignan's Minute : and most certainly such a document, if published by the enemy, without any counter-document on our part, would excite unpleasant impressions in this country. It is, therefore, deemed indispensable to record our sentiments in a producible shape, and I lose no time in instructing you accordingly.

I apprehend, after presenting your note to Metternich, your course will be to transmit a copy to Lord Cathcart for the information of the Russian Government. You will assure the Allies that we act not from the smallest sensation of distrust, but from the necessity imposed upon us of always keeping our case in a shape which, if produced to Parliament, would justify our vigilance and correctness as not having left the enemy a cavil as to our real intentions.

We shall feel much anxiety till an Allied force, adequate not only to its protection, but to assume the offensive towards Antwerp, is assembled in Holland. We consider it of great importance that the Allies should countenance the Prince of Orange as early as possible. Pray encourage the Austrian Government to send a Minister to the Hague. With their support and our arms we may soon hope to have a respectable force established in that most important quarter. If Charles has left you again, impress the same idea upon Prussia. I have not time to write more.

LXVIII. [*F. O. Austria* 103.]
ABERDEEN TO CASTLEREAGH. (No. 53.)
Frankfort, December 9th, 1813.

I am just returned from a long conference with Prince Metternich and Count Nesselrode on the subject of the Treaty of Alliance. The difficulties which I had to encounter, and the irresistible arguments with which I was furnished chiefly from your Lordship's dispatches to Lord Cathcart, rendered the interview sufficiently animated. I placed the question in its true light, reprobated the notion of its being an object more essentially interesting to Great Britain than to either of their respective States, and declared to refuse such a Treaty at the present moment was a policy as blind as it was illiberal. I strongly urged the importance of such a bond of union at a moment when the prospect of negotiation was at hand. The existence of such a Treaty would be of more value in any intercourse with Napoleon than a victory of the most splendid description. It cannot be necessary for me to detail to your Lordship the various arguments and modes of persuasion which I employed to make them fully comprehend the question. It is sufficient to say that I left none untouched of which I was possessed, or which the copious nature of the subject afforded.

Both Prince Metternich and Count Nesselrode professed a strong desire to negotiate the Treaty, provided it was the wish of Great Britain ; but some explanations were required. Prince Metternich made no material difficulty, but Count Nesselrode wished that the subsidiary arrangement should be connected with it. They both appeared to wish that, if Great Britain could not specify what particular conquests might be considered as objects of negotiation at a peace, she would at least declare those which she would never consent to place in that predicament. I represented the folly of such a demand—that it must mainly depend on the state of Europe at the time of negotiation—that it would be tying up our hands to their own injury. Besides which the question was insulting to Great Britain—it betrayed an unjustifiable want of confidence in her. It exercised a right, which considering the unparalleled exertions of Great Britain in their cause, did not belong to them. In short, it appeared to me that such a demand would prove fatal to the project of the Treaty. I had proposed an article which Prince Metternich had approved of, in which the principle was admitted that Great Britain would consider such of her conquests as were not essentially necessary to her prosperity as a resource from which the conditions of a Continental peace might be improved, but that Great Britain must be the sole judge of the respective value of these possessions. Any further proposal on their part I could consider only as dictated by a desire to obstruct the progress of the negotiation and get rid of the Treaty altogether.

With respect to subsidiary arrangements, it appeared to me highly unbecoming to introduce into an instrument, which had for its object the final settlement of Europe, any particular stipulations of this nature. There was no objection to declare generally that Great Britain would assist the Continental Powers both with men and money to the utmost practical extent of her means, but they were too well accustomed to the liberality of the British Government, had too often experienced her generous exertions in their cause, to render a more precise stipulation necessary, even if it were decent and just. On this last point I have reason to hope that considerable impression was made, and that it will not be persevered in, especially as Prince Metternich assisted me in the discussion. I believe, however, that it is intended to present a joint note on the subject, when we shall know exactly what it is they desire.

I see clearly that Prince Metternich, although perfectly ready to sign the Treaty himself, is unwilling to follow the example of Prussia in separating herself from the Allies for fear of giving umbrage to Russia. He therefore will endeavour, if possible, to draw Russia with him. This may be all very right, but I could not help observing to them that they appeared by their conduct almost as anxious to make common cause against us as against France.

LXIX.   [*C. C. IX.*, 107.]
CASTLEREAGH TO ABERDEEN.
St. James's Square, December 22nd, 1813.

The march of events is so rapid, the points at issue so important, and the impossibility of keeping pace, by instructions from home with the necessity for them abroad, is such as to require, were it practicable, that the Government itself should repair to head-quarters.   As it is, they have thought it right that I should, during the recess, proceed there, to make such arrangements as the existing circumstances may require on the spot.   You may, there-fore, expect me early in the month, and I trust we may be enabled to decide on Pozzo's budget more satisfactorily when the dis-cussions can be conducted under a full knowledge of the existing state of affairs.   I shall, therefore, go no further with him or with the other Foreign Ministers here than to ascertain all the points on which they deem it expedient that I should obtain the senti-ments of the Government before my departure for my final decision when we meet.

It gives me the greatest pleasure to observe that a little political controversy has made no change in yours and Charles's mutual confidence.   If I could have foreseen the great questions that were impending, I should certainly have thrown the three Ministers that were at headquarters into a species of commission, and have required them to consider and decide upon subjects of general policy in their collective capacity, transacting the inferior details in their distinct capacities.   What has been wanting was a central authority.   The differences have been fewer than might have been apprehended, but where there are several independent authorities, there must be doubts as to the sentiments of the Government, Whilst I state the evil, and advert to what might have been in a great degree the remedy, I must say that, upon the whole, the Government has been most ably served, and I beg you will be assured we do ample justice you all.   .   .   .

PART II

THE MAKING OF THE ALLIANCE
AND
THE FIRST PEACE OF PARIS

PART II

THE MAKING OF THE ALLIANCE AND THE FIRST PEACE OF PARIS.

LXX. [*F. O. Cont. Arch. I.*]

MEMORANDUM OF CABINET, DECEMBER 26th, 1813.

Present.—The Lord Chancellor, The Lord President, The Lord Privy Seal, Earl of Liverpool, Earl of Bathurst, Earl of Buckingham, Earl of Mulgrave, Viscount Sidmouth, Viscount Melville, Mr. Vansittart, Mr. B. Bathurst, Viscount Castlereagh.[1]

The three Allied Powers having invited the Prince Regent to send a Plenipotentiary to the Continent charged with full powers to treat both with friendly and hostile Powers on all matters which concern the general interests; and H.R.H., having previously received from the Ministers of the said Powers in London satisfactory assurances on the Maritime question, has been pleased, in compliance with the desire of the said Allies, to direct His Majesty's Secretary of State for Foreign Affairs to proceed forthwith to the headquarters of the allies in execution of this especial service.

Lord Castlereagh is charged in the first instance to enter into such preliminary explanation as may be necessary to ascertain with precision the basis on which it is proposed to negotiate. He is to endeavour to establish a clear and definite understanding with the Allies, not only on all matters of common interest but upon such points as are likely to be discussed with the enemy, so that the several Allied Powers may in their negotiations with France, and in perfect concert, and together maintain one common interest.

If called upon for an explanation of the views of his Government as to terms of peace, and the sacrifice of conquests which Great Britain is disposed to make for the general interest, he is to state that with respect to the latter, it must in a great measure

---

[1] These instructions were drawn up for Castlereagh to take with him on the Continent so that he might decide important points without delay. They were submitted to a Cabinet meeting at which, as appears on the document, all the members were present except Camden. See an article by G. W. T. Omond in the "Nineteenth Century," March, 1918.

be governed by the nature of the conditions with respect to the Continent, which the Allied Powers may be enabled to obtain from the enemy. If the maritime power of France shall be restricted within due bounds by the effectual establishment of Holland, the Peninsula, and Italy in security and independence, Great Britain, consistent with her own security, may then be induced to apply the greater proportion of her conquests to promote the general interests. If, on the contrary, the arrangements should be defective in any of these points, Great Britain must reserve a proportionate share of these conquests to render her secure against France.

If called on for a more detailed explanation, he may state that the objects *sine qua non* upon which Great Britain can venture to divest herself of her conquests in any material degree are :—
1. The absolute exclusion of France from any naval establishment on the Scheldt, and especially at Antwerp ; and 2. The security of Holland being adequately provided for by a Barrier under the House of Orange, which shall at least include Juliers and Antwerp as well as Maestricht with a suitable arrondissement of territory in addition to Holland as it stood in 1792, it being understood that Wesel shall also be in the hands of the Allied Powers.

[The Monarchies of the Peninsula must be free under their Legitimate Sovereigns, their dominions at least in Europe being guaranteed against attack by France. The Allied Powers to take engagements to this effect and to stipulate the amount of succour to be mutually furnished in each ease. Great Britain is prepared to confine the *casus foederis* to the Continent. Under these circumstances Great Britain is prepared to consider her conquests as objects of negotiation. But Malta, the Mauritius and the Isle of Bourbon, Guadeloupe and the Island of Les Saintes must remain British, Mauritius being considered as necessary to protect Indian commerce, and Guadeloupe as a debt of honour to Sweden. If Guadeloupe should be made a *sine qua non*, Sweden must be compensated by Bourbon or a Dutch Colony, Holland in the latter case taking Bourbon. If Holland is secured by a Barrier, the Dutch colonies will be restored, but the Cape of Good Hope will be retained and £2,000,000 paid by Great Britain. The Danish conquests, except Heligoland, should be made instrumental to the engagements with Sweden.]

In all communications on the expediency of Peace, the same course to be pursued as heretofore, viz., to evince a desire to conform as far as possible to the general interests of the Continent; to give to the Allies the most unequivocal assurances of a firm determination to support them in contracting for an advantageous peace and to avoid everything that might countenance a suspicion that Great Britain was inclined to push them forward in the war for our purposes. The utmost exertions to be used to prevent any relaxation in the military operations, whilst negotiations are pending.

[He is also to direct force as much as possible from all quarters upon Holland and the Low Countries, but the British force cannot exceed 10,000 men and may be withdrawn. If Austria would like the Archduke Charles to be settled in the Netherlands, the proposal is to be welcomed. But the question depends on the success of the Allies afterwards in the war, i.e., whether he can have the whole of Belgium or not. The Prince of Orange is to be discouraged from attempting to extend his dominions, without the express consent of the Allies. A marriage between the Prince of Orange and the Princess Charlotte of Wales is to be suggested. If the Dutch Barrier is not obtained, then the restoration of the Dutch colonies is to be proportionately reduced.]

As the Barrier for Holland is an object most deeply interesting to all the Allies, Great Britain is willing to purchase it by a double sacrifice, by cession both to France and to Holland. If the Allies should not carry this point, so important to their own security as well as to that of Great Britain, the latter Power will, in that case, have no other alternative than to preserve her colonial conquests as a counterpoise to the dominion of the enemy, and on these grounds to withhold those cessions which she would otherwise be prepared to make to France. The cession of conquests by Great Britain being declared to be contingent upon equivalent securities to result from the continental arrangements, and especially on the side of Holland and the Low Countries, any general stipulation which does not expressly declare the principle by which it is to be regulated and connect it pointedly with these objects, appears objectionable.

[As to Italy, the military line of the Alps and the roads lately opened in the direction of Italy to be specially attended to. It is " highly expedient " that the King of Sardinia should be restored, and he should perhaps, receive Genoa, in exchange for Savoy. If Austria connects herself with Murat, the Sicilian Family is to have Tuscany or Elba. The Pope is to be restored. The Milanese, Modena, Parma and Placentia are to be subject to discussion. Great Britain offers mediation on the internal

German affairs. She is ready to sign a peace with the United States, in a general peace on the *status quo ante bellum* without involving in such Treaty any decision on the points in dispute at the commencement of hostilities. A direct proposition to treat in London having been lately made to the American Government, this offer not to be stated unless the subject should be brought forward. Should such an offer be made to America, a time to be stated within which her acceptance or refusal must be declared. The question as to the arrangement with Denmark to be subject to discussion with Sweden. The distribution of the Command in the North to be reserved for consideration at Head Quarters. A subsidy of £5,000,000 is to be under reserve, 1. As to sending home the Russian fleet. 2. The acceptance of a proportion in credit bills. 3. The signing of engagements especially as to Holland and the Peninsula as may justify to the British Public and the Allies so great an exertion on the part of Great Britain.]

The Treaty of Alliance *not to terminate with the war*, but to contain defensive engagements with mutual obligations to support the powers attacked by France with a certain extent of stipulated succours. The *Casus Foederis* to be an attack by France on the European dominions of any one of the contracting parties. [Spain, and if possible Holland, to be included as contracting parties. Sweden being beyond the Baltick, is less interested in being included, or rather has an interest not to participate.]

Humbly submitted for your Royal Highness' Sanction.

(Signed.) GEORGE P.R.

MEMORANDUM ON THE MARITIME PEACE.[1]

Great Britain in the course of the war has conquered from her enemies the colonies and possessions according to the annexed list.[2] Great Britain has declared her disposition with certain exceptions to sacrifice these conquests for the welfare of the Continent, being desirous of providing for her own security by a common arrangement, rather than by an exclusive accumulation of strength and resources. Her object is to see a maritime as well as a military Balance of Power established amongst the Powers of Europe, and as the basis of this arrangement she desires to see the independence of Spain and Holland as maritime Powers effectually provided for. Upon the supposition that these

---

[1] This document immediately follows the Cabinet Memorandum of December 26th, and may be considered part of it. It was probably drawn up in the course of the discussions to make quite clear to the Cabinet a point in which they were much more interested than in the details of the Continental settlement.
[2] Not given.

two objects shall be obtained in the proposed arrangements, that
the limits of France shall be reduced within proper bounds, and
that the peace of the Continent shall be secured by an amicable
understanding between the Allies, Great Britain will then be prepared also to return within corresponding limits and to throw
her acquisitions into the scale of the general interests.

As nothing is yet defined with precision either as to the state
of the enemy's limits nor as to that of the Allies, it is impossible
to do more than state on the part of Great Britain the nature and
extent of concession she would be prepared to make upon given
data as to the continental arrangement. The object will best be
effected by stating what the maximum of concession might be on
the part of Great Britain upon assuming the reduction of France
within her ancient limits, and the Allies having amicably arranged
their own state of possession. In developing this subject it is
desirable to state, 1st, the classes into which the conquests made
by Great Britain resolve themselves, and 2ndly, the principles
upon which the British Government is disposed to govern its
decision with respect to their restitution.

With respect to the latter point they do not desire to retain
any of these Colonies for their mere commercial value—too
happy if by their restoration they can give other States an additional
motive to cultivate the arts of peace. The only objects to which
they desire to adhere are those which affect essentially the engagement and security of their own dominion.

And first as to the Danish Colonies enumerated in the Margin[1].
If they could be the means of promoting the interest of the common cause in the North of Europe, Great Britain long since
offered to restore them. A treaty of peace has recently been
signed with Denmark by which all their possessions (with the
exception of Heligoland) are surrendered, Denmark ceding Norway to Sweden, in satisfaction of the engagements of Russia, and
joining her arms to those of the Allies.

The next class to be adverted to is the Dutch Colonies as enumerated in the Margin.[2]

In the East Indies, Great Britain shall restore to France, the
different settlements and factories in possession of that Crown as
well on the coast of Coromandel and Orisca, as on that of Malabar,
as also on Bengal at the commencement of the year 1792-3, and
the Government of France engages to erect no fortifications in

[1] Not given.
[2] Not given. The document stops here and is continued on a smaller sheet
simply endorsed " East Indies."

any part of the said settlements or factories, nor to maintain any
military force therein beyond what may be deemed necessary
for the purposes of police, and His Britannic Majesty engages on
his part to secure to the subjects of France, without the limits of
their settlements and factories, an impartial administration of
justice, in all matters concerning their persons and properties and
to adopt such measures as may be judged requisite to enable them
to carry on commerce upon the footing of the most favoured
nations.[1]

LXXI. [C. C. IX., 123.]
CASTLEREAGH TO LIVERPOOL.
Harwich, December 30th. 12 o'clock, 1813.

I have received yours and Lord Bathurst's letters. Wellington's movement seems to have reached its natural limits as a
first operation. . . . The result, upon the whole, as far as
it goes, is satisfactory. I only lament that the wear and tear is
to fall upon the British and the Portuguese, and that the Spaniards
cannot be brought forward. I have read with great interest
Lord W.'s private letter,[2] and shall keep the subject to which it
refers constantly in view. As matters *now* stand, I think *we*
cannot be too careful not to adopt any equivocal proceeding,
which might render our position, both with the Allies and those
in France who might be induced to show themselves, most
embarrassing. If *they* move of themselves, we are fully entitled
to take advantage of that, as of any other incident in war : but,
if we lend ourselves to the measures that are to excite it, it will
be considered as a trick on our part to get rid of the negotiation,
and those French who may be committed will, right or wrong,
conceive themselves entitled to our protection. Should France
reject the Allied terms, we are then all free to do what we like ;
but, having gone the length with our Allies to accept a basis on
which we have declared that we are ready to negotiate, I think
our line ought to be an unembarrassed one till the question of
negotiation is disposed of.

[1] A variant is given of the last sentence as follows : " and to adopt such
measures as may be judged requisite to enable the said subjects to carry on a
safe and independent Trade."
  [2] Wellington had written to Bathurst on November 21st : " I can only tell
you that, if I were a Prince of the House of Bourbon, nothing should now
prevent me from now coming forward not in a good house in London, but in
the field in France." In December a Bourbon emissary arrived at his head-
quarters with a request that a Bourbon Prince should join his army and raise
the standard of Louis XVIII. in the South of France. Gurwood. *Wellington*,
Dispatches XI ; 306, 381, 390.

As soon as I arrive at head-quarters, I will converse with our Allies upon the view Lord W. opens, and apprize you of their sentiments. I think we cannot assume that the view Metternich took of the question, when referred to him two months since, remains the same under the pending negotiations. I have myself so humble an opinion of the effect of a French Prince showing himself in France, without arms and money, wherewith to levy troops, that I cannot feel disposed to risk much, especially in the peculiar situation in which we now stand, to try its effect upon the enemy. I am inclined to believe, when they talk of the effect to be expected from a Bourbon showing himself, they mean a Bourbon with arms and money. Of the latter, I apprehend we have none to spare—not enough evidently to bring the Spaniards forward.

Upon the whole, my impressions are against any step which should, even in appearance, mix our system with that of the Bourbons, whilst we are embarked in discussions for peace, and ignorant how our Allies would relish such a step at the present moment ; and in this view I doubt the prudence even of a declaration as to the armistice by sea and land ; 1st, because it would be considered an invitation to a rising ; and, 2ndly, because I doubt its efficacy even to that object ; as those who reason at all cannot doubt that, were the Bourbons restored, hostilities would immediately cease. We ought always to recollect that we are suspected of having *une arrière-pensée* on the question of peace, and that we should act with the more caution.

I have written very hastily my first impressions upon your letter. They are intended for Bathurst, for whom I have a letter, as well as for yourself. From the early part of Lord Wellington's letter, I think his impressions are the same as my own ; that, with all the objections to such a peace, if Buonaparte will give you your own terms, you ought not to risk yourselves and the confederacy in the labyrinth of counter-revolution. If he will not, you may then run greater risks ; but even then I should wish to see more evident proofs of active disposition to throw off B.'s yoke, before I encouraged an effort.

That some fermentation exists I have no doubt ; that it may increase in proportion as France is pressed is probable ; but if it really prevails to an extent that renders resistance feasible, I am persuaded it will explode, without waiting for a Bourbon to give it birth.

M

LXXII. [*C. C. IX.*, 130.]

CASTLEREAGH TO LIVERPOOL.

Erebus, at anchor in the Rowling Grounds.

2 p.m., December 31st, 1813.

[Feels the importance of despatches just received, but thinks that any step taken on behalf of the Bourbons would be premature. The presence of Monsieur[1] at the scene of Lord Wellington's operations would cause France as well as Europe to suspect an engagement between him and the British Government, and any support he might receive would be given in a confident reliance upon our protection. If Wellington denied authority to countenance his cause, reason to fear that the rising disposition in favour of the Bourbon's might be checked rather than promoted by the Prince's presence thus unsupported.]

It appears to me that, on this occasion, as on many former, the Bourbons are desirous of taking a step prematurely. Lord W[ellington], you seem to infer, wishes one of the family to come, but I apprehend only upon the supposition that, when there, he may be permitted to co-operate with him. If we are not ripe for this, Lord W[ellington]'s task will be a most embarrassing one. Supposing the disposition to move true to the extent stated on ths side of Bayonne, unless it pervades the interior, and the Allies countenance it, on their side, it is more likely to lead to embarrassment than to success. It appears to me that matters have not yet sufficiently developed themselves to make an experiment prudent on a small scale, and in a quarter where we are unprepared to give it direct support. I should doubt the discretion of Monsieur hazarding such a failure as a matter of impression. If one of the family goes, and nothing arises out of it, their cause is essentially prejudiced ; and what can a Bourbon, without arms, money, or the avowed support of the Allies, hope to effect by his personal presence, in a country hating their Government but still dreading its resentment.

Nothing can be more satisfactory than the course Lord W[ellington] is pursuing to ascertain the temper of France, and he cannot follow up the inquiry too actively ; but we must distinguish between the good-will with which he is received and a disposition to bear arms against the existing ruler. His army relieves the people of France for the time from all the evils of their own system : no conscription—no taxes—no requisitions— ready money for all supplies—and kind treatment. We must not wonder at the popularity of such a *régime* ; but it is another

[1] The Comte d'Artois, later Charles X. See *infra.* p. 163.

question whether the people will or can rise in sufficient force to accomplish any great purpose. Of this Lord W[ellington] seems to deem the evidence yet received to furnish but inadequate proofs. They appear to me altogether insufficient to found any proceeding upon which they might, even in appearance, commit us, *without a combined arrangement with our Allies* ; and that, as a French Prince cannot be there for any useful purpose, without our being committed more or less, my opinion leans strongly to the truth of the proposition stated by Lord W[ellington], that things are not yet ripe for a Prince to show himself ; and, if it is expedient that he should be there, it is a question of too great magnitude for us to hesitate in opposing it (at least, till we can consult our Allies) in the most decisive manner. In the meantime, they may pursue their own measures in preparing the interior. . . . .

LXXIII. [*C. C. IX.*, 169.]
CATHCART TO CASTLEREAGH.
Basle, January 16, Sunday, 1814.

. . . . . . The Emperor has charged me to express to you his regret that he cannot await your lordship's arrival here ; and that there are important considerations which oblige him to go away from the conversation which he was so anxious to have with you on your arrival.[1] His Imperial Majesty, however, trusts that you will bear in mind the principles which dictated the request I have by various messengers stated on his part concerning your first audience. He is aware that you cannot now avoid going into business with the Ministers you will find here ; but he requests that you will leave a place in the opinions you may be led to form, and particularly in any communication of them you might be disposed to make, for the results of the conversation his Imperial Majesty hopes to have with you, at an early day, on several important topics.

The first of these is that of negotiation. The general sentiments of His Imperial Majesty are to avoid incurring the charge of neglecting to make peace when a favourable opportunity presents itself ; but to avoid precipitation and to weigh well the question whether more should not previously be done by arms.

---

[1] Alexander had said : " I will engage you to ask Lord Castlereagh to see me before he sees any Minister either of *mine* or of any other Power on the business which brings him here." Cathcart to Castlereagh, Jan. 8th, 1814, C.C. IX., 149.

Secondly, to treat for peace *pure et simple*, proposing boundaries, and reducing the question to a categorical answer—Yes or No—and avoiding mixing in this negotiation those questions which belong to the Allies among themselves, towards ensuring the proper balance of power, and securities for the duration of peace. On this latter subject, His Imperial Majesty, is equally desirous that you should reserve yourself for a conversation with him. And you will find the Emperor equally impressed with a notion of the importance of postponing for the present all complicated questions on this subject.

I know the principal topics have been named to you—Saxony forms the principal feature, and the greatest nicety may be required to adjust that question between Austria and Prussia. I do not know that any difference of opinion has broke out, but everybody wishes to canvass you. What is very singular, Chancellor Hardenberg came to the Emperor within these few days, and reported that Prince Metternich had spontaneously declared to him that he, Prince Metternich, abounded in the same sentiments on the expediency of giving a frontier to Prussia in Saxony[1]. I cannot undertake to say that the frontier was named ; but I think to the Elster and Bohemia. Coupled with other things, the Emperor is a little inclined to think that the Chancellor has either mistaken the Prince, or that there might be an intention of sounding his Excellency.

I see the Emperor looks to a great alliance between England, Russia, Austria, and Prussia, giving to each sufficient means, and prescribing the line of joint operation, in case of the future aggression of France. Russia renounces all idea of extension to the Vistula, in favour of Prussia, but will look to the demolition of the duchy and to the acquisition of so much thereof as may be necessary for her purpose.[2]

It is conceived that whatever is done for the King of Saxony must be on the side of Italy. His Imperial Majesty will talk to you of his readiness to support the King, and the interests of his Royal Highness the Prince Regent in Hanover . . . .

[1] But the agreement is confirmed by an entry in Hardenberg's Diary of January 8th, 1814. cf. Fournier. *Congress von Chatillon*, p. 361.

[2] This is an entirely erroneous report and the fact was soon clear. Nevertheless Castlereagh sent a copy of this dispatch to Alexander at Vienna on October 20th, 1814, as a proof of his continued expectation of Russian moderation. The duchy is, of course, the Duchy of Warsaw.

LXXIV. [*W. S. D. VIII.*, 535.]
CASTLEREAGH TO LIVERPOOL.
Basle, January 22nd, 1814.
[Alexander wished to see Castlereagh before he saw the ministers of the powers, but had to leave Basle before Castlereagh arrived. Castlereagh found letter asking him not to make up his mind on any subjects till he had seen Alexander, and this he has borne in mind in his interviews with Metternich, Stadion and Hardenberg.[1]]

With respect to the spirit which animates the Allies, late events will have sufficiently established the military energy that pervades their councils. . . . [Details of the operations.] I wish I could feel quite satisfied that nothing was likely to occur to suspend the energy of the offensive operations now in progress in the interior of France ; but there are some questions pending of great importance, which, if not speedily and distinctly understood, may lead in this respect to the worst consequences. Some persons contemplate these circumstances with more apprehension than I can bring myself to entertain after the many difficulties we have already surmounted.

The first and most important, and that which will perhaps surprise you the most, is a disposition represented to be felt by the Emperor of Russia to favour the Prince Royal of Sweden's views to the throne of France. I can hardly yet bring myself to give credit to this statement, but it comes to me through so many channels of authority that I cannot hesitate to believe that the project has been countenanced by his Imperial Majesty, although I trust not to an extent that will induce a perseverance in it after the objections have been pressed upon his attention. If there were no other evil in this scheme, its effect in paralysing the Allied arms must be conclusive. I have reason to believe that, until this intention is disavowed, the Austrian army will not advance much farther in the direction of Paris. Prince Metternich's language on this subject is the most decisive possible, and the Prussians feel not less warmly upon it.

The Austrian Minister's confidential language is, that his Court have no objection to bring forward, should the French nation think fit to restore the ancient dynasty ; but that it is another question to have Madame Bernadotte substituted in the room of a Princess of the House of Hapsburgh. He considers this, however, as only a subordinate objection, deeming such a connection between Russia and France to be formidable to the

[1] See LXXIII.

liberties of Europe, and precisely that evil to guard against which the Emperor gave his daughter in marriage to Napoleon.

I have understood, in addition to the éclat of dethroning Buonaparte, and getting rid of a troublesome neighbour, that the Emperor was led to contemplate such a change with more favour upon a late visit he made to the Court of Baden, where he met the Queen of Sweden, and was much struck both with her and her children, and soon after expressed an earnest desire to replace them in Sweden. I still flatter myself that this impression has been a passing one, as nothing could be more discreditable, after extorting Norway from Denmark for the purpose of rendering Sweden independent, than to secure, through an intrigue with such a man, the control of both, and further to aim at establishing a preponderating influence in France itself. It is certain that the Prince Royal has been actively following up some purpose of his nature in the interior of France. He has progressively liberated officers for the purpose of passing into France, and latterly, as he stated, with the Emperor of Russia's concurrence, liberated not less than sixty in a mass. [These men were sent back by Schwarzenberg's orders. Mr. Thornton's correspondence shews that Bernadotte is actively engaged in overthrowing Buona-parte. Castlereagh has ordered Thornton not to countenance his other measures and not to allow him the command in Holland. He did not deem it right to do more than this till he had seen the Emperor of Russia.] . . .

The other questions of delicacy to which I have alluded (exclusive of that of the Bourbons, on which I shall write fully as soon as I see the Emperor) are those of Poland, Saxony, and others of a minor nature connected with interior arrangements. I do not like to flatter myself too much upon so short an observance of the temper in which these delicate questions are agitated, but I augur favourably of the result ; and I am the more anxious, contrary to former impressions, to press an early decision on these arrangements, at least in all their leading features, for the reason I shall now shortly state[1]. [Caulaincourt has been invited to Chatillon, and the Allies are thus pledged to discussion.]

The objects in conducting this are felt to be two : first peremptorily to resist any idea of congress as to the substance of the peace, and, as far as possible, negotiation ; and secondly, to exclude France practically, but in the least offensive manner, from any interference in the arrangements beyond her own

[1] Castlereagh was doubtless led to this premature and erroneous conclusion by Cathcart's letter, LXXIII.

limits. To speak of the last point first, I believe I apprised you before I left London that this was a favourite idea of the Emperor of Russia's. I own that it appeared to me then, as it does now, too strong a measure, calculated to give Buonaparte popular grounds on which to refuse the terms to be proposed, and bearing too much the character of a blind and dishonourable capitulation, as the security or insecurity of any given extent of limits must depend on the relative state of possession in which the other Powers, at least those of the first order, are to be left.

To obviate this difficulty, it is conceived that the relative state of Europe, at least in outline, as proposed by the Allies, might be presented to the enemy at the same time the proposition with respect to his own limits was tendered to him, and that, with this knowledge, he should be called upon within a time to be limited (as was done at Prague) for an answer Yes or No. The advantage of this proceeding, if it can be satisfactorily executed in detail, would be, that all procrastination would be avoided, and the enemy obliged either to accept our own terms or to emancipate us by a refusal from the restraints and embarrassments of the *Frankfort basis*, the inconveniences of which we foresaw at the time, and feel still more now.

With respect to the nature of the arrangement which is looked to, there are various shades of sentiment. I can yet only speak generally ; but I am happy to observe that Metternich's geographical notions are improved, and that he will *listen at least* to modifications of the Rhine in advance of Dusseldorf.

[Assurances have been given by Metternich in a note to Aberdeen (who deserves praise for his zeal), concerning Holland and the desire of Austria to please the Prince Regent in that respect. Castlereagh told Metternich and Hardenberg that the question involved the military position but he thought that it entitled the Allies to confine France within her ancient limits, and that at any rate Luxembourg and Mayence should be obtained and a line drawn embracing Luxembourg and following the Moselle by Treves to Mayence. All this is not necessarily to be given to Holland, and as Austria had given up her pretensions perhaps Prussia, as the second great military Power, might be brought there.] I was induced to throw out the idea of thus bringing forward Prussia, as I recollected it was a favourite scheme of Mr. Pitt [1]. . . . I doubt much the policy of making Holland a power of the first order to which she would approach if she possessed the whole of these territories. I should not

[1] See I. and Appendix I.

wish to say that this Projet was actually *countenanced*, but it did not seem to alarm and I think a good victory at Châlons might make it very popular. The point of Antwerp and an accession to Holland both of territory and military frontier was cordially and fully admitted as indispensable.   .   .   .

LXXV. [*C. C. IX.*, 185.]

CASTLEREAGH TO LIVERPOOL.

Basle, January 22nd, 1814.

I have had, during the last two days, several hours' conversation with the three most leading Ministers here—I mean Metternich, Stadion,[1] and Hardenberg ; but it is too soon to judge of them before I come to closer quarters with them upon the points of difficulty : I have every reason, however, so far to be satisfied, and they seem to feel my arrival as a valuable facility.

I have had a very full confidential communication with Metternich on the Bourbon question : he is highly conciliated by the line we have taken, and the forbearance with which we have used the discretion given to us by his Government through Aberdeen. I am confident that I should have great additional influence over his mind on any practical question connected with this subject that may occur, from the manner in which we have conducted ourselves upon it. My opinion is that, if we meet this event in our progress as a French measure, Austria will not embarrass it from any family considerations, and the less so from the dread she feels of Bernadotte's elevation ; but she will not speculate upon it, or commit herself upon either loose or partial grounds. She will desire always to see the public act, and to frame her decision with reference to its nature and extent, and the state in which the Allied interests at the moment stand in the war. Metternich seems strongly impressed with the feeling that, to take our terms high against France, we must not encumber ourselves with anything that can bear the appearance of an initiative on such a question on the part of the Allies. I have always strongly felt this as applied to our own interests, and that we cannot press *our* demands to the utmost, if we are at the same time *mixed* in a question which, as far as relates to the existing Government of France, supersedes all terms. He also thinks, for the interests of the Bourbons themselves, that it is a question of doubtful policy, to say the least, whether they would not lose

---

[1] Stadion was now on the best of terms with Metternich, but he represented of course the Anti-French Party in the Austrian counsels.

more than gain from showing themselves, in the first instance, in the camp of any of the Allied Sovereigns, and, above all, in the British camp. He seems to dread that great question being ineffectually stirred, and anxious that the Allies should not be encumbered with it, or responsible for it. In other respects, I should not despair of his concurring with the other Allied Powers in turning any public effort the French nation may make in this sense to a good account ; and I am sure my means of giving his mind such a direction will be in proportion to the delicacy we may observe in not precipitating any act on our part which might compromise the Allied counsels prematurely in so vital a question. It is painful and not fair that the Bourbons should have their hands tied, whilst Bernadotte's are free ; but why should they not pursue their views in some quarter which does not locally and in appearance mix them with us ? I shall write more precisely on this subject from head-quarters. I think it material to say thus much now, and the rather as we are endangered not a little in our internal counsels by the number of great State problems that are at the same moment cast upon us . . .

LXXVI. [*F. O. Cont. Arch.* 2.]
CASTLEREAGH TO LIVERPOOL. (Private.)
Basle, January 22nd, 1814.

After closing my former letter I was anxious again to see Prince Metternich in order to remove if possible any impression from his mind which might check the movements of the armies, and I am happy to state that his alarms about Bernadotte are abated. The better to prepare his mind for our discussions at head-quarters I stated to him what occurred to me on the four alternatives to be looked to as to the Government of France. 1st., Buonaparte, 2nd., a French general, suppose Bernadotte, 3rd., a Regency, 4th., The Bourbons. I represented the 2nd. and 3rd. as both peculiarly objectionable, not stable in themselves but likely to lead to some new change—in the meantime calculated to create dissension by appearing to throw an undue weight on the one case into the scale of Russia, on the other case of Austria, perhaps in both exciting jealousy rather than giving real power. I represented that if Austria refused to reassume the imperial crown in order to avoid unconstitutional and odious authority, she ought doubly to deprecate a state of things, in which an Austrian Regency in France would be involving her in endless jealousies and embarrassments. Prince Metternich entered fully into this reasoning and said of the four alternatives he thought it was that which Austria should most deprecate.

With respect to the second, we considered it too objectionable to be very formidable, and from a note he had this day from head-quarters he appeared relieved upon it, and hopes it is not a prospect the Emperor attaches himself to with much eagerness.

I represented that the 1st. and the 4th. alternatives had the advantage of leading to no discussion among ourselves. In the first place we agreed in forcing the best possible peace upon Buonaparte and in preserving it by a defensive union when made. In the last the Government of France would devolve to its ancient and legitimate sovereigns unconnected equally with any of the Allies, and likely to be too weak for years to molest any of them.

Prince Metternich admitted equally this view of the question, and said if a wish could decide between these alternatives he could not hesitate to prefer the Bourbons, but that he would not interfere to decide what belonged to France to regulate. I left the question here having, I thought, done enough when I brought him to admit that there were only two alternatives in fact, namely Buonaparte or the Bourbons, and that the latter was the most desirable, if France took that tone upon it which could alone lead to its successful accomplishment accompanied with the good will and favourable sentiments of the nation.

LXXVII. [*F. O. Cont. 2.*]
CASTLEREAGH TO LIVERPOOL.[1] (No. 3.)

Langres, January 29th, 1814.

[Reports a conversation with the Emperor of Russia, to whom had been previously conveyed, through General Pozzo-di-Borgo, the expectation and confidence of Great Britain in the Emperor.]

Through the same channel I took care that the Emperor should be apprized of the report in circulation that His Imperial Majesty was disposed to give countenance to the Prince Royal's views on France. As it was a point on which I felt myself bound in duty to have an explicit understanding with the Emperor, I thought it desirable that His Imperial Majesty should be previously acquainted with my having heard the report, not without considerable uneasiness, as calculated, though false, to do much mischief. This intimation produced the desired effect, and the Emperor

---

[1] Castlereagh arrived at Langres on the 25th January and most of this dispatch was written on the 28th. See Oncken. *Lord Castlereagh und die Ministerconferenz zu Langres.* Hist. Tasch. VI., 4, p. 5.

was pleased himself to advert, early in our conversation, to this circumstance, and to afford me an occasion of fully submitting to him the serious evils to which such a measure was calculated to lead. I own His Imperial Majesty's conversation on this point was not such as to dispel altogether my anxiety upon this subject—for altho' he disclaimed ever having expressed any intention of taking a step to favor the Prince Royal's claims, it being repugnant to his own principles to interfere in the Government of a foreign State, and assured me that nothing had passed between His Imperial Majesty and The Prince Royal that could give countenance to such a report, yet I could not but be struck with the comparative disfavour with which His Imperial Majesty spoke of the Bourbons for such a trust. Indeed His Imperial Majesty spoke without reserve of the family as not containing one individual competent to such a task, and whilst he admitted that their title had the advantage of legitimacy and whilst he looked with eagerness to the destruction of the Buonaparte's power, he certainly seemed to take no interest but the reverse in the notion of the power of the country passing into their hands, expressing his disposition to be to leave the nation to choose whom they liked.

I ventured to submit after what Europe had experienced from the resources of France being wielded with military ability, that it was not for the Allies to look with any uneasiness (should events lead to a change) to the power of France falling into the hands of an ancient family, in their policy likely to be addicted to peace ; and I suggested that there might be considerable danger, if the Allied Powers could not concur in opinion on what was desireable in such an event, that an intrigue and most probably a military one, might prevail over the real sentiments of the nation. [In this and in a subsequent interview of some length, Castlereagh represented the importance of coming to an agreement on this and other points and suggested that the four great Powers should each appoint a minister to meet officially and prepare a Projet.]

I thought it right to assume the uninterrupted progress of military operations, as a principle which I considered and invariably stated as fundamental, altho' I knew there were strong objections felt in certain quarters to their being pushed to the extent of a decisive battle and a movement upon the capital, till the Allies had determined upon the line of conduct to be observed in the great crisis to which that might lead. . . . I cannot but feel extremely anxious for a discussion face to face, perceiving how progressively points of difference are exaggerated in unofficial interviews. The main points of difference seem to be, that the

Emperor of Russia urges the movement on Paris as indispensable
at all risks, leaving the negotiation to take care of itself in the meantime, and admitting that if he fails in his object, which is the
destruction of Buonaparte's power without any definite idea as to
the future, he may deem it then necessary to make peace on inferior
terms. Austria on the other hand, though now prepared on the
grounds of subsequent successes and improved prospects to raise
her demands largely beyond her former intentions, is not disposed
to turn her back upon the Frankfort overture ; thinks that keeping
Caulaincourt after moving him from Lunéville to Chatillon, any
longer désouevré is not decorous in point of good faith, and
wishes before new councils are taken up, to bring the former to a
peremptory and decisive issue.

[The military leaders, except Blücher and Gneisenau,
are against pressing on till reinforcements arrive.] The
Austrians, naturally anxious for a strong peace on the side
of France, had rather secure that peace by extorting it,
whilst the enemy trembles both on political and military grounds,
than hazard this prospect for indefinite objects, having little
expectation that the Russians would long prosecute the war for
such objects, if foiled in what they call the Emperor's crusade to
Paris. I own I cannot but partake (deeply as we are interested
in the fate of Holland and the Low Countries) to a degree in this
jealousy. If the enemy should refuse the terms to be agreed on,
I think Austria would then embark in any measures directed
against Buonaparte's political existence, that could be reconciled
with sound principles. Upon the whole they appear honestly
to act up to the principles which they have professed and I do not
discover any sort of tenderness in their views to the existing
dynasty ; but they appear to consider it necessary both in policy
and in good faith, that Buonaparte should have refused to the
Allies a peace on their own terms, before they embark in measures
avowedly directed to his subversion.

As far as I have hitherto felt myself called upon to give an
opinion, I have stated that the British Government did not decline
treating with Buonaparte as the existing ruler of France : that no
public act on the part of the French nation had yet taken place to
call in question the character in which he stood, and that having
proceeded to the Continent under the Prince Regent's orders,
upon the invitation of the Allied Powers, to take a part in a
negotiation which was originated by them, I held myself in readiness to do so, and was not prepared on the part of my Court under
existing circumstances, to sanction any principles inconsistent
with such a purpose.

LXXVIII. [*F. O. Cont.* 2.]
CASTLEREAGH TO LIVERPOOL. (No. 4.)
Langres, January 29th, 1814.

When I closed my former dispatch,[1] I felt considerable anxiety upon the temper, which prevailed in the two leading cabinets ; the Austrians announcing an intention of not pushing forward, till ulterior views were ascertained ; the Russians declaring their intention to proceed *to Paris* without the Austrians, if they hesitated to advance. The Council of the four Powers alluded to in my former letter, met this morning, and I have the satisfaction to acquaint you, that, after a long deliberation, the result more than answered my expectations. Austria was represented by Prince Metternich and Count Stadion, Russia by Count Nesselrode, Count Razumoffsky and Pozzo-di-Borgo, Prussia by the Chancellor Hardenberg. These ministers with myself and Baron Binder as Secretary composed the meeting.

The first point discussed was whether upon the military opinions given, coupled with the pending negotiations, a forward movement ought to be made. The paper I transmit[2] will suggest the nature of the reasoning brought forward. On the part of the British Government I deprecated the adoption, on grounds merely political, of a principle wholly inconsistent with the overture which had brought us together, namely that no relaxation should be premitted in the operations, pending negotiations ; that the appearance of standing still, whilst negotiations were in progress, would have the worst effect, and that no sufficient motive of policy had in my judgment been brought forward to induce a departure from the principle agreed upon from the first, viz., that the war should be conducted with vigour without regard to discussions for peace. I stated at the same time whilst I urged a steady adherence to that principle, that I by no means wished to see the army improvidently hazarded, after the close of so great and rapid a movement as had secretly been made, by a direct operation upon Paris in separation from its reserves, now not many days march in the rear ; and that with respect to the enemy's capital, if their army was posted there, against the capital the movement must be made, but that for the capital alone little in my calculation ought to be put to risk : that the arrival of the Allied armies in the Metropolis might certainly serve to bring the enemy to terms, it might enable the French nation to throw off Buonaparte's yoke and seek repose under the rule of the ancient dynasty : but it might also give birth to a Jacobin explosion, or to an effort

---

[1] LXXVII.
[2] A Memorandum of Schwarzenburg, dated January 26th, dealing with the military situation.

in favour of some other military chief, against which the Allies could have no remedy : and I did not hesitate to avow, that my apprehensions on the latter head had been much augmented since I came upon the Continent. The discussion on this point was neither long nor attended with any material difference of opinion. It was unanimously resolved that the operations should take their course, leaving it to the Commander-in-Chief, Prince Schwarzenberg, to conduct them with a due regard to military prudence.

The next point entered upon was the measure to be adopted towards Caulaincourt who had been waiting some days at Chatillon, having been appointed to proceed there by a letter from Prince Metternich, written with the sanction of the three sovereigns. It was as unanimously agreed that nothing had occurred to prevent the negotiation from being entered upon ; and Prince Metternich was requested to address a letter to the Duc de Vicenza (copy of which is enclosed) notifying to him that the Allied Plenipotentiaries would assemble on the 3rd February at Chatillon.

The extent and nature of the terms to be proposed to the enemy were then canvassed, and some details gone into as to the frontier to be required. I thought this a desirable occasion to have the general principle examined, whether we were yet bound to negotiate upon the Frankfort basis, or whether we were not entitled now to stand upon another basis, just in itself and more conformable to our subsequent successes and existing prospects. I submitted that in reserving the rights of war, when that basis was admitted, the Allies as well as the enemy must be considered as entitled to all the legitimate results of successful war, and that in agreeing to a particular basis as the most convenient ground on which the discussions could, according to the then state of occupancy, be pitched, neither party could be considered as thereby divested of the right to push their demands further, even upon the supposition of their enemy being placed at their mercy. That if this principle were true, it was to be considered that the Allies had since terminated their war in the North—They had by the accession of Naples secured Italy, and they had established themselves in force in the centre of France.—They had done this while no illicit delay had been interposed in opening the negotiations. To suppose that the Allies could now rest satisfied with any arrangement substantially short of reducing France within her ancient limits, was to impute to them an abandonment of their most sacred duty, which, if made with a view to peace, must fail of its object, as the public mind of Europe would never remain tranquil under so improvident an arrangement. If this were the case, it was more manly avowedly to claim a new basis, than to do violence in its application to the spirit of the former, and I submitted whether our present military positions did not impose it as a duty to take the ancient limits of France as our basis, subject on either side to modifications for mutual accommodation.

This underwent considerable discussion, and it is due to Prince Metternich to state, that he entered very liberally into the question, and concluded, as did all the ministers present, by acceding to the principle I had laid down, and we may now be considered as practically delivered from the embarrassments of the Frankfort negotiation. Prince Metternich desired to reserve the consideration of some concession to France, neither extensive nor important in itself, beyond the ancient limits. He seemed to point chiefly to some of the flat country of Savoy and possibly to some portion of territory on the left bank of the Rhine. As this suggestion appeared to connect itself with the language of the Allied Proclamation,[1] it was not considered, if taken within moderate bounds, to be inadmissible so far as it did not encroach upon the great territorial outlines to be re-established for the security of Europe.

The form of the negotiation was then considered at much length. The result was that the Allied Negotiants should act as common parties under a general instruction, and that they should consider themselves as maintaining one and the same interest on behalf of themselves and their Allies, now collectively constituting (as opposed to France) the whole of Europe with the exception of Turkey. It was agreed that the Russian proposition of denying to France any right to enquire beyond the question of her own limits was too odious a principle to be maintained. I stated that it was that to which I could not accede on the part of Great Britain. The Prince Regent had declared from the throne, that he was ready to make peace with France, in conjunction with his Allies, in terms just and honourable to both states : that that demand, if attempted to be peremptorally enforced, was precisely what was most calculated to dishonour a nation, whereas the true honour of France could not in any view be prejudiced by her being divested of her revolutionary spoliations. It was left for future consideration in what manner and to what extent explanations under this head were to be afforded ; it being understood that the object was to exclude the enemy's interference in the regulation of our own concerns, a condition to which France must

[1] Of December 1st, promising that France would be left with a greater extent of territory than she possessed under her kings.

submit, if she wished speedily to terminate the war and to deliver her own limits from the presence of an hostile army.

I enclose a copy of the Protocol of this our first conference,[1] which is to be renewed with a view of coming to some understanding, first upon the precise limits to be insisted on as applied to France,—secondly, the general nature of the arrangement to be made by the Allies within their own limits—and thirdly the state of possession to be adopted in the maritime Peace with reference to such a Continental settlement.

I found the ministers perfectly sincere and cordial in the exclusion of the maritime question from the negotiations. Your Lordship will observe from the enclosed correspondence that this determination on the part of the Allies is to form the first commands to be made to the French negotiator.

All unbecoming interference in the internal affairs of France having on all sides been disclaimed, I thought it right before the meeting separated to express my earnest hope, that there was no wish in any of the Allied sovereigns inconsistent with the restoration of the ancient Family, should a change be brought on by the act of the nation itself. In support of this wish I shortly developed the ideas stated in my letter from Basle.[2] I further desired to be understood that, altho' Great Britain was at all times prepared as a general principle to treat for peace with the Government of France, and at this moment ready to do so with Buonaparte as the head de facto of that Government, I must reserve to myself a right to suspend negotiations on the part of my Court, should his character in this respect be called in such a degree into doubt as in my judgment to render him incompetent to afford the requisite security to His Britannic Majesty for the fulfilment of any engagements he might contract . . . .

LXXIX. [C. C. IX. 212.]
CASTLEREAGH TO LIVERPOOL.

Langres, January 30th, 1814.

I have not many minutes to write to you with unreserve. I think our greatest danger at present is from the *chevalresque* tone in which the Emperor Alexander is disposed to push the war. He

[1] Protocol of the Conference of the 29th January at Langres at 10 o'clock a.m. See *Sbornik of the Imperial Russian Historical Society*, XXXI., p. 360. It simply records the decisions described in this dispatch. There do not appear to have been any official protocols of the subsequent meetings.

[2] No. LXXVI.

has a *personal* feeling about Paris, distinct from all political or military combinations. He seems to seek for the occasion of entering with his magnificent guards the enemy's capital, probably to display, in his clemency and forbearance, a contrast to that desolation to which his own was devoted. The idea that a rapid negotiation might disappoint this hope added to his impatience. I hope that this is abated, and that we may not suffer from his precipitancy. Our decision of yesterday has calmed his temper, and given general satisfaction.

You may estimate some of the hazards to which affairs are exposed here, when one of the leading monarchs, in his first interview, told me that he had no confidence in his own Minister, and still less in that of his Ally. There is much intrigue, and more fear of it. Russia distrusts Austria about Saxony ; and Austria dreads Russia about Poland, especially if she is mistress of the question after a peace. I have got some length with both the parties upon this subject, and I shall try to deliver them from their mutual alarms. Suspicion is the prevailing temper of the Emperor, and Metternich's character furnishes constant food for the *intriguants* to work upon. . . .

I thought the negotiation might have been put upon a short issue. It is difficult in itself. Russia leans to delay. I have no notion Buonaparte would or could, as things yet stand, yield to the latest demand ; and, if peace is impracticable, we should be better rid of our plenipotentiaries.

It is right you should know my channels about Bernadotte. They were Russian as well as Austrian ; and could not take the alarm without some cause. The Emperor attacked Charles[1] in a good-humoured manner as to my informants. Charles admitted he was *one*, and that he had heard it from his own people. His Imperial Majesty expressed himself, *even* to him, that he did not consider the Bourbons as the most worthy. On the other hand, Noailles and the emigrants here say the Emperor *has* given them encouragement, promised them not to make peace, and only desired they might not hoist the white cockade within the Allied positions. The Emperor told me, on the contrary, that he had given them no encouragement ; and, from the marked approbation he expressed of *your* having given them none, I must suppose that this is the fact. . . .

[1] Sir Charles Stewart.

N

LXXX.   [*F. O. Cont. 2.*]
CASTLEREAGH TO LIVERPOOL.   (No. 8.)
Chatillon,[1] February 6th, 1814.
[Discussion with the Allied Representatives on the restitution of the colonies.] In stating this question, I thought it material to distinguish between what Great Britain might deem it proper to do towards France, and what she might be prepared to do for the interests of her Allies.   If by the course of the war, the Allies were satisfactorily secured, without aiming at unreasonable advantages, Great Britain might feel herself entitled to retain certain possessions, which, under an adequate necessity, she might be prepared to sacrifice to the nterests of the Continent.   As an example, I mention the island of Tobago.   It being a colony purely British as against France, nothing could be more fair, and becoming, than that we should keep it.   If on the other hand by doing so we put the Continental interests in the larger sense to hazard, Great Britain might not feel disposed to press the retention."
[A statement was then made by Castlereagh as to the lines on which he proposed to proceed, viz., " to restore what France had always set the first value upon and only to retain what was of inconsiderable value to her but which in the hands of another power was liable to be used against us as an instrument both of annoyance and danger."   Thus, besides restoring all the Danish and Dutch colonies except the Cape of Good Hope, he was willing that France should receive back all her West Indian colonies except Guadeloupe, Les Saintes, and perhaps Tobago. In the East Indies France must be limited to commercial stations only.   Malta must of course, as was fully admitted, remain British, but he was prepared to surrender the Ionian Islands so long as France was excluded from them.]
In closing this statement I begged it might be understood, that it was the wish of my Government in peace and in war to connect their interests with those of the Continent—that whilst the state of Europe afforded little hope of a better order of things, Great Britain had no other course left, than to create an independent existence for herself, but that now that she might look forward to a return to ancient principles, she was ready to make the necessary sacrifices on her part, to reconstruct a balance in Europe. Before, however, Great Britain could proceed to the length of actually signing away her conquests, that there were three prelimin-

[1] Castlereagh alone of the principal Ministers proceeded to Chatillon to watch over the negotiations with Caulaincourt.   He was not, however, an official member of the Conference.   The first sitting of the Conference took place on the 5th February.

ary conditions on which she felt herself entitled to insist, all of them being, in her view, essential to that state of things, which would justify the surrender of so much strength and power.

The first was that France should submit to retire, if not literally, substantially within her ancient limits ;

Secondly—that Great Britain should have an assurance by an amicable arrangement of limits between the three great Powers, that, having reduced France by their union, they were not likely to re-establish her authority by differences amongst themselves ;

And thirdly—that we should be satisfied, that the arrangements in favour of the Powers of whose interests we were more especially the guardian were likely to be attended to, and especially those of Holland and Sicily—the point of Spain being abandoned by France herself.

I thought it necessary to make these points now as the two latter depended, not upon the enemy but upon the Allies—a consideration which seemed, in addition to its other advantages, to suggest the importance of an explanation on these subjects proceeding if possible *de front* with the other negotiations.

The explanation throughout was received with evident satisfaction. The possibility of something being found to give to France in exchange for Guadeloupe and the Mauritius was thrown out, and Prince Metternich suggested the idea of such a sacrifice on the part of Spain and Holland. I observed that this was a proposition which could not originate with the British Government— that it was not their practice to call upon their Allies to pay the price of acquisitions made by them—that I saw no reason why France after such a war should be relieved from all direct sacrifice. Since the Plenipotentiaries assembled here, I have again adverted to the necessity of explanations amongst the leading Powers as to their immediate views, and that they should be prepared for such a claim from the British negotiators, when the latter were called upon to state the restitutions, which Great Britain was prepared to state.

LXXXI. [*F. O. Cont.* 2.]
CASTLEREAGH TO LIVERPOOL. (No. 12.)
Chatillon sur Seine, February 16th, 1814.

[The Russian Plenipotentiaries have received orders from Alexander to suspend negotiations.[1]] As the advance of the armies rendered their early arrival in the capital a presumeable

---

[1] By a letter from Nesselrode of the 8th February.

event, I had signified my intention before this order was received of going to Head Quarters for the purpose of arguing the importance of a distinct understanding between the Allies as to the measures to be pursued under the delicate and important circumstances to which their entry into Paris might give birth. I found on my arrival at Troyes[1] that the order had been dispatched without any concert or communication with either of the other Allied Courts on the spot and that it originated in an intention on the part of His Imperial Majesty to suspend any further discussions till he should arrive at Paris where it was his purpose to assemble a representation of the nation to decide on the future sovereignty of France, not meaning however to exclude Buonaparte if the choice should fall on him.

This intelligence Your Lordship may imagine, after what I had occasion to state in former letters, was received with considerable alarm, an alarm which was augmented by learning that the Prince Royal of Sweden was on the point of arriving on the Rhine, with an intention of immediately putting himself at the head of Winzingerode's corps, being the division of his army most advanced in the interior, viz., near Rheims. I also found La Harpe lately returned from an excursion to Paris, attendant on the Emperor's person, as a confidential adviser of this enterprize

The Emperor did not appoint me to attend him till the day after my arrival. I had then, and on the following day, when commanded to dine with His Imperial Majesty in private, two very long interviews, in which the Emperor was pleased to permit (I might say to encourage) me to discuss without any reserve the important questions that arose out of the present state of affairs.

I presumed to express to His Imperial Majesty my regret that the order sent to Chatillon, was not previously concerted with the Allies, and sent according to the understanding as a joint order which would have taken from the French minister the advantage of all comment or inference as to a separation of views amongst the Allied Courts. His Imperial Majesty said he only meant the order as suspensive, but certainly with the intention of attempting during the suspension the dethronement of Buonaparte : and His Imperial Majesty repeated his intention of leaving the nation freely to choose a successor, or even to establish Napoleon on the

[1] The Chatillon Conference was suspended on February 9th, and Castlereagh arrived at Troyes on the 12th. The conversation reported in this dispatch therefore took place on the 13th February. Castlereagh arrived back at Chatillon on the 16th February and then wrote his report of the meeting at Troyes.

throne. Your Lordship will find the Emperor's views fully explained in the official answers given by the Russian Secretary of State to the Austrian Queries.[1]

To an enquiry as to the mode in which it was proposed to collect the sense of the nation, the Emperor said his intention was that the corps legislative and other leading bodies of the State, with such other persons " marquantes," as might be deemed proper, should be invited to assemble and declare the national will as to the Crown of France. I suggested the difficulty as well as the danger that might attend such proceedings. In the first place if the constituted authorities were looked to for an opinion they probably would be gone. Napoleon returning with his army to the Loire would naturally send his Government and his " employés " before him : and if such an assembly could be collected for such a purpose, the Allies might wait long at Paris, before they could constitute such a meeting of individuals even of competent respectability. But supposing the difficulty got over, the assembly was then to deliberate and decide, controlled by no acknowledged principle of preference arising either from possession or legitimacy. They were open to the intrigues of rival pretentions ; chosen by Napoleon, they might from favour or fear decide in his favour, and thus give fresh vigour to his authority ; or they might very probably insist on offering the crown upon conditions to the object of their choice, which would embark the Allies, and the new monarch in all the delays and details of a new constitution.

The Emperor said he never would consent to this. I represented however that if the deliberation was to be free, His Imperial Majesty could have no negative, and the only protection against such evils was to avoid giving existence to their source.

The pretentions of Louis XVIII. were then discussed. The Emperor was still unfavourable to the Bourbons, but particularly to the King, as personally incapable. His Imperial Majesty however said that he saw the prevailing sentiment amongst the Allies was for the Bourbons, and presumed the choice would fall upon one of the family, probably one of the younger branches. The Duke of Orleans was mentioned as possible but not to me.

The Duke of Vicenza's letter,[2] herewith sent, was then spoken

[1] Printed in the *Sbornik* op. cit. p. 377-379. See note on p. 152.
[2] To Metternich of the 9th February asking for an armistice.

of and the difficulty of voluntarily risking such a transaction, as that of exciting a revolution in France, if it could no longer be alledged to be essential to the professed purpose for which the Allies entered France, was examined. Baron de Stein having observed at dinner that the Allies could not with honour desert the people who had already shown them so much good will since they entered France, referring to this remark I ventured to suggest to His Imperial Majesty, if there existed any such claim at present, where no overt act had taken place, what would be the extent of the claim if the Allies, by going to Paris expressly to invite a declaration, were the occasion of calling forth sufficient of public sentiment to sacrifice individuals but not enough either to enable or justify the Allies to commit themselves in a civil war to give a monarch to France. The Emperor professed his intention of acting with great caution, and said he should have the means of judging, when there, what he might hazard without committing either the Allies or individuals. I pressed upon His Imperial Majesty that,this might be so, if in the legitimate pursuit of his own object, he found himself at Paris, but that, if he unnecessarily sought Paris for another object, he would make himself responsible for the consequences ; that it was a risk not to be lightly run, and, if made at all, it should be with decision. I gave him my opinion that, if any attempt was to be made, it could only be creditably or honourably hazarded in favour of the legitimate claimant, and that to support one usurper against another would dissolve the Alliance, and probably end in confusion. I frankly stated that in my opinion such an attempt could not properly originate directly or indirectly with foreign Powers, and that the utmost they could justify was to act according to circumstances upon a self created effort. That as yet no sort of a disposition to a movement had been evinced in any part of France, altho' the concentration of the French and the presence of the Allied Armies had given the utmost facilitites to an explosion, whilst the troops of Napoleon on all occasions fought bravely, and there had yet been no public and decisive proof of disaffection either amongst his military or civil officers.

The Emperor's mind was so bent upon finding himself at Paris, whether the events of the war naturally led him there or not, and the general feeling was so strong the other way amongst the Allies, that I thought it right, in order, if possible, to bring opinions more to a common standard to submit to His Imperial Majesty's consideration the difficulties we should have in sustaining Louis XVIII., if Buonaparte retired with his army and government from Paris.   The first difficulty would be where to find French subjects of sufficient weight in the public opinion, and of sufficient political boldness, to induce them to undertake his Government.   The next would be how to give him an army : to compose it of his own subjects would require large funds and arms. The Emperor thought this impracticable from want of officers, etc.   I then asked His Imperial Majesty how long he would undertake to *keep his army* in France to fight the battles of a Bourbon against Buonaparte, and whether his Allies would engage for theirs.   But there was a more important consideration, supposing the Allied sovereigns agreed upon this point ; how would the people of France feel towards a King supported by Russian, Austrian, and Prussian troops, all living at free quarters, not paying like Lord Wellington but encroaching on the sustenance of the people without reserve or recompence ?   The people bore it now, considering it the inevitable consequence of an invasion professedly made to conquer a peace, in the accomplishment of which they feel the deepest interest, but tell them a peace *on their own terms* has been rejected by the Allies, such a peace as never was before realized, and that, contrary to their declared purpose on entering France, the Allied armies are now living upon them to uphold a Bourbon against Buonaparte, and the consequences must be fatal, possibly to the armies themselves, but at all events to the cause they support.

The Emperor asked me what had been the result of our conferences in the morning (the ministers of the four Powers having met in council).   I stated to His Imperial Majesty that they had come to no decision, but that the leaning of their judgment was strongly against breaking new grounds, and now, for the first time, after inviting him to negotiate, making the dethronement of Buonaparte not the incidental consequence, but the direct object of the war :—that they felt this a course full of hazard, at direct variance with the principles upon which the confederacy had been cemented amongst the Allies, and supported by Europe, —and that they feared it might lead to failure, disgrace, and disunion.

His Imperial Majesty had seen the queries accompanying the Duc de Vicenza's letter to Prince Metternich.   I apprized the Emperor that answers had been given to these queries by the Prussian and Austrian ministers as well as by Count Nesselrode by His Imperial Majesty's orders, and that I proposed, as soon as

I had an opportunity of considering these several opinions, humbly to offer my own.[1]

The Emperor said he observed my view of the question was different from what he had reason to believe prevailed in England.[2] I observed to His Imperial Majesty that in England the wish was strong against the individual and in favour of the legitimate claimant, but that wish was subordinate to the principles upon which the King's Government publicly professed to act : that my persuasion was the proposed change of policy would not under the circumstances of the case receive the sanction of the British Government, but that, acting here in discharge of a responsible trust, I must be guided by the dictates of my own judgment, and not suffer myself to be biassed by any supposed wishes formed in England, in ignorance of the real circumstances upon which we were now called upon to decide. I expressed great regret at perceiving that I had the misfortune not to see this question altogether in the same light as His Imperial Majesty, and the more so from the condescension with which I had been permitted to state my sentiments. The Emperor said he always wished to encourage discussion and His Imperial Majesty's manner of promoting a free examination of all subjects is highly honorable to his character.

[Enclosures give the propositions submitted to the ministers and their answers. The whole was submitted to Alexander with the Projet of the Treaty of Peace, upon which Alexander wrote a confidential letter to Nesselrode. After considering the Duc de Vicenza's letter offering an armistice, it was thought better to compel him to arrive at his object through an arrangement of Preliminaries. He was thus precluded from charging the Allies with an indirect purpose in continuing hostilities. If he was really anxious for peace, he would be prepared to agree to fix the frontiers of France on the basis of 1792 and this was now definitely offered to him.] As this[3] is the document upon which, if the negotiations break off, the appeal will be made, I thought it expedient to put the British terms forward in a liberal shape. If

---

[1] The Austrian queries had asked if an armistice was to be granted and what steps were to be taken to ascertain the views of the French nation as to a change of dynasty, especially if Paris declared for the Bourbons and the Allies occupied it. Alexander wished to refuse an armistice, push on to Paris, and allow the matter to be there decided, the Bourbons being given no special privileges. Austria and Prussia wished to sign peace with Napoleon on the basis of the ancient limits of France if he would do so. They were more friendly to the Bourbons than Alexander. Castlereagh's reply is appended to this dispatch.

[2] See below. LXXXIII.

[3] The projet of a preliminary treaty of peace.

the question had taken the course of the negotiation, I might possibly have contended for an absolute exclusion from the continent of India ; but in my judgment we should have injured our reputation in the Continent by giving France this fact of monopoly to comment upon ; and I, therefore, being driven to an ultimatum, preferred confining to the article as prepared by Lord Buckinghamshire, and lately transmitted to me. . . . [Details as to Colonies.][1] . . . What will be the fate of the whole I cannot guess, but we have acted consistently and honorably : and if we are still exposed to Buonaparte, with a defensive alliance upon which I have made useful progress, and such a peace, we need not trouble for the future.

I flatter myself that in performing the somewhat painful duty of combating the Emperor of Russia's Parisian plans, I have brought His Majesty's mind to look deliberately into the detail of this measure, and that if the events of the war yet lead us to the enemy's capital, our conduct there will be both more united, and more circumspect. To guard as far as possible against the danger, that might [await][2] us upon our arrival at Paris, after much discussion the enclosed projet of a convention[3] was prepared by Prince Metternich, and has been seen and not disapproved by the Emperor of Russia. The mode in which the Bourbon question is treated therein must be considered highly creditable to Austria, and justifies the opinion I had formed upon this point : viz. that their policy is uninfluenced by the family connection. This convention may serve another valuable purpose in bringing back the Emperor of Russia to some fixed and sound principles as to the throne of France. It was intimated to me, that, if I desired it, Great Britain might be a signing party to this Treaty. I thought it upon the whole better to decline it, and to rest satisfied with its being officially communicated. This opinion was founded upon a consideration that the Treaty, tho' other questions were incidentally introduced, was in its main purpose intended to regulate the occupation of Paris. Great Britain having no army engaged on the spot, is not naturally a party to such a measure, and I thought it better not to have a British minister mixed unnecessarily in delicate questions relating to the interior of France.

In concluding this dispatch I think it right to acquaint Your Lordship, that notwithstanding the state of the negotiations, and

---

[1] These do not differ materially from those mentioned in LXXX.

[2] An indecipherable word.

[3] Projet of a Convention as to the methods to be employed on the occupation of Paris, dated February 14th, Oncken, *Zeitalter II*. 768. See below, p. 171.

the delay given to the operations from the successive checks to which Marshall Blucher's army has been exposed, it is by no means yet impossible that the Allies may get possession of the enemy's capital. What may be the extent of the movement, if any, is very differently estimated. I have not myself any information, which justifies me in believing, more especially if Buonaparte avoids a general battle, and retires into the interior, that the spirit of the nation will be so loud against him, as to divest him of the means of continuing the contest.

Your Lordship will observe that Austria, upon a satisfactory case, and upon adequate means and engagements previously secured, is not unwilling to bear her share, in what may be deemed best for the general good. But considering her own and the Prussian dominions as most exposed by any attempt of this nature imprudently made and failed in, she will not embark without new treaties, *especially with Russia*, of the adventurous temper of whose councils it is my duty to inform Your Lordship there is a much more general impression, than of their steady and persevering application to the establishment of a solid peace, particularly on this side of the Rhine.

Your Lordship will not be surprised from what I have stated, and the interests which the adherents of the Bourbons have in circulating such an impression, that attempts should be made, however unjustly, to insinuate that the British Government is insincere in their negotiations for peace, and that they are indirectly exciting a movement in France. I have reason also to believe that an impression prevails and that assurances are circulated, that if the effort against Buonaparte can once be set agoing, English money and English arms may be relied on and that the game of Spain will, on the part of Great Britain, be played over again in France. This is so great a question in all its parts ; it is one which may so easily assume a shape upon which some practicable decision must be taken, and upon which explanations may be required by the Allies from me, of what they may expect of aid from Great Britain on embarking in such a contest ; that I feel it my duty to request it may receive the earliest and most mature consideration of the Prince Regent's Government.

The power of the individual may at once melt away, or be dissolved by a great defeat, but there is no apparent reason as yet to assume such a result ; and, as I consider a protracted contest in the heart of France upon grounds personal to its ruler, to be a very new and different question from that which the nation has maintained for years, with such unexampled firmness in the Peninsula, I have not felt it consistent with my duty to give the smallest countenance on the part of my Court to such an effort, confining my endeavours strictly to the conduct of the negotiation confided to my care, and to the counteraction of any views which appeared to me calculated in the event of a change, to give it a direction prejudicial to the general interests.   The charge with which I have been entrusted is sufficiently arduous to make me desirous of receiving the sentiments of my Government upon the course which has been pursued.   I must likewise request to know in what degree they are prepared to embark with respect of the future, and to what extent in point of resources.   I shall in the meantime not hesitate to act upon my own responsibility in the manner which I conceive may upon the whole be most conducive to the honour and interests of the Prince Regent's Government.

VISCOUNT CASTLEREAGH'S ANSWER TO THE AUSTRIAN QUERIES.[1]

Troyes, February 13th, 1814.
.   .   .   The difference of sentiment which pervades the Allied Councils (I trust an amicable one) on this important question, arises from a doubt whether we should accept from France a peace on our own terms, or pursue the war further for the purpose of rendering the enjoyment of that peace more secure by the dethronement of the individual who now exercises the Government of France.

I am of opinion that in public duty we are precluded from taking up this new object in the war for two reasons.   1st. because it is not wise, and 2ndly because if it were so, we have by public and solemn acts of our Governments precluded ourselves from doing so.   The Allies have entered France avowedly to conquer the peace, which they did not find within their reach on the Rhine. So far from invading France to effect a change in the internal Government, they voluntarily addressed themselves to the existing ruler, they invited him to a negotiation, and they admitted thereby his faculty to treat and in that negotiation they are at present engaged, no public manifestation of national sentiment having since taken place to alter the grounds on which they originally proceeded ; I do not therefore conceive that the Allies can now

[1] F.O. Cont. 2.   There is a French translation in Fournier, *loc. cit.*, p. 285.

recede from the principle of their own venture and render that contest personal, which was understood to be one of conditions alone.

I think it is unwise because it is of hazardous policy in the execution, and it is rendered the more so, by the obvious difference of opinion that prevails amongst the Allies, as to the mode and principles upon which it should be attempted.

The appeal to be made to the French nation at Paris, to adjudge the crown of France appears to me pregnant with danger ; the measure of putting forward the pretentions of Louis XVIII., of very doubtful success, and both to be questions on which the Allies, more especially if the avowed and legitimate objects of their own war should be within their reach, are wholly incompetent to provoke a discussion, involving as it must do, the fate of individuals, as well as the tranquillity of the nation. In justice to their own subjects, I conceive they cannot incur the responsibility, which such a line of conduct would impose upon them, to the people of another State.

I am therefore of opinion that whenever a peace, such as Europe may now command from the enemy can be reduced into proper form by the negotiation now in progress, that both in policy and good faith it ought to be seized, if no intervening act of the nation itself shall bring into doubt the competence of Buonaparte to treat and to contract.

And I am further of opinion that altho' an armistice in the ordinary sense of the term is wholly inadmissible pending negotiations, yet there may be military sacrifices on the part of the enemy, constituting in themselves so complete and perfect a security for the attainment of the objects of the war, as to make it inconsistent for those who would accept the peace, to refuse an armistice so regulated.

I am therefore of opinion that the Allies should entertain the principle of the Duc de Vicenza's proposition so far as to agree to negotiate upon it, but with a determination not to suffer their military operations to be suspended by any armistice, which they do not consider to be in point of security equivalent to a treaty of peace. [Whilst I differ from the opinion which has been expressed on the part of the Emperor of Russia, I am ready to do homage to the sentiments, which induced His Imperial Majesty to interest himself so deeply in the future security of Europe, and the freedom and happiness of the French nation.][1]

---

[1] This last sentence was deleted before the answer was dispatched. Oncken, *Hist. Tasch.* VI. p. 32.

LXXXII.   [*F. O. Cont.* 2.]
              CASTLEREAGH TO LIVERPOOL.   (No. 14).
                              Chatillon, February 18th, 1814.
Considering the stability of any peace which might be concluded
with Buonaparte to depend upon the preservation of the existing
Alliance of the Great Powers and upon their being bound together
by defensive engagements to succour each other hereafter against
an attack from France, I lost no time in comformity to the sentiments of my government to prepare a project of such a Treaty
which I have submitted with the accompanying note to the
Austrian, Russian, and Prussian ministers. The state of the
negotiations and of the campaign has not hitherto admitted of my
officially inviting them to a discussion on this important arrangement, but I have received satisfactory assurances from the respective ministers that their Courts are favourably inclined to the
principle of the measure. Count Nesselrode acquainted me that,
in confining the Casus Foederis to the *European* dominions of
the contracting Powers, I had obviated the principal objection
to which the Emperor of Russia had deemed the arrangement
liable. He further added that he was authorized to enter upon the
discussion whenever he received an invitation from me to that
effect. I shall not fail to take the earliest opportunity of bringing
this measure into regular negotiation.

LXXXIII.   [*C. C. IX.*, 266.]
              CASTLEREAGH TO LIVERPOOL.
                              Chatillon, February 18th, 1814.
[Encloses a letter from Lieven[1] to Nesselrode, which has been
expressly referred to on more than one occasion by Alexander, as
containing the sentiments of the British Government.] It is the
more necessary that you should be in possession of it, and that I
should receive your explanation, from the very embarrassing
publicity that has been given here to this document. The first
knowledge I had of it was from Prince Metternich, to whom the
Emperor had reported its contents, and with the singular candour
of adding that he (Prince Metternich) was personally rather
roughly handled in the despatch. I next heard of it from Hardenberg, the Prussian, and again from Münster, before it was sent
to me. I have since had the mortification to learn that it was

---

[1] Dated 26th January, 1814, which claimed that the Prince Regent and
Liverpool wished the Bourbons to be restored. This was true, so far as the
Prince Regent himself was concerned, and several members of the Cabinet
were of the same opinion, but Lieven had no right to report the conversations.

sent to this place to Count Rasumoffsky, to be communicated
confidentially to Lord Cathcart. It is so much the system of
foreign Courts to act by double and contradictory channels, that
it may make less sensation here, and the knowledge of the transaction rest where it is ; but, as I cannot doubt your sentiments
upon the utter inadmissibility of this system, as it has already
placed me personally in the most distressing predicament, so it
has essentially complicated the business with which I have been
charged, and exposed the Prince Regent's name to be very unpleasantly compromised—I cannot, either in justice to his Royal
Highness, to you, or to myself, avoid placing the whole in your
hands, convinced that you will do what is most proper upon it.

I have felt myself bound, with all deference to Count Lieven, to
express my entire disbelief of the accuracy of his conception of the
sentiments which he has thus attempted to convey. More than
this it was impossible for me to state as to the substance of the
letter. I could only represent to the Emperor of Russia, which I
did, of course, with great pain to myself, that I should feel it my
bounden duty, as the responsible servant of the Crown, acting on
the spot, to deliver my opinion, on the part of my Court, in direct
opposition to the instruction which that despatch was supposed
to convey.

LXXXIV. [F. O. Cont.[1] 2.]
CASTLEREAGH TO PRINCE METTERNICH.
Chatillon, February 18th, 1814.
Count Stadion has been so obliging as to communicate to me
your letter of yesterday from Troyes. I cannot express to you
how much I regret the proposition of armistice which Prince
Schwarzenberg appears to have made under the sanction of the
Emperor of Russia and King of Prussia, but without any authority
from his own government or any adequate necessity which could
justify so precipitate a step. An offer so inconsistent with the
proceedings here, and of so little dignity in itself cannot fail to
invite the enemy to assume a tone of authority.

I feel it more than ever necessary to conjure you and your
colleagues at headquarters, not to suffer yourselves to descend
from the substance of your peace. You owe it, such as you have
announced it to the enemy, to yourselves, and to *Europe*, and you

---

[1] This important letter is a good example of the vigour which Castlereagh
could use on occasion when he was much moved. On Feb. 20th he left Chatillon
for headquarters to reinforce his letter by personal intercourse.

will now more than ever make a fatal sacrifice both of moral and political impression, if under the pressure of those slight reverses which are incident to war, and some embarrassments in your Council which I should hope are at an end, the great edifice of peace was suffered to be disfigured in its proportions. Recollect what your military position is. You have 200,000 men *in France* yet unbroken. You have in reversion the prospect of drawing 100,000 in the spring from Italy. You may rely on above 100,000 on the side of Spain. Including your own reserves, you can assemble 100,000 on the Upper Rhine and between the Prince Royal, the British Dutch and Hanoverian levies, you are certain of 100,000 men on the side of Flanders. If we act with *military* and *political* prudence, how can France resist a just peace demanded by 600,000 warriors ? Let her, if she dare and the day you can declare that fact to the French nation, rest assured Buonaparte is subdued.

I protest, therefore, against any relaxation in our terms of peace. As to the securities to be demanded I desire nothing offensive or dishonourable to France. If the surrender of the three French fortresses is revolting, I should be satisfied to waive it ; our line may be secured by their being observed or blockaded. If the enemy will consent to evacuate all the fortresses with'n the territories to be ceded, allowing the garrisons to remain (if required) within the lines of the Allies till the definite Treaty is signed, which need not occupy much time, I should see no objection to the removal of the Allied army from France progressively as the places were given up, so that French territory should be ceded in exchange for Allied fortresses—France taking no increase of military force from the garrisons extra France till she shall become irrevocably bound to the peace itself.

I shall always be ready to attend at Headquarters when I can be of service to the Allied Cause. In the meantime you may make what use you please of these my sentiments. The Confederacy has already done wonders. There can be in good sense but one interest among the Powers ; namely to end nobly the great work they have conducted so near to its close. They must not differ upon new objects or small shades of policy. Let them be intrepid and persevering upon the object of the war as long avowed and agreed upon, and if on these the enemy breaks off (which is by no means improbable) let the Allies set him at defiance. They need not fear for an early and glorious result if their operations are conducted with common military prudence.

LXXXV. [*F. O. Cont.* 3.]
    CASTLEREAGH TO LIVERPOOL.
        (No. 20. Most secret and confidential.)
                    Chaumont, February 26th, 1814.
    I cannot conceal from you that the internal temper here is very embarrassing, if not alarming.[1]   The criminations and recriminations between the Austrians and Russians are at their height, and my patience is worn out combatting both.   Austria both in Army and Government is a timid Power.   Her minister is constitutionally temporising—he is charged with more faults than belong to him, but he has his full share, mixed however with considerable means for carrying forward the machine—more than any other person I have met with at Headquarters.   Russia could have enormous influence to correct the faults of Austria, if her Emperor was more measured in his projects, more accessible in Council, and more intelligible as to his own views.

    I have been labouring to procure an understanding on the point of Poland but the Emperor always evades it and now Czartoriski is invited here to throw more alarm into the Austrian Councils— perhaps this may be of use ; when things are at their worst, they mend.   If he had been explicit about the Bourbons he would probably have carried Austria with him, but he is with fine qualities both suspicious and undecided and cannot bear to have a minister about him who is capable of serving him.

    After the defeat of the several detached corps the Emperor was the first to descend from the project of Paris to that of armistice, and I received last night a message from His Imperial Majesty by Count Nesselrode, probably embroidered by the bearer, to urge the expediency of an early peace.   But I do not yet altogether despair of his perseverance, and if I can get him to speak out to Austria, and allay all her alarms, real or pretended, I am confident she could not leave us upon the main question.   But we must not go to sea in search of adventures with such a bark as we sail in. The misfortune has been that Russia has spoiled both games in the mode she played them, both that of peace and dethronement.

---

[1] " I was very much grieved   . . .   to learn   . . .   that Prince Schwarzenberg had again recurred to the proposition of an armistice   . . .   I had last night a conference of the four Ministers at the Chancellor Hardenberg's at Bar-sur-Aube.   I could not but perceive the altered tone of my colleagues —their impressions being strongly tinctured with the demoralising influence of a rapid transition from an advance made under very lofty pretensions to a retreat of some embarrassment and of much disappointment and recrimination."   Castlereagh to Liverpool [No. 19] February 26th, 1814.   F.O. Cont. 3.   The situation was saved by Castlereagh insisting on placing part of the troops commanded by Bernadotte under Blücher's orders.

Caulaincourt's letter offering old France required five days discussion before we could procure a decision, and in the meantime the enemy had successes, and we had then the folly to go to him. It is lamentable to look back, and not a little anxious to look forward ; we must, however, not be discouraged.

The Emperor of Russia, not quite satisfied with himself is loud against the Austrians for not giving battle on the Seine near Nogent, and told me that Schwarzenberg had secret orders from his court not to fight a general action in the then state of the negotiations. The fact is the advance from Langres was against the military opinions : Austria agreed to it in hopes of forcing the peace, Russia meaning to defeat the peace in order to reach Paris. Nothing keeps either Power firm but the consciousness that without Great Britain the peace cannot be made. They have all been lowering their tone to me ; but I have explicitly told them, that if the Continent can and will make a peace with Buonaparte upon a principle of authority, for such a peace Great Britain will make the greatest sacrifices : but that if they neither will nor can, we must for their sake as well as our own, rest in position against France.

I thought it necessary to state this sentiment strongly to Prince Schwarzenberg and Radisky[1] [sic.] at the council, having received some very desponding insinuations from them, through Lord Burghersh. Whatever may be the issue I have thought our line to do any good must be alone decided, and I have represented to them all the hopelessness of their future security against France re-established, if they shrink now from the contest when they are reunited, and the enemy, though still formidable, essentially shaken in his military power and resources. The reinforcements drawn from Spain have made an impression which I trust Lord Wellington's early operations will efface.

LXXXVI. [*F. O. Cont.* 1.]
BATHURST TO CASTLEREAGH. (No. 4.)
February 27th, 1814.

[Having received the dispatches relating to the Troyes meeting[2] the Government expects the Allies to adhere substantially to the project of the Preliminary Treaty which has been presented to the French, and in which England announces definitely the sacrifices she is prepared to make.]

The Prince Regent trusts therefore, that if the French Government decline these terms there will be no abatement of them in any material point ; and an appeal to the French nation as to the

[1] *i.e.* Radetsky.
[2] See LXXXI.

sincerity of their ruler in his professed desire for peace will rest, H.R.H. is convinced, satisfactorily upon the ground of these propositions.

The next point for consideration is what should be the policy of the Allies, if these terms of peace should have been rejected. The Prince Regent's Government concur in the opinion of the other Allied Powers that a manifesto should be published, which, they think, should contain the terms which had been proposed and should express the sincere anxiety, which the Allies had felt and still feel, for relieving the French nation from the calamities and burthens of war, and the conviction, which they were persuaded would now be entertained throughout France that the personal ambition of its ruler, which had already carried the horrors of war into so many and such distant countries, was alone the obstacle of tranquillity and repose in the French dominions ; that from the nature of the terms offered, the honor of the French nation could not be involved in the war ; that although nothing could be more foreign to the intentions of the Allied Powers, than any attempt to prescribe to an independent nation, either the person of its sovereign or the form of its Government, yet they could not conceal their opinion founded upon long experience, and confirmed by the rejection of the terms now proposed, that a restoration of the house of Bourbon, would afford the best prospect of procuring permanent happiness and tranquility to France itself and to the rest of Europe.

It might further be added that, compelled to continue the contest against the present ruler of France, by the rejection of the terms now offered, the Allies would think themselves entitled to the advantage of any further success with which Providence might bless their arms ; but that upon concluding a peace with the ancient dynasty they would be ready jointly to guarantee to France the limits described on the terms proposed by the Allies.

Such a declaration could scarcely fail of producing a considerable effect, particularly if the spirit of the Allied armies is unbroken, if their numbers are augmented by powerful reinforcements (now on their way to join them), if they can continue to maintain themselves in the interior of France, and if Lord Wellington should be enabled to advance from the South with the distinguished armies under his command.

In communicating to you the sentiments of the Prince Regent's Government as to the manifesto which it would be expedient under these circumstances to address to the French nation, we are nevertheless of opinion that it would not be adviseable to adopt any measure which would preclude the Allies from making peace upon proper terms with the Government of France *de facto*, in whatever hands it might be placed.

[Great Britain is ready to continue the subsidies for the present year, and beyond it so far as is possible.   Portugal, Sicily, and Sweden should be included as signatories of the Treaty of Peace, so that they may not think themselves neglected by the Allies.]

LXXXVII. [*F. O. Cont. Arch.*, 3.]
       CASTLEREAGH TO LIVERPOOL.   (No. 23.)
                           Chaumont, March 3rd, 1814.
[Military reports.   Napoleon has gone against Blücher.   News that the latter is too scattered, but after his recent experience hopes that he will have learnt a lesson.]   I had a long interview yesterday with the Emperor of Russia.   Allowing for an amicable reference to former points of difference, I was better pleased with His Imperial Majesty's conversation than on any former occasion. It was temperate and firm ; looking to the issue of the war as that to which all were bound to devote their utmost exertions.   Such was the temper of yesterday and I flatter myself it may prove solid.   There can be no doubt of the Emperor's good will to the cause, and if we can avoid *calamity* notwithstanding the Peace faction in his army is strong I think the Emperor will go on with the war.

Monsieur[1] is at Vesoul—he gives out that he has received encouragement, but as yet nothing moves and I can perceive no symptoms nor do I learn that any demonstration of any consequence has taken place.   His Royal Highness has desired an interview with the Emperor of Russia to make to him some important communications ; but, if conviction and not éclat was the object, why press for a personal interview ?

I have had communications with the Princes Czartoriski and Radzivil on the affairs of Poland, and I hope I have succeeded in discrediting their views considering them as in truth a diversion

[1] The Comte d'Artois, later Charles X.

in favour of France—the former who is a person both of principle and merit promised to absent himself from the Headquarters if his presence was considered as calculated to create disunion, which I ventured with every possible sentiment of regard, to assure him was the fact.

LXXXVIII. [*C. C. IX.*, 311.]
CASTLEREAGH TO LIVERPOOL.
Chaumont, March 5th, 1814.

Robinson[1] arrived at Chatillon the fourth day from his leaving London, and joined me here last night. He came by Paris, where he stayed a few hours, without hearing or seeing anything particular.

Your private letter is entirely satisfactory to all my feelings, public and private, and it will altogether remove any possible prejudice which might have resulted to the public service from misconception, as to my language not being sanctioned. I took occasion this morning to show it to the Emperor, saying everything that might protect Lieven against any unfavourable impression as to what had passed. I also read to his Imperial Majesty part of your private letter of the 12th, in order to satisfy him that our views have been consistent and essentially coincident throughout.

The discussions at Troyes were necessarily painful, and gave to my intercourse with the Emperor a more controversial character than I could have wished ; and I have reason to know that he was not a little impatient of the opposition he had met with from me ; but this is all gone by, and His Imperial Majesty now encourages me to come to him without form. I see him almost every day, and he receives me with great kindness, and converses with me freely on all subjects.

. . . I don't know that the negotiation, as it has turned out, has had any effect whatever upon the operations, however it may, from the extraordinary circumstances under which it was brought forward, have tempted the enemy to presume upon the Allies politically ; and, in ending so, I hope we have so managed as to recover our position of authority, which has restored harmony and confidence amongst ourselves. . . .

[1] He had been sent home in consequence of Lieven's dispatch. [See LXXXIII.]

LXXXIX. [*F. O. Cont. Arch.* 3.]
CASTLEREAGH TO LIVERPOOL.   (No. 32.)
Chaumont, March 10th, 1814.

[Encloses the Treaty of Chaumont.[1]]   Your Lordship will observe that this Treaty is founded upon the Projet of Peace delivered on the part of the Allies at Chatillon to the French negotiants, and provides equally for the alternative of a prolongation of the war, or a termination of the contest.   Your Lordship, who has been enabled to observe the shades of feeling to which coalitions are liable in the progress of events, will be enabled correctly to estimate the value of such a measure at the present moment, not only as a systematic pledge of preserving concert amongst the leading Powers, but as a refuge under which all the minor states, especially those on the Rhine, may look forward to find their security upon the return of peace, relieved from the necessity of seeking a compromise with France.   Its influence even upon the restless ambition of the enemy cannot well fail to be important.

For the accomplishment of this object at the present conjuncture I have gone to the full extent of my instructions on the subject of subsidy.   In the 3rd. secret article perhaps I have exceeded them, but I could not hestiate upon the propriety of participating in the burthen of successfully winding up that continental system to the creation of which the nation has so long devoted its utmost exertions.   I am confident this Treaty will have the most decisive and beneficial influence throughout the Confederacy in firmly cementing their union against France.

XC.   [*C. C. IX.*, 335.]
CASTLEREAGH TO MR. HAMILTON.[2]
Chaumont, March 10th, 1814.

I have been a very bad correspondent, but I have found it difficult to supply one intelligible report of the many events

[1] The Treaty was dated March 1st.   It not only bound the Four Powers to continue the present war with armies of at least 150,000 men, but also to maintain the Alliance for twenty years after peace was concluded, with armies of at least 60,000 men.   Castlereagh had thus obtained, though in a different form to that first proposed, the Treaty of Alliance which he had been trying to obtain since September, 1813.   See *supra* p. 24.   There were also three Secret Articles (1) confirming the decisions already arrived at as to Germany, Switzerland, Italy, Spain, and Holland ; (2) inviting Spain, Portugal, Sweden, and Holland to accede to the Treaty ; and (3) agreeing to keep forces on foot for a year after peace with France had been made.

[2] The permanent Under Secretary of State for Foreign Affairs.

passing here. In order to avoid trouble in classing, I have addressed the whole to Liverpool. When I return, I can settle with him what despatches shall be made official, in which case Lord B[athurst]'s name can be substituted.[1]

I send you my treaty, which I hope you will approve. We four Ministers, when signing, happened to be sitting at a whist-table. It was agreed that never were the stakes so high at any former party. My modesty would have prevented me offering it ; but, as they chose to make us a military Power, I was determined not to play a second fiddle. The fact is, that upon the face of the Treaty this year, our engagement is equivalent to theirs united. We give 150,000 men and five millions, equal to as many more— total, 300,000. They give 450,000, of which we, however, supply 150,000, leaving their own number 300,000. The fact, however, is that, sick, lame, and lazy, they pay a great number more. On the other hand, we give to the value of 125,000 men beyond the 300,000. What an extraordinary display of power ! This, I trust, will put an end to any doubts as to the claim we have to an opinion on continental matters.[2]

I am not aware of anything in the treaty which may require revision. As it is an instrument of great moment, I shall, how-ever, stay the ratifications here till the return of the messenger, whom I beg you will expedite. If it can be avoided, better make no change ; if there is any essential error, being all assembled, we could, without any serious inconvenience, execute new copies, and cancel these. As soon as I hear from you, I shall send off the ratification of the three Powers, to be exchanged in London. By laying the treaty before Parliament before the holidays, we can discuss it immediately on my return.

XCI. [*F. O. Cont. I.*]
BATHURST TO CASTLEREAGH. (No. 7.)
March 19th, 1814.

[The Prince Regent warmly approves the Treaty of Chaumont, but has read with deep concern the reports of the Conference at

---

[1] This was never done, and the official dispatches are addressed to Liver-pool though Bathurst signs the official instructions to Castlereagh.

[2] Cf Castlereagh to Liverpool, March 10th, 1814. "If the engagement is safe in itself and par within the scale we have hitherto acted upon or are likely to act upon during the war, there can be no reason why Great Britain should not assume that station in Europe as one of the great military Powers to which the exploits of her armies and the scale of her resources have so justly entitled her to lay claim." *F. O. Cont. Arch. 3.* It was Alexander who insisted on Great Britain accepting the same military responsibilities as the other Great Powers.

Chatillon of the 10th and 13th inst, sent by Lord Aberdeen. He had been persuaded that the original Projet of peace made by the Allies was substantially an ultimatum, and it was upon this condition that he approved of stating the whole of the colonial sacrifices which Great Britain was prepared to make ; but this is not so, if the Projet is not an ultimatum but a document on which the Powers are to negotiate.   The French Plenipotentiary ought only to be allowed to suggest alternatives in details which do not affect the main Projet.   But this has never been done and the original Projet is admitted to be only a basis for negotiation.]   It is not improbable that the negotiation will have been brought to some issue before you receive this dispatch, but the Prince Regent thinks it right to declare that he cannot consider himself bound by anything that has passed to agree to any Treaty with France which shall substantially differ from the Projet delivered by the Allied Ministers on the 17th of February.

The next point to which I am directed to call your attention, is the many inconveniences which arise from the protraction of the negotiation.   When the Projet was delivered on the 17th of February, it was obviously the intention of the Allied Powers, to bring the negotiation to a short issue.   On the 17th of March, after the expiration of four and twenty days, no material progress has been made in it.   Nor will it soon be brought to a conclusion, unless by some peremptory proceeding on the part of the Allied Powers.

The advantages of delay to Buonaparte are incalculable.   He is fully apprized of the ultimatum of the Allies, and he may suppose therefore that he knows the terms upon which under any military calamity he might obtain peace.   On the other hand he has bound himself to nothing so that he may imagine that he can raise his pretensions and improve his proposals at any time, if the fortune of war should happen to favour him.   This delay is likewise productive of another very serious inconvenience.   It has precluded the Allies from taking any step for making an appeal to the French nation against Buonaparte and from giving the assistance which they might otherwise be desirous of affording to those persons, particularly in the Western and Southern provinces of France, who may have manifested a disposition to resist his power.

[Thus negotiations must be brought to a speedy close or Castlereagh is to inform the Allies that the British offers were made on condition that the matter would be quickly settled, and if there is delay that the Prince Regent considers himself at liberty to withdraw them. Protest must also be made against Caulaincourt's declaration in the Conference of the 10th inst.[1] from which it might be supposed the cessions of Great Britain were actually in the possession of France instead of being already at the disposal of Great Britain.]

XCII. [*F. O. Cont. Arch.* 3.]
CASTLEREAGH TO LIVERPOOL. (No. 40.)
Bar-sur-Aube, March 22nd, 1814.

[The Allies felt the necessity of terminating the Chatillon Conference, and thus " it was determined to give the most peremptory character to our proceedings."]

I wish it had been possible with less sacrifice in point of time, to have ascertained in a manner that would satisfy the world of the fact, the impracticability of concluding peace with the existing ruler of France, but it has at length been accomplished in a manner which I am persuaded, can leave no reasonable doubt in the view even of the French nation, that Napoleon is the true and only obstacle to an early, honourable, and solid peace, a truth the more important to establish, as it is impossible the sentiments of the nation should not be speedily pointed, with an active indignation, against those to whom they may be led to attribute the sufferings to which they are now exposed by the presence of such numerous armies in the interior of the Empire. . . . It is due to M. de Caulaincourt to state that his personal conduct throughout the negotiation has been altogether unexceptionable, in the execution of the orders of his Government.

XCIII. [*F. O. Cont.* 3.]
CASTLEREAGH TO LIVERPOOL. (No. 41.)
Bar-sur-Aube, March 22nd, 1814.

There is nothing which has surprised me more, since the entry of the Allies into France, than the total absence of any authenticated communication from the interior, especially from Paris, having for its object the establishment of a concert with the Allies, for the destruction of Buonaparte's authority, as the great obstacle to peace.

---

[1] This refers to an ingenious sophism of Caulaincourt that France had still to cede the *legal* sovereignty over the conquered colonial possessions.

A communication of this nature, which in many respects appears entitled to considerable attention, has, however, within these few days been received. It is conveyed through a channel[1] peculiarly competent in point of ability to develop the views of those concerned ; and he appears to be sent by and to act in concert with persons of no mean weight in France. The general view he presented for consideration you will receive enclosed No. 1.[2] The enclosure No. 2[3] will give you the results of our deliberations on this important question, and I hope before the dispatch is forwarded to accompany it with at least the projet of declaration, which the Allied Governments propose to issue upon the rupture of the negotiation.

The individual alluded to has felt it essential to the object of his mission, to see Monsieur before he returns to Paris : he will report to us the result of his explanations, and receive such communications as the Allied Ministers may have to make to his friends. He attributes the delay in the overture to the expectation entertained in France, that Napoleon would not hesitate to accept the peace offered to him from Frankfort, and that it has now originated in an impression that the negotiation was not likely to end in peace. You will not consider the paper No. 2 as more as yet, than a memorandum drawn up for the consideration and approbation of the sovereigns (upon a full conference, however, amongst their ministers). It has been drawn with much ability as it appears to me, by Prince Metternich, who has throughout this transaction, and in failure of obtaining the peace demanded, acted fairly up to the sentiments, which I reported to Your Lordship as having been expressed by him at Basle, and subsequently.

---

[1] This was the appearance of Baron de Vitrolles. See his *Memoirs*, Vol. I., pp. 119–170.

[2] Vitrolles' demands, as given in this paper, were (1) That the Allies should no longer treat with Napoleon but only either with the representatives of the nation or, better still, with the representatives of Louis XVIII. (2) That a Bourbon " quartier general " should be placed vis-a-vis to each Napoleonic army as a rallying point. (3) That the Allies should supply the Comte d'Artois with funds. In return the Royalists would raise as much of France as possible.

[3] This cautious paper of Metternich's declared that the French people would never take the initiative on behalf of the Bourbons and that the Allies could not impose them on France, but it suggested that Monsieur should be encouraged to take action and given the revenues of any provinces that adhered to his cause. Vitrolles was to tell his Paris friends of Allied sympathy and to promise that if the Bourbon cause were not eventually successful, an amnesty for them would be included in the Treaty of Peace.

Considering that every claim in point of good faith, arising out of the Frankfort overture to treat with Napoleon has been scrupulously satisfied, that the line to be pursued affecting the interior of France, has become solely one of expediency, and that the safety of the Allied Armies in France, as well as the successful prosecution of the war requires the adoption of every justifiable measure, which may have the tendency to point the national resentment against the real author of their calamities, and to conciliate an interest in France to the cause of the Allies, I have not hesitated to give my cordial concurrence to the principles, upon which this question has been considered.

Your Lordship will observe that the Allied Powers are prepared to make a very wise sacrifice in favour of the cause of peace, by surrendering up to their immediate administration the revenues of all such provinces as shall declare in favour of the antient family, even those conquered and now occupied by themselves ; thus proving at once the purity of their views and rendering thereby the cause of the French people truly national. . . .

With such an example of liberality on the part of the Allies, I shall not deem it consistent, either with the good of the public service, or with the known sentiments of the Prince Regent, or his ministers to decline charging myself with the personal responsibility of making such reasonably pecuniary advances as the exigency of the case may at the outset appear to require, but as I know the difficulties of controlling an expenditure of this nature, more especially through British agents, I have expressed an earnest desire, that the three Allied Powers may exclusively charge themselves with the surveillance of whatever means are to be applied to this object, whether arising from revenue, or advances, and that such aid as Great Britain can afford to grant (necessarily limited as it must be in amount by the vast extent of her existing engagements) should be appropriated to this object, under their application, rather than as a direct grant to be made to the French Princes from the British Government.

I consider this course of proceeding as not only the most prudent in a financial point of view, as rendering the expense definite on our part, but as relieving the question from much of the political difficulty, which must always attend, in a Government like ours, the voting a sum of money for effectuating a change in the Government of France. It places the case on its true grounds. The great military Powers of the continent contend for a solid peace. They fail to obtain this object by negotiation. Their armies are in the heart of France. They feel it desireable to ally themselves if possible with the majority of the nation, in prosecution of an object of common interest, viz., peace, and to wage war upon Napoleon and his party alone. Pledged by every principle as well as interest to support the Continental Powers in the war and in the manner most effectual according to their conviction to the end in view, we afford them aid to this effect. The question thus becomes essentially military, and is at once relieved from any imputation of a desire to intermeddle idly and unnecessarily in the political Government of France.

The Projet of a convention,[1] which the Allied Sovereigns framed amongst themselves to regulate their conduct in the event of the occupation of the enemy's capital . . . will with some extension and alteration effectuate the object I have in view, which is, to bring Great Britain forward, in whatever may regard the interior of France, rather as the ally and auxiliary of the continental Powers, than as charging herself in chief, and making herself responsible, for what cannot be conducted under the superintendence of her own Government.

XCIV. [*F. O. Cont. I.*]
BATHURST TO CASTLEREAGH. (No. 8.)
March 22nd, 1814.

[News from Wellington that Bordeaux has been entered by the British. They were well received there and the White Cockade by Wellington's orders was hoisted, though Beresford did not encourage the inhabitants and told them of the risks they ran.] I have further to add, that in no instance have either money or arms been advanced under the authority of the British Government to any inhabitants of the southern provinces of France, who have manifested a disposition to resist the Government of Bonaparte, and to support the cause of the Bourbons. Under these circumstances the Prince Regent is of the opinion that the case has in a great measure occurred for which Your Lordship fought so judiciously, as appears by your dispatch No. 4 at the Conference held at Langres between the Ministers of the Allied Sovereigns on the 29th of January, and that it may now be a matter of doubt how far Bonaparte may continue to be competent to fulfil his engagements which he has or may have contracted. The Prince Regent has commanded me, therefore, to instruct Your Lordship to use your utmost efforts with the Allied Powers to break off the

[1] See LXXXI., p. 153.
[2] LXXVIII. p. 144.

negotiations unless preliminaries shall have been signed previous to the receipt of this dispatch. Such a proceeding can alone put the sentiments of the French nation fairly to the test. We are not now proposing to found our conduct upon the speculation of individuals, but upon the overt act of the second or third city in France directed solely by the impulse of its own feelings and supported, as we are informed from Lord Wellington, by the general disposition of the people in the adjoining provinces.

The delay which has taken place in the negotiation at Chatillon since the middle of February, which is solely to be ascribed to the French Government, will, in the opinion of the Prince Regent, fully justify, under such circumstances and upon such an event, the adoption of the proposed measure. If your Lordship shall, however, find it impossible to prevail upon the Allies to break off the negotiation you will acquaint them that you are authorised to direct the British Plenipotentiaries not to be parties to the Treaty, under these circumstances, without a further reference ; and you will inform me of the sentiments of the several Allied Powers after the whole of the inclosed information shall have been laid before them, in order that the Prince Regent may give such further instructions on the subject as he shall then judge expedient. Lastly, if the preliminaries shall have been actually signed by the several Plenipotentiaries previous to the receipt of this dispatch, I think it right to apprize your Lordship, that it is the Prince Regent's intention to suspend the ratification until he shall have been informed of the sentiments of the Allies, whether the case shall have fully and substantially arisen, to which the reservation made by your Lordship on the 29th of January was intended to apply. In all your communications with the Allied Sovereigns or their Ministers upon this subject you will assure them of the unaltered and unalterable attachment of the Prince Regent to the principles of the Alliance so happily formed between H.R.H. and the great Powers of Europe : and that in the course which he has adopted on the present occasion, he has no other motive than strenuously and cordially to co-operate towards the most complete attainment of that great object of all their efforts, a peace not only just and honourable in its terms, but promising durable tranquillity to Europe.

[Wellington, by his private letters, shows that he considers the Bourbon cause popular, and that, if negotiations with Napoleon were broken off, there would be a general rising, if encouraged.]

XCV. [*F. O. Cont. Arch.* 3.]
CASTLEREAGH TO LIVERPOOL. (No. 45.)
Dijon, March 30th, 1814.

. . . The person[1] therein referred to has not yet returned from Monsieur who was at Nancy when the last courier left that place. The sudden removal of part of the Head Quarters to this town, in separation from the Emperor of Russia, has given some interruption to our proceedings upon this subject, but His Imperial Majesty's general sentiments being sufficiently known, it has been deemed expedient not to wait for an express authority, but to send a *confidential* mission to Monsieur, to concert with His Royal Highness as to the course to be pursued. As it appeared to me of the highest importance to mark, that the Emperor of Austria was prepared cordially to concur with his Allies in the policy to be pursued towards the Bourbons, I strongly urged, that an Austrian agent should be sent, the better to satisfy Monsieur and those who are disposed to support Louis XVIII— that this with His Imperial Majesty is a national and not a family question.

[Bombelles sent to-night to Nancy for this purpose. Encloses his instructions[2] in which the Emperor of Austria's sentiments are sufficiently marked.] In the management of this business, Prince Metternich is anxious to found the cause as much as possible upon a French interest,—that this should be created by the Bourbons accepting the peace which Buonaparte has rejected and thus making themselves the immediate and only resource to which the nation can appeal, to deliver them from their present difficulties. In this view it was the general opinion that the invitation to recur to the antient family ought not, in the first instance, to appear in the Allied declaration, and that their disposition to support the cause should follow and not precede the proclamation of Monsieur.

The declaration of Bordeaux is a providential feature in the question. If Lyons should imitate the example everything may be hoped. I understand Monsieur has been well received at Nancy. In this town there is a good disposition, which the news

[1] The Baron de Vitrolles. See XCIII.

[2] These laid down four conditions, " (1) L'engagement du roi de régner constitutionellement. (2) La sanction royale explicite et sans détour de la validité des acquisitions de biens nationaux. (3) Le sanction de la dette publique. (4) Le maintien des fonctionnaires publics tant civils que militaires."

from all the armies and the London Extraordinary Gazette, reprinted and placarded on the walls, may ripen into a more active sentiment. Marshal Beresford's private letter announcing the "Cocarde Blanche" attracts much attention.

XCVI. [*F. O. Cont. Arch.* 4.][1]
CASTLEREAGH TO LIVERPOOL. (No. 50.)

Dijon, April 4th, 1814.

[Unfortunately the messenger mentioned in the dispatch of the 22nd March[2], after an interview with Monsieur, was taken by armed peasants. However, in consequence of a letter from Castlereagh to a friend in Paris " whom I knew to be with the party likely to conduct the expected movement," a new agent was sent to the Allies, from Paris.][3] Prince Metternich, Baron Hardenberg, and myself saw him together, satisfied all his wishes and sent him back with our joint signatures to establish the fact of our full concert and trusting to his fidelity for a faithful report. His arrival, which we have heard of, has no doubt had the best effects.

The Declaration which has been signed by the Emperor of Russia is not a very orthodox instrument—in so far as it is a pledge to guarantee a constitution without knowing what it is. At the same time I am not afraid of any mischief. The communications we receive are quite decisive in favour of the Bourbons. The Emperor is weaned of his false notions on this point, and we have a secret intimation from Nesselrode through Schwarzenberg, that the Prince Royal's intrigue with Joseph is understood and that Talleyrand and others in authority will counteract it. This is fortunate, as I find Charles Jean[4] (evidently in expectation of a crises) is gone to Headquarters. The plan was an intermediate system ostensibly to favour the return of the Bourbons at the head of which Bernadotte expected to appear as dictator for a limited time, Joseph looking through his influence to some suitable settlement.

I had the satisfaction of stating this morning to a deputation from Lyons the course we have pursued throughout, especially the generous, loyal, and manly language of Lord Wellington to the

---

[1] Sent in cipher.
[2] See XCIII.
[3] I can find no details as to the personality of this second messenger.
[4] Bernadotte.

people of Bordeaux. It is impossible the Prince Regent could wish to add to the sentiments of admiration which his perseverance and liberality to the Continental Powers has occasioned. The prevailing opinion is that, although the natural sentiment has been checked by the conferences at Chatillon, and by a doubt as to the intentions of the Allies, the result will be rendered more certain in consequence of the forbearance shown by them in leaving the initiative to the nation.

XCVII. [*F. O. Cont. Arch.* 4¹.]
CASTLEREAGH TO LIVERPOOL. (No. 54.)
Paris, April 13th, 1814.

[Castlereagh arrived at Paris on the 10th in the evening. Little to add to the reports of Lord Cathcart and Lord Stewart. Explains his attitude concerning the Treaty of Fontainebleau, April 11th with Napoleon. On arrival he found that arrangements with Napoleon were on the point of execution and would have been signed by the Russian Minister had not the arrival of the Allied Ministers been announced.] The motives for accelerating the immediate conclusion of this act were the inconvenience, if not the danger, of Napoleon's remaining at Fontainebleau, surrounded by troops who still, in a considerable degree, remain faithful to him, the apprehension of intrigues in the army and in the capital, and the importance attached by a considerable portion of the officers to some arrangement favourable to their chief, in satisfaction of their own personal honour before they left him.

On the night of my arrival the four ministers had a conference with the Prince de Benevent on the subject of the proposed convention, to which I stated my objections, desiring at the same time, to be understood as not urging them then, at the hazard of the internal tranquillity of France, nor in impeachment of what was due, in good faith, to the assurance given under the exigency of the movement by Russia. The Prince of Benevent admitted the weight of many of the objections stated, but declared that he did consider it, on the part of the Provisional Government as an object of the first importance to avoid anything that might assume the character of a civil war, even for the shortest time : that he also found some such Pont d'or essential to make the army

---

¹ This dispatch was laid before Parliament on April 7th, 1815, when the Treaty of Fontainebleau was first officially communicated. Some of the critical passages were, however, omitted. *Hansard.* xxx. 376.

pass over in a temper to be made use of. Upon these declarations and the Count de Nesselrode's that the Emperor his Master had felt it necessary, in the absence of the Allies, to act for the best in their name as well as his own, I withdrew any further opposition to the principle of the measure, suggesting only some alterations in the details. I desired, however, to decline on the part of my Government being more than an acceding party to the Treaty, and declared that the act of accession on the part of Great Britain should not go beyond the territorial arrangements proposed in the Treaty. My objections to our being unnecessarily mixed in its forms, especially in the recognition of Napoleon's title under present circumstances were considered as perfectly reasonable . . . At my suggestion the recognition of the Imperial Titles in the family were limited to their respective lives, for which there was a precedent in the case of the King of Poland, when he became Elector of Saxony.

To the arrangement in favour of the Empress I felt not only no objection (except so far as it might embarrass our Sicilian indemnities), but considered it due to the distinguished sacrifice of domestic feeling which the Emperor of Austria has made to the cause of Europe. I should have wished to substitute another position in lieu of Elba for the seat of Napoleon's retirement, but none having the quality of security, on which he insisted, seemed disposeable, to which equal objections did not occur, and I did not feel that I could encourage the alternative which Caulaincourt assured me Buonaparte repeatedly mentioned, namely, an asylum n England.

On the same night the Allied Ministers had a conference with Caulaincourt and the Marshals at which I assisted ; and a very singular cabinet it was, as any it has fallen to my lot to attend. The Treaty was gone through and agreed to with alterations ; it has since been signed and ratified, and Buonaparte will commence his movement towards the South to-morrow or the day following.

I felt I own the utmost repugnance to anything like a Treaty with him after his déchéance had been pronounced. The sordid nature of the transaction strips it perhaps of a real danger, and I really hope both his character and his fortunes are now sufficiently lowered to render him but little formidable. I should have wished, however, if he was humble enough to accept a pension, that it had been an act of grace and not of stipulation. It is, however, in all its parts, a question which should not be suffered to cloud for a moment the lustre of the transaction with which it is connected, to which perhaps it may have indirectly contributed.

[Details of Monsieur's entry. Reception of Emperor of Austria arranged.]

XCVIII. [*C. C. IX.*, 472.]
CASTLEREAGH TO LIVERPOOL.
Paris, April 19th, 1814.

In the present state of things, I am anxious, as far as possible, to put you personally *au fait* of *nuances* here, and to possess myself of your ideas, before I am driven to the necessity of acting upon them.

And first, as to our peace[1]—we have agreed to enter upon its negotiation with Talleyrand, under full powers from Monsieur, in order that it may be ready for signature on the King's arrival. With respect to the nature of the arrangement, we shall all be agreed to take our Chatillon *projet* as the basis ; but, in the present state of things, there is just cause for some modification ; and there is disposition in the Emperor of Russia inconveniently to favour a relaxation in our demands.

As far as I can judge, we shall be unanimously disposed to strip the arrangement of any thing bearing upon it the character of particular distrust. We propose to admit the French Ambassador to the general Congress ; and, having the English restitutions necessarily in hand as a security for the peace, we are disposed, by the Convention for the suspension of hostilities, to allow the evacuation of old France by the Allied troops, and of the fortresses beyond those limits by the French troops, to go hand in hand. . . .

With respect to the future limits of France—I hope the Emperor will not be disposed to press any departure from the antient frontier which, in a military point of view, can be objectionable. The flat part of Savoy, not affecting the line of the Alps, and Avignon, are the augmentation to which, from the first discussions at Chatillon, it was thought France might be suffered not unreasonbly to aspire. I believe, upon similar principles, something in the Palatinate had been thought of ; but this must depend upon German arrangements.

[1] Castlereagh wrote singularly little home in either private or public letters about the negotiations for the first Peace of Paris. The reports of Münster throw, however, some further light on events, though details on many important points are lacking.

P

With respect to the power of France so augmented, I see no present cause for alarm ; and there is a strong motive for giving to our peace with the Bourbons somewhat of a more liberal complexion.

With respect to our own peace, I consider Malta, the Cape, Mauritius, and Tobago, as *sine qua non* ; also the regulations limiting the French to a commercial occupation of their factories in the East Indies. I should wish, as at present circumstanced, not to press the Saintes. It is not worth swelling the catalogue with a demand of this nature. It is easily reduced, at the outset of a war, and will not be strengthened by the Bourbons : their finances for years will be deplorably deranged. They have an army of officers to pension, and will find it difficult to keep things going. Points may occur in the discussions upon which I can refer, but I wish to know your wishes as to the spirit in which we should conduct ourselves. I am myself inclined to a liberal line upon subordinate questions, having secured the Continent, the ancient family, and the leading features of our own peace. Let me have an answer to this as soon as you can.

P.S.—I still feel great doubts about the acquisition in sovereignty of so many Dutch colonies. I am sure our reputation on the Continent, as a feature of strength, power, and confidence, is of more real moment to us than an acquisition thus made. The British merchants ought to be satisfied, if we secure them a direct import. Holland cannot well refuse this, nor Sweden, if she acquires Berbice, which ought to satisfy. More than this, I think Holland ought not to lose, even though compensated on the side of the Netherlands.

XCIX. [*C. C. IX.* 478.]
CASTLEAGH TO LIVERPOOL.
Paris, April 20th, 1814.
I still wish you would persuade the Prince to invite both the Emperor of Austria and the King of Prussia to visit England. I am confident we ought not to make Russia our *only* feature, for reasons I will explain when we meet ; nor is it wise for us to make a Power exclusively popular, circumstanced as Russia is both towards France and us. Be assured, the Emperor will not *reciprocate* such a principle.

You can best judge how far this Junta would answer. So far as the King of Prussia is concerned, it would be all smooth : he *wishes* to go—falls naturally into the Emperor's wake—and, I know from the Chancellor Hardenberg, expects an invitation : indeed, he persuades himself that he has already been invited. The Emperor would be more reluctant, but still, I think, would go, if the Prince pressed it, and it was understood through me that it was really wished, and that his situation would be upheld.

The Emperor of Russia, from various circumstances, exploits, manners, etc., must make his brother Emperor, though the first in rank, the second in *éclat*. He always, however, personally treats the Emperor of Austria with the most perfect attention, placing himself *en seconde ligne*.

If the Prince sees the political advantage of this combination, I think he can work it out without any diminution of attention to Russia ; but, in this case, he must either write himself to the three Sovereigns, or direct me *officially* to convey his wishes ; and it ought to be done without delay, as the Emperor of Russia expects to set out from hence by the 15th of May at furthest, for London.

I see no difficulty in executing this measure now, as far as the Prince of Sweden is concerned. We owe him no compliments, and he has business enough in Norway to look after. In this object, for our own sakes, we must assist him. We cannot punish the Swedes for his faults ; and hesitation in our mode of acting will only add to our own difficulties, by encouraging the Norwegians to persevere. This is the feeling both of Russia and Austria. There is no other Allied Sovereign that can take offence ; and the line draws itself, when confined to the four great Powers who have conducted the whole. The conduct of Austria has been throughout so good, under difficult circumstances, and recently so very distinguished, that the Prince will raise himself and his Government by re-echoing the general sentiments ; and I can assure you the influence of Austria in France not only has been, but still is of immense importance to the completion of our work. It is still more important to our views in the Netherlands. You may command her entire exertions on both points by good management, and without any sacrifice.

When I recommend you to dilute the libation to Russia, I am the last to wish it should be less palatable. The Emperor has the greatest merit, and must be held high, but he ought to be grouped, and not made the sole feature for admiration. The interview in England will have a sensible influence on the politics of the Continent. His Imperial Majesty is all kindness to me.

C. [*F. O. Cont. Arch.* 4.]
CASTLEREAGH TO LIVERPOOL. (No. 58.)
Paris, May 5th, 1814.
[Little progress in the Treaty of Peace. It is necessary to examine whether any or what extension could be given to the French frontiers of 1792.] This and a strong desire felt by Prussia and Austria to bring both Russia and France to some understanding upon the main principles of the Continental arrangements, in a secret article or otherwise previous to our stipulating away our conquests, has led to a tedious and elaborate examination of this very complicated and arduous question. I now send you a report[1] upon this subject drawn up by the Chancellor Hardenberg after repeated discussions. It is to be submitted this day to the Emperor of Russia. I am afraid there will be difficulties in that quarter, as His Imperial Majesty has still, I apprehend, more extensive views on the side of Poland than this projet countenances.

[The unsettled condition of affairs and the pressure of business on Talleyrand also prevented progress. . . .]

CI. [*C. C. X.* 8.]
CASTLEREAGH TO LIVERPOOL.
Paris, May 5th, 1814.
I am truly sorry to occasion any embarrassment at home, by being absent from my post ; but I really work as hard as a man can well do, in such a town as Paris, to finish my work ; and I cannot persuade myself that it would be safe to leave it incomplete. Robinson holds himself in readiness, upon the return of the messenger, to join you, if you still think it necessary ; but, in that case, you must spare me Hamilton, as the quantity of business here is considerable. I can hardly conceive the Opposition will persevere in pressing discussion. . . .

You will see, by Lord William's official despatches, that we shall have something to unravel in Corsica, and also at Genoa.[2] It was inconsiderate his making a declaration in favour of the old system, at the latter place, knowing, as he must do, that there is little disposition in the Allies to re-establish it. My persuasion is

---

[1] "Plan pour l'arrangement futur de l'Europe." Paris, April 29th, 1814. This document discussed in detail the whole European settlement.
[2] Bentinck, after his entry into Genoa, issued on the 26th April, a declaration guaranteeing the independence of the Republic which Castlereagh, who had already agreed that Genoa should be absorbed in Piedmont, had immediately to repudiate.

if the war had gone on much longer in France, we should have had a most disastrous complication in Italy, and that Lord William's corps, acting separately, would have been probably the first sacrifice. He seems bent upon throwing all Italy loose : this might be well against France, but against Austria and the King of Sardinia, with all the new constitutions which now menace the world with fresh convulsions, it is most absurd.

Campbell's[1] letter will amuse you. General Schuwaloff, the Russian Commissary, assures me he [Buonaparte] showed little or no fortitude in his difficulties. If his taste for an asylum in England should continue, would you allow him to reside in some distant province ? It would obviate much alarm on the Continent. Joseph, now in Switzerland, has expressly solicited a passport. What am I to say ?

CII. [C. C. X. 17.]
CASTLEREAGH TO LORD WILLIAM BENTINCK.
Paris, May 7th, 1814.
. . . I shall take care not to compromise any of the parties referred to in your secret letter.[2] I fully approve of your giving the Projet no countenance ; nor can I bring myself to wish that the too extensive experiment already in operation throughout Europe, in the science of Government, should be at once augmented by similar creations in Italy.

It is impossible not to perceive a great moral change coming on in Europe, and that the principles of freedom are in full operation. The danger is, that the transition may be too sudden to ripen into anything likely to make the world better or happier. We have new constitutions launched in France, Spain, Holland, and Sicily. Let us see the results before we encourage farther attempts. The attempts may be made, and we must abide the consequences ; but I am sure it is better to retard than accelerate the operation of this most hazardous principle which is abroad.

In Italy, it is now the more necessary to abstain, if we wish to act in concert with Austria and Sardinia. Whilst we had to drive the French out of Italy, we were justified in running all risks ; but the

---

[1] The British Commissioner at Elba.
[2] This dispatch and the next are included as showing Castlereagh's attitude towards the cause of constitutional liberty. It must be remembered, however, that in this dispatch he was writing to a vehement and impractical Whig, whose conduct in Italy had nearly wrecked the Allied schemes for bringing fresh forces against Napoleon in that quarter. The secret letter refers to projects for setting up a constitution in Naples.

present state of Europe requires no such expedient ; and, with a view to general peace and tranquillity, I should prefer seeing the Italians await the insensible influence of what is going on elsewhere, than hazard their own internal quiet by an effort at this moment. . . .

CIII. [*C. C. X.* 25.]
CASTLEREAGH TO SIR HENRY WELLESLEY, K.B.[1]

Paris, May 10th, 1814.

. . . . I entirely approve of the language held by you to the King of Spain, in the present critical circumstances of his affairs. The mode in which your Excellency's advice was asked did not denote, on the part of his Catholic Majesty, any disposition to abide by it ; and, if so, more especially under the extreme difficulties of the question, it would have been highly unadvisable for your Excellency to have made yourself responsible for measures over which you could have exercised little or no control.

Although the conduct of the Cortes and Regency has latterly been marked by a firm adherence to the principles of the Alliance, so far as the mere existence of the Constitution is at stake, it is impossible to conceive that any change tranquilly effected can well be for the worse. We are entitled to pronounce now, upon a certain extent of experience, that, in practice as in theory, it is amongst the worst of the modern productions of that nature.

I am glad to hear that the King is not disposed, in looking to a change, to aim at the restoration of the ancient order of things. I am confident there is not vigour and ability enough amongst his adherents to sustain such a system against the temper of the times, and the party which exists in Spain favourable to a form of Government more or less free. If his Majesty announces to the nation his determination to give effect to the main principles of a constitutional *régime*, I think it is probable he may extinguish the existing arrangement with impunity, and re-establish one more consistent with the efficiency of the executive power, and which may restore the great landed proprietors and the clergy to a due share of authority : but, to succeed in establishing a permanent system, he must speak to the nation, and not give it the character of a military resolution ; in doing which, the language of Louis XVIII. may afford him some useful hints.

I hope, if we are to encounter the hazards of a new constitutional experiment in Spain, in addition to the many others now in progress

[1] Wellington's brother, Minister to Spain.

in Europe, that the persons charged with the work will not again fall into the inconceivable absurdity of banishing from the legislature the Ministers of the Crown ; to which error, more perhaps than to any other, may be attributed the incapacity which has distinguished the march of every one of these systems which has placed the main authorities of the Constitution in hostility, instead of alliance, with each other.

I have every confidence in the discretion with which you will act in the impending crisis. You will not hesitate to afford your counsel and support, where you may be of opinion that the just influence of the British Government can promote the happiness of our Ally ; but, where you cannot see your way clear as to the probable result, I should wish you to abstain, rather than commit your Government by any systematic, precipitate, or too ostensible interference in the internal affairs of Spain. . . .

CIV. [*F. O. Cont.* 4.]
CASTLEREAGH TO LIVERPOOL. (No. 59.)
May 19th, 1814.

[Sends the Projet and French Counter-Projet on the Peace. In the British Projet Castlereagh has adhered to the views of the Government except that St. Lucia is substituted for the Saintes. Calling on Talleyrand for the Counter-Projet, Castlereagh was disappointed to find that the sketch which he had prepared for the King was entirely subversive of all British views. It was silent on St. Lucia and Tobago, demanded compensation for the Mauritius, and did not discuss the Slave Trade.]

It was fortunate I saw the Minister before he went to the King, as it gave me an opportunity of making him distinctly understand the course I should pursue. It was necessary as a considerable change of tone had been disclosed on the preceding day by the Court. The Marshals had talked high language and His Majesty had expressed himself somewhat in the same manner to the Emperor of Austria. I thought it therefore wise to be quite explicit and to recall the French Government to a sense of our claims, to the forebearance shewn, and to the true relations of the parties.

The point of all others upon which I have had the most difficulty to encounter is the Slave Trade, not any indisposition in M. de Talleyrand himself, but from a general sentiment, first that it is derogating to French honor to submit to a *stipulation* on this subject, as the condition of receiving back their colonies ; and secondly from an impression however erroneous, which he describes as prevalent in all the commercial towns, that with such a restriction the cession itself of their Colonies would be illusory. M. de Talleyrand entreated me with great earnestness to impress this view of the subject upon the British Government. He knew the difficulties *they* had to contend with, representing however *his own* as going fundamentally to the authority and stability of the new Government, which must accommodate [sic] to the prejudices of commercial men, if they hoped to revive a spirit in France more congenial with peace, than had grown out of the later system.

I represented all the duties and embarrassments of our situation, and especially the discontent which would follow the importation in islands ceded by us, especially when contrasted with the line adopted towards Sweden and Denmark, and intended to be followed up towards Holland. I told him that to do nothing was impossible, and that I could not answer for my Government being satisfied with anything short of the stipulation I had proposed, but that if France was prepared to make the abolition on her own part absolute at a fixed and remote date, and in the meantime (and especially at the approaching Congress) to unite her exertions and influence with ours to make the abolition general at that period, I would bring under the view of my colleagues fully and fairly the considerations which opposed themselves on the part of France to the abandonment of all discretion with respect to such preparatory measures as the interest of her colonial system might appear to require.

I particularly guarded myself against any committal on the subject. I cannot, however, forbear recommending that our demands should not be pushed to an extreme upon this point. The probable importations into Martinique and Guadelope in the next five years cannot be considerable, circumstanced as their population and cultivation now is. Many people look to the recovery of Saint Domingo but altho' this is a prospect, which the Government cannot afford to damp, and (you will observe) feel it necessary to secure against opposition on our part, yet it appears to me too visionary and impracticable a scheme in its execution to be the occasion of any large importation of slaves in the time limited. Where all trace at least of European property in land is lost, I have no conception that any man would risk money in the purchase of slaves to carry with him to St. Domingo. My feeling is that on grounds of general policy we ought not to attempt to tie France too tight on this question. If we do it will make the abolition odious in France and we shall be considered as influenced by a secret wish to prevent the removal of her colonial interests. The friends of abolition ought also to weigh the immense value of having France pledged to this question, and the subject brought before the Congress with the aid of France and Russia, both of which I can in that case answer for. We have convincing proof how small the progress is that can be practically made in this measure unless the aboliton can be made general. If we get France on our side we shall have a preponderance of authority; without her aid I shall despair of bringing Spain and Portugal into our views.

[Further details of the Treaty discussed. France endeavouring to obtain concessions on the side of the Netherlands.] I have been compelled peremptorily to oppose this as incompatible with the only defence of Brabant, and as disclosing a desire to encroach in that direction, which has been the source of so many wars. I spoke yesterday strongly to Talleyrand on this subject, and shall feel it my duty before I leave Paris, to represent to the King the necessity, if he wishes the peace to last, of extinguishing in the minds of the army this false notion of Flanders being necessary to France. . . .   In order to bring the whole to an early issue I have prevailed upon the Allied Governments positively to fix their departure for the end of this month, after which period, if the peace is not signed, the conference must be removed to London.   [This will encourage the French to hasten the peace.]

CV. [C. C. X. 10.]
CASTLEREAGH TO LIVERPOOL.
Paris, Monday [23rd[1] May.]
I received your letter of the 19th. to-day. I shall discuss the points to-morrow, and you shall then know the result.

I send you the remainder of the Treaty in the rough. You will see I have secured the consent of France to the incorporation of the Low Countries with Holland. I felt it of the last importance not to go to a Congress without having this most essential point acquiesced in by that Power. The annexed map will give you a rough idea of the proposed frontier. The black line is old France ; the red, in advance, the accessions granted ; the brown *enclaves* are the *réunions*—the whole does not exceed a population of 600,000, and concedes no military point.[2] I thought it also material to

---

[1] Undated in the *Correspondence* and placed by the editor among the dispatches of May 5th, but the original in the Archives is dated as above.

[2] See *Hertslet*. Map of Europe by Treaty vol. I. France was reduced to the limits of 1792, with some extension on her North-Eastern frontier and a considerable addition in Savoy.

secure Genoa as a free port, and to extinguish Antwerp as a naval station.

You will see, by the extent of matter comprised, that the pecuniary reclamations have been a most troublesome and difficult concern. After endless controversy, they have all, with a good grace, come into the principle I recommended from the first, viz., clear scores in respect to State claims, France engaging to do justice to individuals whose claims rest upon contract, in contradistinction to military spoliation and warfare.

PART III

THE CONGRESS OF VIENNA

PART III

THE CONGRESS OF VIENNA

CVI. [*C. C. X.* 76.]

CASTLEREAGH TO WELLINGTON.[1]

Downing Street, August 7th, 1814.

I enclose, for your Grace's private information, an extract of a letter received from the Prince of Benevent,[2] together with my answer ; and I have to request that you will, as early as possible after your arrival at Paris, endeavour to learn his Highness's views upon the subjects that are likely to occupy the attention of Congress, and especially upon the points of Poland and Naples. It is desirable that I should be as fully informed of the sentiments of the French Government as possible, before I meet the Allied Ministers at Vienna, where I have promised to be about the 10th of September.

Your Grace will observe that I have explained to the Prince of Benevent the object of these preliminary conferences. So far as you can regulate the Princes' arrival, I should wish him to be there about the 25th. The Emperor comes on the 27th, and we should then have time to discuss the more difficult matters previous to the assembly of the Congress on the 1st of October, having previously methodized the less complicated parts of the arrangement. You will, I hope, be able to obviate any jealousy of these previous deliberations : they are the necessary result of our former relations, which must throw upon the four principal Allied Powers the initiative in most of the arrangements.

It is material your Grace should endeavour to ascertain how far France is prepared, under any and what circumstances, to support her views on these two leading questions by arms. It is particularly desirable to learn whether the French and Spanish Governments limit their hostile views against Murat to a refusal to acknowledge him ; or whether, in the event of other Powers (Austria included) declining to give him aid, they would be disposed to employ their arms to replace the King of Sicily on the throne of Naples.

I should also wish to know whether the French Government has opened itself at all to the Prussian Government on the subject of Poland, as well as on the jealousy they appear, from the enclosed

---

[1] Wellington was appointed Ambassador at Paris on August 6th, 1814, and took up his duties there on the 24th August.

[2] 27th July and 7th August respectively in F. O. France 99.

letter from Sir Charles Stuart,[1] to entertain of the views of Russia in the north of Europe. If not, I should recommend their doing so without loss of time. The position and strength of Benningsen's army justify an apprehension that the Norwegian question may be made, both by Russia and Sweden, a pretext for dismembering Denmark, notwithstanding the King, in the judgment of the Allied Commissioners, has done what depended on him to transfer Norway ; but also from perceiving that the Emperor of Russia, before he left this country, was prone to hostile measures towards Denmark.[2]   . . .

CVII. [*C. C. X.* 93.]
WELLINGTON TO CASTLEREAGH.
Mons, August 18th, 1814.

I received last night your letters and despatch of the 14th.[3]

[1] Chargé d'affaires at Paris, not to be confused with Castlereagh's half-brother, who, however, becomes Lord Stewart on his appointment to the Embassy at Vienna. The letter of Sir Charles Stuart is one of a series by which Talleyrand's views had been placed before Castlereagh.

[2] Castlereagh was also drawing Hardenberg's attention to this point as a letter to him of August 8th shows. . . . " Some of my letters from the North speak of an augmentation of Benningsen's Corps, of plans of dismembering Denmark in favour of the Duke of Oldenbourg, and I hope you keep your eye upon this force. I have reason to believe that the French Government partakes strongly of the general alarm produced by the accumulating armament on the Russian frontier, and by the organisation of a purely Polish army. I have every reason to be satisfied with the conduct of Talleyrand on the late abortive attempt to revive a French party in the Netherlands and believe you will find him very reasonable and disposed to act at Vienna in concert with us. He will view with great displeasure the introduction of Russian influence into the North of Europe : I was much gratified to find this, as I know nothing more fatal to Prussian authority than to have the Russians on both flanks. I hope you will sift to the bottom before we meet the state of force, designs, etc., both on the Polish and Holstein frontier. . . ." F. O. Cont. Arch. 20.

[3] Castlereagh to Sir Charles Stuart, August 14th, 1814.
" The disposition evinced by the French Government is highly important and satisfactory, and we shall be most desirous of turning it to the best account ; but the Prince of Benevente, if he wishes us to do good, must not expect us to separate from our old connexions, in the midst of our concert. We have no partialities that he need be jealous of ; and, if he desires to render our influence a salutary check upon improvident schemes and undue pretensions, in whatever quarter they may be found to exist, he must allow me to work this out without doing violence to habits established under circumstances to which we owe the blessings of having a Government in France, to which we can feel ourselves associated in common views of policy and interest.
" If it is thought desirable, I shall be perfectly ready to confer with him on my way to Vienna, and to look without reserve at the difficulties we shall have to deal with at the Congress ; but he must not expect me to depart from any engagements to meet my former colleagues at Vienna about the 10th of September : nor must he interpret unfavourably our previously conferring upon the system which has grown out of engagements which subsisted long before we could reckon France amongst the number of our friends, and which the Prince himself proposed should be taken as the basis of our discussions at Vienna." C. C. X. 91.

The situation of affairs in the world will naturally constitute England and France as arbitrators at the Congress, if those Powers *understand* each other ; and such an understanding may preserve the general peace. But I think your object would be defeated, and England would lose her high character and station, if the line of Monseiur Talleyrand is adopted, which appears to me to be tantamount to the declaration by the two Powers that they will be arbitrators of all the differences which may arise.

We must not forget that only a few months ago it was wished to exclude the interference and influence of France from the Congress entirely. I believe that your view and mine are precisely the same ; but, however well Stuart and I may understand you, I am convinced that neither of us will explain so satisfactorily as yourself to Monsieur Talleyrand the necessity of your previous interview with the Ministers of the Allies, and the nature of your concert and mediation ; and it is desirable on this ground that you should come to Paris.

Your coming there, and your departure so long previous to his, may occasion the same unpleasant sensation in the public mind at Paris which you observed that the information of your previous conferences at Vienna had occasioned to the Duc de Berri. It must also be recollected that the Allies will be aware of your journey to Paris, and may be jealous of your intimacy with Talleyrand. But I conceive that these considerations are nothing, when balanced with the great object of your establishing a perfect understanding with Talleyrand on your measures, and on the mode in which you will carry them into execution, which, in my opinion, nobody can do for you as well as you can for yourself. . . .

CVIII. [*F. O. Cont. 7.*]
CASTLEREAGH TO LIVERPOOL. (No. 1.)
Geneva, September 3rd, 1814.
[No time to report from Brussels on Paris.] . . . The letters I received at Brussels, especially from the Duke of Wellington,[1] determined me to go to Paris, and I considered that the result has fully justified the considerations which dictated this measure, however inconvenient in its execution, as it enabled me to dissipate many doubts, to bring the French Government to a more temperate view of the description of understanding which ought to subsist between us, and to precede the Prince de Benevent to Vienna with a much more formed notion of the mode of thinking of his court than I could have otherwise obtained.

[1] CVII.

I cannot pretend, in the compass of a despatch, to give Your Lordship, even in outline, the substance of two long interviews with that minister occupying no less than five hours, in which, as he assured me by the King's command, he discussed the various topics likely to come under consideration at Vienna with perfect unreserve. I was honoured also by the King with a private audience of above two hours, in which His Majesty went, seriatim, through the same points. I could observe shades of opinion on some of the points, but as to their desire and determination to cultivate a connection with Great Britain, the King and his minister were equally cordial and explicit.

My task was rather to repress the exuberance of this sentiment, and to prevent its assuming a shape, which, by exciting jealousy in other States might impare our respective means of being really useful. I flatter myself I succeeded in this, and, as a proof, I have reason to believe that M. de Talleyrand, laying aside his former jealousy, regarded with satisfaction my preceding him to Vienna ; and as no inconsiderable indication of confidence, he left me at liberty to use at my own discretion, in my intercourse with the Allied ministers previous to his arrival, what I had found to be the sentiments of his Court.

This authority may be material in my preparatory discussions with Count Nesselrode. I found the sentiments of the French Government with respect to Poland perfectly analogous to our own.—A decided repugnance to the Russian Projet, as the most dangerous and unjust of the three ; a strong abstract preference (especially in the King's mind) for the re-existence of Poland as an independent State in the House of Saxony, but this idea subdued by a sense of the danger of the attempt, into a desire not to subvert but to regulate the existing principle of partition.

My object in examining this and other questions, was to discuss and not to conclude; this was fully understood. The point of Poland gave me a favourable opportunity of opening to M. Talleyrand the Dutch and Swedish arrangements,[1] as affording a salutary influence over the Russian Councils. M. Talleyrand seemed much pleased with the manner in which this had been conducted, and seemed to expect that it would prove a useful instrument. He expressed no objection to the colonial part of the

[1] An Act recognising the Sovereignty of the House of Orange over Belgium was signed on July 21st, a Convention compensating Sweden for her surrender of Guadelope on August 13th, and on the same date a Convention regulating the return of the Dutch colonies except the Cape and one or two minor islands, compensation being paid to Holland in the form of a grant of £2,000,000 for the fortification of Belgium.

arrangement, which I represented not as a measure of original policy, but as arising out of the efforts which Great Britain was willing to make in favour of other States, in which France had her full share.

As I was apparently treated with much candour both by the King and his minister, I regretted that I should have had still a reserve to observe towards them with respect to our Treaty with Spain.[1] I left instructions, however, with the Duke of Wellington not only to take the earliest opportunity, when authorized by the Government of Spain, to remedy this, but to express my personal regret at not having received the sanction I had solicited whilst at Paris. I took, however, advantage of the question of Naples to express that we felt no objection but the reverse to the restoration of this branch of the House of Bourbon, that we were aware that the power and influence of France must be thereby materially augmented; but that we felt no repugnance to the natural and legitimate influence of the family so long as the two principal Crowns abstained from a connection which made them one State for the purpose of aggression. I urged this topic strongly both with the King and Talleyrand, and it was received with complacency at least by both. I told them I pressed it with the more earnestness and unreserve as I considered it indispensible to a good understanding between Great Britain and France.   . . .

CIX. [F. O. Cont. 7.[2]]
CASTLEREAGH TO LIVERPOOL.
Vienna, September 24th, 1814.

My letter of the 21st instant will have apprized your Lordship of my arrival here.[3] I found the Russian Minister, Count Nesselrode, and the Chancellor Hardenberg, reached Vienna the day but one after. The Ministers of the Allied Powers have had four conferences, which have been principally occupied in discussing the form and course of our future proceedings. There has been but one opinion on the point, " that the conduct of the business must practically rest with the leading Powers "; and with the exception of a doubt on the part of the Russian minister, whether the Emperor may not press the introduction of the Swedish

[1] Referring to the secret article in the Treaty of July 5th, by which the Family Compact was expressly forbidden.
[2] Printed, except for the last paragraph, in my Congress of Vienna, Appendix I., where will also be found other documents relating to the organisation of the Congress.
[3] On the 13th September.

Q

plenipotentiary, we are agreed that the effective Cabinet should not be carried beyond the six Powers of the first order, with an auxiliary council of the five principal States of Germany for the special concerns of Germany. You will observe from the protocol [A,][1] that the Allied Powers have deemed it necessary to preserve the initiative in their own hands. I have concurred in thinking this line expedient ; but, considering the complexion of the protocol prepared upon this subject (which is Prussian) to be rather repulsive to France, and a little more conclusive in its expressions than I quite liked, I thought it right to give my acquiescence to it with the qualification contained in the note annexed to it.[2]

The mode of assembling the Congress and conducting business next occupied our attention ; and that you may see the succession of ideas that have prevailed upon this subject, I enclose unofficially and confidentially for your perusal the memoranda which have been given in, rather as throwing out ideas than containing a formal opinion on the part of those who prepared them.[3] The idea that first occurred naturally was to constitute the Congress, and when constituted to propose to nominate a committee to prepare a Projet of arrangement for the consideration of Congress. But this course of proceeding was soon dismissed, as involving us without previous concert in all the preliminary questions of difficulty—namely, what Powers shall be admitted to sit and deliberate, and what only to petition and negotiate ; what are to be the functions and attribution of the Congress ; and by what mode they are to act and conclude. This led to another view of the question, which you will find in two papers of mine,[4] the object of which was to see whether, saving all questions in the first instance, we might not, through a preliminary meeting of plenipotentiaries, get the conduct of the business with a general acquiescence into the hands of the six Powers, with their auxiliary Council for German affairs.

The assembling of such a preliminary meeting of plenipotentiaries is certainly by no means free from objection. You will find this subject investigated in a further memorandum, prepared by Baron Humboldt, who assists Prince Hardenberg ;[5] but the

---

[1] Protocol of September 22nd, 1814. B. and F. State Papers II. 554.

[2] Ibid 555. Castlereagh's qualification was that France was to be treated as a friendly, not a hostile Power and he reserved the right to dissent from the decisions of the " Four."

[3] See the Congress of Vienna. Appendices II. and IV.

[4] Ibid. Appendix III.

[5] Ibid. Appendices V. and VI.

substitute he proposes has its awkwardness, as it too broadly and ostensibly assumes the right to do what may be generally acquiesced in, if not offensively announced, but which the secondary Powers may protest against, if recorded to their humiliation in the face of Europe.

The question remains open till the French and Spanish plenipotentiaries join us. Perhaps the most prudent course may be between the two propositions, and that the declaration of the six Powers should not contain any public avowal of what they mean in point of form to do ; but that it should state reasons why the Congress should not be constituted till the plenipotentiaries, after their assembly at Vienna, have had full opportunity for confidential intercourse, and till there is a prospect that by such communications (without saying of what nature) some Projet of general arrangement may be devised, more likely than anything that could now be hazarded, to meet the sentiments and provide for the interests of all concerned.

I have endeavoured, as much as possible, to effect a coincidence of sentiment between the French and Allied Ministers, and I hope I have in a considerable degree succeeded ; but, whatever may be their differences with each other, the three Continental Courts seem to feel equal jealousy of admitting France either to arbitrate between them or to assume any leading influence in the arrangements consequent upon the peace.

The Emperor of Russia and King of Prussia are expected to-morrow. Count Nesselrode brought with him no authority to make any modification of the Emperor's former plans with respect to Poland : at the same time the impression is that His Imperial Majesty, (without however admitting any stipulation to that effect) will desist from his political but persevere in his territorial views with respect to Poland ; the folly of ever stirring the former point can only be equalled by the total want of judgment in giving a discreditable grasping and menacing character to his councils upon such a point.

CX. [*C. C. X.* 142.]
CASTLEREAGH TO WELLINGTON.
Vienna, October 1st, 1814.
[Hardenberg's proposals for the distribution of territory in Germany : Bavaria to be indemnified on the right of the Maine, Prussia being placed behind the Rhine, with a *lisière* only on the left bank, supported by the Wesel and Mayence. Bavaria and

Austria refuse to agree. Prussia accordingly suggests that Bavaria should reassume the Palatinate, strengthened by the territory and fortress of Luxemburg ; Mayence to be an imperial fortress, with regulations to secure the free navigation of the Maine to the Southern States. This would give the provinces on the left bank of the Rhine a permanent security against France, an impossibility except by giving them a footing beyond the Rhine.]

If this reasoning is solid, there can be no doubt that the support of so highly military a Power as Bavaria on the left flank, with Prussia in second line to Holland, and Bavaria as proposed in the present plan, presents a much more imposing front to France than Holland spread out to the Moselle, as suggested in the former plan, with Prussia behind the Rhine, and the territories between the Moselle and the Rhine *morcellés*, as mere indemnities, between the Grand Duke of Baden and other petty princes.

The arrangement, as suggested, is less liberal, in a territorial point of view, to the House of Orange than could be wished : perhaps in this respect, some modification may be effected, but the great question for them, as well as for us, is to weigh what is the best security for peace, and for keeping the Low Countries out of the hands of France. In this view of the subject, beyond all others the most essential for Great Britain to look to, I doubt the policy of building our system of defence exclusively upon the Prince of Orange's power, enfeebled as it must be for great military exertions by the genius of his people, and by the principles of his Government.

You will weigh this in deciding on the alternatives into which the question resolves itself. We should both wish to press what was most acceptable to the Prince of Orange, but the point ought to be ruled upon larger principles, and, in examining them, I am always led to revert with considerable favour to a policy which Mr. Pitt, in the year 1806,[1] had strongly at heart, which was to tempt Prussia to put herself forward on the left bank of the Rhine, more in military contact with France. I know there may be objections to this, as placing a Power peculiarly military, and consequently somewhat encroaching, so extensively in contact with Holland and the Low Countries. But, as this is only a secondary danger, we should not sacrifice to it our first object, which is to provide effectually against the systematic views of France to possess herself of the Low Countries and the territories on the left bank of the Rhine—a plan which, however, discoun-

[1] 1805 is meant. See LXXIV. p. 135.

tenanced by the present French Government, will infallibly revive, whenever circumstances favour its execution.

CXI. [*F. O. Cont.* 7.]
CASTLEREAGH TO LIVERPOOL. (No. 3.)
Vienna, October 2nd, 1814.

. . . The day after his arrival, I received the Emperor of Russia's commands to attend him and was honoured with an audience of two hours and a half. His Imperial Majesty received me with great personal kindness, which was not abated at any period of the conversation notwithstanding the adverse views of the question I felt myself obliged to press upon his attention. I closed without any relaxation of the sentiments brought forward on the part of the Emperor, but it was distinguished from former interviews on the same subject, by the absence of any decisive declaration in the nature of a decision : on the contrary His Imperial Majesty more than once pressed me to weigh the arguments he had adduced, and expressed a desire to renew the conversation. He expressed a desire to conciliate, and promised me to hear the opinions of the other Ministers here. This, as far as the form of the proceeding is concerned, would justify hopes of a better understanding. I am not however warranted in drawing this conclusion either from the substance of His Imperial Majesty's conversation with me, nor from what I understand from Prince Metternich to have since passed in a still longer conversation with him.

Very early in the interview the Emperor opened his views with respect to Poland in considerable detail—the substance did not vary in any essential degree from what had always been understood to be his plan, namely to retain the whole of the Dutchy of Warsaw with the exception of a small portion to the westward of Kalish, which he meant to assign to Prussia, erecting the remainder together with his Polish Provinces formerly dismembered into a Kingdom under the dominion of Russia, with a national administration congenial to the sentiments of the people.

The Emperor endeavoured to establish how favourable such a system must prove to the happiness of the people ; that he was not prompted to it by any views of ambition. That he was ready to give the neighbouring States every security as to their possessions. That it was a sense of moral duty which dictated the measure and that it could not but prove grateful to the British Nation.

I represented that most certainly the British Government would view with great satisfaction the restoration of Poland to its independence as a Nation, but that they took a broad distinction between the erection of a part of Poland into a Kingdom merged in the Crown of Russia, and the restoration of the whole or greater part into a distinct and independent State. That to the latter measure they would feel every friendly disposition if it could be effected with the concurrence and support of the neighbouring Powers, and if I was not authorised to press such a measure upon His Imperial Majesty's attention, it arose only from the reluctance the Prince Regent felt to suggest any measure for the adoption of his Allies, which might be felt by them to call for an unreasonable sacrifice of interest after the great exertions they had lately been called upon to make—but that if the question of restoring Poland was to be stirred at all, the British Government were of opinion to be either just in itself, or safe in its operation, that it ought to be taken up upon a broad and liberal basis ; and that I had reason to believe neither Austria nor Prussia would hesitate to unite themselves with His Imperial Majesty for such a purpose, however strongly they deprecated the proposed measure.

The Emperor frankly acknowledged that he was not prepared to make this extent of sacrifice on the part of his Empire, but continued to argue the safety of the measure to his Allies—its advantages to the Poles, and favourable collateral influence upon Russia.

In reply to these views of the subject, I represented that it was impossible to suppose that so great a change could be effected in Russian Poland, without the Austrian and Prussian Provinces being involved in its consequences. If, as his Imperial Majesty supposed, it would satisfy his Polish subjects and make them look for nothing more, in the same proportion must their former fellow subjects become discontented and impatient to re-assemble under the same standard. That if, on the contrary, as I had the strongest reason to know, the Poles regarded this qualified restoration under Russia as only a temporary and intermediate arrangement, and if the national spirit was thus aroused to all those intrigues and exertions which were to advance them to their national and never ceasing object—the ten millions of Poles, whilst they did adhere to Russia, would, for all military purposes tell with double force on the side of Russia, whilst the five million belonging to Austria and Prussia now inert would become disaffected. It was obvious that such a state of things must not only sow distrust and jealousy between the three Powers, but destroy in a double or triple ratio, their proportional strength as derived from Polish acquisitions, whilst it must give birth to a political fermentation which could only end in separation.

I further pressed the repugnance felt to the measure by his own Russian subjects, and how arduous the attempt was on the part of His Imperial Majesty, to undertake to conduct two such adverse and rival interests within his Empire. That if his personal ascendancy kept it alive during his reign, it would probably be deliberately destroyed, or perish in the hands of a successor. I ventured to assure His Imperial Majesty that a measure of this partial and disquieting nature would be disapproved by all Europe, and that it was odious and alarming in the extreme to both his Allies : that if the King of Prussia, from personal deference and regard, was apparently more acquiescent, His Majesty's repugnance and that of his subjects was not the less strong. That such was the universal sentiment, His Imperial Majesty would find from all the Ministers present, and were the general impression even founded in prejudice, and not in reason it was in vain to hope that an attempt so repugnant to the prevailing feeling of Europe could be productive of good.

I submitted that I had argued the question more as a Russian than a British Minister, at least than as a British Minister having any sinister view with respect to Russian interests ; that if I wished to involve His Imperial Majesty in internal difficulties, to embarrass his administration and to embroil him with his neighbours, I should urge His Imperial Majesty to pursue the course he had stated ; but that the object of my Government was to promote quiet, and there was nothing they more desired than to preserve their connection with Russia and to see His Imperial Majesty enjoy the fruits of his most glorious labours. . . . .

CXII. [F. O. Cont. 7.]
CASTLEREAGH TO LIVERPOOL. (No. 4.)
Vienna, October 2nd, 1814.

The day after my interview with the Emperor, Count Nesslerode called on me, apparently to learn the impression made upon me by my conversation with His Imperial Majesty. I expressed my sense of the reception I had met with whilst I had to regret that the views of our respective Governments were still so wide of each other.

I thought it material to explain myself to Count Nesselrode upon one view of the subject, which the nature of my discussion with the Emperor did not enable me to touch upon, namely upon the possibility of His Imperial Majesty abandoning the political but adhering to the territorial part of his plan. I told him that, feeling as the British Government did upon the question of Polish independence, it could not be expected that we should consent to bear the odium of any disappointment the Nation might experience, whilst Russia carried into effect her views of aggrandizement against the declared sentiments of her Allies, and, as I believe, equally against the general sense of Europe. That it was not only dangerous but degrading to Austria and Prussia in the eyes of their own subjects as well as of Europe, to deny them the semblance of a military frontier, and it was no remedy for such a menacing arrangement, to hold out to these Courts indemnifications elsewhere, to reconcile them to this undisguised state of military dependence upon Russia.

That such a system originating in a previous unjustifiable pretention on the part of Russia would acquire a character the more obnoxious as being an extension of the principle of partitioning by the three Powers of Europe, which had been sufficiently odious when confined to Poland. That it would have the colour of an attempt to revive the system we had all united to destroy, namely one colossal military Power holding two other powerful States in a species of dependence and subjection, and through them making her influence felt in the remotest parts of Europe. That such an attempt would, in the course of time, probably be in like manner resisted and overthrown, but that its revival in any shape was repugnant to the principles on which the Powers had acted, and although it might not lead to immediate war, its remote effects were not less certain, and its immediate consequences must be to cast a shade over the councils of the Emperor as an object of alarm instead of confidence.

I further pressed the embarrassments it must expose us to in Congress especially the plenipotentiaries of those Powers who had publicly to defend the system to which they gave their sanction : That I ooked with more pain to any difference of this nature, wishing to find myself enabled to act in concert with the Allies throughout, but that to do so, they must give me a system which I cou d defend.

Having effected my purpose of undeceiving Count Nesselrode, if he supposed the concession of the political part of the plan would reconcile my Government to the territorial, I left the question here, without receiving from him any explanation. It was impossible however he should have been insensible to the difficulties I had placed before him.

CXIII. [*F. O. Cont.* 7.]
CASTLEREAGH TO LIVERPOOL. (No. 6.)
Vienna, October 9th, 1814.

. . . I acquainted Your Lordship by my last courier, that I feared no effectual resistance could be made to the views of Russia in that quarter, and that the two neighbouring Powers were more likely to seek their own aggrandisement in other directions, than oppose themselves to the pretentions of their more powerful neighbour.

I was not the less confirmed in this impression, from perceiving that the extravagant tone of war which Austria had held, was accompanied by an equal jealousy of Prussia on the side of Saxony, and of France in Italy, which at once proved, that compromise and not resistance was really intended, and further from knowing, that Prussia, feeling she had no other support than Russia to secure to her Saxony against the views both of Austria and France, could not afford to risk that support, by too decisive an opposition to the Emperor's designs with respect to Poland.

Under these circumstances I conceived, that the only chance of doing good was to take up some ground of opposition short of war, and to endeavour to bring Austria and Prussia to a compromise in Germany, in order that they might unite against Russia upon the Polish question.

The existing Congress appeared to me to furnish a suitable expedient, as it enabled those Powers to represent to Russia, without menacing her with war, that they could not make themselves, in the face of Europe, the instruments of their own humiliation, by recommending *that* as just, wise and proper, against which they had been so long engaged in remonstrances—that it was one thing silently to submit, and another to originate a measure of national danger.

With this view, I desired an audience of the King of Prussia. I found His Majesty, as in England, the advocate of the Emperor of Russia, although personally adverse to his measures. I represented that the evil might yet, with proper management, be arrested without a contest. I pressed His Majesty not to abandon the interests of his monarchy in despair, and begged that he would oppose every obstacle, short of arms, to an arrangement which left his provinces uncovered, and his State in obvious dependence upon another Power.

I then opened myself unreservedly to Prince Metternich and Prince Hardenberg, and endeavoured to make them feel the dangers to which their disunion exposed both their monarchies.

The latter explained himself very frankly, that whilst Saxony was in doubt, and with it the possibility of Prussia being suitably reconstructed it was impossible for him, more especially feeling as his King did, to risk the favour of Russia, but that if Saxony was assured to him by Austria and England, he could then unite with Austria, to oppose such resistance as prudence might justify, to Russian encroachments.

I found Prince Metternich without any fixed plan. In descending from his war language he appeared to me to fall into the other extreme, and to think in fact only of compromise. I represented the necessity of an understanding with Prussia, as the only chance of present good, or possibly of future safety. Prince Metternich, the following day, had an interview with Prince Hardenberg, and professed his willingness to enter into his views with respect to Saxony, provided an understanding could thereby be established with respect to Poland and certain German points of minor importance.[1] The parties profess a mutual desire to understand each other, but there is a certain degree of mutual distrust, and fear of Russia, which does not justify me in speaking confidently of the result.

I endeavoured to derive some aid in this attempt from the appui of France—but, unfortunately, the manner in which Prince Talleyrand has conducted himself here, rather excited apprehension in both the Austrian and Prussian ministers, than inspired them with any confidence in his views. Although adverse to the designs of Russia in Poland, he betrayed not less hostility to theirs in Germany and Italy, and both, perhaps not unnaturally, seem equally to dread the appearance of a French force at present in the field.

The question must then take its course amidst all the difficulties that surround it. I shall do my best to give it a safe and creditable direction. If I fail, I shall endeavour to separate the British Government as far as possible from any share in its determination.

CXIV. [F. O. Cont. 7.]
CASTLEREAGH TO LIVERPOOL. (No. 8.)
Vienna, October 9th, 1814.

I enclose a copy of a declaration which after much discussion has been agreed to by the ministers of the eight Powers who signed

---

[1] The fortress of Mayence which Austria wished Bavaria to have as compensation for cessions to herself, while Prussia wished to garrison it, was, however, scarcely a point of minor importance.

the Peace of Paris.[1] The several inclosures which accompany it
will give your Lordship an idea of the various stages of discussion
with which we have at last arrived at this measure.

Prince Talleyrand's[2] official note of the 1st inst., having transpired, it led to a meeting of 13 of the smaller German Powers who
applied to Bavaria to join them, and to support France in resisting what they called, the usurpation of the great Powers. This
gave a most unpleasant complexion to our discussions, and produced an impression, that the object of the French minister was to
sow dissension in Germany, and to put himself at the head of the
discontented States. Prince Tal'eyrand also urged, a little out of
time, a declaration against the admission of Murat's ministers ;
this the Austrian minister opposed as premature and unreasonable
and the discussion became warm. Your Lordship will perceive
that our first measures have not been without difficulty, and
certainly as yet our prospects are not from any quarter promising.
In proportion as the question was discussed, it was evident, that a
Congress never could exist as a deliberative assembly, with a
power of decision by plurality of voices—that Prince Talleyrand's
proposition of a delegated authority to frame a plan was impracticable, as we should have had a question upon the selection
of the plenipotentiaries on the first instance, and that as the
business must take before Congress the form of a negotiation
rather than of a decision upon a question put, the only course that
could facilitate our formal proceedings was to give time for informal discussion in the first instance. This principle, Prince
Talleyrand at last acceded to, and in announcing it to the other
plenipotentiaries, we have endeavoured to cloath it in language
of as little pretention as possible.

The confidential conferences will now go forward, but until the
question of Poland is disposed of, little progress can be expected
to be made.

CXV. [*W. S D. IX.* 323.]
CASTLEREAGH TO LIVERPOOL.
Vienna, October 9th, 1814.
My public letter[3] will have put you au fait of the state of parties

----

[1] Postponing the opening of the Congress. Talleyrand's protest prevented
the acceptance of the schemes of the " Four " for the regulation of the Congress, but he did not succeed in obtaining a position at their side until January.
[2] Talleyrand, for very good reasons, dropped his title of Bénévente at this
time, and Castlereagh therefore ceased to use it in his public dispatches.
[3] CXIII.

here. I wish I could send you a more satisfactory statement. However unpromising, we must not despair of getting it into some better form.

I had a long interview with Prince Hardenberg this morning. He has made a communication of his views this day to Prince Metternich, which, though in certain points exigeant, may lead to an understanding and concert. The Austrian Minister will have much to retrench.

I afterwards payed Prince Talleyrand a visit. I had a long interview with him, in which I took the liberty of representing to him without reserve the errors into which he appeared to me to have fallen, since his arrival here, in conducting the views of his Court, if they had been correctly understood by me at Paris, when I was permitted to confer upon them with His Highness and the King of France.

That I could not disguise from him that the general impression resulting from his demeanour had been to excite distrust and alarm with respect to the views of France ; and that the effect of this had been to deprive him of his just and natural influence for the purposes of moderating excessive pretensions, whilst it united all to preserve the general system ; that instead of presenting himself here as disposed to cavil, to traverse, and to create a discontented party in Germany, he ought to have come to carry his own avowed object (which I understand he had limited to Naples), and to moderate excessive pretensions from whatever quarter, but with a disposition to support the councils of the confederacy against anarchy and petty intrigue.

That it was not for the Bourbons, who had been restored by the Allies to assume the tone of reprobating or throwing odium upon the arrangements which had kept the confederacy together. That it was impossible to suppose that, in conducting so great and complicated a cause to a successful issue, concessions to interested views were not at moments wise and requisite. That France having been delivered by this combination, and the legitimate family restored, both ought to regard the means which had been applied to this end in the spirit of favour and indulgence, and not endeavour to thwart it upon general reasoning, without any due consideration of the circumstances of the moment.

That in estimating his means of usefully moderating the arrangements in progress, it was a gratuitous sacrifice of influence to be opposing at once the favourite objects of all the respective Powers, instead of suffering the general sentiment to effect its first object, of modifying as far as possible the extravagant pretensions of Russia on the side of Poland ; in the event of succeeding in which it would have been then open for him, without complication and counteraction, to try either to moderate the demands of Prussia upon Saxony, or to urge the union of all the Powers in support of the Sicilian family. But that as His Highness had conducted it, he had sacrificed all useful influence, and united all against himself.

I pressed upon his attention that, more especially with respect to success on the Neapolitan point, conciliation was his duty. That so far from wishing to bring it into early decision, and upon a collateral point, his object should be (so long, at least, as the nature of the proceeding did not involve any concession of principle in favour of Murat) to keep it out of the way till the great Powers, assured of their own objects, felt themselves at liberty to take up such a question as this.

Prince Talleyrand received with perfect good humour my remonstrances except so far as to justify his past intentions ; but he did not combat my statement with respect to the future. On the contrary, he indicated a disposition to take the questions in the order I had stated, and seemed to admit that for any useful purpose the resistance ought not to be pushed beyond what certain of the Allied Powers could support.

I cannot answer for this explanation with the Prince de Talleyrand being a protection against the revival of inconvenient and fruitless controversy ; but I think it has given him more precise notions of the mode in which he may render service, if he be so disposed. The course His Highness adopted at the instant, and the impression produced, left me no alternative but to uphold decisively the authority of the Alliance, which had advanced us to our present position. Whilst this conduct was tempered with every endeavour to conciliate France, it may, I trust, induce Prince Talleyrand to direct his exertions rather to modify our course than to speculate either upon disuniting or overpowering us, if such can have been his object, which I hardly believe to have been the case.

I left him in a temper apparently to be of use ; but I have lived now long enough with my foreign colleagues not to rely very implicitly upon any appearances.

CXVI. [*F. O. Cont. 7.*]
CASTLEREAGH TO LIVERPOOL. (No. 9.)
Vienna, October 14th, 1814.

Since I last wrote, I received the enclosed communication from Prince Hardenberg [1] As there seemed to be much indecision in the Austrian councils, I considered that there ought to be the less hesitation on the part of the Prince Regent, in marking the decided interest His Royal Highness takes in the effectual re-construction of Prussia. I accordingly addressed to His Highness the enclosed letters.[2] Prince Metternich's answer has not yet been received.

I also thought it desirable as the Emperor of Russia was daily committing himself in conversation upon the question of Poland, to ask an audience, in which I might impress His Imperial Majesty's mind with the difficulties of the course he was pursuing, both under his Treaties, and upon principles of general policy.

Having solicited an audience, His Imperial Majesty was so gracious as to signify his intention of calling yesterday on Lady Castlereagh, after which I was honoured with an interview of an hour and a half. In order to avoid the inaccuracy with which such questions are examined in conversation, and that no doubt might rest as to my sentiments (His Imperial Majesty having taken credit in a conversation with my brother, for Prince Metternich's concurrence in his views) I thought it right to address the inclosed letter to the Emperor transmitting it in the memorandum [3] which was forwarded to Your Lordship by the last messenger, and I gave these documents to His Imperial Majesty at the close of our discussion, as an unreserved record of what I felt it my duty to submit to him on this important subject.

I am sorry to have to report to your Lordship that the interview ended without any relaxation of opinion on either side, His Imperial Majesty appearing to adhere with much warmth and tenacity to his views, both political and territorial, than when I last waited upon him. He seemed to reject any idea of compromise with respect to the mode of ameliorating Poland, and put forward his assumption of the crown as indispensible to his object. The Emperor endeavoured to defend his plan, upon the ground that,

---

[1] Hardenberg to Castlereagh and Metternich, October 9th, 1814, formally asking for the assent of Austria and England to the incorporation of Saxony in Prussia. D'Angeberg, *Le Congrès de Vienne*, 1934.

[2] Castlereagh to Hardenberg, October 11th, 1814, giving assent on condition of Prussian co-operation on the Polish point.

[3] A précis of the letter and Memorandum follows this dispatch. The first Memorandum had been drawn up originally by Castlereagh to establish a basis of discussion for Austria and Prussia on the Polish question which he could defend as a British minister.

by thus establishing a Polish Kingdom, he would create a balance and check upon Russian power. That Russia, as at present constituted, was too large, but that when the Russian Provinces were united under a free system, and his Russian army withdrawn beyond the Niemen, Europe would have nothing to fear.

I represented that, with a view to war, the cantonment of one branch of his military force somewhat further to the rear, would make, at most, the difference of three weeks, in its assembly for service at the opening of a campaign ; that the question for Europe was the gross amount of his force, and that so far from being tranquillized by this species of distribution, they would consider it only as a means to actively call forth the military energies of Poland in his support, by flattering the pride of the nation.

In pressing upon the Emperor the rights of Austria under the Treaty of the 27th June [1813] His Imperial Majesty was at first embarrassed, and appeared to have forgot the articles. After some reflection, he attempted to bring his intended arrangement within the words of the Treaty, by stating, that he meant to cede the half of the Salines which belonged to the Dutchy, to Austria, an object too trifling to have deserved notice, much less to be put forward in satisfaction of such an engagement[1].

When driven in argument upon the territorial question, His Imperial Majesty again took shelter under his moral duty, that if it was merely a question of territory, he would yield it without a struggle, but that it involved the happiness of the Poles, and the people would never forgive his ceding them. I asked His Imperial Majesty how he distinguished between his duty to the Poles on one side of his line and on the other, and that, where he could not satisfy his principle without denying even to Prussia any share, he should not do violence to his engagements with Austria, to please the Poles.

I further represented, that if the principle of moral duty was so far limited as to be controlled and even extinguished by deference for Russian interests, which His Imperial Majesty had declared it was, in the instance of making Poland really free, he must not expect other States to admit this consideration as binding upon them, to the sacrifice of interests not less essential.

I met the Emperor afterwards in the evening at court. His Imperial Majesty assumed a very gracious manner, and said he always respected my *franchise*, although he differed with me in

[1] By the Treaty of Reichenbach [See p. 6] Poland was to be partitioned between the three Powers. The Salines are the salt mines of Wiliczka.

opinion. I must reserve till another opportunity to inform Your Lordship of the steps taken by me in consequence of this conversation with the Emperor, and of the impression produced by it upon the ministers of the other Powers.

P.S. I forgot to mention that towards the close of the conversation the Emperor regretted the slowness of our progress, and stated the necessity of giving more activity to our march. I ventured to observe, that it could not be otherwise than slow, when upon the first great question, which was, in its nature, preliminary to all others, we had the misfortune to find ourselves all opposed in sentiment to His Imperial Majesty. The Emperor insinuated that this question could only end in one way as he was in possession. I observed, that it was very true, His Imperial Majesty was in possession and he must know that no one was less disposed than myself hostilely to dispute that possession, but I was sure His Imperial Majesty would not feel satisfied to rest his pretensions on a title of conquest in opposition to the general sentiment of Europe. That Great Britain had not acted upon such a principle as making her conquests the measure of her claims, and that it was perhaps to a very different principle acted upon on her part, that His Imperial Majesty had achieved what he had done and acquired the possession in question.

VISCOUNT CASTLEREAGH TO THE EMPEROR OF ALL THE RUSSIAS.[1]

Vienna, October 12th, 1814.

Since Great Britain is the last Power whose interests could be endangered by any determination of H.I.M. on the side of Poland, Castlereagh may be mistaken in his judgment, but on no question can he be considered a more impartial authority. Although he is opposed to H.I.M.'s pretensions on the Duchy of Warsaw he is not, therefore, against a liberal and important aggrandizement of the Polish frontier, it is only to the extent and method of the increase to which he objects. H.I.M. may receive an ample pledge of European gratitude without imposing upon his neighbours an arrangement inconsistent with the relations of independent States with each other.

Past experience relieves the British Government from any suspicion of a policy adverse to the interests of Russia : Castlereagh refers to their recent policy as regards Norway, in Turkey, and in Persia, as evidence of this. He does so from an anxiety that his motives shall not be misinterpreted if he is compelled in this, " the fourth instance of Russian aggrandizement within a few years," to press for a modification of H.I.M.'s pretensions.

The future fate and interests of Europe are likely to be deeply influenced by the issue of the present Congress : the character of its transactions will depend upon the mode and temper in which it shall be wound up : a million of population more or less must be secondary in H.I.M.'s mind compared to the glory and the service rendered by setting Europe an example of generosity and moderation. Castlereagh declares his " solemn conviction that it depends exclusively upon the temper in which your Imperial Majesty shall meet the questions which more immediately concern your own empire, whether the present Congress shall prove a blessing to mankind, or only exhibit a scene of

[1] Précis of letter in W. S. D. IX. 329.

discordant intrigue, and a lawless scramble for power." H.I.M.'s position in Europe enables him to do anything for the general happiness if he founds his intervention upon just principles : if he should leave public opinion behind him there could be no just and stable order of things in Europe and H.I.M. would be regarded for the first time as an object of alarm instead of confidence.

Castlereagh is persuaded that there is a course open to H.I.M. which will combine his beneficent intentions to his Polish subjects with what his Allies claim at his hands.   They do not desire him to enter into engagements restrictive of his sovereign authority over his own provinces ; they only wish him to ameliorate gradually the frame of his Polish administration, and to avoid that species of measure which may create alarm both in Russia and the neighbouring states, and which, " however it may gratify the ambition of a few individuals of great family in Poland, may, in fact, bring less of real liberty and happiness to the people than a more measured and unostentatious change in the system of their administration."

If the political question could be settled it would only remain for H.I.M. to arrange his frontier according to the Treaty of the 27th June, 1813, which might be done, leaving H.I.M. in possession of the greater part of the Duchy of Warsaw, whilst his Allies would obtain " that species of frontier which no independent Power can forego either with dignity or with safety." . . .

First Memorandum on the Polish Question.[1]

Quotes from the Treaty of Kalisch, signed by Russia and Prussia on February 28th, 1813, the principles on which that Treaty was founded and which were to be the rule for the future conduct of the two Powers, also the Treaties of June 27th, and September 9th[2] entered into by Russia, Austria, and Prussia, by which they bound themselves to procure a friendly arrangement with regard to the future of the Duchy of Warsaw.

Nevertheless, H.I.M. considers himself entitled to dispose of the whole Duchy and, with the exception of territory which he will assign to Prussia as a matter of grace and favour, he intends to unite it with his own Polish provinces and erect a separate monarchy to be governed by himself as King of Poland to the consequent alarm of Austria and Prussia and the general apprehension of Europe. The forced annexation of so large a territory to Russia, already much increased by her recent conquests ; her advance into the heart of Germany ; and the prospect of renewed contests between the Poles and their neighbours, make tranquility impossible and justify these alarms. The public mind is unable to conceive upon what grounds the measure is adopted and alleges that it is in direct opposition to the engagements made with Austria and Prussia.   It cannot be supposed that, when Austria and Prussia stipulated *for the dissolution of the Duchy of Warsaw*, they would have agreed to so dangerous a revival of it under the Crown of Russia, an arrangement much more alarming to their respective States.   H.I.M. must be sensible that his policy is against the faith of his most solemn engagements, and it is trusted that when he seriously examines these engagements he will be the first to recognise them and to desist from any inconsistent projects.

It is no less difficult to conceive how the plan can be regarded as a moral duty. If H.I.M. is seriously impressed with the necessity of ameliorating the condition of the Poles, the power is sufficiently in his hands at present with regard to his own Polish provinces and his fair proportion of the Duchy of Warsaw without attempting an aggrandizement so enormous and so menacing.   If moral duty requires so decisive a change as the revival of the Polish monarchy, let them be rendered again really independent as a nation instead of making two-thirds of them a mere formidable military instrument in the hands of a single Power. Such a measure would be applauded by all Europe and would be cheerfully acquiesced in both Austria and Prussia.

[1] Précis of document in W. S. D. IX. 332.
[2] See *Supra*, pp. 6 and 81.

It is further alleged that, so long as H.I.M. adheres to this project, it is impossible that any plan for the reconstruction of Europe can be brought forward, or that the present Congress can be assembled to discuss any such arrangement. It cannot be expected that Austria and Prussia should come forward of their own accord and propose to leave their dominions without a military frontier. How unfortunate will be the predicament of Europe if H.I.M. shall adhere to his purpose against the general sense, and if the Plenipotentiaries of the other Powers shall be obliged to inform the representatives of all the States assembled at Vienna that they are deprived, by such a line of conduct on the part of Russia, of any hope of proposing such a settlement as they have pledged themselves to give to Europe ! It seems that no other course can be adopted unless H.I.M. shall consider seriously the consequences which must result from his present measure.

CXVII. [*W. S. D. IX.* 342.]
LIVERPOOL TO CASTLEREAGH.
Fife House, October 14th, 1814.

. . . However this question of Poland may now end, it cannot be settled either creditably or satisfactorily. The Emperor of Russia need never have stirred it, and in that case the Powers of Europe would have left the three States most interested to settle the question *à l'aimable* amongst themselves ; but as it has been once mooted, it becomes a question of serious embarrassment, and it is very material that we should lose no character by the part we take in it.

I am inclined to think that the less we have to do with it, except as far as regards giving our opinion, the better. I have sent you a short Memorandum on the subject, containing the ideas which have occurred to me upon it. They very much correspond with what passed at a meeting at your house before you left England ; but the train of reasoning is drawn out with more precision than occurred to me at that time, and the idea of the Duchy of Warsaw being preserved as an independent State under an independent sovereign, I think it may be of importance to put forward, for the reasons given in the Memorandum.

It is impossible to know how far you may have advanced on this and other subjects before you receive this letter ; but at all events the Memorandum can do no harm, and you will make such use of the contents of it as you may judge upon the whole most advisable. . . .

MEMORANDUM RESPECTING POLAND.
October 14th, 1814.

. . . It is obvious that an arrangement may be made with respect to the Duchy of Warsaw upon either of the three following principles :—

1st. It may be divided between the three great Powers, and so made to constitute a part of each of their dominions. Or

2ndly. It may be preserved as an independent State under an independent prince. Or

3rdly. It may be assigned to one of the three great Powers as an independent State, which under the present circumstances would be Russia.

Of these three alternatives, I should certainly consider the third the worst for the general interests of Europe.

The second would preserve the principle of Polish independence, and might lead the inhabitants of the dismembered provinces to look to their reunion at some period more or less remote with the Duchy of Warsaw ; but the weakness of the Power itself would in this case afford a reasonable security to the neighbouring Powers against the accomplishment of any such object, and at all events the three Powers would be upon an equal footing, and have a common interest in opposing any measure which was likely to produce such an effect. But if the Duchy of Warsaw is to be an independent State under the Emperor of Russia, the independent principle will not only be preserved, but it will be preserved under a monarch whose power will be sufficient to give encouragement to the disaffected in the Austrian and Prussian Polish provinces, to seize the first opportunity of resisting their acknowledged Sovereigns, and of reuniting themselves under a head whom they will consider as strong enough to protect them, and who will be the Sovereign of a country which will be regarded as the parent stock of Polish independence.

I cannot, however, conceal from you that this last project would be less unpopular in this country than the measure of complete partition, and consequently of Polish annihilation.   If we are to come to either of these alternatives, I think it would be very desirable that there should, if possible, be some record of our having expressed our opinion how desirable it would be to restore Poland on the principle of 1792, and of our having made some effort for that which we are more entitled to ask, the independence of the Duchy of Warsaw under a neutral Sovereign. . . .

CXVIII. (F. O. Cont. 7.)
CASTLEREAGH TO LIVERPOOL. (No. 11.)
Vienna, October 20th, 1814.

Since my conversation with the Emperor, I cannot report to your Lordship that the negotiations here have assumed any more decisive aspect.

I communicated confidentially to the Austrian and Prussian ministers what had passed, also the letter I had addressed to His Imperial Majesty.[1] They both expressed their sense of the part I had taken, and desired to be permitted to put their respective sovereigns in possession of both the documents, that had been delivered to the Emperor.   Hitherto no decisive explanation has taken place on the part of Austria upon the confidential overture from Prussia. Both courts possess a conviction, that nothing but a strict and intimate union between Austria and Prussia can preserve their independence, but I have not been yet able to bring Prince Metternich to give an answer to Prince Hardenberg's letter.[2] He has, as I learn, made up his mind, and received the Emperor's authority on the point of Saxony, and has given a verbal consent to the provisional administration being assumed by Prussia ; but nothing yet in writing has passed.

[1] See CXVI.
[2] Of the 9th October. See CXVI. p. 206, note 1.

CXIX. [*F. O. Cont.* 7.]
CASTLEREAGH TO LIVERPOOL. (No. 12.)
October 24th, 1814.

[Transmits the Austrian answer to the Prussian demand for Saxony.¹] . . . Having been shown the brouillon of the proposed answer on the night of the 22nd, I took the earliest opportunity of preparing Prince Hardenberg for it, foreseeing that the point of Mayence was likely to prove a serious impediment in the way of an understanding. I found him, when I saw him next morning, extremely warm upon this subject. I did not combat the validity of his reasoning, but represented that, important as this fortress was, it should not be made an obstacle to so salutary a measure, as the union of the two great German Powers at such a conjuncture.

That the wishes as well as the interests of Great Britain must be on the side of the Northern States, but when Austria chose to rely upon Bavaria, and to incur the greater risque upon such a combination, it appeared to me, that Prussia never could persuade the world, that she, bonâ fide, desired the Alliance, if she broke off upon this single condition, after Austria had made to her so great a sacrifice as the Saxon point.

It was agreed that the Austrian and Prussian ministers should meet the following day (Sunday) at my house, and I have the gratification to state, that the result was satisfactory. Prince Hardenberg expressed himself satisfied with the explanations he had received on the point of Saxony, reserving to himself to reply to Prince Metternich's reasoning against the total incorporation of Saxony with Prussia. He stated strongly his objections to entrusting so important a fortress as Mayence to Bavaria alone ; but was ready to reserve these points for further discussion (satisfied that they could not impede the desired union) and proceed at once to act in concert with Austria, and England upon the Polish question.

The measures to be jointly adopted with this view were then discussed : and they desired me to prepare a Memorandum of the result, a copy of which (No. 4)² I now enclose, on which they mean to take the pleasure of their respective sovereigns.

I took occasion to see Prince Talleyrand soon after, anxious to render his course, as far as possible, conformable to our views.

¹ Metternich to Hardenberg, October 22nd, 1814, which, while stating explicitly all the objections to the incorporation of all Saxony in Prussia, gave Austria's consent to the Prussian demands on condition that the Polish negotiations were successful and that Mayence went to Bavaria. D'Angeberg, 1316.
² Appended at the close of this dispatch.

I found he had had an interview with the Emperor of Russia, in which he had been pressing his Saxon views (and if I may credit His Imperial Majesty's confidential report of the conversation to me) with a disposition to make his line on the Polish question subservient to them. The Emperor, however, was equally obdurate with him upon both. In this fact their respective reports concurred, but there can be no doubt that attempts are making, principally through Prince Czartoriski, to play a back game of this description. I have done my best to counteract it, and shall desire the Duke of Wellington, as from himself, to insinuate through M. de Blacas, that any attempt on the part of France to make such a collateral point as that of Saxony a question of war, in subversion of the more important object of opposing a barrier to Russia, must, in all probability, not only destroy their friendly relations with England, but lead to immediate hostilities, and that its obvious and first effect must be to compel England to sign a peace with Murat, in order to place Austria in security on the side of Italy, and thus enable her to direct her efforts to her Polish frontier. Whereas, if France acts upon the broad principles of European equilibrium, instead of fighting smaller points of local influence, in the event of success attending the common effort with respect to Poland, she would have improved means of urging amicably upon Prussia some modification of her demands upon Saxony : that in thus pursuing the questions in the order of their importance, success, more or less, might attend her exertions on the one or on both : but that, in the inverse order, failure and political confusion were likely to ensue.

The Emperor of Russia leaves Vienna to-morrow for Buda and returns on the 30th. The Emperor of Austria and King of Prussia commenced their journey this morning.

MEMORANDUM ON THE BEST METHOD OF HANDLING THE POLISH QUESTION.[1]

The question of Poland, and the Treaties affecting it, having been in the fullest manner under deliberate consideration of the Emperor of Russia, any further hesitation in bringing His Imperial Majesty to a distinct decision, can be productive of no possible advantage, and may lead to an injurious interpretation of the determination of his Allies thereupon.

It is conceived to be of the utmost importance, even before H.I.M. proceeds to Buda, that he should be apprized of the serious purpose which his Allies entertain of pressing upon H.I.M. what they consider themselves as well by their treaties as by general principles of policy and justice entitled to claim from His Imperial Majesty.

That they should further inform the Emperor, that immediately upon His Imperial Majesty's return to Vienna, they propose to make another attempt to

[1] F. O. Continent, 7. French translation in D'Angeberg, 291, where, however, it is wrongly dated.

settle this question amicably and confidentially with him ; in the event of succeeding in which they flatter themselves to be enabled very speedily to bring to a satisfactory arrangement the other affairs of Europe, and would for that purpose desire a further adjournment of the Congress.

If, on the contrary, they should unfortunately fail in arriving at the conclusion which they so much desire, they will in that case feel it their duty to suffer the Congress to meet as now fixed, before whom the subject must be entered upon formally and officially.

It is proposed, in order that the Ministers of the two Powers should be fully prepared to submit to the Emperor their final determination on his return, that they should forthwith meet to settle the minimum of concession on the part of the Emperor that would satisfy their claims.

That in laying this determination before the Emperor, in the names of their respective Courts, they should explain to him, that, for the sake of preserving unimpaired the harmony which had throughout distinguished the Alliance, they had reduced their proposals within the narrowest possible limits.

That in the event of being compelled to adopt a different course, they must be considered as fully entitled to propose other and more extended terms.

That it may be desirable even in this confidential overture to propose to the Emperor, alterations on the political branch of the question in order to keep it always in view, that it is Russia alone, and not the other Courts, which really forms the obstacles of Polish liberation.

In the event of the question becoming one of discussion in Congress, it is suggested that the proceeding may properly originate in an official note from the Austrian Minister, separately or conjointly with the Prussian, addressed to the Ministers of Russia and claiming from that Power the execution of the secret and separate Article of the Treaty of the 27th of June, 1813, and that, the said note, after fully exposing the views, rights, and sentiments of the said Powers, should conclude by offering to the Emperor's option, one or other of the following alterations :—

First.   The complete and entire reunion of Poland under an independent Sovereign as it existed previous to the first Partition, to the accomplishment of which arrangement, if it shall be acceptable to the Emperor, Austria and Prussia are ready to make the requisite sacrifices.

Second.   If the Emperor objects to this measure as involving too great a sacrifice of territory and dominions on the part of Russia the Courts of Austria and Prussia are willing to consent to a similar measure as applicable to the Kingdom of Poland as it stood in 1791, when it gave itself a free constitution under Poniatowski.

Thirdly.   Or if the Emperor of Russia shall reject the erection of Poland upon a territorial scale, however modified, into a Kingdom really independent, and shall prefer adhering to the principle of Partition, then the two Powers (protesting against his right to act with respect to his division of Poland in defiance of the stipulation of the Convention of 1797) are willing to agree to adhere to the said principle of Partition, provided the same be equitably applied and with a due regard to the security in a military point of view, of their respective States.

In execution of which principle they propose that the Vistula throughout the Duchy of Warsaw to Sandomir should be the Russian Boundary, Prussia receiving them on the right bank, if the Emperor should desire to possess Warsaw on the left.

That in addition to the above, Austria should address a separate note to Prussia, claiming her intervention under the Treaty of September, 1813, by which she engages to see the obligations of the Treaty of June, 1813, executed à l'aimable.

That copies of these several notes should be laid before Congress, and that the several Powers of Europe should be invited to support the said overture, and to declare to the Emperor of Russia, to what extent and upon what conditions, Europe in Congress can or cannot admit His Imperial Majesty's pretensions to an aggrandizement in Poland.

It is desirable that the Emperor should be made distinctly to understand, that, however willing the Allies may be to avert so painful an appeal, by every possible modification of their just claims, in the spirit of which sentiment they had agreed to the minimum proposed to His Imperial Majesty, yet that when driven to make that appeal in the presence of Europe, by refusal of such modification, they must then adhere more rigidly to the scale of their just pretensions, and that it would rest with the Powers in Congress assembled to decide upon the measures which should be called for by so alarming an infraction of Treaties, and by an encroachment upon the military security of independent and neighbouring Allied States, in contravention of the express stipulations of subsisting engagements.

CXX. [*F. O. Cont.* 7.]
CASTLEREAGH TO LIVERPOOL. (No. 13.)
Vienna, October 25th, 1814.

I think it right to acquaint Your Lordship, that notwithstanding the Duke of Wellington's repeated agitations of the question at Paris, and my own representations to Prince Talleyrand here, no answer whatever has yet been returned to my official note of the 8th [1] instant on the Slave Trade.

The more I have occasion to observe the temper of foreign Powers on the question of the abolition, the more strongly impressed I am with a sense of the prejudice that results not only to the interests of the question itself, but of our foreign relations generally from the display of popular impatience which has been excited and is kept up in England upon this subject.

It is impossible to persuade foreign nations that this sentiment is unmixed with the views of colonial policy, and their Cabinets, who can better estimate the real and virtuous motives which guide us on this question, see in the very impatience of the nation a powerful instrument which they expect to force, at a convenient moment, the British Government upon some favourite object of policy.

I am conscious that we have done an act of indispensable duty, under the circumstances in which we have been placed, in making to the French and Spanish Governments the propositions we have done, but I am still more firmly persuaded, that we should be at this moment in fact nearer our object if the Government had been permitted to pursue this object with its ordinary means of influence and persuasion instead of being placed in the predicament of being expected to purchase concessions on this point almost at any sacrifice.

[1] This carried on a negotiation begun at Paris. France had been offered the return of a Colony or monetary compensation, if she would abolish the Slave Trade immediately. A similar proposal had been made to Spain through Sir Henry Wellesley.

It will be my duty as it will be my personal pride to employ every possible effort to further this object, but I never can cease to feel, that the manner in which the efforts of the Government in this cause were last year received, and the coldness if not the tone of disapprobation, in which the most efficient arrangements towards a final abolition which had yet been achieved were met both in Parliament and in the Country, has neither augmented our means of discharging our public duties upon this, nor any other question of foreign policy.

I hope in the course of a few days to have an abrégé [sic] of the evidence taken before the committee of the House of Commons, which I have caused to be translated into French, in a state to deliver to the several plenipotentiaries now here. I inclose a short introductory preface to prepare their minds for the measure of excluding, if necessary, from their markets colonial produce grown within the dominion of States who shall refuse to enter into concert for abolishing the trade in slaves.

I received a more compendious abstract of this nature, which was prepared at Paris, I believe by Mr. Clarkson, under the Duke of Wellington's directions, but I did not wish to rely exclusively upon this, as it omitted several of the latter chapters of the work, from which it was taken, and which I am satisfied are not the least important with a view to impression here. I mean those that go to prove the measure of abolition to be consistent with the private interest of the planter and with the due cultivation of the country.

Your Lordship is sufficiently apprized of the state in which matters have hitherto stood here, to be aware that I could not possibly have brought this question hitherto into discussion. I shall seize the first favourable moment for doing so, but for the reasons already stated, I had rather not hazard a decision till the principal questions of a political nature are at least further advanced towards a decision.

CXXI. [*F. O. Cont.* 7.]

CASTLEREAGH TO LIVERPOOL. (No. 14.)

Vienna, October 25th, 1814.

In order that the Duke of Wellington might observe with the more effect the temper of the French Government on the events in progress here, and also that His Grace might be enabled to correct erroneous impressions, I have invariably transmitted all my dispatches home under flying seal for his perusal. I now send Your Lordship copy of a private letter received from His Grace with my answer.[1] My opinion is, that, until the French Government shall be distinctly convinced that they cannot make the Saxon question a point of authority, they will continue to embarrass themselves and us by their mode of treating it.

If France would lay her shoulders fairly to the Polish point, I should not despair of getting additional territorial means on that side, to re-construct Prussia, in which case I should hope, that the unpopularity of entirely extinguishing Saxony might reconcile Prussia to a modification of her pretentions, but to have any weight at the proper moment on such a question, I should deem it highly impolitick in me to enter it by anticipation or to depart from the acquiescence I have throughout the last twelve months, under every change of fortune, uniformly expressed on the part of my Court, that the fate of Saxony should be considered subordinate, after the glorious efforts of Prussia in the war, to the effectual re-construction of that Power.

P.S. The Emperor of Russia told me he was preparing an answer to my communication relative to Poland. I understand that it is written by Prince Czartoriski.

CXXII. [W. S. D. IX. 372.]
CASTLEREAGH TO WELLINGTON.
Vienna, October 25th, 1814.

The events of the few last days, coupled with your letter of the 8th, have rendered me apprehensive that any decisive effort to abate the Russian demands may be defeated by the counter-acting exertions of France on the Saxon point. It has occurred to me that you might keep down any rising temper at the Tuileries by throwing before M. de Blacas[2] the possible consequences to which a hostile interference, such as he appears to countenance on the part of France, might lead.

You will perceive, from my several despatches, that the difference in principle between M. Talleyrand and me is chiefly that I wish to direct my main efforts to secure an equilibrium in Europe ; to which objects, as far as principle will permit, I wish to make all local points subordinate. M. Talleyrand appears to me, on the contrary, more intent upon particular points of influence than upon the general balance to be estab-

[1] Wellington to Castlereagh, October 8th, 1814, stating that France wished to preserve Saxony, W.S.D. IX. 325. Castlereagh's reply follows (CXXII.)
[2] The principal Minister of Louis XVIII, an émigré who was by no means well disposed towards Talleyrand.

lished ; and his efforts upon the Neapolitan and Saxon questions are frequently made at the expense of the more important question of Poland, without essentially serving either of those interests upon which he is most intent.

I was, from the outset, aware of the extreme difficulty of making Prussia a useful ally in the present discussions, connected closely as she has been with Russia ; but it appeared to me that, notwithstanding the King's *liaison* with the Emperor, it ought not to be despaired of, under the known sentiments of the Prussian Cabinet, more especially as it was difficult to found a satisfactory system of balance in Europe, unless Prussia could be induced to take a part.

Two alternatives alone presented themselves for consideration —a union of the two great German Powers, supported by Great Britain, and thus combining the minor States of Germany, together with Holland, in an intermediary system between Russia and France—or a union of Austria, France, and the Southern States against the Northern Powers, with Russia and Prussia in close alliance.

It would have been to be wished that the arrangements upon a peace could have been effected in Europe without giving rise to any combination whatever of this nature, and that, at the end of so long a struggle, the several Powers might have enjoyed some repose, without forming calculations that always augment the risks of war ; but the tone and conduct of Russia have disappointed this hope, and forced upon us fresh considerations.

In weighing the conveniences and inconveniences of the latter of these alternatives, the objections appeared to me strongly to preponderate, and especially as affecting *our* interests. Necessity might dictate such a system, but not choice. It appeared, in the first instance, difficult to cement, on account of the fundamental jealousy existing between Austria and France, especially upon the point of Italian preponderance. If adopted in order to control Russian power, and, with this view, should it be supported by Great Britain, it rendered Holland and the Low Countries dependant on France for their support, instead of having Prussia and the Northern States of Germany as their natural protectors. It presented the further inconvenience, in case of war, of exposing all the recent cessions by France to re-occupation by French armies, as the seat of war might happen to present itself.

These considerations were sufficiently weighty to induce me to be of opinion that, however pure the intentions of the King of France were, and however friendly, we ought not to risk so much upon French connexion, and that it was wiser to preserve, as far as possible, the good-will of France, whilst we laboured to unite Germany for its own preservation against Russia.

I was induced to prefer this course, first, as affording the best chance, if Prussia could be brought forward, of averting the Polish danger without a war ; and, secondly, if we failed in this object, as opposing the best barrier to further encroachments on the part of Russia, whilst it afforded that natural cover to our interests on the side of Flanders, without leaving them at the mercy of a combination formed somewhat out of the natural course of political interest.

I have troubled you with this outline of the policy upon which I have been acting here, that you may use your own discretion, as occasions arise, of preparing and reconciling the mind of the French Government to a concert between the two limitrophe Powers against Russian encroachment and dictation. You will find their minds (at least Prince Talleyrand's is) very averse to Russia, and impatient of the notion of any union between Austria and Prussia ; yet, while they most inconsistently object to such a union, they admit that it is the only mode in which Russia can be kept within due bounds.

If France were a feeble and menaced Power, she might well feel jealous of such a German alliance ; but, as her direct interests are out of all danger, it is unreasonable that she should impede the sole means that remain to Germany of preserving its independence, in order either to indulge a sentiment towards the King of Saxony, or to create a French party amongst the minor States. France need never dread a German league : it is in its nature inoffensive, and there is no reason to fear that the union between Austria and Prussia will be such as to endanger the liberties of other States.

Until the determination of Austria and Prussia is more fully established, I have to beg your Grace will make your reasoning general, and not admit that any negotiation is in progress.

CXXIII. [*W. S. D. IX.* 382.]
LIVERPOOL TO CASTLEREAGH.
Fife House, October 28th, 1814.

I send you enclosed a memorandum of Vansittart's[1] on reading your despatches of the 14th inst. I think his paper contains very much the impression of several of our other colleagues, viz., that we have done enough on this question of Poland, and that if our

[1] Appended to this letter. Vansittart was Chancellor of the Exchequer.

efforts should not have been successful, the time is now come when, according to one of your former despatches, it would be far better that we should withdraw ourselves from the question altogether, and reserve ourselves for points on which we have a more immediate and direct interest.

I am the more strongly inclined to this opinion because I am fully persuaded, as I have already said, that no arrangement respecting Poland can now be either creditable or satisfactory.

I think it very material that we should likewise consider that our war with America will probably now be of some duration. We owe it, therefore, to ourselves not to make enemies in other quarters if we can avoid it, for I cannot but feel apprehensive that some of our European Allies will not be indisposed to favour the Americans ; and if the Emperor of Russia should be desirous of taking up their cause, we are well aware, from some of Lord Walpole's late communications, that there is a most powerful party in Russia to support him. . . .

MEMORANDUM BY MR. VANSITTART.

I begin to apprehend that we are making ourselves too much principals in the disputes respecting Poland. The pretensions of Russia evidently endanger the security and independence of Austria and Prussia ; but those Powers are at least wavering in their resistance, if not disposed to acquiesce, for the sake of securing objects still more interesting to them. We run the risk, therefore, of being disavowed, and represented abroad as actuated by a jealousy of the greatness of Russia, and at home as the advocates and instigators of a system of partition.

I cannot look without apprehension at the means by which (if at all) the views of Russia can be counteracted. I can see no other than by bringing forward France as a leading Power either in war or negotiation, and re-establishing her influence in the centre of Europe, which it has cost us so much to overturn.

After all, we can have no security against some treacherous compromise between France and Russia ; and there is even a great probability that in resentment of our interference, the Emperor of Russia may be disposed to listen to some suggestion for bringing forward questions of maritime law at the Congress.

With respect to the Polish question itself, I cannot help thinking there is some weight in the Emperor's observation to Lord Castlereagh, " that Russia would gain more power by acquiring half the Duchy of Warsaw as a province than the whole as a Kingdom." The Emperor, in accepting the crown of Poland, becomes bound to give the kingdom a constitution ; and whether he restores the constitution of 1790, or the old one, or frames a new one, he will infallibly cripple the powers of his government, and render the Poles much less manageable than when directly subjects of Russia. There is, besides, the greatest probability that in the course of one or two generations, at the utmost, the nominal independence of Poland would become real. A minority, or a weak reign, in Russia would bring about a separation which all the other Powers of Europe would be inclined to countenance.

In the meantime, as far as British interests are concerned, I think the decision of the question of no great political importance to us either way ; and that in a commercial point of view we should reap considerable advantage even from a nominal independence of Poland. Russia, from whatever cause, shows the strongest spirit or hostility against our trade ; and nothing could so effectually defeat her restrictive regulations as the opening the ports of an adjoining kingdom, in which, even if similar prohibitions were nominally imposed, they would be constantly evaded. It is, indeed, well known that previously to the final partition of Poland large quantities of British goods, prohibited in Russia, always found their way there through the Polish ports ; and the same thing, I am told, in a degree takes place at present in the uncertainty of the final settlement.

These ideas occurred to me upon reading the conversations of the Emperor of Russia with Lord Castlereagh and Lord Stuart, and they lead me to this practical conclusion, that though we were bound to support to a certain extent the endeavours of Austria and Prussia to prevent the extension of a dominion dangerous to their independence, yet that we have now fully performed all that could be expected from us, and that we ought to avoid irritating Russia by a pertinacious opposition which is so unlikely to be successful.

CXXIV. [*W. S. D. IX.* 401.]

LIVERPOOL TO CASTLEREAGH.

Fife House, November 2nd, 1814.

. . . . I should hope, however, that you will soon be able to make some way in the negotiations. The first point on these occasions, if not the greatest difficulty, always takes more time in settling than any other. In this case it is the principal, and most complicated difficulty, not only from its own importance, but in consequence of the variety of interests which must be decided with reference to it. The subject in point of argument has, however, been nearly, if not entirely, exhausted, and we must come to some decision upon it. We shall, above all things, I hope, avoid a renewal of the war.

You will have heard from many quarters of the combustible state of the interior of France, and the expectation which exists of some explosion. If the war, under such circumstances, were to be renewed, there is no saying where it would end. It would very probably plunge Europe again in all the horrors from which we have had the credit of extricating it. Between such an evil and any arrangement more or less good for Poland, Saxony, or Italy, I should not hesitate. I do not say that I would not give my opinion fairly as to what was best, but having given it, I would certainly recommend compromise to avoid rupture.

I see little prospect of our negotiations at Ghent ending in peace, and I am apprehensive that they may be brought to a conclusion under circumstances which will render it necessary to lay the papers before Parliament, and to call for a vote upon them previous to the Christmas recess. Of this, however, I shall probably be enabled to speak more positively some days hence.

The continuance of the American war will entail upon us a pro-
digious expense, much more than we had any idea of ; and I
cannot, therefore, avoid pressing upon you the importance of not
entailing upon us any part of the Russian debt to Holland if you
can avoid it. Consider only what this charge will be in addition
to our war expenditure and to our pecuniary obligations to
Holland and Sweden. It would be in principle one of the most
difficult questions to defend that ever was brought forward in
Parliament. If we had been at peace with all the world, and the
arrangements to be made at Vienna were likely to contain anything very gratifying to the feelings of this country, we might
have met the question with some degree of confidence ; but as
matters now stand, everything that is really valuable will be considered as having been gained before, and we shall be asked
whether we can really meet such a charge in addition to all the
burthens which the American war will bring upon us.

I recommend these considerations to your most serious attention. . . .

CXXV. [*F. O. Cont.* 8.]
CASTLEREAGH TO LIVERPOOL. (No. 15.)
Vienna, November 5th, 1814.

The day but one after the return of the sovereigns from Buda,
the enclosed communication[1] was delivered to me by an aide de
camp of the Emperor of Russia. It was prepared during His
Imperial Majesty's absence by Prince Czartoriski, the memorandum being written in concert with M. Anstette, a conseiller
d'état in the bureau. I have reason to believe that Count
Nesselrode was not consulted.

The Emperor has latterly, on the question of Poland, ceased to
act through his regular servants. It is unfortunately his habit
to be his own minister, and to select as the instrument of his
immediate purpose the person who may happen to fall in most
with his views. This has been particularly the case on the
present question, all the Russians, I believe without an exception,
being adverse to his projects, considering them both as dangerous
to himself and injurious to his Allies. With respect to the
Memorandum[1] which I now enclose, there has been a strong
feeling of satisfaction amongst them, considering the Emperor
as compromised, by having been made the channel for so weak
and dishonest an argument.

[1] A précis is appended to this dispatch.

I should certainly have never presumed to address my first letter with its enclosure to the Emperor, if I had conceived that I imposed on His Imperial Majesty thereby the necessity of a reply. I delivered it after a long audience, as containing the substance of the topics that had been urged. The memorandum it enclosed was not originally written to meet the Emperor's eye, but having been given to Prince Metternich and Prince Hardenberg, I thought it more becoming to submit it to His Imperial Majesty, with the apology contained in the letter, than to have any concealment from him, after the encouragement I had received from His Majesty to explain myself on the subject without reserve. The sentiments of the Emperor's own mind certainly never led him to feel any particular umbrage at the communication, nor to think of giving an answer to it, till his Polish advisers pressed it upon him, probably with a view of pledging His Imperial Majesty more deeply to their schemes. I believe I mentioned to Your Lordship that the Emperor, after he had read the letter, expressed himself very graciously to me upon it, and afterwards in a conversation with Lord Cathcart, more pointedly expressed his approbation of the "franchise," as His Imperial Majesty termed it, with which I conducted myself. That he was persuaded that I adopted the same course in other quarters. That he thought he understood perfectly my motives for the course I had taken, namely, that of effecting a compromise ; and His Imperial Majesty was further pleased to add that if he had been in my place, he would have done the same.

Upon the receipt of the Emperor's letter I felt considerable embarrassment with respect to the part it became me to take. I was unwilling to abuse the indulgence of a direct intercourse with a sovereign, and not less so to acquiesce in imputations and principles, against both of which I deemed it my duty to protest. Upon the best reflection I determined to separate the Memorandum as much as possible from both the letter and the person of the Emperor, and to direct my reasoning wholly to that, as a ministerial document, which has reached me through His Imperial Majesty's intervention, but to which he was in no other sense a party. I yesterday accordingly sent the reply[1] which I now enclose, accompanied by an explanatory letter to the Emperor, by my brother, as the most respectful and the least formal channel of conveyance.

I should have wished that this species of discussion had fallen into more able hands, and especially that it could have been con-

---

[1] A précis is appended to this dispatch.

ducted by the minister of one of the Powers more immediately interested in the Polish question ; but when I saw the service suffering from inaction, I found it difficult to be passive, and Your Lordship may be assured that England is still the only Power that either can, or dares, raise her voice against the powerful and the oppressor.

I wish I could lead Your Lordship to expect a favourable issue to these Polish discussions. I shall furnish you with the details of their intermediate progress since my last in a separate despatch. My object has been that, at least, the Prince Regent should stand justified in the eyes of Europe, whatever may be the event, and that if the Powers most immediately interested should find themselves obliged to submit to an unjust and illiberal act of power, that H.R.H.'s ministers may have been found true to those principles, which have distinguished the British Government throughout the war, and which have conciliated to her councils the respect and confidence of the Continent.

THE EMPEROR OF RUSSIA TO VISCOUNT CASTLEREAGH.[1]

Vienna, October 30th, 1814.

Castlereagh has said that he will see with satisfaction a liberal aggrandizement which is not inconsistent with the relations of independent States with each other. The reply to the Memorandum will prove that the Emperor has never departed from this intention. With reference to the assistance which Russia has received from England, he points out that all the acquisitions which Russia has made up to the present have only been of defensive value ; without the tranquillity which they afforded she would have been unable to carry on the war.

The Emperor agrees that on the issue of the present Congress depends the future fate of Europe. The object of all his efforts has been to see the members of the Alliance acquire dimensions capable of maintaining the general equilibrium and he fails to see how, with such principles, the Congress can become a centre of intrigue and hate. It is for the world to judge whether the desires of gaining a million more or less of population or that of assuring himself of a preponderance, were capable of animating him or of guiding any of his proceedings. If he holds to the order of things which he wishes to establish in Poland it is because he is convinced that it would be for the general advantage more than his personal interest.

The details and the reasoning contained in the reply will serve to calm Castlereagh's fears for the future of those States to whom the Emperor is bound by indissoluble friendship and from whom he counts on an equal return. When such elements exist one need not fear that there will not result from the Congress a state of things honourable and tranquil for all. As to that which concerns what he owes to his own subjects, it is for him to decide.

MEMORANDUM.

The writer of the British Memorandum introduces his paper by the preamble of the Treaty of Kalisch. The efforts and the sacrifices of Russia are not the conclusions which he wishes to draw : he wishes to prove that the Emperor is deviating from his first principles, that he is disregarding the faith of Treaties,

[1] Précis of document in W.S.D. IX. 386.

and that he is threatening the safety of his neighbours. H.M. has read with calm these strange charges : his conduct refutes them beforehand, and he hopes that this reply will allay all fears and render superfluous any fresh remonstrances of this kind.

In order to support his reasoning the writer of the Memorandum cites the Treaty of Kalisch ; from that he passes to the conventions of June 27th and September 9th, and infers that in spite of these engagements H.M. considers himself entitled to dispose of the Duchy of Warsaw, that he intends to create a separate monarchy to be ruled by himself as King of Poland, and that this determination is founded on the moral duty of ameliorating the conditions of the Poles. Quotations from the treaty of June 27th show that this treaty was purely " eventual " : its first stipulations were no longer applicable, and in proportion as Austria and Prussia acquired the prospect of immense acquisitions, Russia also acquired the right of claiming compensations less limited. The Allied Powers felt the truth of this fact in the treaty of September 9th ; either the drawing up of that article is insidious or the rights of Russia are clearly recognised there, but in any case it overthrows the article in the Treaty of Reichenbach.

Let us consider the Treaty of September 9th, and see if its conditions are fulfilled. Austria and Prussia have both received parts of the Duchy of Warsaw and Russia's share cannot truthfully be called immense in comparison with the value of theirs. Military questions are equally exaggerated in the British Memorandum which stresses the political evils which must assail Europe as an inevitable consequence of the reunion of the Duchy. To give some weight to his remarks, the writer endeavours to show that Russia has become enormous by acquisitions in Finland, Bessarabia, and Persia. In all these cases the Emperor has only applied himself to establish a system of defence and not of aggression. It is in vain that the writer exclaims that the capitals of Austria and Prussia are threatened without any means of defence, and that he depicts the renewal of the contest between the Poles and their neighbours. These dangers are shown to be imaginary by a consideration of the frontiers of Austria and Prussia.

The objection to the restoration of the name of the Kingdom of Poland in support of which the writer produces the secret article of the treaty of 1797. For this article to remain in force, it would be necessary for things to have remained in the same state. When Austria and Prussia have contributed as Allies of France to despoil Russia of the greater part of her Polish provinces, and when the Duchy of Warsaw is to-day a compensation for the enormous sacrifices of Russia, it becomes a question of a new division and the stipulations of that of 1797 no longer exist. To wish to disregard the public right in this is to seek gratuitously to complicate affairs and to multiply difficulties. No dangers would result for Austria and Prussia from the Emperor's plan since he offers to both a formal guarantee of the parts of Poland which remain under their rule, and since the least attempt on his part against the system of Austria, Prussia, France, or Great Britain, would unite all the Powers against him. The national rights given back to the Poles are not dangerous, but on the contrary will be the secret means of calming their restlessness.

The writer of the British Memorandum must reproach himself that he has accused the Emperor of abusing the language of his Treaties. He can no longer maintain his argument that, because the Emperor thinks to restore the Kingdom of Poland, all the advantages gained by the Allies are lost and the Congress must separate without having achieved its object. If, having read this reply, he still holds these opinions, the Emperor will have nothing with which to reproach himself. It will show to Europe and to England the nature of his demands, and the peoples who have seen him fight for their liberties will learn what is the cause which has been opposed to the re-establishment of order, happiness and tranquillity.

S

VISCOUNT CASTLEREAGH TO THE EMPEROR OF ALL RUSSIAS.[1]

Vienna, November 4th, 1814.

Having received the Memorandum which H.I.M. has transmitted to him, Castlereagh considers it the strongest proof of H.I.M.'s desire still to examine the question in detail. Regarding the paper not as H.I.M.'s but as the arguments of the person who is the advocate of these measures, he presumes to submit some remarks upon it. If they are written in the freedom of discussion, it is only to bring before H.I.M. the principles upon which he dissents from the writer of the Memorandum, and if any expression of warmth is to be traced in those observations it has alone been dictated by an impatience of any statement which could represent him as defective in sentiments of respectful deference to H.I.M.

SECOND MEMORANDUM.

A public duty not to suffer the Memorandum to which this is an answer, to pass without remark, not only on account of the importance of the subject, but as disclosing maxims of public law novel in themselves and subversive of every principle of good faith between States.

The writer denies the Treaty of Reichenbach to be now in force on grounds that in consequence of the successes of the war it ceased to be binding and also that it was annulled by the treaty of September 9th. The treaty of Reichenbach was that by which Austria bound herself to engage in the war if her mediation failed to effect a peace ; she stipulated two conditions : the recovery of her Illyrian provinces, and that she should receive a proportion of the Duchy of Warsaw. As the only grounds for depriving Austria of her rights it is said that the treaty was "eventual"; not "eventual" upon Austria fulfilling her engagements, nor upon there being the means of giving what was promised, but upon the extraordinary principle that, there being more than ample means, Russia had a new right to decide whether Austria should obtain the object stipulated or accept in lieu of it what Russia deemed an equivalent. The question under the Treaty is not whether the Emperor of Austria has received a full compensation, but whether he consented, in consideration of an extension of his former possessions in Italy, to relinquish his rights to be protected on the side of Poland. Did the parties to the Peace of Paris, when assigning the Po as the Austrian boundary in Italy, suppose they were sanctioning this as such an exchange ? Unless that were so the Treaty of Reichenbach is still in force. The same reasoning applies to Prussia.

The Memorandum alleges that, admitting the rights contended for under the treaty of June, these rights were extinguished by the Treaty of Toeplitz,[2] and the claims of Austria and Prussia upon the Duchy were no longer the same. It is impossible to argue from the then state of the campaign that Austria would have signed a new Treaty gratuitously surrendering pretensions to which she had in June attached the first importance. Neither can it be inferred from the mere change in the wording of the article. The treaty of September was not intended to annul that of June but to confirm and extend its provisions ; the fate of the Duchy of Warsaw was again brought forward and the rights of the three Powers to arrange its disposal solemnly recognised.

It is urged that the position of the Duchy in the hands of Russia is not menacing to the other Powers, and that H.I.M.'s known character renders such a course unimportant. Upon the first point it will be difficult to persuade Europe; if Austria and Prussia are to be really independent their claim to have an adequate frontier assigned to them is irresistible and cannot be reasonably combatted on any grounds. The argument drawn from the Emperor's personal character is not less exceptionable, since the liberties and security of States cannot be built upon personal confidence or upon the life of an individual.

[1] Précis of document in W. S. D. IX. 410.
[2] Of September 9th.

The article of 1797 is said to be dissolved by the change of circumstances, the argument being that successful war justifies a demand for additional compensation ; but, admitting the Treaties to be still binding, the arrangements intended by Russia will amply fulfill their stipulations. Castlereagh annexes official tables to illustrate the inaccuracy of the statistics given and protests against the studied misrepresentations of the paper. The appeal to the Emperor's justice is represented there as an appeal to arms whereas it is well known that the question has never been reasoned upon a hostile principle ; the statements concerning the recent acquisitions of Russia are said to be exaggerated, but they were, on the contrary, treated with moderation.

It has been established that the Treaties of Reichenbach and Toeplitz are in full force, that Russia has no right to annul or alter their stipulations except upon the consent of the other parties, and that the success of the war does not entitle any of the parties to aggrandize themselves unduly to the prejudice of weaker States. It should be remembered that the Powers fought for the liberties of Europe and not for the extension of their dominions ; it is a false principle that nations have a right in all cases to claim additional territories in compensation for expenses incurred in war.

[An official Table of Austria's losses in Poland is appended.]

CXXVI. [*W. S. D. IX.* 417.]
WELLINGTON TO CASTLEREAGH.
Paris, November 5th, 1814.

. . . I have this instant had an interview with Monsieur de Blacas. I found him much displeased at the continued obstinacy of the Emperor of Russia respecting Poland, on which he says that he understands that his Imperial Majesty declared, before he quitted Vienna, to go into Hungary, that he considered all matters settled ; that he was to be King of Poland, and the King of Prussia King of Saxony ; and that he had given Monsieur de Talleyrand to understand that he would not depart from his plan on either of those countries. Monsieur de Blacas said that the result would be that the King, and most probably the Prince Regent, would withdraw their ministers from the Congress, declaring that they could not acknowledge these arrangements, and that Europe would remain in a feverish state, which sooner or later must end in war.

I again urged him in the strongest manner to have instructions sent to Monsieur de Talleyrand to lay aside all considerations upon small points, and to unite cordially with you in a great effort to produce the union of all the Powers in Europe against the projected aggrandizement of Russia. Monsieur de Blacas then said that he considered that these were three great objects for arrangement— Poland, Naples, and Saxony—upon which the King felt an almost equal interest, and that he did not think Your Lordship was inclined to act so directly to effect the views which the Government of both countries professed to have as he had expected, and that he wished that you should receive further instructions on the subject from home. I told him that he was quite mistaken ; that I had not the papers to show him, but could assure him that language could not be stronger than that which you had used, both verbally and in writing, to the Emperor of Russia, to dissuade him from his Polish scheme, which was the foundation of all the mischief, and that you were directing all your efforts to connect the ministers of the other Powers of Europe in the same views and measures with you, on this point ; that you considered other points as comparatively unimportant ; and that, moreover, the ultimate decision of them depended more or less on the decision as to the Polish question, which went to whether there should or not be in Europe any system whatever of equilibrium. I reminded him that I had already apprized him that Monsieur de Talleyrand was running after these small objects, instead of looking to that principal one ; and he admitted that he was not himself satisfied with his conduct. He then proposed that Great Britain, France, Spain, and Holland, should agree by treaty not to recognise the Polish arrangement ; and he pressed this point strongly and repeatedly, as being the best mode of drawing with us Austria and Prussia. I told him that all combinations of this description created jealousy, and that the first and immediate effect of such an arrangement would be to separate us from our old Allies.

He gave up this idea, and he went away at last, as he said, convinced that the best method to be adopted was all to unite for the object of opposing the Emperor's views in Poland, laying all minor points aside, and promising to endeavour to remove from the King's mind the impression that you were not decided in your measures on this point. . . .

CXXVII. [W. S. D. IX. 421.]
WELLINGTON TO CASTLEREAGH.

Paris, November 7th, 1814.

. . . I saw M. de Blacas again last night. He told me that he had repeated to the King what I had mentioned to him on Saturday, and that his Majesty had received it with the greatest satisfaction, and gave entire credit to the assurances which I had given him on your determination to give every opposition in your power to the views of Russia, and to endeavour to unite all the great Powers in Europe against those views. He told me that orders were to go this day to M. de Talleyrand, to direct him to co-operate with you in every way to produce an effectual opposition to the Emperor's Polish schemes, which the King concurred with us in thinking the foundation of all the evil which was likely to result from the Congress of Vienna.

They are quite convinced, not only that M. de Talleyrand has acted foolishly himself, but that he has led them into error by encouraging representations of your conduct and views. M. de Blacas desired me to apprize you that you might depend upon the King's concurrence in your views, and upon his support ; and said that, if I was not satisfied with what he had said to me, I might see the King, who would give me the same assurances himself.

Both the palace and I are so much observed, that I thought it better to decline this offer, with which Blacas appeared pleased ; but he told me that he could let me see the King whenever I wished it, without its being known. . . .

CXXVIII. [*F. O. Cont.* 8.]
CASTLEREAGH TO LIVERPOOL. (No. 16.)
Vienna, November 11th, 1814.

I reported to your Lordship in my dispatch No. 12[1] the result of the confidential interview that took place at my house between the Austrian and Prussian Secretaries of State. On the following day, and before the Emperor of Russia's departure for Buda, Prince Metternich had an interview with him, which led to a discussion of much warmth, especially on the part of His Imperial Majesty.

Upon the return of the Emperor of Austria to Vienna, Prince Metternich received His Imperial Majesty's directions to transmit the note, of which the enclosed is a copy,[2] to Prince Hardenberg, as the basis of the intended negotiation with the Emperor of Russia. Your Lordship will observe that in the third alternative, the Austrian Minister proposes to release Russia from all restraint as to the erection of her Polish dominions into a Monarchy, (which would then contain nearly ten millions of people) under the Russian sceptre, provided the two other Powers received the Vistula as their frontier. It was Prince Metternich's intention to have proposed as a fourth alternative, in case Russia insisted upon passing the Vistula, that the two other Powers should accept the Warta and the Nidda as their frontiers, but in this case, that Russia should be called upon to renew the Treaty of 1797. This

[1] CXIX.
[2] Metternich to Hardenberg, November 2nd, 1814. D'Angeberg, p. 379. The proposals follow very much the lines laid down by Castlereagh [CXIX.]

latter proposition was, I understand, struck out by the Austrian Cabinet, who are under very great alarm upon the subject, and blame Prince Metternich for having been too complying and they leave it to Russia to originate such counter propositions, as she might think fit.

That Your Lordship may judge of the degree of importance attached to this question in the Prussian Cabinet, I send you a memoir written by General Knesebeck, whose weight and confidential situation in their councils my brother correctly describes. It was drawn up by him upon an inspection of the military reasoning contained in the Memorandum I received from the Emperor of Russia. There is no military opinion held in higher estimation here than General Knesebeck's, and his authority is the more deserving of attention from the caution that distinguishes his character, and from the reluctance he must feel to embark his court in an unnecessary controversy with an allied power.

Your Lordship will have observed from the Memorandum transmitted in my dispatch No. 12,[1] that the hope then entertained was, that the Emperor of Russia, to avoid an official démarche upon principles that must place him on disadvantageous grounds in Europe as well as in Poland, might be induced to come into some amicable arrangement, to give effect to which there would have existed every disposition to make the utmost sacrifice ; but, as yet, we have no substantial grounds to hope for such a result ; and I fear, that in the manner of attempting to bring the Emperor to reasonable views, so much appearance of indecision has been shewn, as must weaken, if not render abortive, the formal overture should it be brought forward.

The failure of the efforts hitherto made is chiefly owing to the personal ascendancy, which the Emperor has unfortunately acquired over the King of Prussia. When at Buda His Imperial Majesty omitted no exertion to operate on the minds of both the other sovereigns. His usual mode is to represent their ministers as the obstacle to harmony, and that the whole system of their policy ought to be settled by the sovereigns themselves. This language, which was particularly directed against Prince Metternich, made no sort of impression on *his* master, but the Emperor was more successful in a long conversation with Prince Hardenberg, in presence of the King of Prussia, by which he contrived not only to embarrass that minister, but to deprive his intervention of much of its weight.

[1] *Supra*, p. 213.

I was induced when I first arrived here, to undervalue the importance attached by the Austrian and Prussian Cabinets to the Polish question, and to suppose that they both might be more easily reconciled by arrangements elsewhere, to suffer the Emperor to execute his purpose than has proved to be the fact. The prospect of reconciling their differences on German affairs was no sooner opened, than both Austria and Prussia resumed their former earnestness on this point, which was much augmented by a variety of collaterial indications of the intriguing spirit, which actuated the Russian councils in other quarters.

I deemed it of great importance to contribute as far as depended upon me, to this concert : considering the establishment of Russia in the heart of Germany not only as constituting a great danger in itself, but as calculated to establish a most pernicious influence both in the Austrian and Prussian Cabinets ; and I also foresaw, that if these two Powers, from distrust of each other, gave up the Polish point as desperate, the contest in negotiation would then turn upon Saxony, Mayence and other German points, and through the contentions of Austria and Prussia, the supremacy of Russia would be established in all directions, and upon every question ; whereas an understanding previously established on German affairs, gave some chance of ameliorating the Polish arrangement, and, in case of its failure, afforded the best, if not the only means of counteracting the Russian influence in the other European arrangements, to the tendency of which, it was impossible not to look with alarm, whilst she kept an army of 60,000 men under Beningsen upon the Elbe, still treating Holstein, without a pretence for doing so, almost as an enemy country.

It appeared to me of particular importance to our own views on the side of Holland to do so. If the Low Countries could be covered by a German League, we might venture to resent Russian injustice on the side of Poland, by refusing her the beneficial arrangements relative to the Dutch loan, to which we were *sub modo* pledged, without exposing the Prince of Orange's interests by doing so : but if, triumphing in Poland, the Emperor could dis-unite Germany, the motives for refusing this aid might be augmented, but so might the danger in refusing it ; and we might find ourselves obliged to yield this tribute to Russia, under the most humiliating circumstances.

I therefore was of opinion that every consideration of policy combined to make it our particular interest, as well as duty to promote the concert in question, and, for the reasons I have stated, I trust Your Lordship will see, that to have been indifferent to the Polish question would have augmented, instead of diminishing, our own immediate difficulties. On the contrary, it appeared to me, that it was better for Great Britain, in order to secure her own objects, to contend for an European question of great magnitude in the true spirit of the policy that has marked her conduct throughout the war, than to seem indifferent to that policy, and to reserve herself for an object, viz.: the Low Countries, which is regarded on the Continent as particularly connected with her own power, and which, as I have observed above, might have been exposed to a very unpleasant question, under a disunion between the great German Powers.

I have certainly been led, from circumstances, to take a more active share in the discussions on this question, than I should have permitted myself to do, if it had been any part of my policy to push the Polish point to a hostile issue. In preparing for so serious an alternative, I should have felt the propriety, as a British Minister, of preserving a greater degree of reserve ; it being the province of Great Britain to support, rather than lead, on such occasions. But in proportion as I felt that an effort ought to be made successively by conciliation, by moderation, by persuasion, by pressure of argument, and ultimately if necessary by an imposing negotiation, uniting the general sentiments of Europe upon sound and popular grounds, and not by arms, I felt the less precluded from taking a forward part. Some advantages perhaps have resulted from my being the person to do so, as the same arguments, had they been urged by the parties most interested, might have rendered accommodation more difficult. Such are the principles upon which my conduct has hitherto been founded. It will be highly gratifying to me should they be honored with the Prince Regent's gracious approbation, and with the concurrence of my colleagues in the Government.

Since I have been on the Continent, in my intercourse with the several Cabinets, I have conceived it my duty to keep in view the following principles, considering them as those on which it was the intention of His Royal Highness' Government that I should act. In the first place, so to conduct the arrangements to be framed for Congress, as to make the establishment of a just equilibrium in Europe the first object of my attention, and to consider the assertion of minor points of interest as subordinate to this great end. Secondly, to use my best endeavour to support the Powers who had contributed to save Europe by their exertions, in their just pretensions to be liberally re-established upon the scale to which their Treaties entitled them to lay claim, and not to be deterred from doing so, by the necessity of adopting, for this end, measures, which, although not unjust, are nevertheless painful and unpopular in themselves. And thirdly to endeavour to combine this latter duty to our friends and Allies, with as much mildness and indulgence even to the offending States, as circumstances would permit.

I have pursued these views, with a fixed and anxious purpose, if possible, not to suffer the peace of Europe to be disturbed, even upon just grounds, if by any compromise or even reasonable sacrifice it could be avoided. If in discharge of this duty, I have felt myself obliged strongly to remonstrate against the principles and temper disclosed by the Russian councils, I hope I have maintained honest principles, and I am confident that the relations between the two Governments would not have been improved by a more pliant tone on my part, opposed to that in which the Emperor has of late been disposed to dictate.

Your Lordship may rest assured that no effort on my part shall be omitted to prevent disunion, and still more, war ; but I am confident I speak the universal sentiment, when I declare my perfect conviction, that unless the Emperor of Russia can be brought to a more moderate and sound course of public conduct, the peace, which we have so dearly purchased, will be but of short duration.

CXXIX.   *F. O. Cont.* 8.]
CASTLEREAGH TO LIVERPOOL. (No. 19.)
Vienna, November 21st, 1814.

[Castlereagh has attempted to prepare the minds of the plenipotentiaries on the Slave Trade before regular negotiations. France has refused to abolish completely. Spain has agreed to abolish within eight years and at once partially. Castlereagh is negotiating with Portugal for partial abolition in return for money compensations and a new commercial treaty.]

That I may be the better enabled to profit by your suggestion on the best mode of bringing the question of abolition before the Congress, I enclose a Memorandum of what has occurred to me on this subject. I particularly recommend to your consideration the advantage of having a sort of permanent European Congress in existence, as therein proposed upon this particular subject. I am of opinion that this may be made in itself a most powerful instrument to enforce with good faith the engagements of the several Powers, and as I foresee, that from defect of powers or other causes, we may be disappointed in obtaining such an arrangement during the Congress as Parliament would deem satisfactory as a final measure, it may satisfy feelings much as well as contribute to the success of our views, if our exertions are only adjourned over, to be followed up in London and at Paris by the united exertions of the Ministers of the respective Powers.

MEMORANDUM AS TO THE MODE OF CONDUCTING THE NEGOTIATIONS IN CONGRESS FOR THE FINAL ABOLITION OF THE SLAVE TRADE.

The first effort should be directed to effect an immediate and general abolition of the traffick ; with this view a joint representation should be made by the Powers (vizt. Great Britain, Russia, Austria, Prussia, Holland, Sweden, and Denmark) already declared in favour of this measure to France, to induce her to concur in giving at once effect to the system which she is pledged to carry into execution at the end of five years.

Should France decline acceding to this representation an attempt to be then made by the same Powers to induce the French Government to reduce the period from five to three years and to give effect without delay to the abolition north of the line as promised to Great Britain.

In the event of France refusing to depart from the decision she has hitherto pronounced, there being in that case no hope of bringing Spain and Portugal to a more favourable determination, the seven Powers above named may unite their efforts with those of France to induce the Governments of Spain and Portugal to conform themselves to the engagements taken by France.

Should Spain and Portugal refuse to adopt the limitation of five years, but propose to render the abolition absolute at the end of eight years, with an immediate cessation of the traffick north of the line, the question then will be, should the eight Powers acquiesce and consider the whole of the Powers as then embarked in one common interest, vizt. to carry into full effect this regulated measure of abolition, according to the stipulations of the respective Powers or ought the Powers who have engaged to abolish immediately, or at the end of five years, to separate their councils in the Congress from those of Spain and Portugal, and employ all justifiable means still to enforce upon those Powers the necessity of a more early abolition.

The measure of immediate abolition in States growing more colonial produce than they can themselves consume, may be effected in two ways, either by the law of the State itself prohibiting the import of slaves, or by a law on the part of all other States, excluding the colonial produce of such State as shall refuse to comply with the system of abolition.

With respect to the efficacy of this remedy, if adopted sincerely by the eight Powers, there can be no question. There might be evasion of such a law to a certain extent, but a prohibition enforced with ordinary attention in all the principal markets against the produce of the Spanish and Portuguese colonies would at once deter their planters from the further purchase of slaves.

The justice of the remedy if otherwise prudent cannot be questioned, as a means of giving effect to a system to which so many Powers have made a sacrifice of colonial interests, and which are all morally bound with their utmost means to carry into full execution. It may however deserve consideration whether this extreme measure should not be waved in favour of some reasonable compromise with those Powers, or if that cannot be effected during the sitting of the present Congress from their plenipotentiaries being restricted by their instructions, whether the application of the principle of exclusion should be not suspended till further discussion shall have taken place with their respective Courts.

As it is clear, that the final and effectual extension of the traffick in slaves must be a work of some time, and the success of the effort must depend upon the effectual execution of the regulations adopted by the respective States, it is proposed that the ministers of the several Powers engaged in the cause of abolition resident in London and Paris, should by their respective Courts be ordered to act together in concert for watching over the effectual execution of these regulations, that for this purpose, they should assemble together from time to time in each capital to enquire into the progress made and the extent of the evil remaining. That they should consult upon the most effectual means of counteracting evasion, and of promoting the common object, and that they should require on the [   ] of [   ] in each year to draw out a joint report for the information of their respective Courts, stating the result of the former years' exertions, as far as the same can be ascertained. The missions in London and Paris to correspond and act in concert.

There are two further questions of great delicacy and importance connected with the suppression of this unnatural and criminal traffick, which deserves to be examined. The 1st is to what extent and under what regulations the nations of Europe, who desire to effect the abolition, can actually trust each others ships of war with the detention of vessels acting on the coast of Africa in violation of the regulations of their particular states ? For the elucidation of this subject a Projet of treaty is annexed.[1]

The 2nd question is, how far, after the trade in slaves shall have been abolished by all or nearly all Christian States, the Governments of the said States may be justified in consideration of those engaged in the traffick of whatever nation, as engaged in an offence proscribed by civilized nations, and as such not to be peaceably tolerated ? These questions are suggested for consideration without any judgment being pronounced thereon.

CXXX. [*W. S. D. IX.* 438.]

LIVERPOOL TO CASTLEREAGH.

Fife House, November 18th, 1814.

[Transmits a letter offering the Duke of Wellington the command in America, but announcing the determination of the Cabinet to make peace if possible in view of the attitude of Parliament and Wellington's opinion that no material military success is likely to be obtained in America.]

Our Parliamentary campaign has hitherto gone on very well, but the Opposition are particularly rancorous, and evidently mean to find us good employment. We shall most probably be able to adjourn about the end of the first or beginning of the second week in December, and we can carry our adjournment, I think, to about the 7th of February. I still hope that you may be able to settle all that is material before the end of January.

I ought to apprise you that there is a strong feeling in this country respecting Saxony. The case against the King appears to me, I confess, to be complete, if it is expedient to act upon it ; but the objection is to the annihilation of the whole of Saxony as an independent Power, particularly considering the part which the Saxon troops took in the operation on the Elbe. Considering the prominent part which Saxony has always taken in the affairs of

[1] Not given.

Germany, it would certainly be very desirable that a *noyau* of it at least should be preserved, even if it were under some other branch of the Saxon family ; and I am fully convinced that the King of Prussia would gain more in character and influence by agreeing to such an arrangement than he would lose by any reasonable sacrifice which he might make for this purpose of territory. . . .

CXXXI. [*F. O. Cont.* 8.]
CASTLEREAGH TO LIVERPOOL. (No. 20.)
Vienna, November 21st, 1814.

I regret that it has not been in my power to report to Your Lordship a more rapid advance of business, with which we are here charged. The length to which the discussions on the Polish question have gone, and the connection necessarily subsisting between the decision of one territorial question and another, has hitherto prevented a final decision being taken, almost on any one point. Your Lordship must not infer however from this, that the plenipotentiaries have been idle, or that considerable progress has not been made in examining, preparatory to a decision, the several branches into which the European arrangement naturally divides itself.

In framing the successive protocols herewith transmitted of the deliberations of the eight Powers who signed the Peace of Paris, you will perceive that it has not been deemed advisable, in the present state of the business, to assemble the plenipotentiaries at large in Congress, there being nothing as yet sufficiently matured to submit to them for their ultimate confirmation.

In proportion as the subject underwent consideration, it became apparent that the Congress was incompetent to act as a constituted and deliberative assembly, possessing the power of binding dissentient voices by the majority of the votes : that it could not delegate to commissions powers which it did not itself possess, and that the preparatory negotiations must originate with the parties naturally interested.

This has at last led to an arrangement which seems sufficient for every practical purpose and to which there seems no longer any objection. The plenipotentiaries of the eight Powers, in number twenty, vizt: Austria two, Russia three, Great Britain four, France four, Prussia two, Portugal three, Spain one, and Sweden one, meet together occasionally as a directing body. In the interval the several subjects are treated of nearly under the following distribution.

The affairs of Poland are left to the three Powers locally interested, with the intervention of Great Britain: the Prince de Talleyrand and the other plenipotentiaries have always considered this as a suitable mode of discussing that subject, in the first instance, and he has confined himself to occasional explanations of the sentiments of his Court thereupon in his interviews with the sovereigns, and the parties interested. The details of these discussions have already been submitted to the Prince Regent.

At a very early period, a species of commission consisting of the five principal German Powers, vizt: Austria, Prussia, Bavaria, Hanover, and Wirtemberg, charged themselves with German affairs. They have made considerable progress in framing a Projet of confederation for Germany in pursuance of the principle laid down in the Treaty of Paris. The labours of these commissioners are exclusively confined to the constitutional organisation of Germany, but its territorial distribution has been also a subject of frequent discussion between them, and the other European Powers principally interested : and altho' nothing can definitely be settled till we know what is disposable in Poland to be assigned to the two great German Powers, yet the whole has been examined so carefully, and in so many points of view, that I consider material progress has been made towards a final decision, if the principal Powers could agree upon the two fundamental questions of Saxony and Poland, which must, in a great measure determine the quantum of means disposable to satisfy the various claims.

The affairs of Switzerland have been referred to a commission nominated by the four Allied Powers, consisting of Baron Wessenberg for Austria, Baron Stein for Russia, Lord Stewart for Great Britain, and Baron Humboldt for Prussia. These ministers are charged upon communication with the several deputies from Switzerland, to frame a report, which is afterwards to be discussed with the Duke d'Alberg, who has been nominated plenipotentiary of France for this object. The Treaty of Paris having recognized the principle of an arrangement for Switzerland to be founded upon the basis approved by the Allies, no objection was made on the part of France to leave the initiative with the Allied Powers.

The affairs of Italy have formed another subdivision, and in order to gain as much time as possible on the important question of Naples, we have been unanimous in first directing our attention to the affairs of Northern Italy. As the first in order, we have taken measures for giving effect to the provisions of the Treaty of Paris in respect to Genoa.

The protocol will fully explain the course adopted in sending this question also to a preparatory commission, consisting of Baron Wessenberg for Austria, Earl of Clancarty for Great Britain, and the Comte de Noailles for France. The prevailing idea is, that the cession should take place upon a species of constitution securing to the Genoese certain rights and privileges. It is intended in the next place, and without delay, to proceed with the reclamation of the Queen of Etruria upon Parma, and with the question of the Legations.

I have stated this much to explain to Your Lordship the course in which business is conducted. At first there was an extreme susceptibility in the several plenipotentiaries upon anything being done to their exclusion, but this sentiment, from its own impracticability, has subsided, and I see nothing to object to in the manner in which the discussions are carried on : they must have been brought before this time to a satisfactory conclusion, if Russia had acted upon European principles, and directed her powerful influence upon just and liberal views.

CXXXII. [F. O. Cont. 8.]
CASTLEREAGH TO LIVERPOOL. (No. 21.)
Vienna, November 21st, 1814.

In my dispatch of the 11th, No. 16[1], I expressed to your Lordship my apprehensions, that the Emperor of Russia's personal influence had prevailed over the authority of the Prussian Prime Minister, and that our hope of a joint and imposing representation on the existing difficulties of the negotiation was likely to be thereby frustrated.

I had reason to suppose that this was the case, even to a greater degree than Prince Hardenberg had admitted to me, which was confirmed by receiving from His Highness the inclosed confidential memorandum.[2] The sentiments both of Prince Metternich and myself had always been in our confidential intercourse with Prince Hardenberg sufficiently pacifick, to make an appeal of this nature unnecessary ; we could not therefore consider the argument as in truth addressed to us, but rather as a sort of defence of the King which he was directed to make, in excuse for with-

[1] CXXVIII.
[2] Mémoire confidentielle of Hardenberg, November 7th, 1814. F. O. Cont. 8. Partly printed in D'Angeberg, p. 406

drawing from a concert, which your Lordship will observe that His Highness had in his letters of the 17th and 21st October, not only invited, but urged.[1]

It was obvious, from this communication, that Prussia was not prepared to range herself on the side of Austria in an official remonstrance on the Polish question, however she might still wish to negotiate confidentially on the subject. That being the obvious result, I did not feel myself called upon to combat the reasoning, which was the mere vehicle on the part of Prince Hardenberg of disclosing this change of policy.

Under these circumstances which indicated a considerable degree of divergence in the sentiments of the two Courts, I thought it expedient to decline being the bearer of any proposition they might have to address to Russia, as my late correspondence with the Emperor had rendered my interview less conciliatory than the nature of their negotiation might require. I took this opportunity to repeat to both ministers what I had before, on more than *one* occasion, expressed, that I trusted they would not infer from the zeal which I had shown to support what I had understood to be their wishes, that Great Britain had any separate policy of her own to pursue with respect to Poland, or any wish to excite them to any measures which did not originate on their part, in a sense of their necessity. That the British Government felt desirous of contributing, as far as could reasonably be expected from them, to establish that permanent peace and equilibrium on the Continent, for which the British Nation had made such immense sacrifices, and which was the declared object of the Alliance, but that having honourably performed their part, their duty led them to leave the decision with the Powers more locally interested than Great Britain could consider herself to be, in the Polish arrangements.

Your Lordship will perceive that the Austrian minister in his reply, which I enclose,[2] throws the conduct of the negotiation altogether upon Prussia, reserving to himself to act upon the explanation he may receive, through Prince Hardenberg's intervention. I certainly myself strongly participate in the opinion expressed by Prince Metternich, that such a representation as the two Courts had agreed to make to Russia could in all probability have been attended with success ; and if not, that having pushed their efforts to the utmost, short of war, and having given each other the convincing proof of common interest, they might have

[1] The letter of October 9th (*Supra* p. 206) is obviously meant, but I cannot explain the dates given.
[2] Metternich to Hardenberg, November 12th, 1814. D'Angeberg, p. 418.

made, in concert, a concession, for the sake of peace to an Ally, with less hazard than they can do, when in appearance disunited.

The illness of the Emperor has, for the last three days, prevented Prince Hardenberg from seeing His Imperial Majesty upon the business in question. I understood from His Highness last night that the Emperor was better, and that he hoped to obtain an audience in the course of this day or to-morrow.

CXXXIII. [*W. S. D. IX.* 447.]
CASTLEREAGH TO LIVERPOOL.

Vienna, November 21st, 1814.

You may wish to receive, in a private letter, such speculations as to the possible turn of matters here as I can send you.

With respect to the Polish question, you must always combine it, to a certain degree, with that of Saxony, as Austria can ill afford to be foiled on *both* these points. The failure of Prussia to execute the concert as arranged, naturally threw back the negotiation between the two Courts into the state of embarrassment from which I had laboured to extricate it. Austria no sooner saw, or thought she saw, that she was abandoned by Prussia, than her disposition to resist the Saxon arrangement revived. It is the deliberate opinion of many of their officers, and, I may add, ministers, that, rather than have the Russians at Cracovie and the Prussians at Dresden, they had better risk a war with such support as they can get. Whether this is a sound opinion is another question ; but, in point of fact, the war tone was much augmented amongst the Austrians immediately subsequent to the receipt of Prince Hardenberg's memorandum, and I have reason to believe that a dislocation [*sic*] of their troops was ordered in consequence.

Prince Metternich told me that, in his interview with Prince Hardenberg, he had opened himself unreservedly, and declared to him that no Austrian minister could sign a Treaty giving way on Poland, Saxony, and Mayence ; and urging him to modify his views on Saxony, arguing the impolicy of attempting to extinguish totally that monarchy, against the declared purpose of France and the prevailing feeling of Germany.

I need not trouble you with the various arguments which I understand have been brought forward on the present critical state of the negotiation. It is enough to give you the opinion of the two chiefs. Prince Hardenberg told me last night that he thought it would end in an arrangement, and that Prince Czartoriski had promised him to urge the Emperor to make some concessions. Prince Metternich gave me the same opinion, and added that he felt assured that Prussia would listen to modifications on the Saxon arrangement, to which his Court attached the greatest importance. I give you these two opinions as the best, indeed the only means I possess of forming a judgment, stating at the same time that both these ministers are sufficiently sanguine in their mode of viewing things. I think this question must now be brought to a decision, one way or the other, in the course of a few days. . . .

CXXXIV. [*W. S. D. IX.* 446.]
CASTLEREAGH TO WELLINGTON.

Vienna, November 21st, 1814.

. . . I cannot sufficiently express to you my thanks for your most useful and seasonable co-operation. You have succeeded in rendering the French influence here much more accommodating ; and, if I have not been able to bring the Prince de Talleyrand to the point of common exertion, his Highness has been to me personally most obliging and conciliatory, and has ceased to thwart me as he did, possibly unintentionally, at first.

The day after I received your letter of the 7th,[1] Prince Talleyrand called on me when I was from home. I happened to dine with him that day, and we fixed an interview for the following morning. As my hopes of Prussia had considerably abated, I could not give him much assurance of the progress I was making. I gave him a general outline of the state in which things were, and endeavoured to draw from him his ideas upon the future conduct of the negotiation. He spoke, apparently with openness, his mind, always returning to the old notion of urging Austria to finish the Polish question as well as she could, and then to turn the whole combination upon Saxony.

In judging of the correctness of Talleyrand's reports to his Government of my conduct, it is but fair to observe that I have not deemed it prudent to disclose to him my operations in detail, finding that he was not always discreet, and that I should lose useful influence in other quarters, if I was understood to be in too close confidence with the French Minister. I have endeavoured, however, to treat him with all possible regard, and to keep him generally informed of my endeavours to promote our common objects. He is become infinitely more accommodating in our general conferences than at the outset. . . .

[1] CXXVII.

T

CXXXV. [*W. S. D. IX.* 451.]
CASTLEREAGH TO LIVERPOOL.
                                    Vienna, November 25th, 1814.

The insinuation with which the Emperor's last memorandum[1] closes, that the intervention of Great Britain in the questions pending between him and his Allies had not been conducted in the true spirit of mediation, induces me to trouble you with a few observations on this subject.

If the correspondence which has taken place had been the first and only description of proceeding on this subject, the observation might have been just ; but the fact is, that almost from the period of my arrival at the Allied head-quarters in January last I have, at the instance of the two Allied Courts, been employed to endeavour to prevail upon the Emperor more precisely to explain himself, and to adopt a course with respect to Poland less alarming to their interest. That this task was performed in a manner sufficiently conciliatory to His Imperial Majesty is evident from the manner in which the Emperor has always received me ; but that it was wholly abortive to its object is also proved from this simple fact, that the Memorandum in question is the very first instance in which the question has been rendered, on the part of Russia, avowedly one of negotiation.

In all my interviews, as well as in the first paper received from the Emperor, it was treated as a question upon which Russia was alone to pronounce. His Imperial Majesty's language uniformly was, " Je donnerai ce qu'il faut à la Prusse, mais je ne donnerai pas un village à l'Autriche. J'ai conquis le Duché, et j'ai 480,000 hommes à le garder." Having, in successive interviews during the campaign, at Paris, in London, and in two long audiences since His Imperial Majesty's arrival at Vienna, employed in vain every conciliatory representation to place the question upon a footing to which a mediation could be applicable, it appeared to me that the only remaining hope was to try so to place the argument upon the Treaties before him and upon the general aspect of his decision, as to awaken his mind to a sense of the possible consequences to which his conduct might lead.

I was aware that this might place me, as the Prince Regent's minister, on a less satisfactory footing with the Emperor, and render my position less available for purposes of mediation ; but where there appeared nothing upon which a mediation could be built, this was, comparatively, a small inconvenience ; whereas, in giving to my representations a more decided and more earnest

---

[1] A précis of the Memorandum follows this dispatch.

tone, my *appui* became the more authoritative for Austria and Prussia to found a negotiation upon.

Whatever may be the result, I am confident the Emperor would never have submitted himself to a negotiation at all if this course had not been adopted, but would have stood firm upon the despotism of his military tenure. The fruits that may result from this concession may be small or none, but it is something to bring him down in doctrine to a level with other Powers ; and although from my experience of His Imperial Majesty's character, I expect nothing from his friendship to his Allies, and as little from his generosity or his sense of justice, yet I still hope for something from his fears. The general sentiment of dissatisfaction and alarm occasioned by his conduct is becoming too strong and too universal to be any longer a secret from him. It exists extensively amongst his own subjects, and I have reason to believe that this fact has not been concealed from him. Under these circumstances, and profiting by the reflections for which his illness has afforded an occasion, perhaps His Imperial Majesty may moderate his pretensions ; in which case, with all the motives for peace that present themselves, and the danger of a new war arising out of a speculative rather than an actual danger, it certainly will not be my disposition to push him to extremity upon the conditions. The moral advantage of gaining something against such lofty pretensions is not inconsiderable in itself ; it may give a check at the outset to a career to which passive submission might have added an additional impulse. If Prussia and Austria could have taken a tone of authority together, I should have thought the precise terms obtained of still less importance. I am afraid His Imperial Majesty has now ascertained the subserviency of one of his Allies, and will presume upon it.

THE EMPEROR OF RUSSIA TO VISCOUNT CASTLEREAGH.[1]

Vienna, November 21st, 1814.

[He judges it necessary to reply to Castlereagh's Memorandum as much to refute some of its assertions as to give a fresh proof of the purity of his intentions. He wishes this to be the close of this correspondence and official papers to be transmitted in the usual way.]

SECOND RUSSIAN MEMORANDUM.

The second British memorandum, instead of simplifying the question and facilitating an agreement, tends to prolong the discussion. Since this paper is intended to terminate it, the writer will limit himself to rectifying some of the assertions which are recorded there.

Intentions are attributed to Russia which she has never had ; it is not to herself alone that she reserves the decision of the fate of the Duchy of Warsaw but in conformity with the principles of justice and in concert with the Allied

[1] Précis of documents in *W. S. D. IX.* 441.

Powers. To say that the Treaty of Reichenbach is only " eventual " is not to consider it null but to give it its true character. It is so because, in an absolute sense, it cannot in any case settle all the interests which result from the success of the war. It was concluded when it was still not known whether Buonaparte would accept Austrian mediation. He refused it and the Treaty of September 9th was concluded in the height of the war. If he had accepted it the Treaty of Reichenbach would have prompted new combinations and produced different effects. A similar modification would have been necessary in any case, seeing that the proportions of the compensation to be taken in the Duchy of Warsaw were not determined in the stipulation, and that it was as just as it was indispensable to modify these proportions according to the results of the war. History and diplomacy furnish more than one example of Treaties which one of the parties will not consider as binding because of a change of circumstances.

The Emperor has not in this war founded his policy on his own exclusive interests but has constantly worked to assist those of the Powers who rallied to the common cause. The Allies, having obtained considerable concessions of power, cannot legitimately contest to Russia that which she claims, not with the view of augmenting her resources, but as a necessary weight in the balance of the European system. A survey is given of the territories gained by each of the European Powers and Russia's gains compared with them. Russia cannot have security without a good military frontier, and it is of great importance to her to put an end to the unrest of the Poles. Under all these considerations it is not possible to object to Russia making an aggrandizement that is demanded by justice, the maintenance of European balance and her own internal tranquillity.

If it were possible that all the States could be replaced in their former situations, and if all the changes could be considered null, the Emperor would have been the first to give the example of great sacrifices to contribute to this result, but this supposition appears to be contrary to the disposition of the other States. Rather than to plead vaguely the cause of the principles of public right, it would be preferable to endeavour to assure to the nations the relative advantages to which they have a right and upon which one could reasonably hope to found a peace. A Mediator is only useful in a discussion if he tries to conciliate ; otherwise he had better leave the parties concerned alone. Great Britain could render great services if she were a real Mediator.

The statistical tables appended to the second British Memorandum are then stated to be inaccurate and others suggested in their place.

CXXXVI. [*W. S. D. IX.* 285.]
LIVERPOOL TO CASTLEREAGH.
Fife House, November[1] 25th, 1814.

We received yesterday your letters of the 5th and 11th[2] instant. I can assure you that we are fully sensible of all the difficulties in which you have been involved, and entirely concur with you in the substantial points for which you have been contending. We were certainly apprehensive that the course the negotiations were taking with Russia might unintentionally lead us further than we had any idea of going, and eventually produce a renewal of the war in Europe. It may be quite true that if the Emperor

---

[1] Dated in the *Supplementary Dispatches* September, but the context clearly shows that November is the correct month.

[2] CXXV. and CXXVIII.

of Russia does not relax in his present demands, the peace of
Europe may not be of long continuance ; but for however short
a time that peace may last, I should consider it of great advantage.
In the course of two or three years it may reasonably be expected
that the power of Louis XVIII. in France will be consolidated,
and that the revolutionary spirit which still exists to such an
a'arming degree in that country will in a great measure have
evaporated. The people will have returned to peaceful habits,
and the landed and moneyed interests will feel their fate connected with that of the restored government. In two or three
years likewise the Prince of Orange will, I trust, have been enabled
firmly to establish his authority in the Low Countries, will have
raised an army for the defence of his dominions, and have made
some progress in erecting a barrier against his neighbours. But if
war should be renewed at present, I fear that we should lose all
we have gained, that the revolutionary spirit would break forth
again in full force, and that the Continent would be plunged in
all the evils under which it has groaned for the last twenty years.
A war now, therefore, may be a revolutionary war. A war some
time hence, though an evil, need not be different in its character
and its effects from any of those wars which occurred in the
seventeenth and eighteenth centuries, before the commencement
of the French Revolution. In short, this appears to me to be
the precise period in which the sentiment of Cicero, so often
quoted by Mr. Fox, is really in point : " *Iniquissimam pacem
justissimo bello antefero.*" I entertain these sentiments so strongly,
that though I should most deeply regret the continuance of
Murat on the throne of Naples as a sort of *taint* in our general
arrangement, and though I think, therefore, that all means should
be used consistent with our engagements to negotiate him out
of his present kingdom, yet if such means should fail, as I fear
they will, and the question should be whether any of the Powers
of Europe should take up arms to drive him out of his dominions,
my opinion would certainly be against such a measure. I think
the positive benefit resulting from the success of it is not to be
compared, under present circumstances, to the evils that might
arise out of the attempt.

The reasoning in your last paper in answer to the Emperor
of Russia is quite triumphant ; but I believe the truth to be
that he is committed to the Poles ; and the dread of the rein-
tegration of Poland as it existed in 1772 or 1791, and the effect
of such a sacrifice of territory upon the Russian nobility and
Russian people, are the only considerations that will induce him

to give way. He will be quite deaf to every appeal to justice, moderation, or to the engagements which he contracted with Prussia and Austria in the course of the last campaign. We must likewise not conceal from ourselves that we shall have a hard battle to fight against public opinion in defence of any arrangement of which the independence of Poland does not now form a part.

If the arrangements respecting the Duchy of Warsaw could have been quietly settled amongst the three Powers as the result of the Treaty of Kalisch and of that of the 9th September, 1813, we should never have had any serious difficulty on the subject, and it would have been wholly unnecessary, and I think very imprudent, for us ever to have started the idea of Poland or of Polish independence ; but it becomes very different to defend the partition of the Duchy of Warsaw as one of the alternatives to Polish independence, when the question of Polish independence has been once brought forward. We must, however, do our best in this respect, fully satisfied that we have acted from no other motive than that which was likely to contribute most upon the whole to the peace and tranquillity of Europe.

It seems difficult to imagine what course this whole business is likely to take in Congress.[1] I trust the means will exist, however of protesting against what it may not be prudent to resist, or at least that care may be taken that we are not parties to transactions which we have such strong reasons on every account to disapprove.

CXXXVII. [W. S. D. IX. 456.]
LIVERPOOL TO WELLINGTON.
Fife House, November 26th, 1814.

. . . We are very much distressed at the last accounts we have received from Vienna. The course which the negotiation has taken is particularly embarrassing. Lord Castlereagh has been substantially right in all his points ; but I wish we had not been made so much *principals* in the Polish question. I never thought that question could be satisfactorily settled after it had once become a subject of contest.

If the arrangements respecting the Duchy of Warsaw could have been quietly agreed upon amongst the three Powers, as the result of the Treaty of Kalisch, and of that of the 9th of September, 1813, there need have been no difficulty on the subject.

---

[1] Liverpool means " when the matter is formally discussed." All the negotiations so far had been merely informal discussions between the Four.

It would in that case have been wholly unnecessary, and, I think, very imprudent, for us to have ever started the idea of Poland or of Polish independency. This question has, however, now been forced upon us all by Russia It would be visionary to suppose that Poland can really be established, after all that has passed, as an independent country ; and we are thus brought practically to struggle for a question of partition, which is always odious in itself, in which we might have acquiesced as the result of former engagements, but for which it is painful to be obliged to contend on any other ground. Whatever may be the result of this question I sincerely hope, however, that there will be no war on the Continent. It may be quite true that if the Emperor of Russia does not relax in his pretensions, the peace of Europe may not be of long duration ; but considering the present state of France, of the Low Countries, and of Italy, I should regard a peace for two or three years as a great blessing. It might reasonably be expected that during that time the revolutionary spirit in those countries would in a great degree evaporate ; that the restored Sovereigns would find the means of consolidating their authority ; that the populations would return to peaceful habits ; and that, if a war should then arise, it would not be a revolutionary war, but that it would resemble in its character and effects those wars which occurred in the seventeenth and eighteenth centuries, before the commencement of the French Revolution.

CXXXVIII. [*F. O. Cont.* 6.]
BATHURST TO CASTLEREAGH.[1] (No. 3.)
November 27th, 1814.
. . . I am commanded by H.R.H. to acquaint you, that whilst he deeply laments the unfortunate course which the discussions at Vienna have taken respecting Poland in consequence of the unjust demands and dangerous pretensions of the Emperor of Russia, H.R.H. entirely approves of the firm and decided manner, in which you have expressed the sentiments of H.R.H. Government on the different branches of this important question. And in the event of your failing to avert the establishment of such pretensions, you will, as far as possible, avoid making H.R.H. a party to arrangements so injurious to the general interests of Europe.

H.R.H. cannot contemplate the present state of Europe, and more especially the internal state of France, Italy, and the Low

[1] This is the only important official *instruction* which Castlereagh received from the Cabinet while at Vienna. It will be seen that he deliberately disobeyed the last clause.

Countries, without entertaining the most serious apprehensions of the consequences which would result from the renewal of war on the Continent under present circumstances.

H.R H. has no doubt, therefore, that you will use your best endeavours to prevent, by all the means in your power, so great an evil.

It is unnecessary for me to point out to you the impossibility of H.R.H. consenting to involve this country in hostilities at this time for any of the objects which have been hitherto under discussion at Vienna.

CXXXIX.   [F. O. Cont. 8.]
CASTLEREAGH TO LIVERPOOL.   (No. 26.)
Vienna, December 5th, 1814.

In my letter of the 25th ult.[1] I reported to your Lordship the commencement of the negotiation with the Emperor of Russia upon the Polish question, and that the conduct of it had been entrusted to the Prince de Hardenberg. I was not, at that moment, enabled to state more, than the favourable reception Prince Hardenberg considered his proposition had met with from the Emperor of Russia, that His Imperial Majesty had agreed to treat upon the terms proposed, and had promised an answer in a few days.

The precise terms which the Prussian minister was authorised to propose were as follows : That Prussia should receive Thorn, and the line of the Wartha, and that Austria should obtain, in addition to the circle of Zamosc, Cracovie and the Nidda as a frontier. It was added that, provided the Emperor yielded on the territorial question as proposed, the two Powers were prepared to acquiesce in his political views in Poland, under guarantee to be reciprocally agreed upon.

The counter-projet to this overture was communicated on the part of Russia by Prince Czartoriski, and Baron Stein, neither of whom hold any responsible situation under the Emperor. It was limited to a proposition to neutralize the towns of Thorn and Cracovie, by erecting them into free cities, with a rayon round each, but His Imperial Majesty, however strong his professions had been for several days, of a desire to meet the wishes of his Allies, did not intimate any intention of yielding the circle of Zamosc, or the territory intervening between Kalisch and the Wartha, and between Cracovie and the Nidda, adhering, as far

[1] Castlereagh to Liverpool, November 25th, 1814. (No. 24.) F.O. Continent 8, stating shortly as is repeated in this dispatch.

as territory was concerned, to his former line by Kalisch to the west, and by the Vistula on the south, between Cracovie and Sandomir.

It was stated that as these two points had been represented as menacing to his Allies, the Emperor was willing thus to strip them of that character, but that as a condition *sine qua non* of this concession, he must require that the questions of Saxony and Mayence should be simultaneously settled, the former by its complete incorporation with Prussia, the latter by its being rendered a fortress of the Empire.

Your Lordship will recollect that the circumstances which preceded the transfer of the negotiation into the management of Prussia, were not such as to afford much prospect of insisting with effect upon any demand, more especially one of any magnitude. This, as I understand, induced the Austrian minister to represent to Prince Hardenberg the necessity under existing circumstances of Prussia modifying her Saxon pretensions, so as not only to secure the concurrence of the several German Powers, and, if possible, of France, to her arrangements, but also to compensate, in some measure, the disappointment of Austria as to her Polish frontier, by relieving her from that jealousy, which the total extinction of an intermediate Power on her Bohemian frontier must occasion.

I certainly understood from Prince Metternich, when he agreed to the basis of negotiation before stated, that Prince Hardenberg had previously acquiesced in this principle, it being premised that this modification was not to operate a reduction in the quantum of territory which Russia was to receive. By one of those changes of council which are not unfrequent in the Prussian Cabinet, it appears that this facility to an arrangement, however unsatisfactory it might still have remained with respect to the Polish frontier, is now absolutely withdrawn on the part of Prince Hardenberg, and I am afraid your Lordship must be prepared if this is persisted in, of which there is every appearance, to find the negotiation generally assume a most embarrassing, complexion.

You will judge of this, as far as the interests of Austria are concerned, by observing that the Russian counter-projet gives her nothing in point of frontier on the side of Poland. It merely relieved her from the umbrage of two points, by giving them a political instead of a military character. On the side of the Elbe it exposes her to a direct contact with Prussia, throughout the whole line of her Bohemian frontier, the gorges of which will pass into the hands of that Power, and it also embarrasses even her Bavarian frontier by insisting upon an arrangement with respect to Mayence, which, however wise in itself, disappoints the condition upon which Bavaria had agreed to restore to Austria the strong country extending from Salzburg along the Inn to the Danube.

It is not merely in her territorial relations that the spirit disclosed in the late negotiations embarrasses Austria. She feels still greater uneasiness from the temper of the Russian councils, and from the commanding sway the Emperor has acquired, through the King, over those of Prussia. Had Prince Hardenberg been enabled to range himself, as he promised to do, on the side of Austria, in a sincere, open, and undisguised negotiation with Russia upon the Polish question, whatever might have been the success of this effort, the world would have taken it as a proof that Prussia was true to the interests of Germany, and it would have given Austria a strong moral justification for making great sacrifices to her in Saxony ; but the misfortune is, that the impression, as well as the fact, is now the other way, and that Russia and Prussia are looked upon as one, pledged to support each other's objects, whatever may be their effect either upon Austrian or German interests.

Prince Metternich forcibly represented to me yesterday, the difficulty in which he found himself placed under the circumstances above stated. He stated that he felt himself nominally allied with Russia and Prussia, but with the prospect, upon every litigated question, of having both against him ; that under these circumstances, however desirous of bending, as far as possible, for the sake of an adjustment, he did not feel that he could venture to run counter, on the Saxon question, to the moral feeling of Germany, to the sentiments of his own Cabinet, and to the declared opinion of the French Government without the hazard of leaving himself and his Government without the support in Europe, which was become indispensable to its security and independence whilst Russia possessed so commanding an influence over the Prussian Cabinet.

I foresaw, from the first, that these German questions, if they could not be resolved from a sense of common danger, by a union of common interest between the two great German Powers, upon the Polish question, would prove beyond all comparison the most fruitful source of discord, from the complexity of the combinations amongst the German States, worked upon both by Russian and French influence.

The Austrian minister no sooner perceived from the conduct and language of the King of Prussia, and from the retrocession of the Prussian minister upon the Saxon point, that the intervention of Prussia in the negotiation was little more than nominal, than, in despair of accomplishing anything effectual on the Polish question, he only considered how he could best make an accommodation with Russia subservient to a modification on the point of Saxony, which I look upon now as the point practically at issue, however the other may remain open to further discussion.

The considerations I have already stated are not the only difficulties to a settlement upon the Saxon question. The extent to which Russia has appropriated the Polish territories to her own use, narrows very inconveniently the means of satisfying other claims. In meeting the demands of Prussia, and in making provision for those of the Prince of Orange (but in a manner to which I shall have objections to state) there remains only an indemnity for the King of Saxony in Münster and Paderborn of 350,000 subjects. Whether this is placed at Dresden or on the side of Westphalia, the provision is not in extent such as he is likely to accept. Austria and Bavaria are more moderate in their demands, but France requires for him nearly the whole of ancient Saxony, amounting to one million five hundred thousand subjects, consenting only to deprive him of Upper Lusace and the Circle of Wittenberg.

Could Russia have been prevailed upon to take the Vistula as her frontier there would have been ample means to satisfy all fair claims.

CXL. [W. S. D. IX. 462.]
CASTLEREAGH TO LIVERPOOL.
Vienna, December 5th, 1814.

[Unable to confirm the expectations of an early settlement, founded upon the opinions of Metternich and Hardenberg. Convinced that the adjustment of frontier between Russia and the adjacent States must remain unsatisfactory, but wishes to bring the whole arrangement, subject to this defect, to a tolerable close rather than risk a contest. Impossible, however, to answer for the result. Desirous of receiving from his colleagues any instructions or suggestions which might assist him.]

Upon the existing state of affairs, extremely entangled in themselves, my opinion is, that it may unexpectedly assume a better aspect, but that it may equally lead to a total stagnation, and that it may, as Europe is more extensively armed than at any former period, suddenly end in war.

In the first alternative my task will be comparatively easy, and I shall only have to combine, according to circumstances, the fragments of the arrangement, and to give to it the best form.

In the second supposition, if no general decision should be come to, and the ministers of certain of the leading Powers should absolutely decline to concur in the pretentions of others, I should wish, as far as you can instruct me, to learn the sentiments of the Government as to the extent and period of my stay here.

But the object to which I should most wish to draw your attention is to the third case, of actual or impending war ; and to ascertain, if possible, by anticipation, what my province will be, either in endeavouring to avert or, if that shall be impossible, to counteract the dangers with which it may menace our interests.

In the first place it is only a question of absence from my duty at home, the considerations bearing upon which will be best estimated perhaps when we more nearly approach to the period when Parliament must reassemble after Christmas.

The second case is more critical, and by no means improbable, namely, such an adherence, short of war, to their own views, that the leading Powers, remaining armed, may refuse to accede to each other's pretensions, and the Congress terminate either in a general state of provisional occupancy, or in the partial adjustment of particular parts of the European arrangement amongst the Powers locally most interested.

But the most important, and, if we cannot agree upon some general system, the most likely case to occur is that of hostilities ; and where all are armed, and none can long support the burthen of their existing establishments, the chances are that the warfare will be early and general.

Take the case of Russia and Prussia : if they are determined to make common cause on their respective objects, and cannot succeed in prevailing upon the other Powers to acquiesce in their demands, it will not suit the exhausted finances of Prussia to remain long armed and inactive ; nor can Russia expose herself indefinitely to the incumbrance of large armies remaining unemployed beyond or on the verge of her own frontier. I think the probability therefore is, that one or both of these Powers, if they do not relax in their pretensions, will provoke rather than procrastinate the war.

If war should, under these circumstances, arise, I think it has every prospect of becoming general in Germany. That France must and will enter into it, I have no doubt ; and with Holland, the Low Countries, and Hanover exposed, in addition to the interest we must take in the fate of the Continent, it will be difficult for Great Britain long, if at all, to abstract herself from the contest.

The questions I should then wish you to weigh me, whether we should at once appear as a party in the war, or whether we should rather interpose as armed mediators, if possible to stop the war, or remain inactive till, by an attack on some interest of which we are the immediate guardians, our interposition is rendered indispensable.

In examining the first question, I am inclined to be of opinion, that having no duty in point of alliance imposed upon us which the unfortunate divergence amongst our late Allies will not discharge us from, we ought not to contract any new obligations of so serious a nature upon any of the points now in dispute between those with whom we have been recently acting ; for however deeply we think that we may trace in them a new danger to Europe, the nation, after so long a war, could not be brought forward with effect in support of a question either of Polish or Bohemian frontier. Our interposition, must therefore be, if inevitable, not as auxiliaries to any particular State, but as principals upon some grounds of policy which Great Britain will consider it her duty and interest to maintain.

The first and most popular of all interests perhaps that we could look to is that of preventing war. In this view it deserves consideration whether the sense of our justice and the dread of our arms and resources could at any time, and at what, be brought forward in the shape of an intervention to enforce peace upon the contending parties.

It next deserves to be weighed, whether this attempt, if wise, should be made singly or in conjunction with France. There are many points of view in which the appearance of France at all in the field must be viewed as a danger the most serious in itself ; but this will not exclude her from interference ; and the question is, what species of interference will render her *marche* the least prejudicial to the interest of Europe, and give the King, in whose probity and honour we may venture to confide, the best means of preventing his army from imposing upon him, when in operation, a line of policy which his principles would naturally lead him to abjure.

I am inclined to think that the best mode in which France could intervene, if this risk must be run, would, in the first instance, be to avoid war ; and that, in this character, her intervention might be advantageously combined with ours. The two Powers might truly and powerfully put forward to Europe a coincidence of interests and a similarity of views. Neither have any direct interest at issue before the Congress ; both have the strongest and most obvious interest in peace : if such an appeal could be successfully made, every purpose would be answered ; if it failed, the connexion of France with Great Britain would bring her into the war as it were associated to an anti-revolutionary policy. It will be a solemn disavowal, at the outset, of her former wild schemes of frontier and dominion ; and the army would be taught when taking the field that the King was not again embarking them by degrees in their former views of plunder and spoliation, which might be further guarded against by suitable engagements between the two Courts, in which the Prince of Orange might be included.

If there were any clear and definite principle upon which we might hope altogether to keep out of the war without the incumbrance of remaining armed throughout the period of a protracted contest, the policy of engaging either separately or in conjunction with France in an armed intervention might be more than doubted ; but where we are embarked so deeply in the formation and protection of a system in the Low Countries, I can hardly conceive the possibility of our finding ourselves long dispensed from the necessity of maintaining by arms in such a contest either these particular interests or the interests of Europe in the larger sense.

I have suggested the idea of an armed mediation as an expedient short of actual war, because I think there may be an interval after hostilities had commenced during which Great Britain and France might assume this character, to give weight to which the army of the Low Countries and Hanover might be united under the Duke of Wellington on the Lower Rhine, whilst the French army was concentrated on the side of Strasburg. In this situation they might invite other Powers to associate themselves to their object of arresting the war ; whilst Austria and Bavaria, whose united means are represented to amount to 600,000 men, would have to bear, if it did explode, the first shock.

I throw out these ideas for your consideration without any formed opinion which I should wish to press upon the adoption of my colleagues.

CXLI. [*F. O. Cont.* 8.]
CASTLEREAGH TO LIVERPOOL. (No. 27.)
Vienna, December 7th, 1814.
[Interview with Hardenberg.]

. . . I stated to him that there was but one sentiment amongst us all, that Prussia should be reconstructed upon the scale to which her Treaties entitled her to lay claim ; and that the only question was whether the whole of Saxony should be included in the territories to be assigned to her. In observing on the difficulties that opposed themselves to such an arrangement, I delivered to His Highness an extract of Your Lordship's private letter of the 18th ult.,[1] as the best proof not of what those usually opposed to the King's Government in Great Britain might urge in the controversy of debate upon this subject, but of the sentiments deliberately entertained by those most friendly to the interests of Prussia. I requested Prince Hardenberg to lay this extract before the King in corroboration of the advice I had given him some time since, namely, that as Minister for Prussia, he ought to prefer a compromise on this question to a total extinction. I did not, however, conceal from him that I considered the point as now standing on different grounds from what it did when my letter of the 11th of October and Prince Metternich's of the 22nd of October were written.[2]

That in doing justice to the loyalty of his intentions, it was impossible to deny that the concert on the affairs of Poland, which was the basis of the understanding, had avowedly failed through the conduct of his sovereign ; that under these circumstances, neither Austria nor Great Britain could espouse his claims in the manner they might otherwise have done, and wished to do ; and that the question now was, whether, having failed in an attempt to bring Russia to such an arrangement of frontier as had been deemed requisite, he would assert, through her influence alone, a pretention against the general sentiment of Europe.

Prince Hardenberg endeavoured to maintain the hardship upon Prussia, after all her exertions, to find herself thwarted in her views, and that he would run all risks rather than return home under such an humiliation. I represented that this was not a case of war, that he was in the occupation of Saxony, and that I apprehended no one would think of removing him hostilely, from thence, but that he could not regard an unacknowledged

[1] CXXX.
[2] See CXVI. and CXIX.

claim as constituting a good title and that he never could in *conscience* or *honour* advise his sovereign to make the mere refusal of a recognition a cause of war against other States : that Prussia would then remain in a state of disquietude and doubt, compelled to remain armed, and that his return to Berlin would, under such circumstances, be more painful, than if he brought back the accession of all the Powers of Europe to an equal extent of dominion, though differently constituted.

In pressing upon Prince Hardenberg's mind the friendly share Great Britain had always borne in asserting the interests of Prussia, and the successful efforts recently made by myself to prevail upon Austria to sacrifice her objections on the point of Saxony to the larger question of Poland, His Highness became more reasonable and agreed to take *ad referendum* a counter-projet from Austria, showing how Prussia could be secured in her rights without laying claim to the entire of Saxony. The Chancellor also allowed me strongly to impress upon him that, in proportion as the world imputed to his Court whether falsely or not, it was not necessary to decide, an alarming degree of subservience to Russian influence, that it became the more impolitick in him, wishing as I had no doubt he did, to preserve the general confidence of Europe, to attempt to force an arrangement, which several of the principal Powers of Europe might decline to sanction. That in proportion as he had failed to bring forward his King upon the Polish question, he ought to be accommodating on that of Germany, if he wished to be respected among his co-estates, and not to build his authority amongst them upon an external influence.

I left the Prussian Minister more temperate upon the point than I had expected to find him. Having prepared him for a negative from Austria under present circumstances to the total incorporation of Saxony, I afterwards saw Prince Metternich, and urged him to frame his answer to the Prussian paper in such a manner as would present at once to Prince Hardenberg's mind the difficulty of executing his purpose against the prevailing sentiment and would shew him in a counter-projet how his just views could be otherwise realised.

This Prince Metternich promised to do. He was much pleased with the part I had taken, and, as he is but too apt to do, considered an arrangement now as certain. Much will yet depend on obtaining from Russia some further territorial means in Poland : without these I do not see how the various pretentions can be at all adequately satisfied. We must still hope that the

Emperor will not suffer things to get into confusion for a limited extent of territory. If he cedes up to the Wartha and the Nidda it will give essential facilities.

The Emperor of Austria and Prince Metternich severally had interviews with the Emperor of Russia yesterday. The latter assured me they were both quite explicit with him upon the Saxon point, intimating at the same time their desire to accommodate to his views on the side of Poland, if the whole arrangement could be so cast as to procure a general concurrence upon the Saxon question. I understood from Prince Metternich that he laid in [sic] his objection to the erection of Thorn and Cracobie, into neutral towns, considering them as likely in that state to endanger the tranquillity of the neighbouring Powers. This may probably give occasion to a renewed proposition on the part of Austria and Prussia for the possession of those towns with the territory before asked for, upon conditions of their not being fortified, which will fall within the principle upon which Russia proposed to neutralise them, namely, their not being menacing to the new Polish Kingdom.

I have stated to your Lordship the result of his interview. The Chancellor's language might certainly justify a hope, that these questions were yet open to fair discussion ; but I have so often found Prince Hardenberg's candid impressions disappear upon communication with those around him, and when I witness every day, the astonishing tenacity with which all the Powers cling to the smallest point of separate interest, I must entreat your Lordship not to indulge from this report too sanguine an expectation that the very complicated and important concerns which yet mix themselves with the three great questions now combined in a joint negotiation are likely to be either very speedily or amicably regulated.

CXLII. [*W. S. D. IX.* 483.]
CASTLEREAGH TO LIVERPOOL.
Vienna, December 17th, 1814.

Although I cannot announce to you the result of our Saxon negotiation, I think it right to apprise you in a private letter of a diplomatic explosion which has taken place, since I last wrote, between Austria and Prussia, and which has been productive of very animated discussions between these Courts and the Emperor of Russia.

It arose out of Prince Metternich's answer,[1] now sent, refusing Saxony to Prussia. This exasperated the Prussians, and induced our friend Hardenberg to do a very incorrect act, to which he must have been pushed on by others, possibly with a view to his own overthrow, namely, to communicate to the Emperor of Russia parts of the confidential correspondence that had passed between himself and Prince Metternich with respect to Poland, and their concert against the views of Russia. These secret papers were accompanied with an insinuation that Austria now broke faith with Prussia upon the point of Saxony, in consequence of Prussia *refusing* to enter into a hostile alliance against Russia.

Upon the receipt of this intelligence the Emperor of Russia went to the Emperor of Austria and reproached him with the alleged hostile purpose. The Emperor very naturally replied that if his minister had written such a letter, it was without his knowledge, and that he must be called on to explain.

Under these circumstances Prince Metternich had no other alternative but to carry to the Emperor of Russia, in his own justification, all his *own* letters, leaving it to Prince Hardenberg to produce *his* or not, as he thought fit. The fact happens to be, that the only really objectionable letters are the Chancellor's own. Metternich's are perfectly fair diplomatic papers, avowing in very proper terms the objections of his Court to the Russian views ; whereas Hardenberg, in order to escape an avowed opposition to Russia, in which he found himself disavowed, did not simply confine himself to being most unnecessarily the advocate of peace, but undertook to show that the Emperor must soon be ruined by his own politics, that in a few years his military power would become comparatively feeble, and that it was then the Allies *might seize an occasion of doing themselves justice.*

It is hardly credible that with such appendant matter he should venture to risk the communication of Metternich's replies, all of which originate in papers of his own, more or less indiscreet, and infinitely more inconsistent, particularly with the Prussian relations with Russia, than anything Metternich had written. In truth Prince Metternich's letter of the 22nd October,[2] which I have sent home, evinces a sincere desire to conciliate, and not to quarrel with Russia.

The whole, as you may imagine, made for two days a great sensation, but the result perhaps may serve to prove what I have

---

[1] Metternich to Hardenberg, December 10th, 1814. D'Angeberg, 505.
[2] See CXIX.

ventured before to allege, that the climate of Russia is often the more serene after a good squall. The justificatory interview between the Emperor of Russia and Metternich was not the less stormy, from a little *private* note of the latter, denying, in terms not very measured, some reported insinuations of His Imperial Majesty's against *his* fidelity to Prussia. This note was, either most ungenerously or most unaccountably, amongst the papers sent, and served not a little to exasperate. The audience terminated by His Imperial Majesty's saying he should give his answer to the Emperor in person.

The interview between the Emperors took place the following morning, and, according to the report I have received, was marked by peculiar conciliation on the part of the Emperor Alexander ; a wish to settle all differences, and to be the best possible friends ; regret that he could not meet the Emperor of Austria's wishes about Cracovie, which the Poles could not bear he should alienate as the tomb of their kings ; but that in lieu thereof, and as proof of his regard, he would cede the circle of Tarnapol, which he had received from Austria by the Peace of Vienna.[1] This district contains a population of not less than 400,000 subjects ; and although the cession will not serve Austria in point of frontier, it is certainly the most substantial proof of a disposition to treat à *l'aimable* which His Imperial Majesty has yet afforded. The Emperor expressed his hope that Prussia would also accommodate, and that all might be arranged.

I may be mistaken, but I cannot but infer from what has occurred that this disclosure has produced rather a salutary impression on the Emperor's mind. Had these ministers spoken as bold truths to His Imperial Majesty in their interviews as they did to each other in their letters, and had they supported *me* in the clear and decisive tone which their official correspondence entitled me to expect, my persuasion is that the Emperor of Russia would have come to a suitable arrangement with respect to the point of Poland, notwithstanding the embarrassment he had previously created for himself by hopes given to the Poles. In this correspondence the Emperor clearly perceived that I had not been mistaken in representing to him the real feelings of his Allies ; and I have no doubt that they made their impression even after the concert had failed. I am afraid, however, the disclosure will operate prejudicially on the relations between Austria and Prussia.

[1] Of 1809.

CXLIII. [*F. O. Cont.* 9.]
CASTLEREAGH TO LIVERPOOL. (No. 35.)
Vienna, December 18th, 1814.

I am not enabled to add anything on which I can absolutely rely relative to the negotiation. I have some reason however to believe that a new Projet, assigning to the King of Saxony an increased indemnity to the extent of eight hundred thousand subjects, *but not in Saxony*, has been laid before the Emperor Alexander, for his sanction, by Prince Hardenberg. I have heard from another quarter, that the Prussian answer or Projet, whatever it is, was not approved by His Imperial Majesty. Baron Stein is the most earnest opponent in the Prussian councils of any modification of the Saxon point. Prince Metternich declares that nothing will induce his Emperor to give way on this subject ; and as a proof that his Court is determined, he has transmitted his last note to Prince Hardenberg officially to Prince Talleyrand.[1] This is the first regular overture that has been made by Austria to France; the personal intercourse between these ministers has been considerably augmented within these few days.

The Austrian Minister having expressed a wish for my intervention on the point of Saxony, and a similar insinuation coming through Count Hardenberg on the part of Prussia, but accompanied by a doubt whether the recent conduct of that Cabinet might not indispose me to interfere, I thought it right to declare, that no feeling with respect to the past would make me refuse my intervention, if I thought I could be instrumental in bringing the parties to an amicable arrangement, however much I might desire, on personal grounds, to be as little mixed as possible with this question of Saxony ; but that to afford any chance of being of use, my interference must be equally desired by the parties, and I must be previously assured, that Prussia is prepared to admit as a basis, a suitable arrangement for the King of Saxony.

If the information above alluded to is correct, it does not appear that the Prussians are yet prepared to yield on the latter principle. If they were, with Dresden and the half of Saxony, more or less, according to local convenience, I think the King ought to be satisfied. This would place Saxony in Germany rather above what Hanover was in 1792, and a little below what Hanover and Wirtemberg will now be. If the French Revolution has inordinately raised Bavaria, there is no just reason why Saxony may not be depressed in somewhat a corresponding ration by the different operation of such convulsive causes. To maintain that some

[1] Metternich to Talleyrand, December 16th, 1814. D'Angeberg, 540.

States acting with France may gain by such events, but that others should not lose, would be laying down a principle both unjust and dangerous, and throwing the losses of the struggle upon the most meritorious Houses in Germany.

CXLIV. [*W. S. D. IX.* 485.]
CASTLEREAGH TO LIVERPOOL.
Vienna, December 18th, 1814.

. . . I think Murat's pretensions to be acknowledged by us cannot be sustained ; they do not rest upon any formal engagement. The whole claim turns upon an assurance contingent upon two conditions : 1st. His effective co-operation ; 2ndly. The King of Sicily being indemnified. Neither of these conditions have or are now to be realised. If Murat's conduct in the war had been such as we were entitled to expect, it might be urged that he ought not to suffer from the King's refusal of indemnity, even were it possible to propose one for his acceptance, which it is not ; but where the whole course of Murat's proceedings was, in the judgment and view of the whole army, dilatory, wavering, and suspicious, and when we know from the Viceroy, although he will not be an evidence on the question, that he was engaged the greater part of the time in a traitorous intercourse with him, it appears to me impossible to suffer the contingent assurance given by Lord William Bentinck to the Marquis di Gallo on the 1st of April under the authority of my letter from Chatillon of the 21st of February[1]—an assurance which you will observe from the enclosed was given under expressions of pointed qualification at the time—to supersede all the claims the Sicilian family have to the favour and protection of Great Britain, much more to engage the employment of our power, under such circumstances, to secure an usurper against them in their kingdom of Naples.

[Conversation with Talleyrand on the subject. Told him that British Government not bound to Murat, since the conditions not fulfilled on his part. Talleyrand undertook to have search made in the offices at Paris for evidence of Murat's treachery. Stated willingness to contribute to restore the Bourbons to Naples and asked for a confidential Memorandum as to the steps advisable to be adopted to effect this object. Encloses this Memorandum. Urged the importance of distinct proofs of Murat's treachery, and satisfied Talleyrand of our desire to concur with France on this subject. France as little disposed as we are for immediate war to enforce compliance.]

[1] Laying down two conditions for the recognition of Murat—his active assistance in the war and a suitable indemnity for Ferdinand.

Prince Talleyrand's main reliance for getting rid of Murat is the pledge proposed to be taken against his pretensions, and which he hopes all the Powers except Austria would concur in. This would for the time save the honour of his Government ; but I doubt its having any serious effect upon Murat's situation, or inducing him, as Prince Talleyrand expects, to come forward with terms of accommodation. On the other hand, there is always an inconvenience in such abstract declarations, unaccompanied with any practical measure, either of war of negotiation, and which are capable of being represented, in theory at least, an interminable barrier to the relations of peace being re-established between the principal States of Europe and the kingdom of Naples.

It appears to me that this species of declaration would be open to peculiar inconvenience in a Parliamentary point of view. I think it would not be difficult to satisfy Parliament and Europe that Great Britain owed it to herself to concur in a negotiation to remove Murat from the throne of Naples, under all the circumstances of the case, viz., the existing state of Europe, now comprising two great States, viz., France and Spain, who cannot be expected to acknowledge Murat ; the strong, I may say the almost irresistible claims, now incapable of being satisfied in any other manner, which the Sicilian family have upon those States with whom they have co-operated throughout the war, and the very small claim established by Murat by his conduct in the field to be protected against the ancient family.

I should, therefore, prefer an actual offer of terms to Murat, whether successful or not, to a more insulated declaration. If liberal they would reconcile the public feeling to any future policy of a more hostile nature. The case against him in reasoning is abundantly strong to bear out this first step. The mere fact of the negotiation is by inference a denial of his title and a recognition of his adversary. A refusal on his part would justify his non-recognition, and leave open all future measures to prudential consideration. The attempt on the part of so many preponderating States to restore the ancient family must tend to weaken Murat's authority within the country, and call forth a sentiment, if such exists, in favour of Ferdinand IV., without seeming to provoke insurrection by a sentence of illigitimacy passed upon Murat, unaccompanied, however, by any expedient to facilitate a favourable settlement between these rival pretensions.

The future course to be pursued would remain fairly open to decision. The public mind of Europe, once satisfied of the propriety of the first measure, would be gradually prepared for any ulterior proceedings, and we should close the transactions before Congress without any further embarrassment than a dissent on the part of Austria alone to the institution of a negotiation to settle, if possible, amicably a point which certainly in its present shape menaces most seriously the peace of Italy, if not of Europe.

I enclose a short Memorandum,[1] suggesting for your consideration the course which I should myself prefer to that proposed by Prince Talleyrand on this question.

CASTLEREAGH'S PROJET RESPECTING MURAT.[2]

To consolidate effectually the peace of Europe, Ferdinand IV. must be restored to Naples, since it is impossible to find any adequate territorial indemnity to propose to the King, and it is his avowed purpose not to accept any indemnity.

It is fit and proper that a provision of a pecuniary nature should be secured to Murat and his heirs for ever, having regard to the importance of avoiding measures which might compromise the public tranquillity and involve Naples in civil war.

Should Murat consent peaceably to abdicate, assurance is to be given him that he will receive every consideration on the part of our respective Sovereigns and, in the event of his wishing to establish his residence in any of their dominions, a cordial and hospitable reception.

Further efforts will be made to procure a settlement, as a condition of his abdication in favour of Ferdinand IV., by which, under solemn guarantee, a complete oblivion of the past and an abjuration of every vindictive feeling as to the future shall be secured on the part of Ferdinand and his successors, to the Neapolitan people.

A condition is also to be made that Ferdinand shall secure to his Neapolitan subjects such rights and privileges as may be just and reasonable.

A joint commission to be appointed to open communication with Murat upon these principles and to assure him of the amicable character of the overture.

CXLV. [W. S. D. IX. 493.]
LIVERPOOL TO CASTLEREAGH.
Fife House, December 22nd, 1814.

In the event of the discussions at Vienna leading to some general settlement of the affairs of Europe, it has occurred to us that you may be pressed to become a party to the arrangements of the Emperor of Russia with respect to Poland, or rather to his acquisition of the Duchy of Warsaw.

If this should be proposed to you, we have no objection to your agreeing to it, provided it is distinctly stipulated in the Treaty

[1] Précis follows this dispatch.
[2] Précis of document in W. S. D. IX. 488.

that at least the Polish provinces incorporated with Russia since 1791 shall be reunited to the Duchy of Warsaw, so as to form a distinct kingdom of Poland, under a free Constitution.

As this is in conformity to the Emperor of Russia's own suggestion, and to the language which he has invariably held regarding Poland, he cannot, in fairness, object to this proposal ; and if the Crown of Russia is to be aggrandized to the extent now proposed, it would afford some security to Europe, however inadequate, that the empire should consist of two distinct kingdoms, and that the Crown and one of those kingdoms should be subject to the control of a government more or less popular.

In case, however, the Emperor of Russia should object to any such stipulation in a Treaty or instrument to which other Powers were parties, it may be of importance that you should take means of informing Prince Czartoriski and the other Poles who may be at Vienna that you were authorized by your Government to propose such a stipulation.

I feel it necessary only to add that whatever may be now the result of the arrangements respecting Poland, our taking any part of the Russian debt to Holland as a charge on this country will, we trust, after all that has passed, be considered as entirely out of the question.

CXLVI. [W. S. D. IX. 496.]
LIVERPOOL TO CASTLEREAGH.
Fife House, December 23rd, 1814.

[As to Castlereagh's opinion that the French might be won over to our views on other points by our agreeing with them on the point of Naples, the British Government is of opinion that it would not be justified in assisting to dethrone Murat, if he fairly fulfilled his engagements after the conclusion of the peace between him and Austria. It must be left to Castlereagh to decide upon the best evidence he can obtain as to whether Murat's conduct has absolved Great Britain from any obligation towards him. Since Murat has published the assurances given in Castlereagh's despatch to Bentinck of April 3rd, it is essential that the case against him should be such as will justify the change of conduct towards him by Parliament and by the world.]

Supposing, however, his treachery or wilful and culpable inactivity to be clearly established, how are we to get rid of him ? If he will accept of a compensation, and such compensation can be found, the difficulty is solved ; but if he is determined to defend himself, who is the Power to be charged with expelling him ? Would it be safe, under the present circumstances of Italy, and the unpopularity of most of the governments re-established there, especially those of Austria, to revive a state of war in that country ?

We are inclined to think that it would be more safe and prudent for the Powers of Europe to tolerate Murat than for any of them to undertake hostilities for the purpose of expelling him. A war carried on by France, however, in Germany or the Low Countries, would be so much greater an evil to Great Britain than a war carried on by her in Italy, that if the former can be avoided only by the occurrence of the latter, it appears to us incomparably the least evil of the two ; but we can only be justified in encouraging or giving our sanction to such a line of policy by the conviction that the conduct of Murat subsequent to his engagements with Austria had been of a nature to discharge us from all our obligations towards him.

CXLVII. [*W. S. D. IX.* 497.]
LIVERPOOL TO CASTLEREAGH.
Fife House, December 23rd, 1814.

We have received your despatches of the 5th and 7th instant and the very important private letter addressed to me of the former date.[1]

The contents of these papers have been fully considered, and we are decidedly and unanimously of opinion that all your endeavours should be directed to the continuance of peace ; and that there is no mode in which the arrangements in Poland, Germany, and Italy can be settled, consistently with the stipulations of the Treaty of Paris, which is not to be preferred under present circumstances to a renewal of hostilities between the Continental Powers. Such an event could not at this time take place in Europe without the danger of our being involved in it at no distant period unless we were prepared to purchase neutrality by sacrifices which would be neither consistent with our character nor our safety.

With these sentiments deeply impressed upon our minds, we must not disguise from you that it would be quite impossible to embark this country in a war at present, except from a clear point of honour, or for some distinct British interest of sufficient magnitude to reconcile the country to it.

The defence of Holland and the Low Countries is the only objection the continent of Europe which would be regarded in this

[1] CXXXIX., CXL., CXLI.

light, and for which we could reasonably expect the support of Parliament in imposing or continuing those burthens on the country which our being involved in a war would render indispensable.

If the Austrian government is once satisfied that they have no chance of receiving subsidies from Great Britain, they will not be disposed to urge their pretensions to the extent of war, and the differences between them and the other Powers will, I trust, be in some way or other arranged without an appeal to arms.

We are ready, notwithstanding these considerations, to give full weight to the opinion contained in your private letter of the 5th instant, that adverting to the actual situation of the great Powers on the Continent, how generally they are armed, and how little they are all able to support the expense of their existing establishments, a state of war may possibly arise amongst them, if not from any deliberate view of policy, yet out of the circumstances in which they may find themselves placed.

We concur with you that if war should be renewed on the Continent, it would be in vain to expect that France could be long kept out of it; and if France were once embarked without a previous understanding with Great Britain, her efforts might, in the first instance, be directed, if not against Belgium, at least against the countries between the Meuse and the Rhine, which are now principally occupied by the Prussian armies.

We agree, therefore, that a *rapprochement* between this country and France is most desirable at the present moment; and we shall entirely approve of your proceeding to open a confidential communication with the French Government on all the subjects now under discussion, both through Prince Talleyrand at Vienna, and through the Duke of Wellington at Paris. On whatever points France and England might be found to agree, the knowledge of a good understanding upon those points between two such Powers could hardly fail to give their united opinion considerable weight.

With respect to the line of conduct which it may be expedient for us to adopt in the event of the sudden renewal of war upon the Continent, it must depend upon such a variety of circumstances, and must be influenced so materially by the character which the war may assume, that after the fullest consideration we have found it impossible to frame instructions which can be applicable to the various contingencies to which the renewal of the war may give rise.

We are not insensible to some of the advantages which might be derived in such a case from a joint armed mediation on the part of Great Britain and France ; but a measure of this kind would be so novel and extraordinary, and might be attended with so many consequences which cannot now be foreseen, that it appears to us to be quite impossible to determine upon it as a course of policy before we are distinctly acquainted with all the circumstances under which the war shall have originated, with the immediate cause of it, and with the different pretensions and expectations of the Powers who may have engaged in it.

We do not see any considerable inconvenience that can arise from our deferring any decision on this, and on other points connected with it, until the occasion shall arise, especially as we have no particular nor national interest in any of the objects which are most seriously contested at this time, and as the avowed purpose, therefore, of our policy is not to carry any point of our own, but to consolidate the peace concluded at Paris by an amicable adjustment of the differences which have unfortunately occurred amongst other Powers.

It may be of the utmost importance, in the meantime, to anticipate the Emperor of Russia, who, having carried his objects in the East of Europe, may be disposed to purchase the concurrence of France by an acquiescence in her views in other quarters. The known honour of the King of France will, however, be our best security against his contracting any engagements inconsistent with the stipulations of the peace which he has concluded, and contrary to his good faith towards us, provided we treat him and his government with that consideration and confidence which they regard not unjustly as due to them, and which may induce them to look to a cordial understanding with Great Britain as the best prospect of recovering their fair portion of influence in Europe.

We know these were the sentiments of the King of France and of his Ministers when you saw them in your way through Paris in the month of August last, and we have no reason to believe that their sentiments in this respect have undergone any change since that time.

CXLVIII. [*W. S. D. IX.* 494.]
LIVERPOOL TO WELLINGTON.
Fife House, December 23rd, 1814.
I send open for your perusal several letters[1] which, with the concurrence of the Cabinet, I have written this day to Lord Castlereagh ; and, although cross-negotiations are most objection-

[1] See CXLVI., CXLVII.

able, and generally involve the governments which have recourse to them in difficulties, I can see no objection to your seeking an audience of the King of France, to your explaining to him generally the feelings and sentiments of the Prince Regent's government towards him, and thereby preparing him for any communication Lord Castlereagh may make to Prince Talleyrand at Vienna.

The more I hear and see of the different Courts of Europe, the more convinced I am that the King of France is (amongst the great Powers) the only Sovereign in whom we can have any real confidence. The Emperor of Russia is profligate from vanity and self-sufficiency, if not from principle. The King of Prussia may be a well-meaning man, but he is the dupe of the Emperor of Russia. The Emperor of Austria I believe to be an honest man, but he has a Minister in whom no one can trust ; who considers all policy as consisting in *finesse* and trick ; and who has got his government and himself into more difficulties by his devices than could have occurred from a plain course of dealing.

We must not conceal from ourselves, however, that an avowed union between Great Britain and France would be likely to be unpopular in both countries. Questions might arise, and opportunities might occur, which would, not unnaturally, lead to it ; but a measure of this very delicate nature should not be precipitated ; and we gain our purpose sufficiently at present if we can establish a complete confidential intercourse with the French government which will give to neither party any pretence to entei into engagements to the prejudice of the other, or indeed into any engagements at all, which, under present circumstances, it is not willing to communicate to the other.

We should be much obliged to you if you could let us have some information of the present numbers and conditions of the French army, as well as of the progress of the measures which are now taking to recruit it. We understand that the report which had created so much alarm in the Low Countries some time ago, of the assembly of a large force at Lisle, turns out to be unfounded.

CXLIX.   [*F. O. Cont.* 9.]
CASTLEREAGH TO LIVERPOOL.   (No. 38.)
Vienna, December 24th, 1814.
I stated to Your Lordship in my despatch No. 35[1] the desire which had been evidenced directly by Austria, and indirectly by

[1] CXLIII.

Prussia, for my intervention on the Saxon point, and the language I had held upon this subject.

The following day Prince Czartoriski, who although not in any official situation, appears now the actual Russian minister, at least on Polish and Saxon questions, desired to call on me. He did not profess to come in the Emperor's name nor did I wish to impede any object he might have in conferring with me, by endeavouring to give his visit a more formal character than he chose to clothe it with. The object of his conversation was to ascertain the sentiments of my court upon the Saxon question, and to consider how we could best escape from the difficulties in which we were placed.

I explained to him, without reserve, the reasons which made it my duty to express a modification on the part of Prussia, of the Saxon question, as the only means that could now lead to an arrangement, to which all the great Powers would be parties.

The following day, Prince Hardenberg desired to see me, for the purpose of communicating to me his memoir, and to express a wish, after our separate interview was closed, that I would allow him to have a conference with me in Prince Czartoriski and Baron Stein's presence, to all of which I agreed ; at the latter conversation Baron Humboldt also assisted. The object of this conference seemed to be, to ascertain how far I could be prevailed on to support the proposed establishment of the King of Saxony beyond the Rhine, in favour of which they urged all the reasons arising from the evil of dividing that country, and the discontent and intrigues to which it would hereafter give occasion ; the necessity of the whole of Saxony to give solidity to Prussia, and the hardship, after all their hopes, of depriving them of this possession.

To this I opposed the impossibility of procuring the acquiescence necessary to render such an arrangement really beneficial to Prussia. The King clearly would not relinquish his rights for such an establishment as was proposed. France certainly would neither encourage him to do so, nor recognise the possession in Prussia to his prejudice. Austria would be as little disposed to force upon the King of Saxony an arrangement, which would work a particular injury to herself ; and with respect to Great Britain, although I had never held the rights of the King of Saxony to be paramount to the interests of Europe in the larger sense, nor yet to be the just re-construction, according to her Treaties, of Prussia, yet that under all the circumstances of the present case, I could not admit a necessity sufficiently strong to exist, as to justify the adoption of so harsh and strong a measure as the total incorporation of

Saxony in opposition to the prevailing sentiment of Germany, not less so, as I believed, of Great Britain, and the declared opposition of some of the most preponderating Powers in Europe.

That I could the less do so as my conviction was, that Prussia would not gain real strength by such an unpopular measure, even if acquiesced in, whereas, if it led to war, it was unnecessary to argue the impolicy of an act, which might have the effect of bringing a French army into Germany to assail, and a Russian army to defend, Prussia.

That it was true that Prussia had lost considerably of the solidity of her Empire on the side of Poland (for which however Great Britain was not responsible); but that, on the other hand, if she should acquire a considerable proportion of the Northern parts of Saxony, including the fortresses of Wittenberg and Torgau on the Elbe, together with nearly the two Lusaces, and further obtain a full equivalent in Germany for her Polish subjects, it appeared to me that, upon the whole, the construction of her monarchy would be improved.

This discussion lasted nearly two hours, during which time I had to sustain the united efforts of those present, to convert me, and to impeach the conduct which Austria had pursued. It ended, however, in my contributing, as far as the weight of the British Government could operate, to produce more temperate councils on the part of Prussia, and in making the Russians more correctly appreciate the course that had been pursued towards Prussia; I added that whatever opposition I had given to the Polish arrangement, and although I must still reserve to myself the right to protest against that measure, yet that being once acquiesced in by the Powers most interested, I should be found not the less desirous to promote a conciliatory settlement on other points. Having reason to believe that nothing passed in this interview to abate the desire that I should interfere to promote a settlement, I addressed the Memorandum of which I enclose a copy,[1] to the three Allied ministers communicating it also to Prince Talleyrand. My object in doing so was twofold, first to put an end to the existing discordance as to facts, and secondly that we might be enabled to specify to Prussia more precisely than has hitherto been done, *how* she was to be re-constructed, before we called upon Prince Hardenberg formally to accede to the principle of abdicating a part of Saxony. Prince Talleyrand having made it a request that a French

---

[1] This was a proposal to set up a Statistical Committee. See my *Congress of Vienna*, p. 165.

Plenipotentiary should attend this commission, his wishes have been complied with.

The commissioners met to-day—vizt. : Lord Clancarty, Baron Wessenberg, Duc d'Alberg, Count Münster, and Messrs. Hoffman and Jourdan for Russia and Prussia, and proceeded with their enquiry. I shall press the conclusion of their labours as the only means of correctly estimating either our means or the claims upon them.

The Austrian note,[1] which I enclose, has, for the present, I think, injudiciously narrowed the scope of their inquiry. This, however, can be corrected, and I augur favourably, both of the result, and of the temper in the Russian councils, which has induced an acquiescence in this appointment.

If I might venture an opinion, it would be, that the probabilities of an amicable arrangement are within these few days considerably increased.

CL. [F. O. Cont. 9.]
CASTLEREAGH TO LIVERPOOL. (No. 41.)
Vienna, December 25th, 1814.

Since I closed my secret and confidential despatch No. 37,[2] I have seen Prince Metternich, and learnt from him, that another interview had taken place of a conciliatory nature between the Emperors—in which the Emperor of Russia repeated his former expressions of wishing to finish everything amicably, and without delay ; and that he had appointed Count Razumoffsky as his plenipotentiary to arrange on the Polish question with Austria and Prussia. His Imperial Majesty expressed his hopes, that the King of Prussia could also accommodate upon the point of Saxony, and encouraged the Emperor of Austria to have a personal interview with him, upon the adjustment of their mutual interests.

Prince Metternich also informed me, that he had prepared by order of the Emperor his Master an answer to Prince Hardenberg's last paper, adhering strictly to the principles of his note as communicated officially to France. That the Emperor of Austria, not choosing to adopt the practice of an intercourse between sovereign

[1] Dated 24th December, 1814, D'Angeberg, p. 561, insisting that " l'evaluation de la population elle-même ne sera pas faite sous le simple rapport de quotité ; elle le sera aussi sous celui de l' espéce ou de qualité." No other consideration but that of population was to be taken into account by this commission.

[2] Of December 24th, which merely communicated Hardenberg's note of the 19th December, enforcing and re-butting the Prussian claims on Saxony.

and sovereign, instead of between Cabinet and Cabinet, had directed him to transmit this reply (of which a copy will be forwarded to Your Lordship by the next messenger) through Count Nesselrode, to be laid before the Emperor Alexander.

When I saw Prince Metternich, he was just come from the King of Wirtemberg, who desired not to be considered, on this question, as adopting either the politicks of Prussia or Russia. That his wish, in the event of a contest, would be to preserve a neutrality, but that if the Emperor of Austria put himself at the head of a German League, he would join it. Considering the intended marriage between the Prince Royal of Wirtemberg and the Duchess of Oldenburg,[1] and the active part I know His Royal Highness has been lately taking in concert with Baron Stein, this is a strong indication either that the spirit in Germany is strongly against Russia, or that the King of Wirtemberg thinks His Prussian Majesty intends to accommodate.

CLI. [*W. S. D. IX.* 511.]

CASTLEREAGH TO LIVERPOOL.

Vienna, December 25th, 1814.

I am always unwilling to think sanguinely of things in progress, but various concurring circumstances induce me to consider the probabilities of a settlement greatly increased. This feeling transpires from so many quarters, and the irritation so visibly subsides, that if France and the King of Saxony will assist us in assigning liberally to Prussia out of Saxony, I think we shall at last work it through. Russia, notwithstanding the embarrassment in which Prince Repnin's proclamation has placed her, will not encourage Prussia to resist, now she has secured her own arrangement in Poland. We must be as liberal as we can to Prussia, notwithstanding her shabbiness. Humboldt's *calcul*, I always suspected, was *to take great care* not to save so much of Poland as to weaken their claim to the whole of Saxony. I was aware of this device when I wrote my letter of the 11th of October,[2] which expressly bars the precise case which has occurred as not giving any claim for British support, viz., Saxony being the compensation for an excessive cession of territory to Russia on the side of Poland.

You will see that the correspondence between Austria and France essentially alters the posture of the latter Power. France is now a

---

[1] Catharine, the Tsar Alexander's sister.
[2] See CXVI.

principal in the question. Talleyrand's note[1] is written for impression. He was urgent in his language to me two days since to begin with an engagement between France, Austria, and England. I told him that I thought we were already united in opinion, and that to form an alliance prematurely might augment the chances of war rather than of an amicable settlement, which I trusted was the object we all had in view. His tone was very high and hostile to Prussia. Austria is, on the contrary, as conciliatory as is consistent with the preservation of a substantive position in Saxony to the King.

CLII. [*W. S. D. IX.* 503.]
WELLINGTON TO LIVERPOOL.
Paris, December 25th, 1814.

You will see my despatch to Lord Castlereagh about Murat,[2] the duplicate of which I send to Vienna, with a request to Lord Castlereagh to say nothing upon the subject till he hears from you.

I concur very much in opinion with the King, that the chances of disturbance, particularly in this country, are very much increased by leaving Murat on the throne of Naples. If he were gone, Buonaparte in Elba would not be an object of great dread. You must be the best judge whether you ought or can come forward on this occasion. If you should determine to do so, what follows will show you the means which are requisite, which are in your power, and my opinion of the probable expense.

[1] *Lettre du Prince de Talleyrand au Prince de Metternich, en date du 19th decembre,* 1814, *mandant que le voeu de Louis XVIII. était que l'oeuvre de la Restauration s'accomplit pour toute l'Europe comme pour la France, et considerant comme pernicieuse la disposition qu' on veut faire du royaume de Saxe.* D'Angeberg, 540.
[2] Of December 26th.
" I send you the copy of a letter which I have written to Lord Liverpool, with my despatch regarding Murat. The King is anxious that nothing should be said upon the subject at Vienna, until I shall receive an answer from England.

" Blacas explained to me, last night, how it happens that the King can give only 40,000 men. He says that they cannot venture to employ upon this service either generals, officers, or troops, who have served immediately under the command of Murat, and that they must therefor select them.

" Adverting to the temper prevailing in England, and to the state of the finances. I think it most probable the Government will not enter into this scheme, and that Murat will escape. After all, our coming forward as principals is rather a delicate matter, under all the circumstances of the Austrian Treaty, and the suspension of hostilities ; and the Austrians being so far satisfied with Murat's performance of his engagements as not to join in an attack upon him. However, of this I am very certain, that Murat's continuance at Naples increases the chances of disturbance in France, which would again disturb all Europe "
C.C. X. 228.

x

If the British Government should undertake this operation, it should be performed by the armies of the Allies of the Peninsula, which might be got in the following proportions, viz. : 10,000 infantry from Spain ; 12,000 infantry from Portugal ; 20,000 of all arms from Great Britain ; and 10,000 of all arms from Sicily ; with sixty pieces of field artillery and a battering-train from Great Britain ; the whole to assemble in Sicily, in transports to be found by Great Britain. This force, with 40,000 men, which might be sent from the southern ports of France, by sea, into the Roman States, would be more than sufficient to ensure the object almost without striking a blow. . . .

CLIII. [*F. O. Cont.* 10.[1]]
CASTLEREAGH TO LIVERPOOL. (No. 42.)
Vienna, January 1st, 1815.

Having, for the reasons stated in my despatch No. 40[2] deemed it expedient no longer to suspend proceedings on the subject of the Slave Trade, I addressed the inclosed letter to the Austrian, Russian, and Prussian Ministers requesting to be admitted to an audience of their respective sovereigns.

The Emperor of Russia received me the following evening, and I had an opportunity of explaining to His Imperial Majesty at considerable length the objects with which I was charged, the importance attached to them by the Prince Regent, and the mode in which His Imperial Majesty could most contribute to their successful accomplishment.

I began by satisfying the Emperor that Great Britain had left no means untried which depended on her to effect a complete and total abolition of this odious and criminal traffic. That the British Parliament had now, for some years, in opposition to every prejudice and suggestions of national interest abolished absolutely the traffic throughout the whole extent of the British Dominions— That they had further made it an invariable object in all their negotiations to promote this measure ; that, in consequence, engagements had been entered into by Sweden, Denmark, and Holland immediately to abolish, and by France at the end of five years ; that France had, since the Treaty of Paris, consented to abolish forthwith to the North of Cape Formoso, and that we were in negotiation with Spain and Portugal, for the purpose of deliver-

[1] Printed in *British and Foreign State Papers* III. 941 as an official dispatch addressed to Bathurst and dated January 2nd.
[2] Of December 25th. Portugal had refused to make further concessions.

ing, without further delay, this portion of Africa at least from the evils of the Slave Trade.

That our endeavours had not been confined to mere representations, but that offers of direct and considerable value had been held out by the Prince Regent's commands to France, Spain, and Portugal, in order to reconcile them, if possible, to the measure of immediate abolition.

Having explained the nature and extent of the exertions which Great Britain had made to effectuate this object, I represented to the Emperor, that our means of being of use were, in a great measure exhausted, and that it depended much more upon His Imperial Majesty and the other sovereigns who had no colonies, now to act, than it did upon Great Britain.

The Emperor listened with much attention to every part of my statement, and particularly to this, in which I endeavoured to show that, upon reasonable notice, the great Powers of Europe would not only be justified, but bound in morality and sincerity, to exclude from their ports colonial produce grown within the dominions of states who, within a reasonable period refused to adopt the principle of abolition. That to do so must at once be effectual and to do less was to make themselves parties, in breach of their promises, to the crimes and scandal to which their demand for colonial produce gave occasion, and which they ought preferably to supply from those countries where the culture was not carried on by newly imported slaves.

The Emperor gave me every assurance of support, and directed Count Nesselrode to consult with me, on the measures to be adopted. With respect to the period of abolition to be urged, His Imperial Majesty declared his desire if possible, to prevail upon France to reduce the period of five years, and that Spain and Portugal should be urged to conform to whatever period France might be prevailed on to adopt. The Emperor expressed satisfaction at the idea of constituting a standing commission in London and Paris, composed of the ministers of Powers friendly to this object, whose duty it should be to follow it up with the undivided weight of their respective Governments, till finally effected. His Imperial Majesty received my representations throughout in the most gracious manner, and authorized me to assure the Prince Regent that His Royal Highness might rest satisfied he should do his utmost to second his exertions on this interesting subject . . .

CLIV.   [*F. O. Cont.* 10.]
CASTLEREAGH TO LIVERPOOL.   (No. 43.)
Vienna, January 1st, 1815.

In conformity to the information contained in my despatch No. 38,[1] of Count Razumoffski's nomination to negotiate, and the wish that prevailed with respect to my bearing a part in these negotiations, the accompanying correspondence[2] has taken place.

Before I gave my consent to be present, I thought it right to have an explanatory interview with Count Razumoffski and Prince Hardenberg for two objects. The first was to desire that it might be understood, that by assisting at the arrangement of the details of the intended Polish measure, I was not to be considered as altering or withdrawing any part of the opposition I had felt it my duty to give to the principle of that measure on behalf of my Court, that, with this reserve however, I was perfectly ready to contribute, as far as lay in my power, to render the arrangement as little exceptionable as possible in its minor provisions.

The second point which I desired to press was that France might be invited to take a part in the Saxon negotiations, not to the abandonment of confidential discussion between the Powers that had been allied in the war, but that the former Power might not feel that she was deliberately excluded from the consideration of a question on which she had professed to take so strong an interest.

After this business was concluded there was much general discussion on the point of Saxony—the Prussian Ministers adhering tenaciously to the principle of total incorporation, but declaring their willingness to consider any other Projet that might be brought forward for adequately re-constructing Prussia under her Treaties.

To this it was replied by the Austrian and English Plenipotentiaries, that although they were of opinion that the means existed of fulfilling their engagements to Prussia, without divesting the King of Saxony of the whole of his dominions, yet that until France was combined in the negotiation, we had not the means of concerting a counter projet, which, by uniting the appui necessary, might induce the King of Saxony to cede what was required, that Prince Talleyrand would not concert modifications with us in our individual capacity, and that to postpone communicating with him till the four Powers had come to a previous decision, was calculated to provoke opposition, instead of conciliating the important Power

[1] CXLIX.
[2] Formal notes arranging the official Conference.

he represented, to assist in settling *à l'aimable*, a question upon which we were unfortunately divided in opinion.

It was urged by the two other Powers, but principally by Prussia, that France had no right to take umbrage, if the point was previously negotiated amongst the Allies, whose Treaties bound them to reconstruct Prussia upon a principle agreed upon, to which engagement France was no party. This distinction was argued to be by no means founded, as the first secret article of the Peace of Paris, by recognising " les bases arrêtées entre elles " rendered the Treaty of Kalisch, which established the rights of Prussia as binding upon France as upon any of the other Powers. After some further discusison the point was taken ad referendum, and the Russian and Prussian Ministers, who appear to act completely in concert, promised at the next meeting, which is fixed for Monday, to communicate the decision of their Courts.

CLV. [*F. O. Cont.* 10.]
CASTLEREAGH TO LIVERPOOL. (No. 44.)
Vienna, January 1st, 1815.

Although I have had strong reason to hope that a disposition existed in the Prussian Cabinet to accommodate on the Saxon point, should a liberal offer be made them, yet there are indications which justify the utmost vigilance with respect to their ultimate policy.

The language of their entourés is very warlike, and strongly against yielding any part of Saxony, Baron Humboldt's particularly so. His reasoning yesterday in our conference, which he attends as one of the Prussian Plenipotentiaries, went every length, but that of refusing to discuss such alternatives as might be proposed. They are organising their army for the field, and, I have heard to-day, are employed in fortifying Dresden. This may be all menace to sustain their negotiation, but they may also meditate some sudden effort, in conjunction with Russia to coerce Austria, and place themselves in a situation to dictate their own terms on all other points—the conduct of their employés on the left bank of the Rhine has been extremely vexatious of late towards the Prince of Orange's Government, and no attention has yet been paid here to any of their reclamations.

These indications have attracted the more seriously my attention, from a declaration incidentally made by Prince Hardenberg in yesterday's conference, that should Prussia continue to consider the annexation of the whole of Saxony necessary to her re-construction, she could not, in point of expense, submit to remain in a state of provisional occupation, and that Russia and Prussia would, in such a case, consider a refusal to acknowledge, as tantamount to a declaration of war.

I took occasion to protest in the strongest terms against this principle as a most alarming and unheard-of menace ; that it should be competent for one Power to invade another, and by force to compel a recognition which was founded upon no Treaty, and where no attempt had been made to disturb the possession of the invading Power in the territory to which he laid claim. That such an insinuation might operate upon a Power trembling for its existence, but must have the contrary effect upon all that were alive to their own dignity ; and I added that if such a temper really prevailed, we were not deliberating in a state of independence, and it were better to break up the Congress.

This unguarded declaration was afterwards softened down, and, to a degree, explained away ; but it has not failed, coupled with other expressions used in private, to create a strong sensation and alarm, that if Prussia should not ultimately yield, she will attempt, as is the practice of her Government in lesser concerns, some bold and desperate coup to deliver herself suddenly from the embarrassments of a protracted state of armament and questioned occupation.

This sort of principle, openly announced in a formal conference in the name of two great Powers avowedly ready to act, has appeared to us to call for some precautionary corrective by which the other Powers may be induced to feel that, in the discharge of their functions in Congress, they are not exposed individually and in detail to the destructive effects of such a domineering dictation.

Under these circumstances I have felt it an act of imperative duty to concert with the French and Austrian Plenipotentiaries a Treaty of Defensive Alliance, confined within the strict necessity of this most extraordinary case. Without some such bond, I feel that our deliberations here are at an end ; and although I flatter myself that the necessity will never arise for acting upon these engagements, yet, after what has passed, I should not consider myself justified in leaving either our common councils here, or the great interests we have at stake in other quarters, at the mercy of states promulgating such principles, without providing for them in time the best protection in my power.

I indulge the confident hope that my conduct upon this occasion may appear to the Prince Regent and his Government to have been justified by the circumstances of the case, and the exigency of the occasion.

CLVI. [*F. O. Cont.* 10.]
CASTLEREAGH TO LIVERPOOL. (No. 45.)
Vienna, January 1st, 1815.

I enclose the Projet of the Treaty of Defensive Alliance alluded to in my despatch No. 44.[1] I have just gone through it with Prince Metternich and Prince Talleyrand, and it has received their entire approbation. The latter has charged himself with the French redaction.

It is due to Prince Talleyrand to state, that his conduct throughout all our late transactions, has done the utmost honour to his Court, and altho' his official correspondence takes an inconveniently lofty tone upon the point of Saxony, yet I do not doubt that he will ultimately lend himself to what may be wise and practicable on that question. I have expressly declared, that whilst I concur with him in opinion that Saxony ought not to be wholly absorbed in Prussia, that I will not suffer, as far as Great Britain is concerned, the peace of Europe to be sacrificed upon any principle of modification, of which the question may be reasonably susceptible.

With respect to all the stipulations calculated to secure and cover our interests in the Low Countries, etc., I have not only found His Highness *coulant*, but ready to go before my wishes ; and I am confident, whatever bad principles may prevail in the French nation or in the army on this point, the King's Government is sound upon it.

When I read to him that article of the Treaty which goes to regulate the Peace of Paris, in the event of war, the future frontiers of the contracting parties, he expressed the great satisfaction he would feel in signing, and the King would have in making, in the face of Europe, this declaration, so conformable to all his principles and determination.

I hope we shall be enabled, in the course of to-morrow or the day following, to sign the Convention. I shall then forward it to Your Lordship, but as I do not foresee that it is likely to experience any very material alteration, I shall despatch the present messenger, in order that Your Lordship may be prepared for its reception, and that the return of the ratifications may be accelerated as much as possible.

[1] CLV. This does not differ substantially from the Treaty of January 3rd by which Great Britain, Austria, and France bound themselves to defend one another against attack.

CLVII. [*W. S. D. IX.* 523.]

CASTLEREAGH TO LIVERPOOL.

Vienna, January 2nd, 1815.

Our conference this morning was postponed till to-morrow. I understand they mean to give way upon the point of admitting France. I had an opportunity, in a private conversation with Baron Humboldt, of re-enforcing what I stated in conference upon Hardenberg's menace. I told him he may rely upon it that it was a pretension Great Britain would resist with her whole Power and resources, and that every man in Parliament, of whatever party, would support the government in doing so. I thought it material above all things to extinguish, if possible, this project of a *coup de main*, as Prussia will treat about Saxony rather than remain armed and inactive. I believe they are shaken by the tone in which their menace has been met. . . .

I hope you will not think my Treaty[1] an improvident one. It pledges you absolutely to nothing beyond the value in money at which the force is calculated, whilst it puts Holland, etc., under, I trust, a friendly protection. Should the case on which the Treaty is founded ever, for the disgrace of the times, arise, it is quite out of the question that we should remain quiet spectators ; and I know no mode in which more could have been secured and more effectually, and by which we could have remained more completely masters of the species of exertion in which we may think it wise to engage, the principle on which is such as could create no difficulty in Parliament, whilst it may save Austria, and consequently the Continent. Pray expedite the ratification.

CLVIII. [*F. O. Cont.* 10.]

CASTLEREAGH TO LIVERPOOL. (No. 48.)

Vienna, January 3rd, 1815.

Our third conference took place this forenoon. It was principally occupied in the detail of Polish affairs—Prince Metternich presented a counter-projet, copy of which will be forwarded by the next messenger, varying rather the form than the substance of the Russian projet. This counter-projet was taken ad referendum and is not likely to create any difficulty.

At the close of our sitting a renewed attempt was made by the Russian and Prussian ministers indirectly to exclude France from our Saxon negotiations by desiring that her introduction might be delayed till we had first discussed and agreed upon the point

[1] The treaty of January 3rd.

amongst ourselves. This being opposed, and upon Prince Metternich and myself declaring peremptorily that we would not negotiate in the absence of the French minister, the Russian and Prussian ministers again desired to receive the orders of their sovereigns upon the point.

Since the breaking up of our conference, Prince Hardenberg has positively assured me that he will to-morrow recommend the immediate introduction of the French Plenipotentiary, I consider this as decisive that we shall have no more difficulty on this most essential point.

CLIX. [W. S. D. 525.]
CASTLEREAGH TO LIVERPOOL.
Vienna, January 4th, 1815.

I send you enclosed a copy of my letter[1] to the Duke of Wellington. In the present state of the negotiation, I feel myself bound to urge that I should not be withdrawn from hence at least till the important discussions now pending are closed.

With every deference to the Duke of Wellington's ability and great personal authority, he cannot at once replace me in the habits of confidential intercourse which a long residence with the principal actors has established, and which gives facilities to my intervention to bring them together, which could not attach to another for a length of time, whereas the fate of Europe may depend on the conclusions of the ensuing month.

I must naturally have a strong desire to conduct to their close measures for which I stand so deeply responsible ; but, independent of all personal considerations, I feel that the conduct of the negotiation ought not to pass, as things now stand, into other hands, except upon some necessity, upon which the Prince Regent's Government can alone decide ; and which, under the new circumstances that have arisen both at home and abroad, I cannot myself consider to exist, since our peace with America has been secured.

I think it is probable that I shall be enabled, in the course of four or five weeks, to bring all the territorial arrangements of Europe to a close. The constitutional system of Germany may run into more length ; but this I have no doubt we shall separate and refer to a special enquiry. The point of Naples here, at least, will be a short one, after I receive an answer to my letter[2] of the

---

[1] Dated January 4th, asking him to defer his departure from Paris.
[2] CXLIV.

18th, as the object, whether it is to be pursued by arms or negotiation, cannot occupy more time at Vienna than belongs to the decision of the principle.

CLX. [*W. S. D. IX.* 527.]
CASTLEREAGH TO LIVERPOOL. (No. 49.[1])
Vienna, January 5th, 1815.

I have every reason to hope that the alarm of war is over. I understand the point was considered on Sunday last in the Prussian Cabinet, and the opinions were in favour of a suitable modification of the Saxon question.

I last night had, at his request, a long interview with Prince Hardenberg. Preserving that reserve which it was wise for him to do in order to maintain the pretensions of Prussia to a large share of that country, the Chancellor explained himself to me unreservedly in favour of a settlement, and desired my good offices to effect it.

He intimated the intention of Prussia and Russia to admit France ; they would, however, as a preliminary, call upon Austria and Great Britain to declare on the Protocol what I stated in our last conference : that we considered the question of Saxony not one to be negotiated with the King of Saxony, but that the Powers were bound to decide upon the arrangement which, all things considered, they deemed just between him and Prussia, and to leave the option of acceptance with the King. I was glad to find from Prince Talleyrand this morning, that he concurred in this principle and that although nothing but the King of Saxony's act could effectually close all pretensions hereafter, he nevertheless felt himself bound to support Prussia in her occupation till that consent was obtained to what the Five Powers might deem just and reasonable.

In my conversation last night with Prince Hardenberg, I understood that an attempt was to be made to induce the King of Saxony to desire to be placed on the left bank of the Rhine. Although I have no notion His Saxon Majesty would listen to such a proposal, I thought it material to dissuade the Prince from a plan so inexpedient. To place a weak Prince, from a variety of causes likely to be dependent on France, in so advanced a position, occupying Luxembourg and the countries between the Meuse and the Moselle, was to expose all our defences on the left bank of that river to be turned, and to place that family in the situation the most calculated,

[1] Number given in F. O. Cont. 10.

at a future day, to be an instrument in the hands of France to invade Saxony with a view to its resumption. Prince Talleyrand has expressed himself with great propriety upon this point. He said, for purposes of ambition and conquest he must favour the plan ; but as his sincere desire, and that of his Court, was to put a restraint upon any extension of the existing boundaries of France, he was against the project. His wish is that the Prince of Orange should have Luxembourg rather than the Prussians.

It is difficult to describe to your Lordship the impression produced here by our pacification with America.

CLXI. [*F. O. Cont.* 10.]
    CASTLEREAGH TO LIVERPOOL.   (No. 50.)
                                    January 8th, 1815.

The importance of counteracting by every possible effort, and without loss of time, the attempts in progress to prevail upon the King of Saxony to accept an establishment on the left bank of the Rhine, determined me to solicit an audience of the Emperor of Russia, for the purpose of representing to His Imperial Majesty, my sentiments upon this subject.

I had an opportunity yesterday morning, in a very long interview, of going fully into the subject, and I have since understood confidentially from Count Razumoffsky, who saw His Imperial Majesty after I left him, that my reasoning had served to give him a new view of this question, and that my objections were considered to have great weight. I did not however deem it prudent to rest the point merely upon the argument, but represented the impossibility, under the negative expressly reserved to Great Britain by the Convention of Chaumont with respect to the disposal of the territories on the left bank of the Rhine, that I could consent, on the part of my Court to place a Prince in circumstances so dependent upon France, in the very centre of our line of defence. That the obvious policy in military prudence, was either to place there a great military Power such as Prussia, or if that could not be, to bring forward some secondary Power such as the Prince of Orange, the mass of whose dominions being interwoven in another system, became a pledge, especially when supported by Russia en seconde ligne, for the faithful maintenance of these possessions against France ; but that to create a feeble and discontented state there, was to pave the way for a future cession of those territories to France, in consideration of the re-conquest of Saxony for the family. I urged that the policy of Austria was necessarily so much in favour of Saxony being independent of Prussia—that such a scheme very possibly would be either supported or acquiesced in by her, and could only be successfuly opposed by His Imperial Majesty sending a powerful army at a vast expense into the heart of Germany.

I told the Emperor I should have felt some delicacy in urging this subject so strongly, knowing the warm interest His Imperial Majesty took in supporting the views of Prussia, if I had not first stated my sentiments to the Prussian Minister; and convinced myself that whilst the plan was bad for us all, it was pre-eminently menacing to Prussia in her possession of Saxony, and in this view, I entreated the Emperor to represent it to the King.

After this subject was disposed of, the Emperor went to other matters, and rather to my surprize, referred to reports that had reached him of an Alliance between Austria, France, Bavaria, and Great Britain. Not feeling myself authorized to avow the Treaty, and not choosing to hold a language of too much disguise, I assured His Imperial Majesty that acting upon the pacifick principles which he had avowed in the early part of our conversation, he had nothing to fear from those Powers : that as His Imperial Majesty had condescended to speak to me without reserve, I would frankly avow to him, that the language held by Prince Hardenberg in a formal conference in the name of both Courts, and not disavowed by His Imperial Majesty's ministers then present, had seriously, and I thought justly, alarmed the Powers alluded to. It was evident the Emperor was not unacquainted with the declaration in question, from the manner in which he endeavoured to soften it down. I expressed my satisfaction that the principle was not adhered to, as I could not conceal from His Imperial Majesty, that I would have imposed upon those Powers, and I thought upon all others who valued their independence, the necessity of giving it the most determined resistance.

Having got upon this warlike ground, I thought it the more material to convince the Emperor, by giving another direction to the conversation, that it was to an early and amicable adjustment of the subjects in discussion that all my thoughts and efforts were directed. I happened to have with me the documents which I had prepared, to show how Prussia could be reconstructed without incorporating the whole of Saxony. His Imperial Majesty went with much interest into this question, was anxious to know whether France would consent to such an arrangement, and whether Great Britain would support it, if necessary, against her. The Emperor said that he should be satisfied with it if Prussia was.

His Imperial Majesty repeatedly asked me, whether I thought France really desired peace. I expressed my conviction that the King and his ministers sincerely did, but that as certainly, if a war broke out, that they would take a part. In this the Emperor agreed, and deprecated the risk. I then urged the immense advantage to be derived from prevailing upon Prussia to listen to such an arrangement as all the five great Powers could support, which I looked upon as within our reach, if Prussia was reasonable and if Prince Talleyrand was treated with the consideration to which, as the representative of so great a Power, he was entitled.

I afterwards went through the other German arrangements, and showed the Emperor how the whole might be equitably settled. I asked him, in the event of being pressed for means, whether he could give something more to Prussia on the side of Poland. His answer was that the subject was both a painful and an embarrassing one to him with the Poles, to whom he had given assurances. I did not think it advisable then to press the point further lest I should receive a positive refusal. The Emperor throughout the interview seemed to look to an accommodation, and discussed the several subjects in a temperate and conciliatory manner.

We held our fourth conference this forenoon. The Russian minister announced that there would be no substantial objection, on the part of his court, to the counter-projet as delivered in by the Austrian minister on the affairs of Poland. The Russian and Prussian ministers also signified their concurrence in the introduction of the French minister.

The first conference of the five Powers is fixed for Wednesday next, when Prince Hardenberg will present his Projet founded upon the total incorporation of Saxony. To this the three Powers will reply in a counter-projet, and I indulge a hope that we shall be enabled to frame it upon principles so liberal and advantageous to Prussia as to induce that Court to acquiesce in the general wishes.

CLXII. [*F. O. Cont.* 10.]
CASTLEREAGH TO LIVERPOOL. (No. 51.)
January 11th, 1815.

. . . . It has been evident for some time, that one great difficulty with Prussia in listening to the principle of modification, has arisen from an apprehension, 1st, that neither France nor

Austria would be liberal in the extent of cession ; and 2ndly, that France in particular held the rights of the King of Saxony so high as to throw the point of authority in case of negotiation, very much into his hands. I thought it therefore material to reduce the question to a precise issue, to make the Powers, and not the King of Saxony, judges in the case and further, to obtain for Prussia a reasonable security for the execution of the award when made. With this view I prepared the enclosed memorandum,[1] declaratory at once of my opinion on the propriety of inviting the French minister to assist at our deliberation, and of the course to be pursued on the Saxon question. I produced it at our conference yesterday, and it was entered on the protocol. Prince Metternich acceded to it, and the Russian and Prussian ministers declared themselves entirely satisfied with the explanation therein given and ready to assist at our future conferences.

I had taken the precaution of communicating this memorandum confidentially to Prince Talleyrand before I gave it in, and succeeded in bringing him very nearly to the same view of the question. I send you his opinion,[2] written after our conversation. You will see that he comes almost to the same practical conclusion, but in the tone of an Ally of the King of Saxony. We say that we will *support* the King of Prussia, our Ally, in Saxony, till the suitable sessions are made to him. France says that she will *cease to support* her Ally, the King of Saxony, if he refuses to make good the cessions agreed upon. The distinction is not unreasonable ; the latter form accords perhaps better with the King of France's position, and I am happy to find that it is not objected to by the Prussian minister, who has expressed to me his perfect satisfaction with the understanding thus established.

In form the question of modification is not yet admitted by Prussia, nor can the King's pleasure be taken upon it, till Prince Hardenberg brings forward his Projet, and a counter-projet is given in ; but I consider that it is in substance admitted, and that this question which menaced so seriously the tranquillity of Europe, is now happily reduced to a question of terms, the difficulties of which may be surmounted, if France and Austria shew the same spirit of accommodation in arranging the details, now affairs are promising, that they gave me reason to expect, when matters looked more serious.

---

[1] The Memorandum attached to the Protocol of the meeting of the Conference of the Four Courts of January 9th is as stated in the dispatch. *British and Foreign State Papers*, II., 601.

[2] Talleyrand to Castlereagh, January 8th, 1814. As stated. F. O. Cont. 10.

CLXIII. [*F. O. Cont.* 10.]
          CASTLEREAGH TO LIVERPOOL. (No. 52.)
                                        January 11th, 1815.

I had occasion in my dispatch No. 43,[1] to report to your
Lordship the explanations under which I consented to attend the
conferences on the affairs of Poland.

I now transmit to your Lordship a note[2] which I have thought
it my duty to enter upon the protocol, in order that the sentiments expressed by the Minister of Great Britain on this important subject may remain officially on record, the correspondence
which passed between the Emperor of Russia and myself, not
possessing in strictness perhaps that character.

I am convinced that the only hope of tranquillity now in
Poland and especially of preserving to Austria and Prussia their
portions of that Kingdom, is for the two latter states to adopt a
Polish system of administration as a defence against the inroads
of the Russian policy. I have pressed this in both our last conferences, and Prince Metternich acquiesced in the principle.
My object in this note has been to avoid, as much as possible
the revival of unavailing contention and to confine myself within
the limits of an explanation equally due to my Court and to
myself.

CIRCULAR TO THE PLENIPOTENTIARIES OF THE CONFERENCE.[3]
                                        Vienna, January 12th, 1815.
   The undersigned, His Britannic Majesty's Principal Secretary of State for
Foreign affairs, and Plenipotentiary to the Congress of Vienna, in desiring the
present Note concerning the affairs of Poland may be entered on the Protocol,
has no intention to revive controversy, or to impede the progress of the arrangements now in contemplation.
   His only object is to avail himself of this occasion, of temporately recording,
by the express orders of his Court, the sentiments of the British Government
upon an European Question of the utmost magnitude and importance.
   The undersigned has had occasion in the course of the discussions at Vienna,
for reasons that need not now be gone into, repeatedly and earnestly to oppose
himself, on the part of his Court, to the erection of a Polish Kingdom in union
with, and making a part of, the Imperial Crown of Russia.
   The desire of his Court to see an independent Power, more or less considerable in extent, established in Poland under a distinct Dynasty, and as an intermediate State between the 3 great Monarchies, has uniformly been avowed ;
and if the undersigned has not been directed to press such a measure, it has only
arisen from a disinclination to excite, under all the apparent obstacles to such
an arrangement, expectations which might prove an unavailing source of
discontent among the Poles.
   The Emperor of Russia continuing, as it is declared, still to adhere to his
purpose of erecting that part of the Duchy of Warsaw, which is to fall under His
Imperial Majesty's Dominion, together with his other Polish Provinces, either

[1] CLIV.
[2] Appended to this dispatch.
[3] *B. of F. State Papers II.* 642.

in whole or in part, into a Kingdom, under the Russian sceptre, and their Austrian and Prussian Majesties, the Sovereigns most immediately interested, having ceased to oppose themselves to such an arrangement ; the undersigned, adhering nevertheless to all his former representations on this subject, has only sincerely to hope that none of those evils may result from this measure, to the tranquillity of the North, and to the general equilibrium of Europe, which it has been his painful duty to anticipate.   But in order to obviate as far as possible such consequences, it is of essential importance to establish the public tranquillity, throughout the territories which formerly constituted the Kingdom of Poland, upon some solid and liberal basis of common interest, by applying to all, however various may be their political institutions, a congenial and conciliatory system of administration.

Experience has proved, that it is not by counteracting all their habits and usages as a people, that either the happiness of the Poles, or the peace of that important portion of Europe, can be preserved.   A fruitless attempt, too long persevered in by institutions foreign to their manners and sentiments, to make them forget their existence and even language as a people, has been sufficiently tried and failed.   It has only tended to excite a sentiment of discontent and self-degradation, and can never operate otherwise, than to provoke commotion, and to awaken them to a recollection of past misfortunes.

The undersigned, for these reasons, and in cordial concurrence with the general sentiments which he has had the satisfaction to observe the respective Cabinets entertain on this subject, ardently desires, that the illustrious Monarchs, to whom the destinies of the Polish Nation are confided, may be induced before they depart from Vienna, to take an engagement with each other, to treat as Poles, under whatever form of political institution they may think fit to govern them, the portions of that Nation that may be placed under their respective Sovereignties.   The knowledge of such a determination will best tend to conciliate the general sentiment to their rule, and to do honor to the several Sovereigns in the eyes of their respective Governments.

If such should happily be the result, the object which His Royal Highness the Prince Regent has most at heart, namely, the happiness of that people, will have been secured ; and it will only remain for His Royal Highness most anxiously to hope, that none of those dangers to the liberties of Europe may ever be realised, which might justly be apprehended from the reunion of a powerful Polish Monarchy with the still more powerful Empire of Russia, if at any time hereafter the military force of both should be directed by an ambitious and warlike Prince.

Austria, Russia, and Prussia all sent formal answers agreeing with the sentiments of the note, taking care, however, not to commit themselves to any specific point.

CLXIV. [*W. S. D. IX.* 533.]
LIVERPOOL TO WELLINGTON.

Bath, January 11th, 1815.

. . . Upon the question of our engagements to Murat I think we are quite agreed. There can be no difference of opinion likewise as to the policy of removing him from the throne of Naples, if it is just and practicable. The only question that can occur on this part of the subject is, how far we are likely to succeed, and whether the chances of failure, or the chances of his continuing in undisturbed possession of Naples, are most to be apprehended. I am satisfied that those who are on the spot must be better judges on this subject than we can be here, and we can therefore have no hesitation in leaving these considerations entirely to your discretion. The only point which I wish to impress upon you is, the absolute impossibility in the present state of the circumstances and feelings in this country of our engaging in military operations for the purpose of expelling Murat. I do not mean that it is either necessary or would be prudent to make any such avowal public, least of all that Murat himself should be apprised of our difficulties ; but it may become indispensable that some of our Allies should know on what they have to reckon, and at all events it is fit that you should be fully informed of our situation.

I have never thought that Austria would make any serious difficulty in consequence of her Treaty with Murat, if the other Powers of Europe were determined to get rid of him : her real interest must be to destroy every remnant of the revolutionary system in Italy.

She may likewise feel considerable apprehensions about the march of a French army through the north and centre of Italy ; but if security is given to her (as appears to be intended) on this head, and if the other Powers are determined to declare against Murat, she will, I am persuaded, throw no obstacles in the way of their operations, and I should not despair of her even joining in the cause.

It will remain, therefore, to be seen whether he will submit willingly, or be compelled to submit by the Neapolitans, to the general voice of Europe declared at Vienna. I shall be sanguine on this head if a good provision is held out to him, and it must surely be the interest of the Powers of Europe to get out of such an embarrassment in such a manner. If he is determined, however, to risk everything for the purpose of keeping his throne, the labouring oar of expelling him must rest on France. Spain can afford little aid ; we might blockade his ports by sea ; Russia might send a body of troops, or at least threaten it ; and I should think that with such a combination of external means, the country itself would be led to declare against him. The English name has always been, and is still, particularly popular in Naples. The alarm I entertain is not about Naples, but about other parts of Italy, where a very different spirit exists, and where Austria is unfortunately very much disliked.

I have thus given you my sense on this subject, and I should hope that after talking the matter fully over with Lord Castlereagh, you may be able to put this very delicate and difficult question into as satisfactory a course as the nature of it will allow.

CLXV. [C. C. X. 240.]
LIVERPOOL TO CASTLEREAGH.
Bath, January 16th, 1815.

. . . You can have no idea how much ground the Government lost in the House of Commons, in the short session before Christmas ; and the unfortunate circumstance in our present situation is this—that the debates of most importance which are likely to occur during the session, must take place before the beginning of April. The questions of contest will be the questions of finance, and the political questions will principally be discussed and brought in as auxiliaries. . . . I can assure you that I feel, in common with my colleagues, the greatest reluctance in proposing to you to withdraw at this moment from Vienna. Last year we could spare you ; everything was quiet in Parliament—everybody waiting for the result—and no symptom of party-spirit appeared. Now, very few persons give themselves any anxiety about what is passing at Vienna, except in as far as it is connected with expense ; and I never have seen more party animosity than was manifested in November, and, I understand, still appears at the Clubs and in private societies . . .

CLXVI. [W. S. D. IX. 539.]
LIVERPOOL TO CASTLEREAGH.
Bath, January 16th, 1815.

In consequence of a passage in a private letter which I have received from Cooke,[1] I feel it necessary to trouble you with a few lines on the subject of Poland.

When we said that we should not object to your agreeing to the Emperor of Russia's arrangements respecting Poland, provided the provinces incorporated with Russia since 1792 were detached from that empire and re-united to the Duchy of Warsaw, we were desirous of putting the sincerity of His Imperial

---

[1] Cooke to Liverpool, January 4th, 1814. . . . " You see how the Russian projects of a Polish Kingdom have dwindled. I do not see how the Allies can stipulate to regulate the Emperor's conduct as to the former Polish incorporations : it would be an attempt *ad invidiam*, which he has a right to resist, whatever he may have said." *W. S. D. IX.* 527.

Majesty's professions to the test, but we did not suppose that there was much chance of his acceding to any such proposal. If, however, an arrangement to this effect should be found impracticable, it becomes of very great importance that you should be no party to the stipulations respecting Poland ; and though the manner and degree in which you may think proper to protest against the Polish arrangement must materially depend upon circumstances, I am satisfied that some protest will be absolutely necessary to render the proceeding on the subject palatable in this country.

CLXVII. [*F. O. Cont.* 6.]
BATHURST TO CASTLEREAGH. (No. 5.)

January 18th, 1815.

I am commanded by H.R.H. to express his entire approbation of your Lordship's conduct under circumstances very critical and deeply affecting the tranquillity of Europe.

The spirit with which your Lordship resisted the menacing language of the Prussian minister, upheld the dignity of the Court you represent, and was well calculated to check an impetuosity, from which much might have been apprehended, had it not been so seasonably rebuked.

A defensive Alliance for the purpose of maintaining the sound principles established by the Treaty of Paris, is one, to the formation of which the British Government cannot object, however much we may lament that the conduct of those Powers, to whose splendid exertions that peace is so much indebted, have unfortunately made the Treaty necessary.

I have therefore received the commands of H.R.H. to acquaint your Lordship that the Treaties of Alliance concluded by you on the 3rd inst. will be forthwith ratified, and the acts of ratification will be transmitted to your Lordship as soon as they can be prepared.

Your Lordship's dispatch of the 5th[1] inst. leads us to hope that matters may be amicably adjusted in a manner creditable to the parties concerned : and your Lordship acts with much commendable discretion in providing that the measures taken to restrain the unjust pretensions should not interfere with the fair claims of the Prussian Monarchy.

[1] CLX.

CLXVIII.   [*F. O. Cont.* 10.]

CASTLEREAGH TO LIVERPOOL.   (No. 57.)

January 22nd, 1815.

I stated to your Lordship in my dispatch No. 51 [1] that I entertained a strong hope that the question of Saxony might be arranged without prejudice to the peace of Europe, if Austria and France, now affairs have assumed a more promising aspect, were as accommodating in the details of the arrangement, as they had given me reason to expect, when appearances were more adverse.

I certainly was prepared when I signed the Treaty of Defensive Alliance on the 3rd to expect that this measure of strength and union might, if improperly understood, excite in the Austrian councils a disposition to enterprise anew upon objects of local policy, instead of turning it, as was intended by me, into the means of extricating herself with honour and safety, from the difficulty in which the menace of her opponents had placed her. I was not, however, deterred by this consideration from adopting what appeared to me indispensable to check the intemperance of the two Northern Powers at a critical moment of the negotiation, whilst I reserved in my own hands the means of effectually correcting at a future period any misconception of this nature should it arise.

The inclosed official memoir [2] presented to the Emperor by Marshall Prince Schwarzenberg, the Minister at War, will shew that I was not mistaken in this supposition. I have reason to believe that similar views prevail amongst other members of the Austrian Cabinet, particularly Count Stadion, and I have lately observed Prince Metternich's tone and language to be proportionately changed, indicating a disposition to aim at objects which before he had considered as unattainable.

Having examined this paper attentively, I thought there was no time to be lost in having a full explanation with Prince Metternich, both upon its contents, and the attitude in which I felt myself placed under our recent Treaty and the existing state of the negotiations. I represented to His Highness that I considered the principles therein laid down as not sound in themselves, whilst they were calculated to throw us back in our discussions and to retard, if not defeat, our hopes of an amicable settlement.

That admitting the facts alleged, namely, that the Eastern frontier of Germany was menaced by Russia, and that its Western frontier would be endangered, if the King of Saxony was placed

[1] CLXII.
[2] Undated, advancing strategic reasons for reducing Prussia's share of Saxony. F. O. Cont. 10.

on the left bank of the Rhine, it did not therefore follow, that the security of Austria depended upon depriving Prussia of Torgau and Erfurth.

That if the danger to be provided against was an united attack from Russia and Prussia, it was not a small fortress on the Elbe in the hands of a weak Power, or a position like Erfurth that could enable her to meet it. Such a combination could only be resisted by a counter-alliance, and it was to France and to Great Britain she must look for support in such a crisis, and not to a solitary fortress the more or the less beyond her own frontier.

But this question was different if the hostile attitude was supposed to exist between Austria and Prussia as single Powers. In that case it was an exaggeration to describe Torgau and Erfurth as points offensive and menacing on the part of Prussia against Austria ; they may, with more truth, be described as necessary defences to the weaker and extended state of ten millions of people, against the stronger and concentrated state of twenty-five millions.

That Saxony in its natural politicks appertained to the system of the North, preserving, however, an independent existence to a certain extent between its two powerful neighbours. To endeavour to combine it with the Austrian system and to take Torgau and Erfurth as advanced and menacing points, appeared to me the surest means of permanently uniting Prussia in close alliance with either Russia or France, and rendering her return to German connection hopeless, which I could by no means consider to be the case, however established the influence of Russia might, for the moment, appear to be.

That in looking to the defence of Prussia against France, the line of the Elbe was imperfect, if Torgau was denied to that Power, and that with respect to Erfurth, whilst the Prussian Monarchy was spread out from the Niemen to the Rhine, and broke into two masses but slenderly connected in the centre, such a fortress as Erfurth was essential to cover her extended line of communication, and to afford a point of appui between Juliers beyond the Rhine, and the line of the Elbe.

I added that both these fortresses appeared to me indispensable to give to Prussia under the new territorial arrangement to which we required her to submit, an independent existence, and if such an existence was not secured to her, she would always be driven to seek that independence in a distant and dangerous support, which she might otherwise be desirous of finding in the system to which she belonged.

I hope these representations will have the effect of bringing back our views to their true standard, namely, to make an arrangement which, by sufficiently saving the honor and interest of all the principal Powers, may admit of its receiving a general sanction, and that we should make the best bargain we can for the King of Saxony, placing him in his own states where he may do some good and no harm instead of breaking down our whole system of defence on the left bank of the Rhine by placing him there.

I fully explained to Prince Metternich that, having saved the general principle, and protected his Court by a decided measure of support, when Austria was menaced with invasion, if she refused to acknowledge a new King in Saxony and to transplant his predecessor to a position the most fatal to our whole system, that I could not suffer my Government to be involved in hostile measures upon a mere question of details, to which I now considered in fact the issue was brought ; and that if he expected my support, he must not negotiate upon the principles laid down in Prince Schwarzenberg's memoir—to which I should feel it my duty to object.

I further represented, if he did not clearly see his way in contending these points with Prussia and Russia, how much mischief might result from an ineffectual attempt to do so, if it had no other consequence than betraying a disunion amongst those Powers, through whose joint and imposing influence more moderate sentiments appeared to have been latterly introduced into our deliberations, the salutary consequence of which it was not too much to presume would operate not only throughout the remainder of our discussions at Vienna, but materially contribute, after their close, to the preservation of peace.

CLXIX. [*F. O. Cont.* 11.]
CASTLEREAGH TO LIVERPOOL. (No. 63.)
January 29th, 1815.

Having reason to believe, that the party in the Austrian Cabinet who adhere to Prince Schwarzenberg's views, were employed in urging their opinions strongly upon the Emperor, I availed myself of a confidential channel, to intimate to Prince Metternich that, unless the negotiation was replaced without delay upon the only grounds that I thought were calculated to lead to peace, and such as were consistent with the principles upon which the late Treaty had been brought forward on the part of Great Britain, I should feel it my duty to present a note explicitly disavowing all concert in these new measures, and taking my Court out of the predicament of either being charged with a breach of engagement, or of being insensibly involved in a system to which I must decline to be any party. I desired that it might be also understood, that, in that case, I should request an audience to explain myself to the Emperor.

I received from Prince Metternich that evening an intimation that His Imperial Majesty desired to see me on the following day. I found him extremely *monté* upon the military question, and his general tone more warlike than on any former occasion. His Imperial Majesty received, with his usual condescension, however, my representations of the advantage of exhausting every expedient to preserve peace, and, if we failed, the indispensable necessity, if he looked for support from Great Britain, that the occasion of war should either be founded upon the maintenance of some principle of clear and indisputable importance, or an actual attempt by force to disturb the equilibrium of Europe.

The Emperor repeatedly pressed to know whether Great Britain would support him, 1st, in refusing Torgau and Erfurth to Prussia ; 2ndly, in requiring that the former at least should be razed ; and at the close of our interview, His Imperial Majesty gave me the enclosed proposition,[1] in his own handwriting, as what he was ready to agree to. For the reasons already stated, I felt myself obliged humbly, but most expressly to reply to His Majesty in the negative on both his demands.

The following day, in an interview with Prince Talleyrand, Prince Metternich renewed his endeavours to urge the same view of the question, and stated that the Emperor adhered to his opinion. Prince Talleyrand agreed with the Austrian minister, but stated his sentiments with moderation. I adhered to mine and the interview ended by the Austrian minister declaring his intention of taking the final orders of the Emperor.

There was a good deal of rather warm discussion upon the impossibility of conceding largely to Prussia in Saxony. Prince Metternich's Projet did not go to one third of the whole contents. I stated that it was a little hard the British minister, who had no other possible interest in the question than to save the Continental Powers, and especially Austria, from war, should have the odious task thrown upon him of urging severe measures towards Saxony, but that whilst I would do my best to save the Saxony family

[1] By which Austria offered to cede a number of " souls " to Russia equivalent to what Prussia lost in Torgau. Prussia could then recover from Russia on the Polish frontier. F. O. Cont. 11.

from unnecessary rigour, I would not sacrifice the peace of Europe to preserve to them two or three hundred thousand subjects more or less.

We then discussed the counter-projet to be given in—and I agreed, in consequence of the Emperor of Austria having rendered his Polish acquisitions on the side of Tarnapol an object of negotiation, to frame *our first* proposition on a scale more favourable to Saxony, but I declared that I could not be a party to any counter-projet, which did not assign the fortresses of Torgau and Erfurth to Prussia.

The following morning Prince Metternich acquainted me, that notwithstanding the military advice the Emperor had received, His Imperial Majesty was ready to acquiesce in both Torgau and Erfurth being Prussian, if the British Minister pronounced it necessary, to effect an amicable and honourable arrangement ; but that he expected Prussia to be proportionally moderate and conciliatory on other points, and especially not to press the session of Leipsick. Upon this the counter-projet I now inclose, extending to a certain degree the cessions in Saxony beyond the Austrian projet, was agreed upon between Prince Metternich, Prince Talleyrand, and myself, with the reserve, on my part, of its only being considered as a proposition for discussion, and not as an ultimatum. In all these deliberations the French minister took, I think, a fair and not an unreasonable part. The day but one after was fixed for our conference with the Russian and Prussian Plenipotentiaries, to deliver in the counter-projet, and I undertook, in the meantime, to see the Emperor of Russia and Prince Hardenberg, and to prepare them for its favourable reception.

My interview with Prince Hardenberg took place first. I begged him not to give me any opinion, but to hear calmly what I had to represent, and to reflect upon it. I stated the principles upon which the counter-projet was framed, both as to numbers, composition, and locality, and endeavoured to remove the objections to which I thought the Prussian minister was likely to deem it liable.

In representing to His Highness the strong military grounds of resistance that had been given to Prussia having Torgau and Erfurth, and the mode in which the Emperor's opposition had been waived, I told the Prince that, strongly as I had opposed myself in support of what I deemed to be just and essential for Prussia to possess in a military point of view, I would oppose myself with equal energy to any attempt on the part of his Government to render the Saxon arrangement either unnecessarily severe or painful in its detail, to the Powers who were expected to acquiesce in it, and that I must specially protest against Leipsick being torn from Saxony.

Prince Hardenberg warmly resisted the idea of parting with *this trophy*. That Prussia ought to have at least one of the Saxon capitals, and that he could not return to Berlin under such a mortification. I contended that one of the capitals was precisely what Prussia in sound policy ought not to desire to possess : that it was her interest not to strive to create two Saxonies ; if she did, one would be always Austrian and opposed to the other ; that, on the contrary, the Prussian object should be to render all her acquisitions as Prussian as possible—to give every possible unity to the State which was to remain, and to treat it with kindness, by which means a little sooner or a little later it must adhere to Prussia, and she would then have the benefit of both.

That Prussia would defeat her own purpose, if she pushed her demands upon Saxony too far ; she might lose the appui of some of the great Powers, delay, if not prevent, the King of Saxony's acceptance, and drive the Saxon nation into a permanent feeling of hostility against her.

That the sentiments of Berlin were less material than those of Great Britain, France, Austria, and Germany, and that if the British Government had listened to a popular sentiment instead of to considerations of moderation and prudence, we still should have been at war with America, in pursuit of an object not essential to our honour, and too dearly purchased, even if accomplished, by a protracted war.

On the same evening I was admitted to an audience of the Emperor of Russia, and presented the outline of the intended arrangement, in the light which I thought would best serve to interest him in its favour. Although I begged to be understood as not asking for an opinion till the plan was regularly before him, together with His Prussian Majesty's sentiments, it was impossible not to perceive that the Emperor received it favourably, and wished Prussia might listen to it.

I represented that much would depend on His Imperial Majesty, whose sentiments without indelicacy to Prussia on a point which principally concerned her interest, could not but have the greatest weight, and that if His Imperial Majesty could so manage as to transfer a portion of the Austrian acquisitions in Poland, to Prussia, I did not see how the King could refuse the proposal.

The Emperor repeated to me the difficulties in which his promises to the Poles had placed him with respect to any further cessions in the Duchy of Warsaw. He said that to him as sovereign, it would be a matter of perfect indifference to make the exchange proposed, but that his hands were tied. I urged that the Poles might be reconciled by a corresponding extension on the other side of the Vistula joining the Duchy, and that with this facility His Imperial Majesty had the fate of the arrangement in his hands.

It is due to the Emperor to state, that he shewed every disposition consistent with the delicacy he feels due to Prussia, and to his Polish entanglements, which already begin to manifest themselves, as I understand, at Warsaw, to meet my wishes. He was particularly gracious in his reception of me, and will, I have no doubt, encourage and not obstruct an arrangement.

The intelligence I have received privately of the reception of the counter-projet by the Prussian Cabinet is not unfavourable. Prince Hardenberg has intimated to me, that the King proposes to see me upon it before he gives an answer.

CLXX. [*F. O. Cont.* 11.]
CASTLEREAGH TO LIVERPOOL. (Private.)
Vienna, January 29th, 1815.

Since I closed my letter marked private on Sicilian affairs I have received your letter of the 12th[1] addressed to the Duke of Wellington. The Prince de Talleyrand having immediately after renewed his importunities on that subject, this communication came in time opportunely to relieve me from considerable difficulty ; as I should not otherwise have been enabled to satisfy the French minister sufficiently on this point, to draw from him the concurrence we require to bring our German arrangements to a satisfactory termination.

I explained to him that with respect to engaging in war to expel Murat, it was a point upon which I could pledge my Government to nothing, they must be guided by circumstances now impossible to estimate.

That I was authorized to concert with him and the other Powers as to the steps most expedient to be taken here in favour of the Sicilian family.

That we thought the question should not be stirred, till that of Germany was finished.

[1] CLXIV.

That a negotiation was preferable to a declaration, such as he proposed, which was too unqualified a pledge.

That having been ready to accede to Murat's keeping Naples, had he acted in the war up to the spirit of his engagements we could not take the principle of legitimacy so high as his court.

That our position was nearer that of Russia, and perhaps that a joint intervention on the part of Russia and Great Britain might be the best channel through which a liberal proposition could be made to Murat, founded upon the impossibility of the Kingdom of Naples being tranquilized under his dynasty.

That the Prince Regent was desirous of favouring the return of the legitimate family and the more so, because the King of France wished it. That His Royal Highness would do what in prudence he could to promote it, but that we must be cautious in our proceedings.

I think Prince Talleyrand was satisfied with my explanation. It was agreed to say nothing further on the question, till the German negotiations were closed, and then to confer with the Emperor of Russia upon the subject.

CLXXI. [*C. C. X.* 247.]
CASTLEREAGH TO BATHURST.
Vienna, January 30th, 1815.

Many thanks for your letter. You may rely upon my joining you as soon as I can, without essentially endangering the point immediately at issue ; but you might as well expect me to have run away from Leipsick (if I had been there) last year, to fight Creevey and Whitbread, as to withdraw from hence till the existing contest is brought to a point ; and I think you do both injustice to your own supporters, and too much honour to me, in supposing my presence so necessary. . . .

P.S.—I beg you will not give any money at present to any of the Continental Powers. The poorer they are kept, the better, to prevent them from quarrelling. Time enough to settle accounts, when we know who deserves it.

CLXXII. [*F. O. Cont.* 11.]
CASTLEREAGH TO LIVERPOOL. (No. 66.)
February 6th, 1815.

Considering your Lordship's letter to me from Bath of the 16th ult.[1] as an intimation that, in the judgment of His Majesty's

[1] CLXV.

confidential servants, the public service rendered my presence in England expedient, I lost no time in making the necessary preparations for delivering over the business of this mission to the Duke of Wellington, and for obeying with the least practicable delay the orders of the Prince Regent.

I apprized your Lordship in my dispatch of the 29th ult.[1] of the delivery of the Austrian counter-projet. Its reception, as I stated, was so far favourable as to induce the Russian Government to acquiesce in the principle of the King of Saxony being placed in his own states.

Immediately after the presentation of the counter-projet, I had an interview with Prince Hardenberg, with a view of apprizing him of the points, which I did not consider as admitting of any modification, viz., Leipsick and the re-entering angle into Bohemia by Bautzen and Zittau.

I was directed to attend the King of Prussia on the following day, and I had with His Majesty an audience of an hour and a half, the most painful in all respects, that it has been my fate to undergo since I have been upon the Continent. It is inconceivable to what a degree His Majesty had been worked upon on the point of Leipsick, the false importance he attached to it, and the deep disappointment, if not resentment, with which he spoke of our espousing the cause of the King of Saxony against him. I found it difficult to attract his attention to the obvious embarrassments in which the line His Majesty was disposed to pursue towards Saxony would place him, and I did not escape without some severe personal reproaches for the representations I presumed to make. However, my duty was to discourage the King from any false move, which might compromise us all, and as I wished to execute this without reserve, my audience terminated as unpleasantly as it had begun.

The following morning I thought it right to see the Emperor of Russia, to apprize him of the temper in which I had found the King of Prussia, and to beg His Imperial Majesty's assistance in calming it. The Emperor was very reasonable, and promised to do what in delicacy he could, and as some means of assisting the negotiation, he placed Thorn and its rayon at my disposal, to make such use of with Prussia as I might think fit. Thorn being a position on the Vistula to which Prussia had always attached

[1] CLXIX.

considerable importance, I lost no time in communicating to Prince Hardenberg the Emperor's intentions. The following day he told me that with the aid of Thorn, he had overcome the King's reluctance to leave Leipsick with Saxony.

In the evening he communicated to me the conditions attached by the King to this concession, which contained such a severe infliction upon Saxony territorially, that I was obliged to declare to him my utter despair of bringing either the Austrians or Prince Talleyrand to listen to it; that the King would not venture to accept his country under the fermentation it would occasion, and that we should all, and especially Prussia, be plunged in difficulties.

Prince Hardenberg requested me to make the same confidential communication of his intended Projet to Prince Metternich and Prince Talleyrand, which he had received from them. I undertook to do so, but under a declaration of the reception I was sure it would meet with.

I did so the following day, but requested before they took any steps upon it, they would allow me to see the Prussian minister again, and to try whether I could induce him to relax, in some measure, upon Saxony, by offering him a liberal compensation in some other quarter. In this state of things I felt it necessary, and I conceived would be approved by the Prince Regent, that some sacrifice should be made of interests directly or indirectly appertaining to His Royal Highness, from the difficulty of finding by any other means adequate resource. After conferring with Count Münster, I proposed to reduce in the amount of fifty thousand, the claims of Hanover under Treaty, and to add a sacrifice of equal amount to those already made on the part of Holland. Uniting these with the slender means otherwise available, a fund was created which might operate a salutary reduction in favour of Saxony.

I prepared upon this principle a new Projet of arrangement which I submitted confidentially to both parties. When I first carried it to Prince Hardenberg, I found him again inflamed upon the point of Leipsick, and desirous of making it at least a free town. I represented that, in this state it would only prove a focus of discontent, and probably render the general arrangement equally embarrassing to Prussia and Saxony. It is certain that many of the Prussian officers, and the *Friends of Liberty* as they are called, who abound in the King's dominions, were indignant at losing Saxony, where a new constitution was to be set in motion ; and it was evident a struggle was still making, which became formidable in proportion as it might, from the tone of His Majesty, and many of his most distinguished officers, assume the character of a military and national sentiment.

After some effervescence, Prince Hardenberg received my proposition with calmness, and examined the details with attention. The proposed sacrifice on the part of the Prince Regent allayed his impressions, that I was sustaining the interests of the King of Saxony instead of trying to procure an arrangement practicable and reasonable in itself with respect to his territory. This morning he gave me his answer, accepting with insignificant modifications the plan laid before him. I afterwards had a conference with Prince Metternich and Prince Talleyrand. The former accepted the arrangement without hesitation ; the latter, in consequence of a recent letter from the King, pressing that the sacrifices to be imposed on Saxony might not go so far, had more difficulty. His Highness, however, very honourably considered it his duty not to separate on this occasion from the two other Powers, his own opinion being, that every prudent effort and every becoming sacrifice had been made to fulfil the wishes of his Court, and Prince Talleyrand stated that he had no inclination to withdraw from his fair share of the responsibility. He therefore fully acceded to the measure proposed, which will to-morrow be submitted to the approbation of His Prussian Majesty.

The arrangement in contemplation will give Prussia about eight hundred and fifty thousand subjects in Saxony, together with the fortresses on the Elbe. The King will have about one million two hundred thousand, including Leipsick. His Majesty will thus nearly range in Germany with Hanover and Wirtemberg in territorial possession, and he will also have the Ducal Principalities of Saxe as an indirect support to his system.

I hope, under all the circumstances of this difficult transaction, the Prince Regent will not disapprove the part I have taken. His Royal Highness will personally have the satisfaction of having contributed to the settlement of a question which has now for a length of time continued to threaten the peace of Europe, and, in doing so, His Royal Highness's best interests will, I trust, have been consulted.

In closing the question with Prussia, I consider the territorial arrangement on this side of the Alps as in fact settled in all its essential features, and I hope in the course of this week it will be reduced into official form.

CLXXIII. [*F. O. Cont.* 12.]
CASTLEREAGH TO LIVERPOOL. (No. 71.)
February 13th, 1815.

[Encloses the final settlement of Poland, Saxony, Holland and Hanover, reduced to articles and placed on protocols ready to be inserted in the Treaty.]

Your Lordship will observe that the Hanoverian arrangement will not only give that power the command of the Ems, but place it in direct contact with Holland, throughout the greater part of its eastern frontier—an arrangement which in an European point of view must be considered of the utmost importance for the purpose of strengthening Holland and of securing the Low Countries.

The general arrangement of the Prince of Orange's interests has given great satisfaction to his ministers here, and I trust by his contiguity with Hanover, with Prussia advanced beyond the Rhine, and with Bavaria on the other flank, a better defence has been provided for Germany than has existed at any former period of our history.

P.S. Some exchanges of territory between Austria and Bavaria are the only points of a territorial nature in Germany that remain to be settled.

CLXXIV. [*F. O. Cont.* 12.[1]]
CASTLEREAGH TO LIVERPOOL. (No. 70.)
February 13th, 1815.

I consider that the Defensive Treaty signed on the third ultimo with Austria and France, and since acceded to by Holland, Bavaria, and Hanover, has been productive of all the good consequences, I may say more, than I ventured to hope for, when I proposed that measure for the adoption of those Powers. I attribute this chiefly to the temperate manner in which this Alliance has been acted upon, viz., the not pushing the line of policy founded upon it beyond the legitimate purpose for which the Treaty was intended, whilst sufficient transpired of some engagement of this nature being in existence, confirmed by the attitude in discussion which the Powers assumed, to command respect

---

[1] The substance of this and the next two dispatches were published in the Transactions of the Royal Historical Society, Third Series, Vol. VI. Though a failure, this attempt to give a special sanctity to the Vienna Treaty is not without a special interest. As is seen in CCXXVIII., it first suggested to Alexander the idea of the Holy Alliance. Castlereagh undoubtedly meant it to fulfil the promise of Pitt's paper of 1805. See Appendix I., p. 393.

and to arrest the march of the Northern Courts ; the course of our policy has been conciliatory and unvaried, and it has been marked with enough of impartiality on the part of Great Britain, in the details of the arrangements, to give the whole the character of a sincere but commanding effort to execute with justice and fidelity the engagements taken at Paris. The consequence has been that the leading territorial arrangements have been wound up with a degree of good humour which I certainly did not expect to witness among the Powers, from what had passed in the earlier stages of our proceedings, and it is but justice to the Emperor of Russia to state, that the course of his conduct latterly has materially contributed to this honourable result. It has also enabled me to bring our discussion upon the Slave Trade to a more satisfactory issue than I could have hoped for under a less effectual and cordial appui on the part of so preponderating a Power.

In the course of yesterday the Emperor received the Duke of Wellington and myself and we had an opportunity in an audience of nearly two hours, to go over the several points upon which no official decision has yet been taken, viz., those pending in the North of Italy, the question of Naples, including the Ionian Islands, and the execution of the Treaty of Kiel in the North ; on all of which points His Imperial Majesty shewed an evident desire to have an understanding and to combine his march with that of the British Cabinet. Upon the whole the conversation was satisfactory both to the Duke and myself, and left us both not without considerable hope that by adopting a line of conduct conciliatory towards Russia, without, however, relaxing in those precautionary connections to which we owe our existing position, that the Emperor may be induced to occupy himself at home, where he has enough to do, and that Europe may be at peace.

From what I had myself before observed from what dropped from His Imperial Majesty in a former conversation with the Duke of Wellington and also with the Emperor of Austria, it was obvious that the Emperor of Russia's purpose was to try and renew the Quadruple Alliance before he left Vienna. I thought it material to dissipate this notion by representing the objections to the formation of any Alliance at this moment to the exclusion of France. That on the contrary, after the proofs which we had received on the Saxon and other points of the desire felt by the Cabinet of the Tuilleries to pursue a conciliatory and moderate line of policy, our interest and duty equally required that we should encourage such a disposition, and thus strengthen the king's authority against the bad principles that must still abound in France, and I submitted to the Emperor that the best Alliance that could be formed in the present state of Europe was, that the Powers who had made the peace should by a public declaration at the close of the Congress announce to Europe, whatever difference of opinion may have existed in the details, their determination to uphold and support the arrangement agreed upon ; and further, their determination to unite their influence and, if necessary, their arms, against the Power that should attempt to disturb it.

The Emperor entered cordially into this idea and desired a Projet of Declaration to be prepared. The other ministers, viz., Princes Metternich, Talleyrand, and Hardenberg, to whom this suggestion has since been communicated, equally approve it, and I hope we shall by this expedient have avoided without offence, lending ourselves to any exclusive system of Alliance at present, which I found an equal desire in the Austrian minister to press upon us, but in the spirit of the late Treaty. Prince Talleyrand urged the same idea with me, but was perfectly reasonable, when the objections were explained to him.

I must reserve till my arrival a more detailed exposition of the state of affairs here, which I have no doubt under the Duke of Wellington's superintendence will be brought to a satisfactory conclusion.

P.S. I enclose the Projet of Declaration[1] alluded to in this dispatch. It has been prepared by M. Gentz on my suggestion. The Emperor highly approves of it, as do all the ministers of the other Powers. Prince Talleyrand only wishes to soften the reference to revolutionary France by rather referring to her regeneration. I hope in approving the sentiments contained in this declaration, that the remaining deliberations will be conducted by the Imperial Powers in its spirit.

CLXXV. [F. O. Cont. 12.]
CASTLEREAGH TO ROBERT LISTON.[2]
Vienna, February 14th, 1815.

. . . I have since been honoured with a personal interview with the Emperor of Russia, and have received from His Imperial Majesty the most distinct and satisfactory assurances of his

---

[1] A verbose document which met with a good deal of criticism. It has been published by D'Angeberg, p. 864, and others.

[2] Ambassador at Constantinople. The Porte rejected the overture entirely, so that, even if the return of Napoleon had not prevented the matter from being completed, the special guarantee could not have included the Ottoman dominions.

z

disposition to concur with the other Powers, including the Ottoman Porte, in the general Guarantee to which the present Congress is likely to give occasion, reserving only for a distinct settlement the points of difference now pending, for the amicable adjustment of which the Emperor is willing to accept the intervention of Great Britain, Austria, and France. His Imperial Majesty expressed his wish thus to terminate every misunderstanding that might either menace or disturb the general tranquillity.

You will take the earliest opportunity of opening this important communication to the Porte and you may acquaint the Turkish Government that I have communicated this overture both to Prince Metternich and to Prince Talleyrand, and that they concur with me in the opinion that the Porte ought to lose no time in giving authority to their Minister here to take advantage of an offer so favourable to the general tranquillity and to the particular interests of the Ottoman state.

You will not fail to represent the commercial facilities required as nothing more than the just and liberal execution of existing rights, whereas so solemn a Guarantee cannot but be considered as an inestimable boon—on the other hand, to deny to the Powers of Europe the commerce of the Black Sea by any evasive expedient at such an epoch as the present could not fail to prejudice the Porte in the view of all other Powers.

P.S. I have communicated to the Turkish Chargé d' Affaires the substance of the above overture. As the negotiation for terminating the existing differences between Russia and the Porte might require more time than remains during the assembly of Congress, perhaps the better course to pursue will be to prevail upon Russia to give the general Guarantee subject to an adjustment of the existing differences on certain points to be specially named—the said adjustment to be made under the intervention of Great Britain, Austria, and France.

CLXXVI. [*F. O. Cont. Arch.* 8.]
CIRCULAR LETTER TO AMBASSADORS.
Vienna, February 13th, 1814.

I deem it my duty to inform you, that the negotiations at Vienna are in a favourable train of amicable settlement.

The territorial arrangements of Prussia (including those of Poland and Saxony) are adjusted and also those of Holland and Hanover. Some exchanges between Austria and Bavaria are still pending, but with this inconsiderable exception the territorial arrangements on this side of the Alps are already agreed to and reduced into articles, and as Austria, Russia, Great Britain, France, and Prussia, notwithstanding some difference of opinion upon points when in progress, concur in cordially supporting the proposed arrangement as a whole, you may venture to dissipate all remaining uneasiness lest the peace of Europe should be disturbed. . . .

It affords me great satisfaction to acquaint you that there is every prospect of the Congress Terminating with *a general accord and Guarantee* between the great Powers of Europe, with a determination to support the arrangement agreed upon, and to turn the general influence and if necessary the general arms against the Power that shall first attempt to disturb the Continental peace.

CLXXVII. [*W. S. D. IX.* 573.]
LIVERPOOL TO CASTLEREAGH.
Fife House, February 20th, 1815.

I have received your letter from Vienna of the 6th instant, and have been very glad to find that you had determined to return to England through Paris. Your audience of the King of France may be particularly useful in smoothing difficulties on the Neapolitan question.[1] [The absolute impracticability of Great Britain engaging in war for the purpose of driving Murat from Naples. England at this moment peace mad and thinking only of the reduction of taxes ; impossible, after so long a contest, to expect them to be favourable to a renewal of war, even in a just cause.] I am fully sensible of all the inconveniences of leaving Murat on the throne of Naples, and enter into all the personal feelings of the King of France on this subject ; but I think for his own interest and for that of the French nation His Majesty ought to consider well before he embarks in military operations for the pupose of expelling Murat. Any attempt of this sort might be fatal to the Bourbons in France, if it failed of success, and should be made, therefore, with such an overpowering force as to render resistance hopeless. But

[1] This was in reality the final touch to a separate negotiation which Metternich had been carrying on with Blacas behind the back of Talleyrand, concerning the method by which Murat was to be overthrown. Castlereagh succeeded in inducing Louis XVIII. to accept Metternich's terms. The details of the whole matter are given in M. Weil's *Murat*, III., p. 12 ff. See also my *Congress of Vienna*, p. 126, and the forthcoming *Cambridge History of British Foreign Policy*, Vol. I.

is it certain that a French army could be trusted on this service ? I know there are many persons attached to the Bourbons who are of opinion that the greater part of such an army would desert if opposed to Murat, especially if there were any prospect of Murat being joined by Buonaparte.   This opinion, whether true or false cannot at least be regarded as improbable, when the spirit which is known to actuate so large a part of the French army is taken into account, and ought to be most seriously weighed by the King of France and his ministers before they embark in an undertaking which must, at all events, be extremely hazardous.

I should have the less difficulty in bringing these considerations under the serious view of the French government, as I have no scruple in avowing that the keystone of all my external policy is the preserving the Bourbons on the throne of France.   I am satisfied that this alone can prevent the recurrence of the costs which we have suffered for the last twenty years, and that all other dangers may be regarded as contemptible when compared with those which would arise out of another revolution in France.

I am happy to find that, with the exception of this question of Naples, you will have been able to have brought all the material points to a conclusion before you left Vienna.

CLXXVIII.   [*W. S. D. IX.* 583.]
CASTLEREAGH TO WELLINGTON.
Paris, February 28th, 1815.
. . . You may tell Prince Metternich that the King received his overture,[1] as a proof of the Emperor's desire to establish a good understanding with him. His Majesty admitted the principle that Austria, actively assisting to restore the King of Sicily to Naples, was entitled to his good offices in the North of Italy ; but still there is a difficulty concerning the Queen of Etruria, whom he cannot wholly sacrifice, and cannot provide for by any cessions at the expense of France.   Upon the Valteline and Plaisance, both being military points interesting to Austria, he will make no difficulty.   I think he will also agree to Marie Louise retaining Parma and Guastalla for her life, if the Queen of Etruria, with Lucques as a present possession, obtains the reversibility of these two latter possessions in the event of Marie Louise having no male heir other than the son of Napoleon, against whose succession

[1] See CLXXVII. Note 1.

Austria offers effectually to provide[1]. In this case, perhaps, Lucques might then be made to devolve upon the Tuscan family, and Plaisance upon the Imperial. Upon all other details the King will be content. I thought it better not to enter into these points further : there are none of them, it appears to me, such as should obstruct the main object. Prince Talleyrand will receive instructions to treat personally with Prince Metternich, without communication with his colleagues. . . .

CLXXIX. [*W. S. D. IX.* 590.]
CASTLEREAGH TO WELLINGTON. (No. 3.)
Foreign Office, March 12th, 1815.
[Encloses copy of instructions sent to Lord Fitzroy Somerset,[2] chargé d'affaires at Paris in Wellington's absence, for the direction of his conduct with respect to the landing of Buonaparte.]

The re-establishment of Buonaparte's authority is deemed by the Prince Regent incompatible with the peace and security of Europe ; and he trusts that the Powers who have so gloriously conquered the peace will concur with him in such efforts as may be necessary to preserve it. With this view, it appears to His Royal Highness desirable that the Sovereigns assembled at Vienna should publish a joint declaration, announcing their determination to maintain inviolable the Peace of Paris, and, as the only security for the due observance of the same, the irresolution to support the lawful Sovereign of France against Buonaparte.

It appearing to His Royal Highness that this can best be done by assembling an imposing force on the French frontiers ; that the burden may fall as equally as possible, your Lordship will propose that the whole or such part of the 75,000 men as the Four Powers are liable to furnish under the Convention supplementary to the Treaty of Chaumont shall be appropriated to this purpose ; and that the charge may be more equally distributed, the Powers of Germany, whose accession to that Treaty has not yet been obtained might be required to furnish a reasonable quota.

The efforts of Austria being now so largely directed to Italy, it cannot be expected that she can also appear in force upon the

---

[1] Castlereagh subsequently admitted, however, that the succession to the young Napoleon was secured in the Treaty of Fontainebleau. See CXCI.
[2] Dated 12th March and stating that the British Government considered the peace of Europe to depend upon the preservation of the authority of Louis XVIII.

Rhine ; but no inconvenience will arise from this. If all the other Powers, including Russia, furnish their contingents, I think the gross force on the Eastern frontier ought not to be less than 200,000 men.

I should hope, from the state of the business at Vienna, that your Lordship would find no great difficulty connected with the instructions you will receive by the present courier on Italian affairs to prevail upon the Powers to sign at once a Treaty placing, by an early ratification, all the arrangements already agreed upon out of the reach of doubt. This will give great confidence, and excite little jealousy.

[If this is effected, assurances may be given to the Emperor of Russia that the half of the Dutch loan, as agreed upon will be defrayed by us, it being understood that H.I.M. will act in concert with us in the other measures remaining to be settled. Wellington is to judge where his personal presence is likely to be of most use. It is left to him to remain in Vienna or to put himself at the head of the army in Flanders, only reserving that he is not to expose himself by returning to the interior of France, unless in the command of troops.]

CLXXX.   [*W. S. D. IX.* 592.]
CASTLEREAGH TO WELLINGTON.
Foreign Office, March 12th, 1815.
.   .   .   Since my return I have had a letter from Count Blacas, copy of which I send with several enclosures. You will find in these papers ample proofs, in addition to the detailed reports from General Nugent and Lord William Bentinck, of Murat's treachery, at least of his double dealing.[1]   It is quite clear that Buonaparte, the Viceroy, Fouché, and other members of the family believed him to be false to the Allies. Your Grace will find the reports above alluded to among the papers at Vienna. These reports, together with the letters I now send, will enable your Lordship to satisfy the other Powers of Murat's treachery. It is particularly important that Austria should have the means of justifying herself in considering the treaty as violated by Murat.

The intelligence received from Your Grace of Murat's recent conduct, coupled with Buonaparte's descent in France, has re-

---

[1] These papers were subsequently laid before Parliament. Those found in the French Archives so far as they were genuine, were not, even in the opinion of Wellington, of sufficient value to convict Murat of treachery.

moved all remaining scruples on the part of the British Government. They consider that Murat has forfeited every claim, and that there is no safety, especially for Austria, while he is at Naples. They are therefore prepared to enter into a concert for his removal, and, under proper security as to the system to be established, to support the pretensions of Ferdinand the Fourth to the throne of Naples, whom they have never ceased to acknowledge and to describe in all formal acts as King of the *Two Sicilies*.

As there will be some nicety in giving to our line on this question the form most likely to prove satisfactory to Parliament, it might be desirable that we should accede, according to our own form, to the Treaty previously agreed to by Austria and France, in the negotiation of which you will assist with a view of rendering the details as little objectionable as possible.

The substance of our line will be as follows :—We shall continue to consider Ferdinand the Fourth as Sovereign of Naples, and agree to concert measures with the other Powers, having the like views, for the removal of Murat, either by negotiation or force. This concert ought to include Spain, Russia, and Prussia, although they may not all furnish troops.

In the event of actual hostilities, it is plain and understood that the weight of the military effort must fall upon Austria, and that France and Great Britain can only aid collaterally and by maritime demonstration. The King seemed willing to give 40,000 or 50,000 men, or the equivalent of a part in money.

The government here is very reluctant to bind themselves by Treaty to furnish troops : circumstances may enable them to do so ; but they wish in the first instance to contract no larger engagement as to Naples than they lately had with regard to Norway, which you will find detailed in our treaty with Sweden. I conceive this will not make any difficulty, as *our* military aid must be but a secondary question, if we help them a little in corn, ships, and money. In the former article we can, I have no doubt, do something, and in the latter I have an expedient by which I hope to give them £70,000 a month, for about four months, without going to Parliament to ask for a subsidy : that is, by not deducting the value of the stores supplied to them from the Chaumont subsidy.

This whole question is now put upon a footing that you may press it to a conclusion, preserving, if you can, to us the form in which our accession is to be given.

CLXXXI.   [*F. O. Cont.* 14.[1]]

WELLINGTON TO CASTLEREAGH.   (Private.)

Vienna, March 12th, 1815.

I have little to add to my dispatch regarding Buonaparte's invasion of France. The intention is, as soon as it shall be ascertained that he can make head against the King, to assemble three large corps, one in Italy, solely Austrian, which will consist of 150,000 men ; one on the upper Rhine, Austrian, Bavarian, troops of Baden and Wurtemberg, which will eventually consist of 200,000 men, but will at first consist of only the troops of Bavaria, Baden, and Wirtemberg ; the third on the Lower Rhine, consisting of the Prussian corps of Kleist, the Austrian garrison of Mayence, and other troops on the Moselle, to be joined to the British and Hanoverians in Flanders. Of this corps they wish me to take the command. The Russian army, 200,000 men, is to be formed in reserve at Wirtemberg, &c., &c. ; the remainder of the Prussian Army in reserve on the Lower Rhine.

(The Emperor of Russia at first took the field with the plan of being Dictator. Razumoffski spoke to me of this notion as one of his own ; and I recommended to him never to speak of it to any other person. The Emperor however did mention it to others, among whom the Emperor of Austria, who was much alarmed by it ; but I suppose finding the idea not relished by any, and above all knowing that I should object to it, I found him very quiet and easy this day in a long conversation I had with him at my own house. He seems reconciled to the notion of the old system of managing the great concern in a council, consisting of himself, the King of Prussia, and Schwarzenberg.) He expressed a wish that I should be with him, but not a very strong one ; and, as I should have neither character nor occupation in such a situation, I should prefer to carry a musket.

The Emperor intimated to me this day that, in case the movement of his troops became necessary, he could do nothing without the assistance of money from England. I told him I should write to your Lordship upon the subject by this courier ; and that, in my opinion, the first measure to be adopted was, one something of the nature of the Treaty of Chaumont, in which he agreed ; and afterwards to think of subsidy, if England could grant such a thing.

It is my opinion that Buonaparte has acted upon false or no information, and that the King will destroy him without difficulty,

---

[1] Also in Gurwood. Wellington Dispatches XII., 267, but the portions in round brackets are there omitted. The draft in F. O. Continent is in Wellington's own handwriting.

and in a short time.   If he does not, the affair will be a serious one, and a great and immediate effort must be made, which will doubtless be successful.   All the measures above stated to be in contemplation tend to this effort ; and it will remain for the British Government to determine how far they will act themselves, and how far second the efforts of the Continent.

I now recommend to you to put all your force in the Netherlands at the disposition of the King of France ; (if you can trust the officers at the head of it.)   I will go and join it if you like it, or do anything else the Government choose.   I think we shall have settled our business here, and signed the Treaty if the Spaniard docs not impede us, by the end of the month.   We shall have finished everything that is important much sooner, so that I shall be ready whenever you please to call for me.

CLXXXII.   [W. S. D. IX. 597.]
CASTLEREAGH TO WELLINGTON.
Foreign Office, March 16th, 1815.

[News from Paris unfavourable.   Although Paris and the country generally are tranquil, Buonaparte's progress unchecked by any opposition from the army in some parts of which there are strong signs of disaffection.   Unless a force brought speedily against him, the dissolution of the King's authority may be quickly effected.]

The alarming aspect affairs have so suddenly and (when compared with all the early reports) so unexpectedly taken, will no doubt have been notified to your Lordship direct from Paris.   In the judgment of His Majesty's ministers these circumstances form only so many additional motives for the Powers of Europe to assemble without delay a most powerful force upon the Rhine, and in advance of that river, as the only means of securing the peace of Europe, in the event of Buonaparte's resumption of the government, or, if the French nation shall stand by their lawful Sovereign, of encouraging and supporting them in doing so.

The great change which has taken place in the state of the question may however suggest more caution to be observed in the issuing of any declaration from Vienna till the character of the contest is more precisely established ; for although interference on the part of the great Powers of Europe would, in the judgment of His Majesty's government, be both wise and necessary if sustained by an adequate national support, yet, consistent with the principles on which the Allies have hitherto acted, it would be a very different question to march into France for the purpose of restoring a Sovereign who had been betrayed and abandoned by his own troops and subjects.

I state these principles for your Grace's consideration, leaving the application of them to your judgment, as circumstances arise, upon conference with the ministers of the other Courts. You will, however, lose no occasion of calling their attention to the Treaty of Chaumont, as the only safe basis upon which their conduct can now be founded. If Buonaparte is again to appear upon the stage, and to wield the power and resources of France, more especially under the intoxication of such a restoration, there is no safety for Europe but in a close and indissoluble union of the Four Great Powers, supported by all the other States, who will rally round their standard.

[Dispatches from Stuart reporting that the Prussians have withdrawn a considerable part of their force from the country between the Meuse and the Moselle, weakening the garrison of Luxembourg. The importance of providing adequately for this part of the frontier, including the provisioning of the fortress. Wellington to endeavour to terminate the differences between Austria and Bavaria, and to secure the aid of the latter Power.]

Whatever differences of opinion may have prevailed under other circumstances, I trust that every minor consideration will be buried in the common interest which all must feel to preserve, at least so far as concerns the existing boundaries of France, the glorious results of the late war.

CLXXXIII. [*W. S. D. IX.* 609.]
CASTLEREAGH TO WELLINGTON.
Foreign Office, March 24th, 1815.

[Enclose a communication received from Murat.[1] No answer given to this overture in London ; the decision to be taken by Wellington in concert with the other Powers in Congress.]

In referring this question to your Grace, to be decided on the spot as may be best for the general interest of Europe, I am to inform you that, in the judgment of His Royal Highness's confidential servants, the Neapolitan question has assumed a new shape under the late extraordinary events in France. Whilst Louis XVIII. was supposed to be firmly established on his throne, the difficulty was to consolidate the peace of Europe so long as

[1] Through M. Tocco, the unofficial representative of Murat's interests at London.

a dynasty remained at Naples which neither France nor Spain would acknowledge. The case is different now ; it is a question of public safety in Europe ; and neither the King of France, nor even the King of Sicily, can expect that the policy to be observed towards Murat can be regulated upon considerations of minor importance.

If the Powers of Europe should consider this overture to be *bona fide* on the part of Murat ; if they should be of opinion, under the actual circumstances of Europe, that it is prudent to take advantage of it ; and they find that Murat adheres to his professions notwithstanding the extent of success which has attended Buonaparte's usurpation, your Lordship has full powers to conclude a Treaty with him ; but you will endeavour to combine it with such arrangements as may appear best calculated to insure Murat's fidelity, to secure the tranquillity of Italy, and to leave the Austrian army free to operate on the south of France in force.

If Murat's only object is to secure his footing in the kingdom of Naples, and if a Treaty with England is the security he most covets to obtain this quietus, he ought to submit to such arrangements as are necessary to inspire confidence in his intentions. With this view it appears to me deserving of consideration, instead of remaining in force towards the North of Italy, and consequently holding a menacing position, which, being liable to abuse, must impose upon Austria the necessity of rendering a proportional force inactive in that quarter, whether he might not be required to unite his proportion of active force to the Austrian army intended to operate in the south of France (say to the extent of 20,000 or 30,000 men), and to retire the principal part of his force to the southward, making such reductions in it as a recognition on the part of Great Britain, Russia, and Prussia must render prudent on his part.

Your Grace will of course have no concealment towards the Prince de Talleyrand with respect to this overture ; but, whilst you give all due weight to His Highness's reasoning, the Prince Regent's government does not consider that either the French or Spanish plenipotentiaries can expect the other Powers to submit to their judgment upon this question at the present moment, when the tranquillity of Italy may so essentially influence the general security of Europe, and contribute even to the maintenance of the Bourbons on the throne of France.

On the other hand, however wise the measure may be, there may be a delicacy on their part in being immediately parties to it. If such should be the case, I do not conceive, if all the other Powers concur in preserving him at Naples, that this will make any essential difficulty on the part of Murat, as, when his recognition has been once obtained generally from the other Powers of Europe, there will be not only an increased motive but an honourable justification for the Bourbons at a suitable moment to acquiesce in an arrangement which circumstances have rendered inevitable.

P.S. I have the honour to forward to your Grace a despatch from Mr. Tocco to the Duc de Campochiaro, by which he transfers, on the part of his Court, the negotiation on the subject of this despatch to the Duke.

CLXXXIV. [*Gurwood. XII.* 278.]
WELLINGTON TO CASTLEREAGH.
Vienna, March 25th, 1815.

I found it much more difficult than I imagined when I wrote my dispatch, No. 18, to conclude a Treaty with the Allies on the plan of the Treaty of Chaumont, which work I have accomplished only this night, and now enclose. It will be signed to-morrow night.[1]

The occasion of the delay has been, first, the desire of all the Powers to connect with the engagement for employing a large force, one for the grant of a subsidy from England ; and secondly, the extreme jealousy regarding the command of the contingents of the small Powers in the North of Germany. An endeavour was made to dispose of the contingents of those Powers by an entry on the protocol of the military conference held here in presence of the Emperor of Russia ; and as I refused to sign this protocol, upon finding it contained an arrangement which had not been mentioned, and to which I had not agreed, they have delayed to sign the Treaty for a week.

Your Lordship will observe, that the article providing for Great Britain paying a stipulated sum instead of furnishing men is separate, and the Allies are desirous that it should not be made public till it should be necessary. I found it impossible to frame this article, as I wished, to keep, by agreement, in the power of Great Britain the selection of the Power which should be paid for the deficiency of her contingent, as the treaty of Chaumont was different. The article, however, as it stands, does not deprive her of this power.

I likewise enclose the protocol of what passed at the conclusion of the Treaty this night, in which you will see the urgency with which they all desire to be assisted by subsidies. I believe your

[1] It is dated March 25th.

Lordship is perfectly aware that it will be quite impossible for these Powers to make an effort adequate to the occasion, unless they should obtain this aid. With such a force as they will bring into the field, there is every reason to hope that, if there should be any resistance at all to Napoleon on the part of the Royalists party in France, the contest will be a very short one, and decidedly successful. Nothing can be done with a small or inefficient force ; the war will linger on, and will end to our disadvantage. Motives of economy, then, should induce the British Government to take measures to bring the largest possible force into action at the earliest and the same period of time.

CLXXXV. [*W. S. D. IX.* 623.]
CASTLEREAGH TO WELLINGTON.

London, March 26th, 1815.

I have nothing material to add to my letter. We wait with impatience for intelligence from all quarters. The great question is, can the Bourbons get Frenchmen to fight *for them* against Frenchmen ? If they can, Europe may soon turn the tide in their favour ; and, the process of fermentation once begun, they may create real partisans, instead of criers of *Vive le Roi!* and doers of nothing.

If we are to undertake the job, we must leave nothing to chance. It must be done upon the largest scale. With Mayence, Luxembourg, and Lille,[1] you start on solid grounds, and no fortresses in the rear to blockade as before. But you must inundate France with force in all directions. If Buonaparte could turn the tide, there is no calculating upon this plan ; and we must always recollect that Poland, Saxony, and much Jacobinism, are in our rear.

I wish you would turn in your mind the principles to be acted upon in France. The applying those you acted upon in the South to the force you will now command of all nations, is out of the question. The utmost we could attempt would be to be honest ourselves, and this would make our Allies more odious. My notion is, that France must pay the price of her own deliverance ; that the King should consider the Allied troops as auxiliaries ; that every corps should be accompanied by a French ordonnateur, through whom all requisitions for forage and subsistence should be made ; the value to be paid in bonds, the liquidation of which should be assured upon a peace, either in whole, or in the greater proportion, at the expense of the French Government.

[1] Lille was, however, soon lost to Louis XVIII.

Unless some system of this kind is agreed upon, the war will either degenerate, as it did last year, into an indiscriminate and destructive pillage, or *we* shall be bankrupts, and driven out of the field in three months. I know the difficulties of what I suggest ; but the alternative in the less objectionable sense leads at once to impossibilities and ruin. . . . We long to hear of you in Flanders.

CLXXXVI. [*W. S. D. IX.* 626.]

CASTLEREAGH TO WELLINGTON.

London, March 27th, 1815.

It is to be presumed, in the hurry of their departure, the Foreign Office at Paris has not been stripped by the King's Ministers of any of its contents, and consequently that our Secret Treaty with France and Austria, as well as all Prince Talleyrand's correspondence, will fall into Buonaparte's hands. He will of course try to turn this to account, first in privately sowing discord ; and, if he fails in this, he will expose the whole in the Moniteur. I have desired Sir C. Stuart to ascertain from Blacas how the fact stands, and leave it to your judgment to take such steps as you deem most suitable for counteracting any unfavourable impression.

I flatter myself, after all he knew long since,[1] it cannot produce any unfavourable impression upon the Emperor of Russia's mind. He must feel assured that the whole grew out of differences now settled, and a most indiscreet declaration of Prince Hardenberg's. The Treaty is, upon the face of it, purely defensive ; and all our proceedings since have proved this beyond a doubt.

CLXXXVII. [*F. O. Cont.* 17.]

CLANCARTY TO CASTLEREAGH. (No. 1.)

March 29th, 1815.

[Interview with Wellington who left this morning. Encloses a note of communication from the Duke.]

NOTE OF COMMUNICATION FROM THE DUKE OF WELLINGTON.

March 28th, 1815.

His Grace commenced with the affairs of Naples and stated that there was to be a conference this day at 3 o'clock upon the subject with Princes Metternich and Talleyrand. That at this he was desirous of entering upon the execution of his instructions contained in Lord Castlereagh's letter of the 12th inst.[2] and should propose that the Austrian and French Plenipotentiaries should commence the negotiation of a Treaty for the removal of Murat and restoration

[1] See CLXI.
[2] CLXXX.

of Ferdinand to the throne of that kingdom, to which we should become acceding parties. In order to this that we should assist at the negotiation, and endeavour to reserve to ourselves the freedom of acceding in our own form a Declaratory Article to be inserted in the Great Treaty stating the grounds and the fact that the Powers of Europe could not recognize Murat as King of Naples. With respect to the North of Italy that the Duchies of Parma, Placentia and Guastalla should remain with the Archduchess Marie Louise for her life, recognizing, however, the legitimate *inhabitants*[1] of these to be in the son of Donna Marie Louise. The town of Plaisance, however, to remain with Austria in absolute property and sovereignty.

[During the life of the Archduchess, Lucca, other minor states, and parts of Tuscany to be united into one State in favour of Donna Marie Louise and her son, payment of a perpetual pension being made to the original holders. Efforts to be used for the cession of Olivenza from Spain to Portugal. The three Legations to be given up to the Pope ; other cessions to be made to France, the King of the Two Sicilies, and Austria. In connection with the latter, the Seven Islands to remain under our protection till Ferdinand is restored, after which the protection shall devolve upon Austria. Upon all these points, with the exception of the Seven Islands which had not yet been discussed, Russia in agreement. Marshal Wrede better content with the last Austrian Projet for the exchange with Bavaria. The subject to form part of this evening's conference. In order to have sufficient disposeable territory, it was proposed to require from Wirtemberg and Baden further cessions to the amount of country containing 100,000 more inhabitants. A note prepared from the Five Powers to the Swedish Plenipotentiary on the subject of Denmark and Sweden.]

CLXXXVIII. [*C. C. X.* 301.]
CASTLEREAGH TO WELLINGTON.

Foreign Office, April 8th, 1815.

Our discussion in both Houses last night[2] was sufficiently satisfactory. Until we can open the whole extent of our confederacy, we must have a reserve ; and it is better that our friends should be brought by degrees to look at the prospect of a renewed contest.

My dispatches by this messenger to Sir C. Stuart will give you Caulaincourt's overture and my answer.[3] The general intelligence from France agrees with the enclosed report, and justifies a hope that the Allies, if enabled to move early, may keep alive an important diversion in the South and West. You will best judge whether any and what steps can be undertaken to encourage early exertions. If war is actually decided on, a movement into the interior cannot be too soon made, as far as it can be pushed forward without military improvidence. Its effect must be proportionably decisive.

[1] *Sic.* There is a pencil note in the margin : " Inheritance, I believe he means."

[2] The Government refused to commit itself to immediate war, but only to measures of " military precaution " in concert with its Allies. A summary of the Debate is given in *The Dynasts*, Part III., Act V. Scene V.

[3] Dated April 4th and April 8th. An answer was declined to Buonaparte's appeal to the Prince Regent and the letters forwarded to Vienna.

I have received your renewal of the Treaty of Chaumont.[1] It will be immediately ratified, but we mean to accompany it with a declaration of the nature herewith sent. The latter branch of Article 3, which you very properly endeavoured to qualify, we think may be sustained as declaratory of the object of the concert. It is an engagement, although onerous in its nature, taken between parties who have a common interest in its execution. That which arises out of Article 8, stands somewhat on different grounds. In inviting the King of France, more especially when out of France, to accede to the Treaty, we deem it material to mark that the object of the alliance and concert is to destroy Buonaparte's authority, and not to impose on France any particular Sovereign or form of government. We deem this declaration not less advantageous to the King's interest in France than to the maintenance of the contest in Parliament against Buonaparte. . . .

CLXXXIX. [C. C. X. 301.]
CASTLEREAGH TO CLANCARTY. (No. 5.)

April 8th, 1815.

I send you a copy of my private letter,[2] with its enclosure, to the Duke of Wellington. You will fully appreciate the Parliamentary importance of not having imputed to us that Louis XVIII., by being made an Ally against Buonaparte, has been made master of the confederacy for his own restoration. His Majesty cannot wish us to feel more decisively the importance of his restoration than we do ; and most assuredly every effort will be made so to conduct the war so as to lead to this result, but we cannot make it a *sine qua non*. Foreign Powers may justly covenant for the destruction of Buonaparte's authority as inconsistent with their own safety, but it is another question avowedly to stipulate as to his successor. This a Parliamentary delicacy. By a despatch from Sir C. Stuart, it appears that the King of France perfectly enters into this distinction. I am much hurried, and can add no more.

[1] The Treaty of March 25th. See CLXXXIV. By Art. 3 the Allies engaged not to lay down their arms until Buonaparte was rendered unable to renew his attempts for possessing himself of the Supreme Power in France. Art. 8 invites the co-operation of Louis XVIII. The British declaration expressly stated that these articles were " not to be understood as binding His Britannic Majesty to prosecute the war, with a view to imposing on France any particular Government."

[2] CLXXXVIII.

CXC. [*F. O. Cont.* 17.]

CLANCARTY TO CASTLEREAGH. (Private and Confidential.)

Vienna, April 8th, 1815.

[The policy described in my No. 12[1] entirely accords with views of Wellington.[2]]

My own opinion, and those of my colleagues here, were so entirely in unison with the views of His Grace, that I had the less hesitation in adopting the course pursued by me. But had my judgment even been in opposition to that of the Duke upon this question, from the confidence with which he is so justly honoured by His Majesty's Government, and from the immediate discretion rested in him upon this particular point, I should have felt it my duty to have foregone my own, in favour of his opinion.

I have not intimated the receipt of the instructions conveyed in No. 6[3] to Prince Metternich, or to any of the Plenipotentiaries here ; the different state of circumstances would in my judgment have rendered this unnecessary but after the repeated assurances I had received from Prince Metternich of the peremptory commands to their army in Italy to advance and attack that of Murat, the communication of instructions of this sort appeared to me, only calculated to distract and render more wavering the councils of one, at no time very certain or decided.

This precaution has however in some degree been in vain. Altho' I have withheld Mr. Tocco's dispatch from the Duc de Campochiaro, a similar despatch has reached him through some other channel, and he has given out publicly that instructions to treat with Murat have reached the British Embassy, thus fortifying in a considerable degree the reports published by Murat that the best understanding reigns between him and Great Britain. This Duke called here the day before yesterday and in Lord Stewart's presence stated the notification sent by M. Tocco to him of instructions similar to those conveyed to His Majesty's Ministers

[1] Of the same date as this dispatch intimating that Clancarty would take no action on M. Tocco's dispatch [See CLXXXIII.] as affairs had changed since it was written.

[2] Wellington to Clancarty, April 1st, 1814 (Private). " I enclose a letter from Lord Castlereagh regarding Murat. In my opinion he has by his conduct rendered impracticable the line of policy preferred by Lord C. . . . The Austrians are strong enough to beat Murat if they choose it, and present and future policy should induce them to do so. If I was at Vienna I should not act upon this dispatch, particularly if Murat has attacked or his conduct should still be dubious. The principal point of all is, however, the capacity of the Austrians to get the better of him and keep the peace of Italy at the same time. If they are not certain of that, of which I entertain no doubt, you might act upon this dispatch." F. O. Cont. 17.

[3] CLXXXIII.

A2

here, he then went into a long detail respecting the course pursued by Murat, endeavouring to excuse his advance, altho' he admitted that the invasion of the Pope's territories was an hostile act, to all which I merely replied that any instructions received by me were applicable to a totally different state of circumstances from those which at present existed.

[The Duke since had an interview with Metternich of which he has given not details. Clancarty will seek explanation from Metternich and will] give him the same assurance I have already given to the Duc de Campochiaro, that whatever instructions have reached me relative to Murat were applicable to a state of circumstances very different from those now existing.

[Metternich also notified an interview with Campochiaro with a view to having Mr. Walker removed from Naples to obviate the report of our being in a state of amity with Murat.]

This looks like a determined resolution to go on, nevertheless we have not yet succeeded in procuring the preparation, much less signature, of a Treaty between Austria and France on the subject of the Neapolitan provinces,—which in truth I have the less pressed since the commencement of actual hostilities, and the receipt of the Despatch No. 6.

P.S. *Midnight, April 8th.*

I have seen Prince Metternich this evening. He acquainted me with the subject of the Duc de Campochiaro's interview with him, which was partly, as I suspected, to inform him of the overture announced to him by M. Tocco, and partly to endeavour to explain Murat's conduct. I told Prince Metternich that the instructions I had received were adapted to so totally a different stile of things, that I regarded them as *non avenues ;* and I then asked him how he answered the Duc's apology to Murat : He said that this was to be done by note, stating the fact of Murat's attack upon the Austrian advanced guard :—that the Emperor considered this as a declaration of war, accepted thereof, and therefore he was to send the Duc his passports to return home.

CXCI. [*C. C. X.* 305.]
CASTLEREAGH TO CLANCARTY.
St. James's Square, April 12th, 1815.

You will see by the papers that, although in this country we are disposed rather to take our tone from the Continent, we shall not fail them in our due scale of exertion ; but the Powers of

Europe must not expect us to subsidize all the world, or to go beyond certain limits in point of expense.

These limits now are held by the Treasury to be £5,000,000 subsidy, and 150,000 men, or their equivalent, under the Treaty. If to this you add all our extra expenditure in arms, clothing, ammunition, &c., to Holland, France, &c., you will perceive the effort is not an inconsiderable one at the close of an expenditure which, for past charge, independent of this new catastrophe, has rendered it necessary to fund, in the course of this year, nearly 40,000,000 sterling.

As the confidential *projets* which were exchanged between the Austrian and French Governments, with respect to Italy, were reserved for discussion at Vienna, as I was too much hurried, when they passed under my inspection, to give them any minute attention, I wish to call your attention to one or two points which require to be attended to.

Upon referring to the Treaty of Fontainebleau, I perceive that an interest is expressly created in favour of Marie Louise's son after her death, in the Duchies of Parma, Placentia, and Guastalla.[1] So far as Buonaparte's return to France may be deemed to have annulled the whole Treaty, a right may be held to accrue to the Allies to agree upon a new distribution ; but, admitting the validity of the Treaty, as we are bound to do previous to the escape from Elba, we do not see how a consent on the part of Marie Louise could in good faith prejudice the succession of her son. Pray look carefully into this point before any stipulation comes for our ratification. An exchange of territory, for a valuable consideration, or the cession of a part of any State to save in war the whole, may reasonably be argued to be inherent in the sovereign authority ; but a gratuitous extinction of a minor's right of succession by a mother, at the instance of friendly parties, or by such parties without her consent, does not seem maintainable, particularly when the engagement was contracted with the father. Such a forfeiture, I apprehend, can only be defensible as incurred by Napoleon's act ; and if Marie Louise is suffered to possess these duchies for her life, with remainder to the Queen of Etruria's son, to the exclusion of her own, it must be held to be a new grant to her, founded upon other considerations than those which influenced the Treaty of Fontainebleau.

Whenever the *projet*, prepared by the Italian Commission whilst I was at Vienna, was agitated, I always considered that the decision must have ultimately depended upon Marie Louise's

[1] See CLXXVIII.

consent and such was my assurance, and also the Emperor of Russia's, to her plenipotentiaries ; but, upon looking more narrowly into the question, I doubt the validity of this to extinguish any *essential* interest in the son.

With respect to the Seven Islands, I see no objection to leaving the future arrangement to be amicably settled between the British and Austrian Governments, as you propose. . . .

CXCII. [*F. O. Cont.* 17.]
CLANCARTY TO CASTLEREAGH. (No. 17.)
April 15th, 1815.

It was thought that the change of circumstances which had occurred since the publication of the declaration signed upon the 13th ultimo[1] would render it politic again to publish to the world what were the views of the coalesced Powers of Europe under the actual state of things. This opinion was corroborated by the reports made by several ministers lately returned from Paris, more particularly by that of General le Baron Vincent, the late Austrian Minister at that Court. All of these united in strongly recommending the renewal of an address prior to the meeting of the assemblies convened by Buonaparte for the first of May and that this publication should particularly set forth assurances, that the several Powers of Europe were free from any intention of interfering with the independence of France. In consequence of this the French mission have prepared the projet of a declaration with which the Duc d'Alberg waited upon me on Saturday last.

I must own that neither the reports above alluded to, nor the Duc d'Alberg's arguments presuaded me of the policy of this measure, or that we could rationally flatter ourselves with any probable benefit to be derived therefrom. But the Projet as originally framed appeared to me extremely exceptionable—in as much as it pointed the whole objects of the Allies to be the removal of Bonaparte and second to have directly and immediately in view the encouragement of the Jacobin party to raise their own on the ruin of his power and dominion. With this apparent intent all mention of the King seemed carefully excluded, and his party which we were pledged by our last declaration to protect apparently deserted. And yet on his party now said to be in some force in the South of France our best hopes of interior co-operation are founded.

These observations were candidly urged to the Duc and seemed to make some impression. They have likewise been adduced at

[1] Made before Bonaparte's success was known, and declaring him a public enemy.

the subsequent conferences of the Five, at which the consideration of the policy of an address, and its particular redaction have formed a principal feature. At these conferences the Projet was proposed by Prince Talleyrand on the ground of its probable effects being of the utmost important advantage to the King's interests, most strongly and warmly supported by M. de Nesselrode on that of its effectual tendency in the Emperor of Russia's opinion to destroy the power of Buonaparte—and supported also by Prince Metternich in consequence of the united recommendation of all the ministers lately returned from Paris. In these discussions the Prussian Plenipotentiaries were neuter, rather however appearing to doubt than to adopt the policy of any further declarations till the moment of action.

I felt it my duty to state fully my general objections to the publication of any new address till that period, as serving to weaken the former declaration ; and my particular objections to the redaction of that proposed, principally for the reasons shortly above stated. The extreme anxiety, nay even warmth, evinced upon this subject particularly by the Russian Plenipotentiaries led me however (in entire concurrence with my colleagues) rather to yield my own opinion in consenting to sign an address, than to hazard any interruption in the harmony so necessary to be fostered among all the Allies and those in their service at this critical period. After some considerable discussion, such alternatives were adopted in the redaction as appeared to me essential to obviate, at least in some degree, the detrimental impressions which in my opinion the original Projet was calculated to convey ; and the declaration, a copy of which I have the honour to enclose, was adopted on the night of the 11th and was signed by the Five, and it was afterwards put in circulation to receive also the signatures of the several Plenipotentiaries from the crowned heads of Europe. Some of these, however, especially the Ministers from Spain and Portugal, having objected to sign it in its then shape, it has not yet been published, and it has latterly been thought requisite either to postpone its emission, or so to alter it as to render it more accordant with the former declaration.

CXCIII. [F. O. Cont. 17.]
CLANCARTY TO CASTLEREAGH. (Private and Secret.)
April 15th, 1815.
[A Projet of declaration brought to Clancarty by the Duke D'Alberg. Clancarty against any further publication till the military preparations were more advanced, and considered this

Projet exceptionable as placing the coalition in the hands of the Jacobin party to the discouragement of the Royalists and consequently not likely to be approved by Great Britain or any other of the Powers. A similar declaration proposed by Talleyrand at the evening conference ; an amendment proposed by Clancarty and vehemently opposed by Nesselrode as tending to defeat the object in view, that of gaining the Jacobin party at Paris. Clancarty did not object to this object, but doubting its success, not inclined to hazard the loss of a party actually in existence in arms upon this uncertain chance. Nesselrode finally took the amendment *ad referendum*.

The next day Nesselrode withdrew his objections to the amendment ; the declaration accordingly signed by all the ministers, and sent in circulation for the signatures of the ministers of the other crowned heads, some of whom, particularly those of Spain and Portugal, declined.

This mentioned at the Conference of the 13th, when it was proposed that it should merely be stated that a declaration had been issued in consequence of Buonaparte's landing and that to this declaration the Powers adhered now that he was in Paris. The treaties of March 28th also to be published. Clancarty still of opinion that immediate action should follow any declaration, but objects less to one in this form. Metternich undertook to submit a plan at the next meeting. Talleyrand consistently shewed anxiety for the original form, and the Russians warm in its support ; Prussia apparently indifferent, though more inclined against than for it ; Metternich in support of it in Congress, but against it everywhere else. Private information received by Clancarty perhaps explains all this.

A Frenchman returning to France is said to have had interviews with the Emperor of Russia, Nesselrode, Talleyrand, and Metternich, and to have been charged with negotiations to Fouché and the Marshalls assuring them that there was no intention of interfering with the choice of a government for France so long as Buonaparte was destroyed. Metternich admitted this interview but treated lightly his message to Fouché. He did not think that the Emperor of Russia had had an interview, but did not deny that the other might. Clancarty strongly objected to these proceedings. It is also suspected that a Frenchman staying at the French Embassy, was there on a mission from the Jacobin ministry at Paris. Probable that Talleyrand wishful to be secure both on the side of the Jacobins and of the King. Only this fact explains the conduct of Talleyrand and Nesselrode on the subject of the declaration.

Clancarty to interview the Emperor of Russia, who desires to see the despatches read by him at the former meeting. Wrede has stated that Alexander complained to him that the British minister had impeded the issue of the declaration with a view to pledging the Sovereigns to the specific measure of forcing Louis XVIII. on France. At the interview Alexander said all were agreed in the necessity of bringing up the largest possible degree of force.] but that it was necessary when we are going jointly into the war, that we should also agree and understand each other in the particular object of that war ; that he had understood that in the conferences of the Five I had apparently endeavoured to pledge the Allies to the support of a particular dynasty, this in his opinion counteracting the object which all had in view, viz : the over-throw of Buonaparte, by leading the French nation to a thorough union against us for the purpose of defending their independence. Without suffering him to proceed, I here interrupted him by observing that he had been totally misinformed, for that far from having endeavoured to pledge the Allies to the support of any particular dynasty or system, my sole object had been to keep them free and unshackled, to enable them under such circumstances as might arise to take such line as they might hereafter and accord-ing to the issue of the war, think it expedient to adopt ;—that this had been one of the grounds on which I had objected to the declaration in the form in which it had been produced ; and that I should ill perform the duty which I owed to my Government if I had endeavoured, totally uninstructed as I must necessarily be upon this subject, to tie up theirs and the hands of the Allies, under any state of circumstances, to sustain the interests of any one individual or of any particular line, and I added that if the declara-tion had contained a specific pledge to replace Louis XVIII. on the throne of France, I should have objected and on this very ground to sign it, without direct instructions from my Court. He said he was glad to hear me make this avowal, and that he should now proceed with what he was going to say when I had interrupted him. That he had been anxious for a declaration, and for this particular declaration on these grounds.

That there were three parties in France

1. The Army
2. The Jacobins
3. The King's Party.

That the first were from interest generally attached to Buona-parte, but that among these were many, and some of considerable influence, who were of the second or Jacobin party, and who could therefore be detatched from the first, and led to act in concert with the Jacobins, and if these were gained, with the Allies.

That the Jacobin party, were men of considerable talent, indefatigable activity, extensive influence, and some of them (as Fouché) in situations of great trust, and in which, if they should be gained the most essential services might be rendered by them to the general cause ; that, enriched and enobled as many of them were, it could no longer be apprehended that they were desirous of prolonging civil commotion, and civil struggle, and that they should now seek to renew the attempt heretofore tried in vain, to establish a Republic in France, that the greatest possible advantage might be expected from gaining over this party to the general cause, and that with this view, he had been and still was desirous of the publication of the [declaration of the] 11th.

That with respect to the King's party this was generally composed of *Campagnards* and husbandmen, men who loved the ease and quiet of their usual occupations and who it had been seen, and would still continue to be seen would not lend themselves to any exertion for the restoration of the King. He did not therefore conceive it difficult to determine under these circumstances, that it would be highly adviseable to endeavour to conciliate the Jacobin party. I answered that it appeared to me two separate questions arose on this subject : the first whether any declaration at all ought to be issued at the present moment ; the second in what way, if to be issued, such declaration should be framed.

With respect to the first it appeared to me, on various grounds, as very doubtful policy, to issue any address till the Allies were in a state of readiness to follow up the same with immediate action, and I was going to state the reasons on which I founded this opinion when His Majesty interrupted me by saying that this doubt had also forcibly struck him, and that upon the whole he was inclined to adjourn the publication till the forces were in a collected state, and ready to follow up the manifest. I told him I was greatly relieved by finding His Majesty of this opinion, as it would afford me sufficient time to seek instructions from my Court, with respect to the points which such a declaration should contain, that he must be aware that his plenipotentiaries and those of other Powers possessed a considerable advantage over us in being near and able to consult the opinion of their Sovereign under every change of circumstances, while we could necessarily only act by general inference, and this under a heavy weight of responsibility, that it was my intention to send a courier to-night to England, and to press for the earliest instructions upon this subject, while for the present it was unnecessary for me to detain His Majesty by entering into an examination of the second question into which the subject in my mind resolved itself.

He told me that he thought my conduct perfectly fair, and that it was but just I should have an opportunity of consulting my Government upon such a subject, that in sixteen days I could have an answer, and that this would in his view be sufficiently early to fulfil his objects, he added that I was at liberty to state as much of the conversation he had held with me as I pleased, and desired me particularly to convey to my Government, in order to obtain their answer, what he was about to say.

He then said, if we should be successful—je suis tout à fait contre l'elevation de quelques un [sic] des Maréchaux ou Généraux français au trône de la France, comme Soult, le Prince Eugene et autres de cette trempe ; that he did not like Republics, but that a Republican form of Government as being weaker would be less likely to disturb the peace of Europe, and that if the French wished for the return of the King, et bien ! if the Duke of Orleans, as one born of the Revolution, there was nothing to object, and then fixing me, as if to discover what impression his proposition was likely to make he said—suppose the Regency of Marie Louise, avec ce petit bonhomme de Prince, qu'en pensez-vous ?   I stated that speaking only from myself, as he had well judged by desiring me to write to my Court that I could have no precise instructions.   I conceived His Majesty perfectly justified in his opinion of the impolicy of elevating any of the Marshalls and Generals to the Crown of France ; that any Government of this nature, experience had shown, must necessarily seek its establishment at home by the diversion of public attention to foreign wars and foreign conquests.   I took the liberty of recalling to His Majesty's memory that the same policy had likewise been followed during their Republic by the ephemeral parties in the direction of affairs in France, pending [sic] which period a considerable portion of their conquests had been made, and however different to each other and violently opposed with respect to the interior, the exterior policy of war and plunder had uniformly been the same under all ; that with respect to the Regency (here he fixed his eye steadily upon me) and succession of Buonaparte's issue, I had thought that this had been a point already decided by the Treaty of Apr.l, 1814,[1] and latterly by the declaration of the 13th March, but that at all events, I should much doubt the policy of uniting France with the Austrian monarchy even for such a portion of

[1] The Treaty of Fontainebleau.

time as the Regency would subsist. He seemed much pleased with this, told me that he had latterly seen the Archduchess Marie Louise two or three times, who had expressed to him abhorrence at the idea of returning to France, and that he was sure as far as she was concerned, she had not the least desire to realize the alternative he had latterly put.

This, My Lord, is a summary of the conversation I had with His Majesty on the subject of the declaration and the war with France, and I am sure I need not request the earliest signification of the wishes of Government with regard to the conduct I am to observe upon the points stated in it. . . .

I have no doubt that the Treaty of January 3rd is known[1] to the Emperor Alexander. Marshall Wrede told me to-day that it was so to his knowledge, in as much as the King of Bavaria had told him the Emperor Alexander had good-humouredly reproached him with it, stating that tho' His Bavarian Majesty had wished to be at enmity with Russia, Russia would be in amity with Bavaria. If the Emperor should speak to me upon the subject I will avow the fact, and excuse it upon the necessity of the case for the freedom of Congress under the Chancellor's threat.

CXCIV. [*W. S. D. X.* 80.]
CASTLEREAGH TO WELLINGTON.
London, April 16th, 1815.

I have communicated to my colleagues your private and secret letter of the 11th.[2] Various circumstances have come to our knowledge tending to confirm your Grace's information that the Duke of Orleans has a very considerable party, both civil and military, in his favour ; and without impeaching his Highness's honour to the King, it is not less evident that the line he is now taking has a tendency to distinguish, and so far to separate himself from the other branches of the family.

With respect to the course to be pursued by the British government, we are of opinion that we must not be *pledged* beyond the main object of our concert, viz., the destruction of Buonaparte's power. That, on the other hand, in conducting the Alliance, we must and can only act prudently to the King as the immediate object of our support. In the course of the struggle a necessity may arise requiring the Allies to submit to have another branch of the

---

[1] See CLXXXVI.
[2] Written at Brussels and concerning an emissary of Fouché's who had been sent to urge on the part of the Jacobins their desire for the Duc d'Orléans as King. *W. S. D. X.*, 60.

family placed upon the throne as a middle term, better calculated to allay the internal divisions of the country. This case, should it arise, which is by no means improbable, must be judged of at the time. The only object now to be supported is the King : any appearance of hesitation on this would divide and chill the South and West. The dissolution of the alliance between Buonaparte and the Jacobins may produce other combinations. Our hands must not be tied, however cordially we may desire to employ them in support of the legitimate Monarch, so as to preclude us from adopting a different course of policy under other and adequate circumstances.

I shall be anxious to hear from your Grace further upon this subject. I apprehend we now see it altogether in the same point of view, and I join in your regret that the King's virtues do not give him the ascendency which his position requires ; but with the single exception of Buonaparte, whose influence is derived from a thousand sources, the individual in power, whosoever he may be, is likely, in a country so corrupted as France, to have to sustain the shock of a great combination of interests. The King's habits, unfortunately, do not easily amalgamate with the existing order of things ; but were the Duke of Orleans in power, more especially if brought forward improvidently, his authority probably would soon prove incompetent to repress the factions of the country, and it is not the interest of the Allies, if obliged to enter upon war, to encourage an early and hollow compromise.

CXCV. [*State Papers*[1] *II.*, 301]
CLANCARTY TO CASTLEREAGH.
Vienna, May 6th, 1815.

In Conference on the 3rd inst., Metternich produced some unopened letters which the Emperor had directed him to unseal in the presence of the Plenipotentiaries of the Allied Powers. These, together with a letter to His Imperial Majesty, had been forwarded by a M. de Strassant, who had been stopped on his way hither from not having proper passports. They proved to be a letter from Buonaparte addressed to His Majesty, professing a desire to continue at peace and to observe the Treaty of Paris, and a similar one from Caulaincourt to Metternich. After reading these papers the general opinion was that no answer should be returned and no notice taken of the proposal.

One opinion has directed the Councils of the several Powers upon this and upon all other occasions subsequent to the return of

[1] *British and Foreign State Papers*, edited by the Librarian of the Foreign Office.

Buonaparte, when the present state of the Powers with regard to France has been discussed. They adhere to their Declaration of March 13th, that they are in a state of hostility with the actual ruler of France not from choice but from necessity, because experience has shown that no reliance can be placed on his professions. They feel that if they were now to listen to this desire for peace, for the purpose of relieving their people from the burthen of supporting immense military masses, they would be failing in their duty to themselves and to their people, since they are convinced that, as soon as they were disarmed, advantage would be taken of their want of preparation to renew the former aggression and bloodshed. They are at war for the purpose of securing their own independence and for the reconquest of a permanent tranquillity, because France under its present chief can afford no security whatever. They do not desire to interfere with any legitimate right of the French people to choose their own Government, but they consider that they have a right to contend against the re-establishment of an individual whose past conduct has demonstrated that in such a situation he will not suffer other nations to be at peace. However general the feeling of the Sovereigns may be in favour of the restoration of the King, they do not seek to influence the French people otherwise than may be essential to the safety of the rest of Europe.

These the general sentiments of the Sovereigns and Ministers here assembled, and their previous forebearance should prove to the French that this is not a war excited by any ambition or desire of conquest, but one of necessity urged on principles of self-preservation. . . .

CXCVI. [F. O. Cont. 18.]
CLANCARTY TO CASTLEREAGH. (No. 41.)

Vienna, May 13th, 1815.

[In spite of the arrangements agreed to on March 28th,[1] an attempt now being made to set up the Treaty of Fontainebleau and place the Archduchess and her son in permanent sovereignty of the Duchies. At the above conference all the arrangements for Italy, with the exception of the Neapolitan question and that of the Seven Islands, were acceded to and the articles accordingly drawn up were ready for signature on April 1st. The termination of the business always avoided on the grounds of the uncertain state of Italy during Murat's advance, which seemed reasonable, but no hint of any alteration in the opinions of any of the Pleni-

[1] See CLXXXVII.

potentiaries. Metternich, in conversation with Clancarty, had even admitted the necessity of some plans for avoiding the difficulty of the minority and agreed to consider the latter's proposal to regard the Treaty of Fontainebleau as at an end.]

Such was the state of things when Count Nesselrode yesterday desired to see me ; he began by stating it to be the Emperor's opinion that the Treaty of Fontainebleau remained in full operation, as applicable to the Archduchess and her son (this proved to me that Prince Metternich and he understood each other on this subject, and that the former had communicated to the latter my conversation above referred to.) He then stated his hope that no difficulty could occur with any of the Plenipotentiaries in carrying the beneficial arrangements of this Treaty into full effect in her favour ; and that he was particularly desirous of opening this business in the first instance with me. I told him that I could scarcely suppress my surprise at what I had heard ; that so long ago as the 28th of March, and thence to the present moment I had considered this matter as finally and irrevocably settled—that the Duke of Wellington was present at the meeting at which the arrangement was made ; which, though not absolutely, yet in the form of a Protocol, appeared to me equally binding, the substance having been admitted by all, and the form only of drawing up a protocol séparé of the proceedings of that meeting had been delegated to others ; that prior to that meeting the Duke of Wellington then on the eve of his departure, had given me detailed instructions for my conduct here, which were precise upon this point, in direct unison with the arrangements made upon it on the 28th March, and that Your Lordship's were uniformly of the same nature ; that I could not now feel myself authorized to diverge in any respect from the arrangement then made,—that with respect to the Treaty of Fontainebleau we could not consider it as in any respect subsisting, but utterly annihilated by the subsequent conduct of one of the contracting parties, and that I should not act with that degree of candor which I hoped he had observed in my conduct, if I afforded him the slightest ground to suppose that any reference I should make to my Government could alter their opinion in this respect, especially as I knew that declarations had been made of this opinion openly to Parliament. His reply was not encouraging. He said the Emperor of Russia was decided upon this subject, and proposed as the only expedient for arranging matters, that no notice whatever should be taken of Parma, etc. in the final Treaty. To this I peremptorily objected, as being in truth the most effectual mode which he could have devised for obtaining our formal recognition of the substance of the Treaty of Fontainebleau.   Much more passed, but before he left me he so far softened as to say that nothing short of the Archduchess' request could induce His Imperial Majesty to swerve from the line he had adopted in her favour, and recommended my conversing with Prince Metternich, in order through him to obtain if possible the expression of her desire for the arrangement of this matter according to my views.

[Articles of the Sardinian treaty presented for signature last night.   Clancarty withheld his signature on the grounds that it excluded some part of the arrangements originally agreed to. His conversation with Metternich on the whole subject.   Complained of the apparent breach of faith and want of confidence, and stated that he could not suffer any arrangements to be disturbed which had long since been concluded, or hold out any hope that the British Government would re-open the business. Metternich admitted that the Emperor of Russia was responsible and that he had made promises to the Archduchess at variance with the arrangements of March 28th.   He proposed that Parma, etc., should be passed by the final Act of Congress to the Archduchess and her son, and that Austria should sign a secret Treaty with Great Britain, France, and Spain for the reversion of the Duchies to Don Carlos on her death.   Clancarty's absolute refusal to agree to this or to sign the Sardinian Articles.   Nesselrode's suggestion broached to Metternich who undertook to speak to the Emperor of Austria and to induce him to persuade his daughter to give her assent.

Clancarty's reasons for his determined attitude notably, that to have given in would have been to admit that the proceedings of Congress might be altered at the will of Russia, and that he suspected the Emperor's motive for his interest in the Archduchess to be a desire for a political alliance with France in the event of her becoming Regent, an alliance which it would not be to the interest of England to further.]

CXCVII.   [F. O. Cont. 18.]
        CLANCARTY TO CASTLEREAGH.   (No. 49.)
                                    May 19th, 1815.
    .   .   .   [No satisfactory intelligence on the subject of the Duchies.   Interview with Metternich who was to see the Archduchess and who lamented the difficulty of his position in having

to induce her to set aside her son, in order to satisfy the scruples of a foreign prince who had pushed the matter contrary to the desires of Austria. Clancarty's view that since he had obtained the consent of the Archduchess in the former instance he was responsible for the continuance of it ; he did not question the good faith of Austria, but assured him that this change was attributed by many to a desire on her part to seize upon everything in Italy and to take ungenerous advantage of the present situation of the King of France.

Conversation previous to yesterday's conference with Nesselrode, who stated that the Emperor was more than ever resolved and that the Archduchess had written to him declining to relinquish the interests of her son. Nesselrode's endeavour to maintain that his agreement on March 28th had only been *ad referendum* ; Clancarty could not admit this and stated his inability to proceed with anything until he had received instructions from home.[1] Nesselrode, on his part, afforded no hope that the Emperor would alter his course.

Clancarty stated in Conference that he could execute no Treaty till the point of Parma was settled or till he had received further instructions. Later he consulted with his colleagues and pointed out the impossibility of proceeding on this line to any length of time without producing serious difficulties. As an alternative it was proposed to carry into effect all that had been settled by the Treaty of Paris, together with all the territorial arrangements of Europe, which had been absolutely agreed upon and protocoled, comprising in effect all but the Austrian and Papal arrangements in Italy, excepting perhaps the last ; Clancarty peremptorily declined to sign any Treaty in which the other Italian arrangements should be inserted till either the Parma question should be settled or instructions be received, and suggested that the settlement of the North of Italy should remain over till the end of the war. In spite of its disadvantages, no medium maintainable on any valid

---

[1] His attitude is best shown in a private letter of the same date as this dispatch.

" . . . Upon the Parma question, I beseech you to stand our friend, and to send us your opinion without delay. I never yet was so embarrassed. Will you set a precedent of placing Buonaparte's bastard on a throne ? Will you re-make the Treaty of Fontainebleau *quoad* this offspring of a usurper ? Will you make a present to the Emperor of Russia of the sole dictatorship of all the affairs of Europe ? and play into his hands, so as to further alliances for him hostile to the existence of any European balance ? Will you, now the poor King of France is down, give him an additional blow, by reversing those things which, while he was in prosperity, you had desired to see carried into effect ? These are questions for your decision, which I attend with the utmost impatience. . . ." *C. C. X.* 353.

principles seemed possible between this and Nesselrode's proposition of going on with all other things and leaving the three
Duchies out of the Treaty. His colleagues were in agreement
and considered that this policy should be avowed, at least to
Metternich. In the conversation that accordingly followed with
Metternich, the latter stated that the Emperor had been rather
too peremptory in his interview with his daughter with the result
that she had not only resisted his wishes but had written to throw
herself upon the protection of the Emperor of Russia. Metternich was to see the Archduchess the next day and would do his
utmost to induce her consent.

Clancarty's urgent request that the directions of the Government should be expedited with as little delay as possible.[1]]

---

[1] Castlereagh approved this attitude, and there was no mention of the
succession to the young Buonaparte in the Treaty. Nevertheless Austria,
Russia, and Prussia signed a secret protocol to carry out Alexander's views,
which had later to be disavowed. The succession of the Spanish claimant
was only assured in 1817.

PART IV

THE SECOND PEACE OF PARIS

PART IV

THE SECOND PEACE OF PARIS

CXCVIII. [*W. S. D. X.* 630.]
LIVERPOOL TO CASTLEREAGH.[1]

MEMORANDUM.

June 30th, 1815.

In considering the course of policy which it may be expedient for the Allies to adopt under the present circumstances, there are obviously three alternatives which present themselves to our view.

First, Louis XVIII. may be restored, Buonaparte being dead or a prisoner in the hands of the Allies.

Secondly, Louis XVIII. may be restored, Buonaparte being still alive and having escaped to America or elsewhere.

Thirdly, the difficulties in the way of the restoration of Louis XVIII. may have rendered that event, however desirable, impracticable ; and it may become, therefore, necessary to treat with some other government as representing the French nation.

Upon the first alternative it will be necessary to consider whether the previous declarations and engagements of the Allies compel them to consider the integrity of France as settled by the Treaty of Paris, as a question concluded by what has already passed ; or whether it will admit of any modifications which it may be judged expedient to adopt after the experience of the last twelve months for the general security and permanent tranquillity of Europe. Upon this point it does not appear possible to give any precise or positive instructions until we are more particularly informed of the sentiments of the Allies in consequence of recent events.

In the second alternative it is to be hoped that there would be no difference of opinion. We must all be sensible that, if Buonaparte is still alive and at large, we can have no security that he will not again make his appearance in France in the course of a few months, and we may, therefore, be again involved in a war as critical and burthensome as the present, without many advan-

---

[1] Castlereagh proceeded to the Continent soon after the news of Waterloo was known and reached Paris on July 7th.

tages which have attended the renewal of the contest at this time. We shall have a clear right, therefore, under such circumstances, to require some additional securities ; and although Louis XVIII. should be restored to the throne of France, we should be entitled to provide for the future security of Europe by insisting upon taking from France some of her frontier fortresses, including Lille ; and the only modification which should be admitted of this principle is that it might perhaps be provided that, instead of being actually ceded in sovereignty by France to the Allies, they should be retained by the Allies during the life of Buonaparte or for a given number of years, and then revert again to France.

With respect to the third alternative, it would leave the discretion of the Allies entirely unfettered ; and if they cannot have the security for peace arising out of the character of the government with which it is concluded, they would be fully justified in attempting to obtain it by a reduction of the power and territory of the enemy. As this alternative, however, is not likely under present circumstances to occur, it does not appear to be necessary to say more upon it. The principle as above laid down cannot possibly be disputed ; the expediency of acting upon it to a certain degree will hardly be denied ; but the extent to which we may carry it must depend upon contingencies of which at this time we cannot have the means of forming any judgment.

It appears to be quite indispensable that in the event of the restoration of Louis XVIII. a severe example should be made of those commanding officers of garrisons or corps who deserted the King and went over to Buonaparte. Such a proceeding is not only become necessary with a view to the continuance of the power of the House of Bourbon, but likewise for the security of the object for which the Allies have been contending, a safe and lasting peace. The true principle, taken in its full rigour, would be to consider all the officers commanding garrisons or corps as subject to the penalties of high treason who had gone over to Buonaparte previous to the King leaving the French territory ; but it might be as well to modify this principle by confining it to those who took that step before the King was known to have quitted Paris, considering the elements for conspiracies and rebellion which must exist in France for some years, there can be no chance of stopping them but by an exemplary punishment on the present occasion of those who were forward to join the standard of Buonaparte.

With respect to the conspirators who were not military, it might be proper, likewise, to make an example of those who are most dangerous, subjecting the most criminal to the pains of high treason, and those who were less so to that of banishment.

Whilst measures of just severity are adopted with regard to the authors or abettors of the late revolution, it is of the utmost importance that the King should take the most public measures for allaying the fears of the purchasers of national property. The apprehensions of this class of the King's subjects were productive last year of the very worst effects ; and it will be in vain for the King to think that he can consolidate his authority unless by the security of property as it now exists, without reference to the title by which it was acquired.

CXCIX. [C. C. X. 419.]
CASTLEREAGH TO LIVERPOOL.
Paris, July 8th, 1815.

As I have no doubt that every endeavour will be made to poison the minds of the Sovereigns and especially the Emperor of Russia's, on the steps taken by the Duke of Wellington to accelerate the advance of the King and his restoration to this throne previous to their arrival, I have concerted with the Duke to send General Pozzo di Borgo to meet the Emperor at some distance from Paris. He will carry with him copies of the papers that have passed ; and, having been present at all that has occurred, he will have the means of giving his Imperial Majesty a correct view of the whole before he reaches Paris.

The immediate difficulty is now to keep Blücher and the Prussians within any bounds towards this town. They have notified to the Duke to-day that they had laid on the city of Paris a contribution of 110,000,000, and equipments for 110,000 men ; and they are at this moment mining the bridge of Jena, with a view of blowing it up. The Duke has written to urge them at least to suspend all measures of this nature till the arrival of the Sovereigns ; and we propose to-morrow morning to pay the Marshal a visit at St. Cloud, together, to stop, if possible, these measures of arbitrary and unconcerted severity. . . .

CC. [F. O. Cont. 21.]
CASTLEREAGH TO LIVERPOOL. (No. 5.)
July 12th, 1815.

. . . I have the satisfaction of stating that I have never observed the Emperor of Russia to be in a more cordial, contented, and at the same time reasonable disposition—perfectly well affected to the King, disposed to keep the Jacobins at a distance as you will see from the enclosed letters, and prepared to pursue a precautionary system with all due regard to the King's authority. [Agreed to suspend the march of his army if this was the general wish ; hopes to arrange a council soon to revise our military means.] We continue to have considerable difficulty with the Prussians, who last night proceeded to arrest some of the banners in Paris, in order to enforce their demand of contributions. As the Emperor of Russia co-operates with us I hope we shall succeed in bringing them to reason, and that the conduct of the respective armies will be rendered in all measures of this nature, entirely subordinate to the direction of the cabinets now united. There is a republican spirit in that army, which is very little amenable even to its own Government.

[Jaucourt and Fouché wish the British squadron to help to arrest Napoleon.] From what has occurred in conversation on this subject, it appears to me that the King of France's Government will not, and perhaps have not sufficient authority to charge themselves with the judging and executing Buonaparte as a traitor. If so, and he should fall into our hands, there is no other course than to confine him as a prisoner. The Emperor of Russia asked me this morning whether the British Government would undertake the charge. I told him that the task was not a very pleasant one, but that I had no doubt they would be disposed to meet whatever might be the general wish. I think it is quite clear he must not be in France and that he is better beyond sea, than in any more accessible point of Europe, but if we are to take charge of him I think it is desireable it should be as the prisoner of the principal Powers, France included, who should each nominate a Commissary to exercise a joint surveillance over him.

CCI. [F. O. Cont. 21.]
CASTLEREAGH TO LIVERPOOL. (No. 7.)
July 14th, 1815.

. . . The intervention of the political cabinets of the respective Powers appeared to the Duke of Wellington and to myself the most effectual instrument to restrain the armies and to preserve them in an uniform and correct system. The Provisional Government being dissolved and the King's restored, it is proposed that the ministers of the respective Powers should confer daily with the chiefs of the armies at Paris, or such of their staff as they may appoint to attend, and that the former should serve as a channel of communication between the Allied armies and the Government of the King on all military measures which may be considered as directly involving political consequences, as well as to convey to their respective armies the orders of their particular Governments, connected with the events passing in France. [General Knesebeck (acting for Hardenberg) took the Projet *ad referendum*. I have no doubt it will be agreed to, although they may struggle for some part of what has been already laid on to replenish their military chest which they complain is very low.]

It was easy to see that the requiring France to defray their war extraordinaries would be a very favourite *measure of precaution* with the Allied Powers, and I perceive they will not leave France without obtaining a considerable indemnity. I have not felt myself called upon to oppose this pretension on their part in principle. I have only desired that at a proper time when we know what the state and position of France is, this question may be weighed in combination with other precautionary guarantees which Europe may have to require from France, and that whatever is to be imposed on France beyond the immediate subsistence and supply of the troops with necessaries may be demanded and regulated as a measure of state by a common accord of the four great Powers, instead of each army making arbitrary impositions for itself in such towns or districts as it may happen to occupy without any knowledge or regard to their relative abilities to pay ; and that when the amount of the contribution to be required of France is once fixed, the assessment of it should be left to be effectuated by the King's officers and local authorities. With this reserve in its application a reasonable imposition at a proper time may have a very salutary moral effect upon the minds of the people. It is the Duke's opinion[1] that the Allies will in a short

[1] Wellington to Castlereagh, July 14th, 1815.

" . . . It is my duty, however, to apprize your Lordship, in order that you may make such suggestions as you may think proper to the Ministers of the Allied Courts, that it is my decided opinion that we shall immediately set the whole country against us, and shall excite a national war, if the useless, and if it was not likely to be attended with such serious consequences, I should call it ridiculous, oppression practised upon the French people, is not put a stop to ; if the troops of the several armies are not prevented from plundering the country, and the useless destruction of houses and property ; and if the requisitions and all the contributions levied from the country are not regulated by some authority besides the will of each individual General commanding an army.

" I assure your Lordship that all the information I receive tends to prove that we are getting into a very critical state ; and you may depend upon it that, if one shot is fired in Paris, the whole country will rise in arms against us. I hope that some measures will be adopted without delay which shall put an end to this state of affairs." Gurwood. XII. 558.

time find themselves circumstanced in France as the French were in Spain, if the system pursued by the Prussians and now imitated by the Bavarians, shall not be effectively checked.

CCII. [*F. O. Cont.* 21.]
CASTLEREAGH TO LIVERPOOL. (No. 8.)
July 14th, 1815.

[The position of the King is now considered safe, but he has no army on which he can rely. War will be vigorously carried on by the Allies against those parts of the army which do not surrender.]

With respect to the arrest and punishment of the principal traitors, civil and military, I think there is a great repugnance to shed blood, the result in a great measure of fear and party compromise, and that they look rather to an extensive deportation and outlawry. Prince Talleyrand told me yesterday, upon my urging the importance of adequately indicating the King's authority and the authority of the laws, that they meant to be severe when they had the means of acting, but that until they could estimate what was the temper of their new assembly, they could not judge to what extent or in what manner they could best proceed to deliver France from the individuals they consider it indispensibly necessary should be got rid of. In the obvious state of weakness in which the Government yet stands, it was impossible for me to do more than represent, how much the King's authority must be brought into contempt, so long as the most notorious criminals were not only at large, but seen abroad defying the laws. . . . Upon the whole, up to the present moment, considering their means, I don't know what the King's Government could have done more, and in judging them, your Lordship and the Prince Regent's ministers must make allowances for the infancy of their authority.

CCIII. [*C. C. X.* 430.]
LIVERPOOL TO CASTLEREAGH.
Fife House, July 15th, 1815.

We have received this morning your despatches of the 12th instant.[1] Before I enter on other matters, I am desirous of apprizing you of our sentiments respecting Buonaparte. If you should succeed in getting possession of his person, and the King

[1] CC.

of France does not feel sufficiently strong to bring him to justice as a rebel, we are ready to take upon ourselves the custody of his person, on the part of the Allied Powers ; and, indeed, we should think it better that he should be assigned to us than to any other member of the Confederacy. In this case, however, we should prefer that there were no Commissioners appointed on the part of the other Powers, but that the discretion should be vested entirely in ourselves, and that we should be at liberty to fix the place of his confinement, either in Great Britain, or at Gibraltar, Malta, St. Helena, the Cape of Good Hope, or any other colony we might think most secure. We incline at present strongly to the opinion that the best place of custody would be at a distance from Europe, and that the Cape of Good Hope or St. Helena would be the most proper stations for the purpose. If, however, we are to have the severe responsibility of such a charge, it is but just that we should have the choice of the place of confinement, and a complete discretion as to the means necessary to render that confinement effectual.

CCIV. [C. C. X. 431.]
LIVERPOOL TO CASTLEREAGH.

Fife House, July 15th, 1815.

We have had a long sitting this day on the several dispatches which have been received from you since your arrival at Paris. It is satisfactory to find that the Emperor of Russia is in so reasonable a state of mind, and so likely to co-operate with us cordially in the great objects we must all equally have in view.

The more we consider the various circumstances which have attended the return of the King of France to Paris, the more strongly are we impressed with the opinion of the impossibility of giving that strength to his Government which can afford any real security to the Allies, or to Europe. The forbearance manifested at the present moment can be considered in no other light than weakness, and not mercy ; and, though the King may follow the advice which has been given to him by disbanding his army, I am afraid that very little dependence will be able to be placed on any army formed out of the same materials ; and, if an army could even be otherwise constituted, what dangers might not be apprehended from forty thousand officers unemployed— men of desperate fortunes, and possessing a large proportion of the talents and energy of the country ! A severe example made of the conspirators who brought back Buonaparte could alone have any effect in counteracting these dangers : but this is not now to be expected, and perhaps would have been very difficult, considering the share in the Government which the King has been obliged to assign to some of the members of the Jacobin party.

In this state of things we must look to other measures for our security, and we shall never be forgiven if we leave France without securing a sufficient frontier for the protection of the adjoining countries. The prevailing idea in this country is, that we are fairly entitled to avail ourselves of the present moment to take back from France the principal conquests of Louis XIV. It is argued with much force that France will never forgive the humiliation which she has already received—that she will take the first convenient opportunity of endeavouring to redeem her military glory—and that it is our duty, therefore, to take advantage of the present moment to prevent the evil consequences which may even flow from the greatness of our own success. It might have been not unwise last year to try the effect of a more magnanimous policy ; but in the result of that we have been completely disappointed ; and we owe it to ourselves now to provide, in the best manner we can, for our own security.

These, I can assure you, are the generally received opinions in this country at present, and I think it is material that you should sound our Allies with respect to them. If, however, you should find them not disposed to proceed to such lengths, we think we are completely entitled to an arrangement upon the principle which I am about to state ; and, indeed, their interests will be found as much involved in it as our own.

Supposing Buonaparte to be dead, or a prisoner in the hands of the Allies, we might be induced to waive any permanent cession of territory on the part of France, upon the following conditions :

First. That a considerable part of the Northern barrier of France, including Lille, should be placed in the hands of the Allied Powers, until such time as a sufficient barrier for the Netherlands was completed, and the expenses thereof defrayed by the French Government. The period of seven or five years (as the Duke of Wellington might judge necessary) might be definitely fixed as the time for completing the barrier, and the sum of five millions as the expense : the French fortresses to be restored, at the time fixed, and as soon after as the money should be paid, to Louis XVIII., or to his descendants in line direct, but to no other sovereign of France.

Secondly. The same principle to be applied in such degree as the Allies may think proper to the Eastern frontier of France.

If Buonaparte should escape, and should, therefore, be alive and at liberty, the French frontier above alluded to should be retained during his life, as well as during the time necessary for erecting the new frontier, and for the liquidation of the expenses of it.

These propositions appear to be founded upon a principle perfectly equitable. The French nation is at the mercy of the Allies, in consequence of a war occasioned by their violation of the most sacred Treaties. The Allies are fully entitled, under these circumstances, to indemnity and security. We might not unreasonably claim a security that was permanent, such as France has so frequently enforced under similar circumstances ; but we are contented to limit the extent of the security to the necessity of the case, and, having delivered the adjoining territories from invasion, and being in possession of a considerable part of the kingdom of France, we feel that we have a right to retain such part of the kingdom of France as is necessary for the security of adjoining countries, until that security shall have been provided for in another manner, and the enemy has defrayed the expenses of it.

This arrangement would have the advantage likewise of affording some security to the Government of the King of France, as the restoration of the fortresses would be limited to him and to his legitimate successors. I sincerely believe that this proposition would be far short of the expectations of the country at this time ; but I state it to you, on the part of the Cabinet, as one which, we are convinced, under all the circumstances, is reasonable in itself, as the lowest point to which we ought to go, and as one to which we have little doubt, after all the expense they have incurred, and the dangers to which they may hereafter be exposed, our Allies may be reconciled.

CCV. [F. O. Cont. 21.]
CASTLEREAGH TO LIVERPOOL. (No. 13.)
July 17th, 1815.

At our conference this morning I thought it right to call the attention of the Allied Ministers to the necessity of urging the Government of Louis the XVIII. without further delay, to adopt some measure of vigour against the most criminal of the traitors ; there was but one opinion, that the King's authority would be brought into utter contempt if some step of this nature was not taken without loss of time, and General Pozzo di Borgo was authorized to wait upon the Prince de Talleyrand with a representation in the name of the Allied ministers to this effect. [Castlereagh afterwards had an interview and gave Talleyrand a memorandum as to the necessity of punishing the " traitors."] Prince Talleyrand did not attempt to combat any of its positions, and promised me that the measures to be taken against the most criminal of Buonaparte's adherents should be forthwith decided, and that his own view of the policy to be adopted entirely coincided with that which the Allies recommended.

It is perhaps unlucky that Fouché's office should be at this moment that of the police, as, although the most competent of any to discharge its functions in an ordinary sense, it is difficult for him to be otherwise than indulgent to those who have been supporting the same cause as himself. The great service performed by Fouché was in the last fortnight of the Provisional Government. He had the merit of acting with great personal courage and address, opposed successively to the resentment of Buonaparte, of the army, and of the assemblies ; with a majority against him in the executive government, he succeeded in saving himself, dissolving them, and bringing in the King. It is not that he is not now hearty in the King's cause : I believe he really is and must be from interest, but having always played a game of personal popularity, by covering his friends when they got into a scrape, he has now additional motives for endeavouring to screen them, that he may retain some character, or perhaps what he more values, influence with his party. Talleyrand assured me he had spoken to him very strongly this morning upon this subject.

[Rumours concerning Buonaparte.] As the escape of Buonaparte to America may yet be effectuated, it is worth weighing every collateral aid that can be derived towards the accomplishment of this object. The first that occurs, and it is one to which the Russian minister inclines, is to address a strong note on the part of all the Allied Powers to the American Government, calling upon them to arrest and surrender Buonaparte to them. Such an appeal could do no harm ; at the same time I should expect little good to result from it. I do not see how the President could of his own authority take such a step, and the utmost that our influence might perhaps accomplish, would be to effect his removal from the United States. It is however a measure worth considering, and I should be glad to be informed of the sentiment of the Government upon this point.

What appears to me of more importance, however, is to accumulate every possible difficulty in the way of his ever again finding a party ready to receive him in France. To effect this, in addition to renewing the defensive branch of the Treaty of Chaumont against France, it appears essential to render the 3rd and 8th articles of the Treaty signed at Vienna on the 25th of March[1] a part of the permanent Law of Europe, extending the exclusion to the family at large. There can be no doubt that before we retire, the nation will have felt deeply what it is to be invaded by all Europe. If we make an European invasion the inevitable and immediate consequence of Buonaparte's succession or that of any of his race, to power in France, I am confident, after the experience they have had of his impotence against such a confederacy and their own sufferings, that there is not a class in France, not excepting even the army, that will venture to adhere to him at the hazard of being again overrun by the armies of Europe, with the certainty of being dismembered, and loaded with contributions. We committed a great error when last at Paris, in not opposing the barrier of such a stipulation against his return, for there is no doubt he had address enough to make both the nation and the army believe, that he might be restored and the peace nevertheless preserved. I understand from Fouché that to the last he tried to deceive his ministers by affecting to have an understanding with Austria, with Russia, and even with Great Britain.

I do not suggest this expedient in substitution of the system of interior securities referred to in my instructions, and with a view to which I have already taken steps to prepare the sentiments of the Allied Courts. I am desirous of only adopting it still further to enforce the principle of exclusion, because if we can once lead the publick mind of France completely to dismiss Buonaparte and his race, as pregnant with calamity to the nation, we give the stability to the King's title which it wants. Except Buonaparte the King has no real rival. If he can quiet the alarm of the proprietors of national lands, break down the parties who are struggling for office, by using them according to their means of rendering him service, and organize a new army comprehending much of the old material, I do not despair of his establishing himself and the succession.

I should wish to know if the Prince Regent's servants feel any objection to my endeavour to negotiate a defensive Alliance, upon the principles above laid down.

[1] See CLXXXVIII.

CCVI.   [*F. O. Cont.* 21.]
CASTLEREAGH TO LIVERPOOL.   (No. 14.)
July 17th, 1815, at night.

[News of Buonaparte's surrender received.]   You must make up your mind to be his gaolers.   The French Government will not try him as a traitor, and there is nowhere a place so suitable for his confinement as in Fort St. George[1] under a joint surveillance.

The Emperor of Russia approves this plan, so does Austria, so does France, and so no doubt will Prussia.   He will be less exposed in England to any sudden change in European politicks, and after fighting him for twenty years, as a trophy, he seems to belong to us.   . . .

I have had another interview with Talleyrand and Fouché this evening upon the necessity of acting with more vigour against traitors, and I hope my representation of the sentiments of my Government has produced a salutary effect, and that we may expect without delay some measure of this description.

CCVII.   [*W. S. D. XI.* 122².]
CASTLEREAGH TO LIVERPOOL.   (No. 16.)
Most Secret and Confidential.
Paris, July 24th, 1815.

. . .   Too soon to give any decided opinion of policy which Allies may adopt towards France, as yet only tendency to their respective dispositions can be traced.   Amongst the Powers which border on France there is an evident desire for strong measures, even to the extent of a partial dismemberment.   This is the tone of the King of the Netherlands ; of the Prussians, loudly ; of the Bavarians, Würtembergers—all probably influenced by the double motive of securing their frontiers and augmenting their respective possessions.

Russia, on the contrary, being remote, rather inclines to protect France : the Emperor's principles naturally lead him to this line ; he may also be inclined to keep up a connexion, and not to see France reduced too low.   In a long conversation with him the day before yesterday, could perceive he was averse to any permanent reduction of the territory of France, and that as a measure of

---

[1] In Scotland.

[2] Précis of a number of dispatches are given in the *Supplementary Dispatches*.   The précis are in most cases almost as full as the originals in the Record Office with which I have compared them.   Where the words left out appear to be material I have incorporated them in the text now given.   These additions are indicated by being printed inside round brackets.

security he looked with more favour to dismantling than temporarily occupying certain of her fortresses. Austria is nearer our mode of viewing this question ; but the Austrian Minister fears, moreover, to give Russia so much the lead in point of conciliating the French Government as to produce between France and Russia too close a connexion.

In meantime French ministers not idle in taking advantage of these shades of difference amongst the Allies. Talleyrand has hinted that whilst they are prepared for pecuniary sacrifices within certain bounds, neither the King nor his ministers will ever consent to sacrifice the smallest portion of Frenchy territory. As this declaration reached me through the Russians, as a counter principle I protested against that of a simple pecuniary sacrifice ; that security, not money, was the object of the war ; and that unless concessions of this description were combined with a satisfactory system for securing and permanently covering Europe by a counter-line of defence against France, the Allies would never be forgiven by their own subjects. Unfortunate that the Prussians cannot be restrained, as their conduct tends to unite the French and divide the Allies. Requests that what has been stated may be received with caution, as they are not yet sufficiently advanced to speak with confidence as to the final judgment of the parties.

CCVIII. [C. C. X. 445.]
LIVERPOOL TO CASTLEREAGH.

Fife House, July 28th, 1815.

We have considered your despatch of the 24th instant.[1] We are not at all surprised at the different shades of opinion which subsist amongst the Allied Powers as to the measures which it may be proper to adopt respecting the frontier of France. It is quite natural that the Powers bordering on France should look to their own security in some permanent reduction of the territory of that country.

It is quite intelligible, likewise, that the Emperor of Russia should be desirous of being considered as a protector of the French nation ; but this disposition on the part of His Imperial Majesty should be kept within reasonable bounds. He should recollect that those who are near to France, and consequently in the post of danger, have the deepest interest in the issue of the contest. And, though it may be very proper that he should so far act the part of a mediator as to keep down extravagant and unreasonable pre-

[1] CCVII.

tensions, he ought not to sacrifice what may be necessary for the security of his Allies to the pretensions of the French nation, particularly as that nation has never acted upon those principles of permanent territorial integrity with respect to other countries, when the fortune of war has placed the power in its own hands.

With regard to the two alternatives of dismantling the French fortresses, or their occupation for a given number of years by the Allied Powers, there appears to us to be no question which of these propositions is the most advantageous to Europe and even to France.

In the first place—the dismantling of fortresses has rarely ever been completely effected. The works are partially destroyed, and may be restored for a small part of the expense at which they had been originally constructed. In the second place—though dismantling the fortresses on the frontier of France would uncover that country, expose it for a time to invasion, an advantage as far as it goes, it would not materially protect neighbouring countries which had no fortresses ; and the contest, if it should arise, would depend in that case upon which Power would bring into the field the superior army. Whereas, if the French fortresses were occupied by the Allied Powers, till such time as a barrier could be created by the Allies, they would have the advantage of the security of the French frontier till such time as they had been enabled to create one of their own. In the third place—the occupation of the French frontier by the Allies, to be restored at a given period to the King and his legitimate successors, would be some security for the continuance of his Government ; whereas the dismantling the fortresses could not be productive, at anything like the same degree, of such an advantage.

If, therefore, the principle of security ought to be the rule of our conduct, the option between these alternatives is clear. We do not feel that we should discharge our duty, if we did not urge this opinion upon you with all possible earnestness, and desire you to urge it upon the Allies.

We are strongly impressed with the idea that the continuance of the King of France's authority and Government, after the evacuation of the country by the Allies, must be very problematical, and if his Government should then be overturned, and be followed by a Jacobin or revolutionary system, though not that of Buonaparte, what will be thought of those who, with France at their mercy, had left that country entire in point of territory, enriched by all the plunder of Italy, Germany, and Flanders, and had provided no additional security for the rest of Europe, though in the instance of the Low Countries such security is admitted to be indispensably necessary ?

[Castlereagh the best judge of the time to bring forward this question, but inconvenience in delay.   French ministers will endeavour to gain influence over the Emperor of Russia and important that there should be some understanding amongst the great Powers before he commits himself to their Government. The policy should be decided before a meeting of the new Assemblies.]

CCIX.   [*W. S. D. XI.* 123[1].]
CASTLEREAGH TO LIVERPOOL.   (No. 21.)
(Secret and Confidential.)
Paris, July 29th, 1815.

Refers to letter of the 14th, No. 8[2].   In this state it appeared most desirable, if possible, to come to some understanding in the first instance with the Emperor of Russia.   Accordingly had another interview with His Imperial Majesty, in which he entered fairly into the question, and seemed disposed to concert his measures with the British government before he should commit himself in any other quarter.   If his Imperial Majesty could be brought to adopt the principles for which Lord Castlereagh had contended, thought highly desirable that he should be prevailed upon to take the initiative in imposing them to the other Powers ; that by giving him the lead, it would pledge him the more completely to enforce them upon France ; whilst the measure being thus made his own, the British negotiators would not have the task thrown upon them alone of repressing the eagerness of the *limitrophe* Powers, who desired to profit by the present state of things to aggrandize themselves at the expense of France.

The paper now enclosed[3] was prepared by His Imperial Majesty's command, and has been since modified, after full discussion between the Russian ministers, the Duke of Wellington, and Lord Castlereagh.   In this shape it is agreed to be communicated to the Austrian and Prussian ministers ; and that whilst the general principle is thus brought under consideration the same parties should frame together a Projet upon the two

[1] Précis.
[2] CCII.
[3] See CCXI. This " Russian " Memorandum was, as Pozzo di Borgo admitted, largely inspired by Castlereagh and Wellington. Cf. *Sbornik*, CXII. 297.

C2

important practical questions, viz., the military positions to be occupied by the Allies in France for a time to be limited, and the amount and appropriation of the contribution to be required.

Will lose no time in concert with the Duke of Wellington in endeavouring to bring the Emperor of Russia to a satisfactory decision on these points in which, if we succeed, the difficulties in other quarters may be comparatively easy to surmount.

CCX. [*W. S. D. XI.* 123[1].]
CASTLEREAGH TO LIVERPOOL. (No. 27.)
(Secret and Confidential.)
Paris, August 3rd, 1815.

May be desirable to be informed of progress in settling plan of the Allies, preparatory to a negotiation with the French Government.

Austrian minister has prepared a Memorandum explanatory of the sentiments of the Court on the Russian paper, which adopts substantially the integrity of France as the basis of the arrangement ; adheres to the principle of occupying a line of fortresses for a period of years, but reinforces the Prussian views by giving countenance to the permanent separation of the exterior line of fortresses on the side of Flanders from France ; or if that should not be thought expedient, it recommends that Lille should be absolutely dismantled. To the southward it proposes to give Landau to Germany, and to dismantle Strasburg and Huningen.

The Prussian paper is in preparation : it will, of course, go beyond the Austrian in some points ; but (from a conversation with Hardenberg) I have reason to believe Prince Hardenberg's views do not essentially differ from those of the other Allied Ministers. Sends a memorandum of the Duke of Wellington, prepared by His Grace for discussion, on the military proposition to be made to France. Thinks his own opinion is in favour of the concentrated position in the North, rather than taking up the more extended line of fortresses along the whole frontier, including Lille. In examining this question, adverts to the force of 100,000 men which the Duke proposes should be kept up for the first year to watch France, and to hold the fortresses retained. Both attach much importance to the military attitude of the Allies being rendered at the outset imposing. If it is, France may subside into inaction ; if not, their pride may be encouraged to some new effort to wipe away their disgrace, re-seize their fortresses, and liberate themselves

[1] Précis.

from other onerous stipulations required in our ultimate Treaty. To counteract the impression in France that the Allies would never give up these fortresses it is proposed to occupy them with the troops of the remote Powers.

If Russia and Austria and Great Britain, including Hanover, should furnish the 100,000 men, these, supported *en seconde ligne* by the armies of the Netherlands, of Prussia and Bavaria, would render any sudden offensive project on the part of France hopeless. If such a plan is adopted, and a force of 70,000 men be concentrated in the seven or eight fortresses in front of the valleys of the Scheldt and Meuse, all Europe would have sufficient time, roused by the preparations of France, before she could bring forward a sufficient force to venture into Flanders, etc. [Strategic question then discussed.][1]

CCXI. [*C. C. X.* 454.]
LIVERPOOL TO CASTLEREAGH.

Fife House, August 3rd, 1815.
I send you an official Memorandum, in consequence of the Russian paper transmitted in your despatch No. 21[2]. Although our reasoning, in some respects, differs from that of the Russian Minister, I trust it will be found there will be no practical difference in our conclusions. But I am convinced that we have not overstated the just pretensions arising out of our situation, and that it will be by not underrating them that we shall have the best chance of bringing the French Government to agree to the arrangement which is proposed, and which is as advantageous for the permanent authority of the King of France as for the general security of Europe.

OBSERVATIONS ON A RUSSIAN PAPER MENTIONED BY LORD CASTLEREAGH IN No. 21.
[Russian Memorandum somewhat obscure and some of its reasoning liable to serious objection. If France had responded to the declarations issued from Vienna and had contributed to the overthrow of Buonaparte, the Allies might be bound by the Treaty of Paris, and could not have claimed any permanent acquisition ; but considering the strong resistance of France and the extent of the sacrifices made by the Allies, no doubt that, within just limits, they are entitled to such acquisitions as are necessary for their own security. Although they may not press this principle if the French Government is ready to agree to a satisfactory arrangement, it is material that it should be held out as one to which they have a right to revert in case unreasonable expectations of that Government should leave them no other alternative.]

[1] Encloses a Memorandum by Wellington on the strategic points involved.
[2] See CCIX.

To come, however, to the practical result of the paper, the Prince Regent's Government have no difficulty in acquiescing in the Russian propositions, provided they are correctly understood in the following sense :—

First.   In the present convulsed state of France, no Government whatever, not even that of Louis XVIII., can, in itself, afford to the Allies and to Europe that security which they are entitled to expect.

Secondly.   This security, therefore, must in part be obtained by diminishing the means of aggression possessed by the French nation, either through permanent acquisitions of territory by the Allies, or by the temporary occupation of a military line within the country.

Thirdly.   If the Allies are willing, under all the circumstances, to waive the demand of any permanent cession of territory, and consequently to acknowledge the integrity of the kingdom of France, as it existed before the Revolution, or as it was settled by the Treaty of Paris, it must be on the express condition that the French Government agrees to the occupation by the Allies of a part of the frontier of France, including some of the fortresses of the first and second order, until such time as a barrier can be created, for the protection of the neighbouring countries, and until the expense of it has been defrayed by the French Government.

Fourthly.   It is not unreasonable that the French Government should expect that the contribution which they are to pay should be fixed in its amount, and that, provided it is duly paid, the time for the occupation of their frontier should be limited.

It might be stipulated, therefore, that the amount of the contribution should be [——]¹, and that the time for occupying the frontier, provided the contribution was paid, should not exceed seven or five years.

Fifthly.   In order to secure, as far as possible, the continuance of the legitimate authority in France, it should be provided that the Allies were only bound to restore the parts of the frontier of France which they are admitted to occupy, to Louis XVIII. and his successors by rightful inheritance.

Sixthly.   The French frontier should be occupied by the forces of the neighbouring Powers ; but the French Government should have the advantage of the guarantee of those Powers which do not occupy the frontier, that the territory will be restored at the time limited, upon the conditions which have been stipulated being duly performed.

The Prince Regent's servants are inclined to believe, notwithstanding the ambiguity which pervades the Russian paper, that the summary of principles above laid down is conformable to the intentions of the Emperor of Russia, as meant to be set forth in that paper.

If they are not mistaken in this respect, an arrangement, founded upon a fair application of these principles, will, as far as regards the question of territory, be perfectly satisfactory to the Prince Regent's Government ; but the value of the arrangement will essentially depend on the strength of the military positions which the Allies are to occupy.

As the arrangement, after being agreed to in principle, might be defeated in detail, by providing military positions inadequate for the three great objects for which they were intended, viz., security for the neighbouring countries against fresh aggression, indemnity for the expense of the new barrier, and the more effectual maintenance of the legitimate monarchy of France, it appears to be very desirable that there should be, as soon as practicable, an understanding with the Allies as to the mode in which it was intended to carry those principles into effect.

¹ Blank in original, and a note appended : " This sum should be sufficient to pay for the expense of the new frontier, and for the occupation of the French fortresses, in the meantime."

CCXII. [*Gurwood XII.* 596.]
WELLINGTON TO CASTLEREAGH.
Paris, August 11th, 1815.

[After perusal of the various Memoranda my opinion is, that the French Revolution and the Treaty of Paris has left France in too great strength for the rest of Europe, weakened as all the Powers of Europe have been by the wars in which they have been engaged with France, by the destruction of all the fortresses and strongholds in the Low Countries and Germany, principally by the French, and by the ruin of the finances of all the Continental Powers.]

Notwithstanding that this opinion is as strongly, if not more strongly, impressed upon my mind than upon that of any of those whose papers have lately come under my consideration, I doubt its being in our power now to make such an alteration in the relations of France with other Powers as will be of material benefit.

First : I conceive that our declarations, and our Treaties, and the accession, although irregular in form, which we allowed Louis XVIII. to make to that of the 25th of March, must prevent us from making any very material inroad upon the state of possession of the Treaty of Paris . . .   The French people submitted to Buonaparte ; but it would be ridiculous to suppose that the Allies would have been in possession of Paris in a fortnight after one battle fought if the French people in general had not been favorably disposed to the cause which the Allies were supposed to favor.

In the North of France they certainly were so disposed, and there is no doubt they were so in the South, and indeed throughout France, excepting in Champagne, Alsace, parts of Burgundy, Lorraine, and Dauphiné.   The assistance which the King and his party in France gave to the cause was undoubtedly of a passive description ; but the result of the operations of the Allies has been very different from what it would have been if the disposition of the inhabitants of the country had led them to oppose the Allies.

In my opinion, therefore, the Allies have no just right to make any material inroad on the Treaty of Paris, although that Treaty leaves France too strong in relation to other Powers ; but I think I can show that the real interest of the Allies should lead them to adopt the measures which justice in this instance requires from them. . . .

But my objection to the demand of a great cession from France upon this occasion is, that it will defeat the object which the

Allies have held out to themselves in the present and the preceding wars. That which has been their object has been to put an
end to the French Revolution, to obtain peace for themselves and
their people, to have the power of reducing their overgrown
military establishments, and the leisure to attend to the internal
concerns of their several nations, and to improve the situation
of their people. The Allies took up arms against Buonaparte
because it was certain that the world could not be at peace as long
as he should possess, or should be in a situation to attain, supreme
power in France ; and care must be taken, in making the arrangements consequent upon our success, that we do not leave the
world in the same unfortunate situation respecting France that it
would have been in if Buonaparte had continued in possession
of his power.

[The situation of the Allies, whether the cession is agreed to or
not by the King, very embarrassing. If he refused and were to
throw himself upon his people, divisions in France would cease,
and there could be no possibility of the Allies' disarming. If he
agreed, which seems improbable, the experiences of last year
provide an illustration of the situation in which we should find
ourselves. Last year the Allies were obliged to maintain establishments to guard the cessions ; in France, the general topic of
conversation was the recovery of the left bank of the Rhine, and
the unpopularity of the Government was attributed to its
supposed disinclination to go to war to recover these possessions.
With these facts in view, and with the knowledge that the justice
of a demand for a great cession is doubtful and that it would be
made against the inclinations of the Sovereign and his people,
there could be no hope of peace. If we take the cession, war
must be considered as only deferred, until France shall find an
opportunity of endeavouring to regain what she has lost.] In my
opinion, then, we ought to continue to keep our great object, the
genuine peace and tranquillity of the world, in our view, and shape
our arrangement so as to provide for it. Revolutionary France is
more likely to distress the world than France, however strong in
her frontier, under a regular Government ; and that is the situation in which we ought to endeavour to place her.

With this view I prefer the temporary occupation of some of the
strong places, and to maintain for a time a strong force in France,
both at the expense of the French Government, and under strict
regulation, to the permanent cession of even all the places which
in my opinion ought to be occupied for a time. These measures
will not only give us, during the period of occupation, all the

military security which could be expected from the permanent cession, but, if carried into execution in the spirit in which they are conceived, they are in themselves the bond of peace.

There is no doubt that the troops of the Allies stationed in France will give strength and security to the Government of the King, and that their presence will give the King leisure to form his army in such a manner as he may think proper. The expectation also of the arrival of the period at which the several points occupied should be evacuated would tend to the preservation of peace, while the engagement to restore them to the King, or his legitimate heirs or successors, would have the effect of giving additional stability to his throne. . . .

CCXIII. [W. S. D. XI. 126[1].]
LIVERPOOL TO CASTLEREAGH.
Fife House, August 11th, 1815.

Acknowledges the receipt of No. 27[2], with the Duke of Wellington's Military Memorandum on the proposition to be made by Allies to French Government. With respect to the two Projets in the Memorandum, the Cabinet disposed to place entire confidence in whatever may be the ultimate military judgment of the Duke.

However desirous of seeing Louis XVIII.'s Government popular in France, does not feel that they should be justified in sacrificing for this object anything deemed important for the general security of Europe. Doubts whether forbearance on the part of the Allies would have the effect of rendering the King popular, and decidedly of opinion that government may thereby deprive themselves of the means of affording him that support on which his authority must for some time essentially depend. Wishes, therefore, that this question should be decided on military principles, according to what may best contribute to general security.

While ready to give discretion on the non-demand of Lille, if the Duke of Wellington shall be of opinion that the object can be better or as well accomplished without it, the Cabinet is nevertheless of opinion that Lille should in the first instance be required, and that we should only give up our claim upon the French Government consenting to such arrangement as shall be considered entirely satisfactory.

[1] Précis.
[2] CCX.

Not yet having seen the Austrian and Prussian Projets, ignorant of the extent of the views of those governments ; but informed that they adopt the principles of permanent cessions by France, at least as far as regards the external line of fortresses. We should not forget that these governments have more of common interest with us in the whole of this question than the government of Russia ; and though we have all at heart the consolidation of the legitimate government in France, we should consider that our success in this object must necessarily be very uncertain, and that the security of the neighbouring countries against France may be much more easily attained than the rendering France orderly and pacific

CCXIV. [*W. S. D. XI.* 125¹.]
CASTLEREAGH TO LIVERPOOL. (No. 31.)

Paris, August 12th, 1815.

Forwards Austrian and Prussian remarks on the Russian note ; also the opinions which have been given in on the part of Great Britain by the Duke of Wellington and him.²   Not yet had answer to No. 27. Question of Lille, however, still remains open in the alternative of places. The Duke appears to prefer the concentrated position, and in this believes Prince Schwarzenberg concurs.

Has sounded the Ministers upon the principle of restraining France within the frontiers of 1790 ; assigning the *enclaves* to the territory in which they are enveloped. This would restore to Sardinia and the King of the Netherlands the districts severed by the Peace of Paris, and to Germany the important fortress of Landau. These acquisitions, with the dismantling of Huningen and possibly Condé, seems as much as can be attempted without changing the complexion of the measure.

The objection of his proposed measure is the difficulty of execution : is certain it cannot be well executed in other hands than those of the Duke of Wellington. This is the decided opinion of both Emperors : the Emperor of Russia is disposed even to make it a condition *sine qua non* of his leaving a Russian contingent. The Duke is willing to accept the chief command ; his only reluctance is a doubt whether he can manage the Prussians, and whether they will be willing parties to the arrangement. His Grace having the command will render the plan less unpopular in France, and less injurious to the King.

¹ Précis.
² Memorandum follows.

As the charge will be borne by France, no objection will probably arise to our furnishing our quota in British troops : they will be particularly acceptable in France.

(That you may see how very far the Prussian ideas of dismemberment go, I send)[1] Knesebeck's Memoir,[2] with explanatory map, whence it may be judged what prospect there would be of forcing the King to assign away for ever all the great places of the monarchy.   Thinks he had better leave the country.

Has reason to hope the Emperor of Russia will go as far as the Duke of Wellington's proposition ; and if so, how much better it is for Europe to rest its security upon what all the Powers will stand to, than to risk the Alliance by aiming at measures of *extreme* precaution !

MEMORANDUM OF LORD CASTLEREAGH.[3]

August 12th, 1815.

[Advocates the policy of Temporary Occupation.]

. . . Strong reasons may no doubt be alleged to prove that the military power of France has long been too great for the peace and security of Europe ; that the principles of the Peace of Paris are not strictly obligatory under existing circumstances ; and that Europe owes to itself now to repel the encroachments made by France upon its limits for a century past.   Were it clear that what Europe could now reclaim would in itself constitute security, and not provoke new wars by affording to the military temper of France, at no distant period, fresh motives for enterprise, it might be politic to incur the hazard of creating disunion amongst the Allies themselves by the difficulties to which these new distributions of territory would infallibly lead : but as the influence of such a measure is at best problematical ; as the spirit of the Treaty of the 25th of March, if not the formal acts since executed with Louis XVIII., place that monarch so far in the character of an Ally as to limit the demands which the Powers of Europe can honourably make upon him within the principles *of a sound necessity ;* as the occupation of a commanding position on the French frontiers for an extended period of years carries with it most of the advantages, whilst it obviates many of the evils, incident to the more hostile course of policy, it seems upon the whole to be the wisest principle upon which the Powers of Europe can now act.

It may be stated as an additional motive in favour of this system, that it necessarily preserves Europe in a continued state of alliance for the surveillance of France by imposing upon the Allied Powers as a common duty the occupation and defence of what is ceded for a fixed period to all ; whereas, were the cessions final in their nature, when once melted down into the sovereignties of other states, the probability of uniting all to maintain the point which might be attacked by France would be infinitely diminished, and the question would thus cease to be European.

The continued excesses of France may, no doubt, yet drive Europe at a future day to a measure of dismemberment ; and Europe will effect with vigour and preserve with unanimity such a change in its constitution in proportion as it shall become in the view of mankind a measure of clear and admitted necessity.   To effectuate a change so fundamental was certainly not

[1] F. O. Continent 23.
[2] Which demanded that Lille and all Alsace-Lorraine should be ceded by France.
[3] W. S. D. XI. 147.   Where, however, a wrong date is given.

the end or purpose contemplated when the Allies entered France ; it has rather grown out of the rapidity and extent of their successes.

The overthrow of the French army, the capture of Buonaparte, the continued union of Europe, and the protracted occupation of a military position in France, seem to provide adequately for the immediate danger, and at the same time to avoid the agitation of any new question which might disturb the settlement so happily effected at Vienna. Let the Allies then take this further chance of securing that repose which all the Powers of Europe so much require, with the assurance that if disappointed in this their primary object by the military ambition of France, they will again take up arms, not only with commanding positions in their hands, but with that moral force which can alone keep such a confederacy together, and which has hitherto proved its greatest strength.

CCXV. [C. C. X. 484.]
CASTLEREAGH TO LIVERPOOL. (Private and Confidential.)
Paris, August 17th, 1815.

I mentioned, in my despatch No. 31[1], that I had sounded the Allied Ministers here upon the principle of permanently restraining France within the frontier of 1790, assigning the *enclaves* to the country in which they respectively stand insulated ; and this with a view to acquire for Germany the important fortress of Landau, and to recover for the Kings of the Netherlands and Sardinia the cessions made by the Treaty of Paris of certain portions of Belgium and Savoy. I have since had reason to assure myself of the Emperor of Russia's support in favour of this demand, as well as that of the other two Powers. The Emperor thought this suggestion the more reasonable, as it rested upon a principle, and did not open an arbitrary selection of points, in which the local pretensions of the Allies might either stand in competition, or the general demand be swelled by their collective demands.

As I originally adverted to the probability of the Emperor putting himself forward as the protector of Louis XVIII., I think it due to him to observe that he has not shown himself disinclined, after fair discussion, to the adoption of such measures of salutary precaution as have been proposed to him ; and I still think that, by the course I adopted towards His Imperial Majesty, as reported in a former letter, I not only deprived him of that character of being the *exclusive* protector of the King—a relation in which, for the general politics of Europe, it is of great importance he should not be permitted to place himself—but that I have gradually brought him publicly to adopt all the principles of the Allied Powers as his own, and to push them as far as it is at all clear they can be pushed without a dangerous reaction.

[1] CCXIV.

I quite concur with the remark contained in your last letter that the true interests of Great Britain are much more identified with those of Austria and Prussia, in the existing crisis, than with those of Russia ; but I must, at the same time, observe that both these Courts require to be narrowly watched at the present moment, with respect to the mode in which they pursue their particular views, in order that we may not be involved in a course of policy in which Great Britain has no principle of common interest with them but the reverse.

[1] [The first point is that neither Austria nor Prussia may, and certainly none of the smaller Powers have any sincere desire to bring the present state of things to a speedy termination, so long as they can feed, clothe, and pay their armies at the expense of France, and put their English subsidies into their pockets, of which last nothing can deprive them previous to the 1st of April, 1816, but the actual conclusion of a treaty with France.

The Austrians, it is true, have latterly halted a corps of 15,000 men in Lower Austria ; but they have brought the whole of Bianci's army into Provence, to feed upon that poor and loyal country.

The Prussians have not only brought an entire new *corps d'armée* of 40,000 men forward, much to the annoyance of the King of the Netherlands, on whom they have been feeding by the way, but have reinforcements to an equal amount in full march to fill up their other corps, making their force in France, according to their own returns, 280,000, for which they draw rations.

The Bavarians also, not to lose time, have forwarded troops from Munich to the Loire in waggons, at a moment when their service in the field was out of the question.

The Prussian Minister of Finance, Bulow, told him yesterday that he calculated the Allied force now in France at 900,000 men, and their expense, including forage and waste, at not less than three livres per man per day, which is about 112,000*l* per day, or 36,000,000*l* per year, exclusive of pay and clothing, the latter being provided by distinct requisitions, the former by the revenues of the department occupied.

To this must be added the final contribution to be demanded, which, from what he can gather, is not likely to fall short of 600,000,000 of livres ; and if to this is added the charge of 100,000 men to occupy the intended positions in France for a number of years, the pressure is likely to be as heavy in a pecuniary shape as the country can be expected quietly to submit to.]

[1] Précis, Wellington. **Supplementary Despatches XI. 127.**

I have adverted to the ultimate contribution, for the purpose of observing that there is another point of view, in which our views will not be found altogether in unison with those of the two Powers in question, namely, in appropriating a considerable portion of the contribution to fortifications. You reason the justice of throwing upon France the expense of providing those defences which her position and conduct render indispensable to the security of the neighbouring States. Austria and Prussia state the justice as strongly and preferably in favour of being indemnified for the expenses of the war and for former contributions levied upon them by France. It is quite clear that France cannot meet all these demands ; that the charge upon her must be limited in amount ; and that it will be a question amongst the Allies, in appropriating this fund, which pretension is to give way.

From what fell from Prince Hardenberg, some time since, I apprehend much opposition to my proposal in that quarter ; and I have found Prince Metternich more impracticable upon this point than on any I have ever discussed with him. I hope, however, I have made some impression upon him ; but you must not suppose that this is a question between us and France : it is, in truth, a question much more between us and our Allies, in which, as I foresaw before I left England, we should have to contend, upon grounds of remote precaution, against the immediate pressure of avarice and poverty.

[1] [Has, in addition to support, received assurances from the Russian Minister that the Emperor will agree to his proposition of appropriating one-third of the contribution to fortification, which, considering the remote interest of Russia, is a very liberal proceeding.

In the management of his troops, the Emperor has been as little open to reproach. His second army was put in motion without any bargain, and previous to the assurance of any assistance from us ; and their march was stopped, and orders sent for their return, upon a representation from Lord Castlereagh. His Imperial Majesty now urges (and for the economy of our subsidies we must be anxious for the same) that a prompt settlement should be made with France, being anxious to march his army back as early in the next month as the state of the negotiations will permit.

Another point in which we must be guarded with those Courts is the impulse they receive from the public sentiment in Germany,

[1] Précis, Wellington. Supplementary Despatches. XI. 127.

from the temper of the smaller Powers, and the desire each feels not to yield to the other the influence in Germany which belongs to what is most popular.

The prevailing sentiment in Germany is favourable to the territorial reduction of France. After what the people have suffered, this is not wonderful ; but it is one thing to wish a thing done, and another to maintain it when done. None of these Powers can for any time keep up war establishments, or, having laid them down, easily resume them. If, then, this course increases the chance of early war, the acquisitions may be of short duration ; and whilst the chances of peace diminished, we may be obliged, in order to keep France within due bounds, to take the weight of the war on ourselves.]

The more I wish the alternative, the more I am impressed with the wisdom of what the Duke of Wellington states upon this subject, in his letter to me,[1] when he says that he deems the possession of a certain number of French fortresses, for an extended period of time, in itself preferable to the actual cession of the same places, and for this obvious reason, that the one is compatible with French connexion, the other leads to unite all Frenchmen against us, or rather against the Power that shall be found in possession of their spoils ; and, as the King of the Netherlands would probably be the first to be attacked, we have more reason to weigh well the course to be pursued.

When I state that the temporary occupation is not incompatible with preserving a useful influence in France, I do it from knowing that the King and his Ministers do not wish to see France without foreign troops—that they admit the Allies cannot leave their troops in France, without the security of a certain number of their fortresses. My belief and hope, then, is, if the arrangement is made with some attention to the feelings and interests of the country, that the King, his Government, and the loyal party in France, will ally themselves with you ; and that, thus sustained, the King will be able gradually to establish his authority, which, if accomplished, is valuable beyond all other securities we can acquire. If he fails, we shall not have to reproach ourselves with having precipitated his fall, and we shall have full time to take our precautions. If, on the contrary, we push things now to an extremity, we leave the King no resource in the eyes of his own people but to disavow us ; and, once committed against us in sentiment, he will be obliged soon either to lead the nation into war himself, or possibly be set aside to make way for some more

[1] CCXII.

bold and enterprising competitor. The whole of this view of the question turns upon a conviction that the King's cause in France is far from hopeless, if well conducted, and that the European Alliance can be made powerfully instrumental to his support, if our securities are framed in such a manner as not to be ultimately hostile to France, after she shall have given *protracted proofs* of having ceased to be a revolutionary State.

I don't know what impressions the Austrian and Prussian papers may have made in England in opposition to this reasoning ; but, if you should deem it necessary to demand securities against which all Frenchmen must protest, which I do not consider to be by any means the case, with respect to those recommended by the Duke of Wellington, my advice then will be to you and to the Allies to have no reserve towards France. You cannot— you must not. In that case, calculate upon the submission of France but for the shortest interval ; and the only objection I should then to have to state against General Knesebeck's plan is that it does not go far enough. It leaves France nearly entire, both in population and resources, whilst it deprives her precisely of those objects which will revive in every Frenchman, whatever may be his principles, a desire of war at the first favourable moment.

I have troubled you with this long letter, because I think we must make up our minds whether we are to play a game with any portion of France, or against France collectively. If we mean the former, the duty of the negotiator will be to get as much direct security as he finds compatible with that object, in order to gratify what, I have no doubt, is the prevailing temper in England, as well as in Germany. The Cabinet ought to instruct the Duke of Wellington not to look to secure a fortified place the more or the less, which seldom tells for much in the contest of nations, but to confer with the other Powers how we can best reduce the power of France, and most effectively disqualify her from again making the attempt to assail Europe. I have no doubt the middle line would be the most popular, and that, in extorting the permanent cession of one or two fortresses of great name, our labours would carry with them an *éclat* which is not likely to attend them, according to the course we recommend. But it is not our business to collect trophies, but to try if we can bring back the world to peaceful habits. I do not believe this to be compatible with any attempt now materially and permanently to affect the territorial character of France, as settled by the Peace of Paris ; neither do I think it a clear case (if we can, by imposing a strait waistcoat upon that Power for a number of years, restore her to ordinary habits, and weighing the extraordinary growth of other States in latter times, and especially of Russia) that France, even with her existing dimensions, may not be found a useful rather than a dangerous member of the European system ; but these are the problems you are to weigh. You have now all the materials before you ; you know the Duke of Wellington's sentiments and my own ; and, if you wish us to alter the view we have taken of the question, or have to make any change in the instructions given me on leaving England, there is no time to be lost.

As far as we have gone, I apprehend the securities proposed exceed in amount (Buonaparte being in our hands) what was then required, in the event of his being at large ; but this is no objection, if the thing is right in itself.

CCXVI. [*W. S. D. XI.* 130.]
LIVERPOOL TO CASTLEREAGH.
Fife House, August 18th, 1815.

We have received your letters of the 12th inst.,[1] enclosing the Prussian and Austrian Projets on the terms to be proposed to France, and your Memorandum and that of the Duke of Wellington upon them.

I entirely concur with you and the Duke of Wellington in your opinion as to the extravagance of the Prussian propositions under all the present circumstances. I certainly think that the reduction of the power of France proposed in their Projet would be more beneficial to Europe than it would be disadvantageous to France ; and I should not be surprised if events were now to take such a turn as might render it just and expedient for the Allies to insist on the Prussian demands to their full extent. But the contest must in that case assume a new character. The Projet in question is in no way consistent with the relations in which we stand at present to Louis XVIII.

On the other hand the Austrian Projet does not appear to us unreasonable. It is founded on no principle of dismemberment, nor on that of reducing the power of France or violating the integrity of their territory beyond what is absolutely necessary for the security of the neighbouring states. I confess I think that, under all the circumstances, the most wise arrangement would be a combination of the Austrian Projet with that of the Duke of Wellington. . . .

[1] CCXIV.

An arrangement on this principle would have nothing in it which could really be considered as humiliating to France. The proposition for temporary occupation, on which we are agreed, is in fact more humiliating than what it would be proposed to retain. We should ask no more than what a successful war on the frontiers might entitle us to demand, and I doubt very much whether the French expect to be let off more easy than they would be by a proposal of the nature of that above stated.

You have, however, been apprized in the Memorandum of the 3rd August[1] of the arrangement in which we are ready to concur if nothing further can be obtained. But I think that while we attend so much to what is due to the feelings of the French Government, we ought not to be insensible to what we owe to Austria, Prussia, and our other Allies, and likewise to the public feeling in this country, which I cannot conceal from you will be grievously disappointed by the acknowledgment.

[The question of the statues and pictures withdrawn from other countries ; very desirable in principle that they should be restored, but aware that this cannot be effected without some prejudice to the King and his Government. If the King is to be called upon to make other sacrifices for the security of Europe, possible to understand the repugnance which may exist to pressing him too far on this point, but if the integrity of French territory is to be observed, he ought to give up the plunder of the Revolution. The intention of conferring on Wellington the command of the force to be kept on the French frontier highly judicious ; no objection to furnish a quota of British troops.]

CCXVII. [C. C. X. 495.]
LIVERPOOL TO CASTLEREAGH.

August 23rd, 1815.

I have laid before the Prince Regent and the Cabinet your very able letter, marked Private and Confidential, of the 17th instant.[2] Under all the difficulties which unavoidably attend our present relations with the French Government, we are prepared to concur in the alternative stated in your letter, to which both the Duke of Wellington and yourself give so decided a preference, and, instead of urging the permanent cession of any part of the

[1] CCXI.
[2] CCXV.

French territory by the French Government, we shall be satisfied with an arrangement which secures to the Allies, for a time sufficiently extended, the military occupation of certain of the French fortresses, according to the *projets* in the Duke of Wellington's paper, and which provides at the same time for the rectification of the French frontier, by restoring France to the situation in which she stood in the year 1790, and giving the fortresses *enclavés* in the neighbouring territories to the States to which those territories belong.

We cannot conceal from ourselves and from you that an arrangement on this principle (which I believe to be entirely novel in its character) may be subject to many serious inconveniences ; and we should be most desirous that there should be added to it, therefore, a stipulation for the dismantling of Lille and Strasburg. Such a stipulation need not, in our judgment, mortify the pride of the French nation. It would in no way affect the permanent interest of France, whilst it would add considerably to the temporary security of the Allies ; and we are of opinion that this object is the more deserving of attention, as the other part of the arrangement might, in a great measure, fail, in the event of differences unfortunately arising amongst the Allies, from any change in the policy of their respective Courts, by which any one of the considerable Powers might separate itself from the Alliance during the period specified for the occupation of the fortresses, and might thereby throw the whole arrangement into confusion, or defeat the purpose of it altogether. In short, the principle of temporary occupation must necessarily be so complicated in its nature, that we feel all the importance of annexing to it something which may afford security to the neighbouring States, independent of the contingencies above stated, till such time as measures can be adopted for placing their own frontiers in a respectable state of defence.

You will understand me as not bringing this proposition for dismantling Lille and Strasburg forward as a *sine qua non*, but as wishing it to be urged with all the weight which we feel is due to it ; and, considering how very short our propositions fall of the Austrian and Prussian *projets*, I cannot but entertain a confident hope that, when the French Government are aware, as they must be, of the extent of sacrifice which would have been demanded from them, if it had not been for the moderation of Great Britain and Russia, they will not feel it possible to make any serious resistance to a concession of this nature. . . .

CCXVIII.   [*F. O. Cont.* 24.]
CASTLEREAGH TO LIVERPOOL.   (No. 38.)
August 24th, 1815.

. . . [As to the demand for expenses of St. Helena, does not think it wise.] Buonaparte gave himself to us. The Allies, feeling they had to tranquillize the public sentiment in their respective States with respect to this man, desire that Napoleon may be deemed to be the prisoner of the Powers generally, and that they may have a right to send Commissaries to verify his existence, etc. None of them pressed the custody upon us. I took care not to let suffer any question to arise about his passing into any other hands, because in no other could he safely for our own interests be placed. If the custody had been brought in doubt, I have no doubt other Powers would have been willing to take and shut him up in one of their fortresses without making any charge upon us, but we should then have been placing a most serious instrument in hands always of dubious import in the fluctuations of Continental affairs. . . .

CCXIX.   [*W. S. D. XI.* 137[1].]
CASTLEREAGH TO LIVERPOOL.   (No. 40.)
Paris, August 24th, 1815.

Lord Castlereagh requests instructions to bring the negotiations to a conclusion. Despatches Lord Stewart to England. Hoped to have sent a paper of Prince Metternich's upon the idea of Lord Liverpool's letter of the 18th.[2] Prince Hardenberg has not explained himself. Difficulties of restraining the Prussian army, which Prince Hardenberg (*finds himself so wholly incompetent to control, or direct the violent party in the army, that he did not hesitate to avow to Lord Clancarty two days since that he felt himself in the midst of Praetorian bands. At the same time although this state of affairs may give trouble, and occasion delay, the desire of union will, I have the strongest hope, with a proper interference on the part of Great Britain, in the end prevail.*) Refers to his own paper, with " Principles " and " Observations,"[3] and encloses Count Nesselrode's vote of the Emperor of Russia. Views of Prussia. Councils wholly military. Spirit of vengeance against France. Dangerous spirit in the Prussian army *quoad* Europe and their own government. Prussia meditates change in her position. Knesebeck, when he brought his Projet to Lord Castlereagh, etc.,

[1] Précis.
[2] F. O. Continent 24.
[3] *W. S. D.* XI. 138. Recapitulates all the arguments in favour of a moderate policy.

professed moderation ; but it was clear he thought of extension on the side of Hanover and the Pays de Liege ; Hanover to be indemnified by the Duchy of Luxembourg, and the King of the Netherlands by part of French Flanders. The Prussian object is to augment their possessions ; put Hanover and the Pays Bas between them and France, for their own security ; and involve Hanover and the King of the Pays Bas so irreconcileably with France as to render them dependent on Prussia for support, and then to demand her own terms for her support. Lord Castlereagh advises strongly against such a state of things as can produce this result. It is said France will covet Belgium ; Lord Castlereagh says the Revolutionary party in France will ; but if you take part of old France and add it to Belgium, all France will, as a point of honour, be anxious to regain it. Lord Castlereagh thinks the King of the Pays Bas had better trust to Europe for seven years, and to his fortifications afterwards, for protection. The same principle operates respecting all the small States bordering upon France : it is bad policy to encourage them to endeavour to get a small line of territory, which will only offend France and give them no security. Views of Austria right : desirous of peace ; inclined to court popularity at our expense in Germany ; to give fortresses in France to the King of the Pays Bas ; to secure more of contribution to themselves, as less will be necessary to complete the frontier line of the Pays Bas. She will agree finally with England. Lord Castlereagh and the Duke of Wellington wish for decision upon these points. Language of the British here and British newspapers do the King's government great harm. Requests the consideration of the Cabinet on the means of preserving the peace of Europe, and destroying revolutionary spirit in France. Seven years' peace necessary for England. Wishes to share with the Emperor of Russia the credit of supporting the King of France, and prevent the too great union of France and Russia, which would be a serious evil. The difficulties of settlement are becoming daily greater. Prussia has made a requisition for 58,000,000 of livres and 24,000 horses.

CCXX. [*C. C. X.* 500.]
BATHURST TO CASTLEREAGH.
Downing Street, August 25th, 1815.
[Persuaded that the British principle in regard to the negotiations for peace a sound one, yet strong arguments in the memorials of the Austrian and Prussian Ministers in favour of a more rigorous policy. Nothing, however, more unfounded than

Prussia's objections to a part of the contribution imposed on France being allotted to the construction of a barrier for the Netherlands. The Allies have an unquestionable right to be indemnified by France, but only for the expenses incurred by the violation of the Treaty of Paris ; Prussia takes into calculation all that they suffered in the previous wars, but the Treaty must be understood as having settled the account up to that period. The expenses of Great Britain during this last war far greater than those of any of the other Allies, since in addition to her own expenditure she had subsidized all the other Powers. Does Great Britain forfeit right to her share of the proposed contribution because she is willing to devote it to the defence of the Netherlands and the security of Europe, instead of confining it to her immediate advantage ? Determined not to give way in this particular. No possibility of reconciling the public to the peace if Great Britain is to pay for the expense of making a barrier when one might have been obtained at the expense of France herself. The public could never understand why Great Britain should be severely taxed in order to preserve the integrity of France. Since the policy of preserving that integrity is to be adopted, it is essential that there is laid upon France the charge to which this forbearance would otherwise expose either Great Britain or her most immediate Ally. Holland cannot undertake it ; therefore can now be but one alternative, either France or Great Britain must bear the expense and the British determination is therefore natural.]

CCXXI. [*C. C. X.* 506.]
LIVERPOOL TO CASTLEREAGH.

Fife House, August 28th, 1815.

Your brother, Lord Stewart,[1] arrived in London yesterday morning, and came down to me soon after to Combe Wood. I had the opportunity there of a long conversation with him on all the points concerned in your dispatches, and we have had a Cabinet this morning, at which he has attended, in order that such of our colleagues as were in town might be correctly apprized of your sentiments and those of the Duke of Wellington upon the present state of our negotiations.

I was inclined at first to hope that my letter of the 23rd[2] instant, which must have reached you after your brother left

---

[1] He had been sent to England to win over the Cabinet to Castlereagh's views.
[2] CCXVII.

Paris, would have relieved you from all difficulties, inasmuch as it distinctly gives up all idea of permanent cessions from France, except as far as such cessions had been suggested by yourself : and although we recommend the proposal being made for dismantling Lille and Strasburg, it is distinctly stated that this demand should not be brought forward as a *sine qua non ;* nor was it our intention that it should be urged in such a manner as might materially retard the conclusion of an arrangement between the different Powers.

The explanations, however, which we have since had with Lord Stewart have convinced us that considerable embarrassment might arise from a proposition of this nature being even brought forward under the present circumstances, and in the existing state of the negotiation—that it is far better, in the situation in which we now stand, to advance no demand to which we are not determined to adhere—and that it is most expedient therefore, to confine our proposition to the principle of *temporary occupation,* and to that of the rectification of the frontier, according to the suggestion contained in your dispatch, and approved by the Emperor of Russia in the Memorandum delivered by Count Nesselrode. . . .

The terms of *the King or his legitimate successors* may be open to cavil, as it may be contended that any successor approved by the nation is a *legitimate* successor. It was to avoid this objection that the Chancellor suggested, in the memorandum of the 3rd of August, the terms, *Louis XVIII., or his successor by rightful inheritance ;* and we wish you would attend to the adoption of this phrase, or designation, in the instrument which may be to be signed.

We are further of opinion that it cannot be too clearly expressed that the fortresses are not in any case to revert to France, except it shall be under the Government of Louis XVIII., or his successors by rightful inheritance. The explicit recognition of this principle, whilst it explains the motives which have actuated the councils of the Allies, affords one of the best securities for the continuance of the King's authority. I am not aware that I can have anything further to add on this most important branch of your negotiations.

. . . .

Whatever may be the first popular impression on the result of the negotiation according to the principles which have been agreed upon, your brother will be authorized to assure you that you will be most cordially and zealously supported and upheld by all your colleagues in this country.

CCXXII. [*Gurwood. XII.* 622.]
WELLINGTON TO CASTLEREAGH.
Memorandum
On the Temporary Occupation of part of France.

Paris, August 31st, 1815.

The principal points of difference between the scheme proposed by [Prince Hardenberg[1]] and that proposed by the Ministers of the other Courts for the settlement with France consists, first, in the Prince's desire that certain French fortresses should be ceded to the Allies, and others razed ; and, secondly, in the difficulties which exist, according to the Prince's notion, in the execution of the measure of temporary occupation, and in His Highness's notion of its inefficiency to effect its object. In regard to the first point, it is a political rather than a military question, and it is not my intention to say much upon it. I wish, however, that some principle should be fixed regarding the right and expediency of demanding from France the cession of several separate fortresses distributed on the line from the sea to the Alps. I have already taken an opportunity of discussing the right of demanding these cessions, which must be founded upon the clear omission in the declarations and treaties of the Allies of anything to preclude the demand. The expediency of making the demand will depend upon a variety of political and military considerations, among which will be the following : whether the possession of the fortresses named is that which gives France the formidable strength complained of, or if transferred to the Allies would give them severally the wished-for strength ; whether it is not a combination of population, pecuniary resources, and artificial strength, which makes France so formidable ; and whether the transfer of the last only to certain of the Allies, leaving the two first unimpaired in the possession of France, that is to say, to give the Allies fortresses without additional resources in men to form garrisons and armies to defend them, and resources in money to maintain those garrisons and armies, would not tend to their weakness rather than to their strength, at the same time that the measure would afford to France a just pretence for war, and all the means which injured national pride could give for carrying it on.

If the policy of the united Powers of Europe is to weaken France, let them do so in reality. Let them take from that country its population and resources as well as a few fortresses. If they are not prepared for that decisive measure, if peace and tranquillity for a few years is their object, they must make an arrangement which

[1] F. O. Cont. 26.

will suit the interests of all the parties to it, and of which the justice and expediency will be so evident that they will tend to carry it into execution.

All persons appear to agree that the maintenance of the authority of the King is essential to the interests of the other Powers of Europe ; and, notwithstanding the difference of opinion regarding the extent of the force which ought to be maintained for a time in France, and regarding the difficulties of executing this measure, and after all that has been said of its inefficiency in affording security to the Allies in general, it appears to be generally admitted that it is necessary to adopt it. It is necessary to adopt it with different objects in view ; first, to give security to the Government of the King, and to afford him time to form a force of his own with which he can carry on his government, and take his fair share in the concerns of Europe ; secondly, to give the Allies some security against a second revolutionary convulsion and reaction ; and, thirdly, to enable the Allies to enforce the payment of those contributions which they deem it just towards their own subjects to lay on France in payment of the expenses of the war.

I have enumerated the objects of this military occupation in this order as being that of their several relative importance. In discussing them I will consider that first which I have adverted to in the second instance, viz., the security of the Allies. . . .

CCXXIII. [F. O. Cont. 26.]
CASTLEREAGH TO LIVERPOOL. (No. 47.)
September 4th, 1815.

. . . .[Encloses letters from and to Clancarty concerning the feeling in Brussels.[1]] You may rely upon it, that to have more money to spend and less to set apart out of the contributions for new fortifications, is the true motive which makes these Powers

[1] Castlereagh to Clancarty, September 4th, 1815.
" Your letter of the 30th reached me last night by Gagern, whose mission was managed without my knowledge, in that little spirit of German intrigue which is but too prevalent here.
" It is curious to observe the insatiable spirit of getting something without a thought of how it is to be preserved, there is not a Power, however feeble, that borders France from the Channel to the Mediterranean, that is not pushing some acquisition under the plea of security and ratification of frontier. They seem to have no dread of a kick from the lion, when his toils are removed, and are foolish enough to suppose that the great Powers of Europe are to be in readiness always to protect them in the enjoyment of these petty spoils. In truth their whole conception is so unstatesmanlike, that they look not beyond their sop ; compared with this the keeping together an European force has little importance in their eyes. This spirit of plunder has been the misery of Germany for the last century." F. O. Cont. 26.

so very fond of French fortresses. I asked Baron Gagern, on his return, how the king would relish having these fortresses without the guarantee of England, for that I thought it was a very different question for Great Britain to agree to guarantee the Low Countries to the King, and to include in that guarantee some French fort-resses ; that the one was an engagement fundamental and in-separable from our policy,—the other was in its nature only incidental and auxiliary, a mere question of expediency, of means to an end, and to the adoption of which, objections of great magnitude existed. This view of the question appeared altogether to damp His Excellency's appetite for such acquisitions.

The fact is that we have now before us demands from every State, however feeble, that either borders or approaches, France desiring to have some portion either directly or indirectly of permanent accession at her expense, and for the conservation of which it is taken for granted that we are to be guarantees :—the more I reflect upon it, the more I deprecate this system of scratch-ing such a Power. We may hold her down and pare her nails, so that many years shall pass away before they can again wound us. I hope we shall do this effectually, and subject to no other hazards of failure than must, more or less, attend all political or military arrangements, but this system of being pledged to a continental war for objects that France may any day reclaim from the particular States that hold them, without pushing her demands beyond what she would contend was due to her own honor, is I am sure a bad British policy,—and that if the States who ambition [sic.] these objects choose to fly at such small game, it ought to be at their own risk, and with their own means and not with ours, but unfor-tunately if they once get into a scrape with such an enemy, Great Britain may, and probably will, sooner or later be involved, and hence it becomes necessary for us not only to refuse them our guarantee for such purposes, but to dissuade them from pursuing them.

CCXXIV. [F. O. Cont. 27.]
CASTLEREAGH TO LIVERPOOL. (No. 53.)
September, 11th, 1815.
[Idea of dismissing Fouché has been put forward by the Ultra Party, especially the Comte d'Artois and the Duke and Duchess d'Angoulême.]

I own there is nothing I regard with more apprehension than the enterprizes of the party in France, at the head of which M.

and Mme. d'Angoulême are disposed so indiscreetly to place themselves. It is even now a great protection to the throne, and may in time when it acquires public men capable of conducting it, and better disciplined to the existing order of things, become capable of governing, but at present it is a mere rope of sand without leaders habituated to office, without any fixed system, but with an inordinate infusion of passion, resentment and spirit of inversion. The weight this party will certainly possess in the assembly, the general power of the Crown and the influence of the Allies, will deter the democratic party from any dangerous projet. In truth I do not believe that those in the Government have any disposition to a republic or to an order of things more popular than that which now exists and in their hands I think the power of the Government so guarded may for the present be safely left, whilst the other party will gradually require consistency. If the existing ministers fail upon trial, the King has a resource which he will use with a better chance of success if he does not precipitate the change, and the reproach of the failure will not be his. If on the other hand without giving them a fair trial the King was to take his own friends—I really believe such is the public feeling, and such their natural intemperance that they would not have a chance to stand a month and that their fall would leave the King almost without resource.

There is also a view of the question which affects intimately the position of the Allies. If the high royalist party get into power you may rely upon it they will drive things to extremities, and that not having the mass with them they will either be the victims of their own rashness or the Allied troops must interfere. I look to the necessity of such an interposition as so great an evil, that I deem it of the greatest advantage to keep the power in the hands of men whom the nation will not so easily confound with the foreigner and the emigrant, a consideration which becomes the more pressing, if we are to have 150,000 men posted in France. . . .

CCXXV. [C. C. XI. 16.]
LIVERPOOL TO CASTLEREAGH.
Fife House, September 15th, 1815.

I can assure you that I am fully sensible of the injurious effect which must result from the general line on present politics taken by our daily papers, and particularly by those which are supposed

to be Government papers.[1] You know, however, full well that
there are papers, which are vulgarly called Government papers,
in consequence of the support which they give to the Government
rather than to the Opposition of the day : there are no papers
over which we have any authority, or even any influence on which
we can depend.

It is supposed by many at home, and, I have no doubt, generally
believed on the Continent, that these papers are in the pay of
Government ; whereas no paper that has any character, and
consequently an established sale, will accept money from
Government ; and indeed their profits are so enormous in
all critical times, when their support is the most necessary, that
no pecuniary assistance that Government could offer would
really be worth their acceptance. The only indirect means we
possess of having any influence over the editors is by supplying
them occasionally with foreign intelligence, and by advertise-
ments ; but, with respect to the former, it is notorious that
some of the papers which are not connected with Government
have always had the earliest foreign intelligence ; and, with regard
to the latter, they know full well that the public offices will
necessarily be obliged, sooner or later, to insert their advertise-
ments in the papers which have the greatest sale, and they hold
in consequence very cheap any menace to deprive them of this
advantage. . . .

CCXXVI.   [*W. S. D. XI.* 165.]
CASTLEREAGH TO LIVERPOOL.

Paris, September 21st, 1815.

In my dispatch No. 54[2] I informed your Lordship that Prussia
stood out upon three points : 1st.   The demand of 1200 millions,
under the head of contributions, instead of 600 millions ; 2nd.
The transfer of Luxembourg to Prussia ; and 3rd.   The cession
by France of Saarlouis to the same Power.

[1] Talleyrand had protested to Castlereagh about the tone of the English
Press.   Castlereagh forwarded the protest home " in the hope that some means
may be adopted of keeping some at least of the English papers a little more
correctly informed and of moderating a system of defamation which can be
productive of nothing in France, as far as the British Press can have any influence, but confusion and civil war.   I understand from the other ministers that
the intemperance of the English newspapers does even more mischief in Germany by aggravating the passions especially of the middling ranks, already
sufficiently exalted by their sufferings and by their successes." Castlereagh
to Liverpool, September 11th, 1815.   F. O. Cont. 27.

[2] Of September 14th, as stated above.   F. O. Cont. 27.

The importance of preserving harmony amongst the Four Powers, and a desire to be enabled at last to make our proposition to France before the assemblies met, made us all desirous of sacrificing somewhat to procure unanimity.   It was accordingly agreed, after much discussion, that Prussia should reduce her pecuniary demands to the level of the other Powers ; and that they, in return, should undertake to press the point of Saarlouis upon France, and to use their good offices with the King of the Netherlands as to Luxembourg.   The King of Prussia urged the cession of Saarlouis with the more earnestness, as the Military Council were of opinion that no equivalent position for a fortress presented itself within his own frontier.

This concession to Prussia necessarily entailed an extension of our demand beyond the ancient frontier in other quarters. Having once opened the principle, we could not, in justice to the King of the Netherlands, omit to demand Condé and Givet as points immediately interesting to him.   It was also thought right to include an improved frontier for Switzerland, and the military possession of Monaco for the King of Sardinia, in our proposition to the French government.

I have reason to believe that the Plenipotentiaries on the part of France will reject the principle of making any cession whatever of the ancient territory ; that they will admit the principle of ceding their late acquisitions ; that they will admit the principle of temporary occupation ; and that they will admit the principle of pecuniary indemnity.   Beyond this I do not believe the King will go without the express advice of the assemblies ; nor will his Ministers, in the present posture of the government, be disposed to make themselves responsible for any measure which does violence to the national prejudices.

CCXXVII.   [F. O. Cont. 28.]
CASTLEREAGH TO LIVERPOOL.   (No. 65.)
September 25th, 1815.

[The change of government in France,[1] which has created general alarm in the public mind.   Probable that the ministers anticipated their dismission by resigning.   Extraordinary and unjustifiable that, in such a state of things, a negotiation with the Allies should have been undertaken since the ministers could hardly consider themselves as in office when they offered to receive

[1] The resignation of Talleyrand and Fouché.   Richelieu was not appointed to succeed Talleyrand till the beginning of October.

our overture. The King not sufficiently firm to pursue a line of principle and, distracted by family and party impulses, has all the disadvantages of a popular government without taking the benefit of being sheltered by the constitutional system in the difficulties which surround him. . . .

Castlereagh's interview with the King.] I found His Majesty at first tres exalté in his manner and shewing great soreness upon the propositions made to him. I represented that the Allied Sovereigns would never have thought of making any proposition to his Majesty which they conceived could be either dishonourable or ruinous for him to accept. That their proposition appeared from the answer to have been misconceived, that they founded their claims in no degree upon the right of conquest, but upon the two principles of indemnity and security, the power of which the French note admitted, whilst upon the second, by far the most important of the two, it was wholly silent ; and yet of this latter principle after such a convulsion, the dangers of which could not be expected soon to pass away, even the ties of friendship and alliance could not exclude the consideration.

I stated to the King how long and diligently we had laboured to reduce the precautionary arrangement to the minimum that could be reconciled with the safety and feelings of our respective nations. That in order to avoid the necessity of demanding the permanent cession of an extended proportion of the defences of France, the system of temporary occupation had been devised. That it was necessary however to combine this with some system of permanent security and that, in framing this, instead of asking for any fortress that detached any considerable portion of the ancient territory from France, we had asked for none that were not either without or upon the frontier, and that, in order to limit as for as possible the amount of our demand, we had adopted the expedient of accepting money as the means of construction within our own frontier.

I found that the separation of the demand for fortification from the contributions, had been felt as a great humiliation, viz., the giving money to erect defences against themselves. I told the King the motive of so stating the proposition was to justify the Allied Governments in the eyes of their own people for not pushing their views further, by shewing them that measures had been taken to effect the same end though by other means, but that if His Majesty wished to give an equal sum under another name, I was persuaded the Allies would cheerfully accommodate in the form, provided the substance was secured.

[Upon the pecuniary part[1] of the arrangement the King was more *coulant*. Castlereagh insisted that they were moderate, and that France had easy means of meeting them by selling the forests, adding to the debt, etc.] Before I withdrew the King returned with considerable earnestness upon the wounded pride of the nation, and the eternal reproach he should incur by ceding any part of the ancient territory. I ventured to submit that there was a just and rational pride which it would be unwise in the Allies to expose His Majesty to the necessity of wounding, but there was a pride growing out of and belonging to the Revolution, to which violence might reasonably be done and perhaps ultimately with advantage to His Majesty's interests. I instanced the dispersal of the Louvre collection as falling within the latter principle, as also that principle of inviolability which France since the Revolution had attempted to assume in favour of her possessions, without admitting the same in favour of any other nation, that to maintian such a principle in the extreme was offensive to other Powers, whilst it was the interest of His Majesty, by conciliating and managing feelings on both sides to encourage Europe to persevere in the support of His Majesty and of the cause of order and good government in France. [Told the King his instructions precluded him from negotiating on the basis he wanted, viz., the inviolability of France. The King asked Castlereagh to write home for fresh instructions, but he said that recent events were more likely to strengthen than to weaken them. Left the King in a better humour than he had hoped for at the beginning.]

[1] The demand had been reduced to 800 millions of francs. This was shortly afterwards reduced to 700 millions. By October 1st the outlines of the Treaty had been agreed with the Duke of Richelieu, though the Treaty was not signed till November 20th. Castlereagh summed up the results in a dispatch of October 1st.

(1) Entire defeat of the French Army and capture of the French capital " principally by the armies of Great Britain."

(2) Surrender and imprisonment of Napoleon Buonaparte.

(3) Entire dissolution of the French Army.

(4) Permanent cession of 5 fortresses and all the territory acquired beyond the frontiers of 1790 by the first Peace of Paris.

(5) Temporary occupation for five years of 14 French fortresses. [The period could be, however, and was reduced to three years.]

(6) Maintenance of an Allied force of 150,000 men by the French.

(7) Indemnity of 700 millions of francs.

(8) A total charge of 70 or 80 millions sterling imposed on France before she could get back her fortresses. (Because she had also promised to satisfy certain private claims, but the total amount was eventually settled in 1817 for 200 millions.)

(9) Renewal of the Treaty of Chaumont.

(10) Restitution of the works of art to their previous owners.

And he hoped that the Cabinet would be satisfied with his work. F. O.

Cont. 28.

CCXXVIII.   [*W. S. D. XI.* 175.]
CASTLEREAGH TO LIVERPOOL.
Paris, September 28th, 1815.

You will receive enclosed a *lettre autographe*[1] from the three Allied Sovereigns addressed to the Prince Regent, which I have been desired to transmit.   It was delivered to me by Prince Metternich, the communication being understood to be made to His Royal Highness through the medium of the Emperor of Austria, as the senior Emperor.

To explain the nature of this rather novel proceeding, I have obtained copies both of the letter and its enclosure, deeming it material to accompany it with such explanations as may assist His Royal Highness in making to it a suitable reply.   I have, then, to acquaint you that although the Emperor of Austria is the ostensible organ, the measure has entirely originated with the Emperor of Russia, whose mind has latterly taken a deeply religious tinge.   Since he came to Paris he has passed a part of every evening with a Madame de Krudener, an old fanatic, who has a considerable reputation amongst the few highflyers in religion that are to be found in Paris.   The first intimation I had of this extraordinary act was from the Emperor himself ; and I was rather surprised to find it traced back to a conversation with which I was honoured with the Emperor when leaving Vienna.   You may remember my sending home a Projet of Declaration[2] with which I proposed the Congress should close, in which the Sovereigns were solemnly to pledge themselves in the face of the world to preserve to their people the peace they had conquered, and to treat as a common enemy whatever Power should violate it.   The Emperor told me that this idea, with which he seemed much pleased at the time, had never passed from his mind, but that he thought it ought to assume a more formal shape, and one directly personal to the Sovereigns ;   that he had communicated that morning to the Emperor of Austria his sentiments upon this subject, and that he would speak to me further upon it in a few days.

Prince Metternich, the following day, came to me with the projet of the treaty since signed.   He communicated to me in great confidence the difficulty in which the Emperor of Austria felt himself placed ;   that he felt great repugnance to be a party to such an act, and yet was more apprehensive of refusing himself to

---

[1] This forwards the famous Treaty of the Holy Alliance by which the three Sovereigns promised to act towards one as Christians and recommended their peoples to do the same.
[2] See CLXXIV.

the Emperor's application ; that it was quite clear his mind was affected ; that peace and goodwill was at present the idea which engrossed his thoughts ; that he had found him of late friendly and reasonable on all points ; and that he was unwilling to thwart him in a conception which, however wild, might save him and the rest of the world much trouble so long as it should last. In short, seeing no retreat, after making some verbal alterations the Emperor of Austria agreed to sign it. The Emperor of Russia then carried it to the King of Prussia, who felt in the same manner, but came to the same conclusion.

As soon as the instrument was executed between the Sovereigns, without the intervention of their Ministers, the Emperor of Russia brought it to me, developed his whole plan of universal peace, and told me the three Sovereigns had agreed to address a letter to the Prince Regent, to invite him to accede, of which intended letter His Imperial Majesty delivered to me the enclosed copy. The Duke of Wellington happened to be with me when the Emperor called, and it was not without difficulty that we went through the interview with becoming gravity.

Foreseeing the awkwardness of this piece of sublime mysticism and nonsense, especially to a British Sovereign, I examined with Prince Metternich every practical expedient to stop it ; but the Emperor of Austria, with all his sobriety of mind, did not venture to risk it. When it reached me, in fact, the deed was done, and no other course remained than to do homage to the sentiment upon which it was founded, and to the advantages Europe might hope to derive from three such powerful Sovereigns directing all their influence to the preservation of peace ; that I was confident the Prince Regent would unite, *coeur et d'âme*, with his august Allies in making this the basis of all his policy, and that I would lose no time in laying before His Royal Highness this solemn pledge of the pacific and moderate spirit which actuated their councils.

I ventured to express to the Emperor my satisfaction that the Sovereigns had not given to this instrument an official character ; that this might have rendered its production as a State document necessary ; that it was better it should pass as an autographic communication of sentiment between Sovereign and Sovereign, binding upon their own consciences in the general management of their affairs, than that it should be exposed to public discussion as an act advised by their Ministers. I had, in truth, taken pains, through Prince Metternich, to keep it, if it must go forward, in this channel ; foreseeing that, as Wilberforce is not yet in posses-sion of the Great Seal, even if I should receive the Prince's command to countersign it, it might find some difficulty in passing through the ordinary course of office.

Upon the whole this is what may be called a scrape ; and yet in the long run it may be attended with more beneficial results than many of the acts which are in progress, and which are of a character better to suit the eye of Parliament.   The fact is, that the Emperor's mind is not completely sound.   Last year there was but too much reason to fear that its impulse would be to conquest and dominion. The general belief now is, that he is disposed to found his own glory upon a principle of *peace* and *benevolence*.   Since the point of Poland was disposed of, there has been nothing in his political conduct in the progress of arrangements which indicates another purpose, and he really appears to be in earnest.   It is, at all events, wise to profit by this disposition as far as it will carry us ; and this is peculiarly the feeling of Austria and Prussia, who hope to keep down, " now that they are compatriots," much of the spirit of frontier jealousy which has hitherto embarrassed them.

With the letter and Treaty you will also receive a Projet for the Prince's accession which the Emperor sent me this morning, before his departure.   I am desired by the Emperor of Austria, through Metternich, to express his earnest hope that the Prince will not refuse himself to this overture, however much he may feel, with him, the embarrassment of the proceeding ; that he thinks good may come of indulging the Emperor, and that real danger might result to the Alliance from a refusal.   My own opinion very much concurs with that of His Imperial Majesty ; and in weighing difficulties on both sides, I think no person will blame the Prince for not refusing himself to *a proposition so made to him*, where the objection lies rather against the excessive excellence than the quality and nature of the engagement : but then, I think the Prince must take it upon himself, and sign it without the intervention of his Ministers, as an autographic avowal of sentiment between him and the Sovereigns his Allies, tending to preserve the tranquillity of Europe.   To decline doing so, after a late explanation might produce very unpleasant consequences.

The Emperor told me with great delight that there was nothing had given him so much satisfaction as to affix his signature to this bond of peace, in, he believed, the most *irreligious* capital in Europe.

I confide this communication to your management, and hope the Prince Regent may find himself enabled to avoid disturbing the harmony which at present subsists between him and his Allies.

CCXXIX. [*W. S. D. XI.* 183.]

LIVERPOOL TO CASTLEREAGH.

Walmer Castle, October 3rd, 1815.

I have received your letter[1] with the enclosures, containing an autograph letter from the Emperors of Austria and Russia and the King of Prussia to the Prince Regent ; the copy of a Treaty signed by their Majesties at Paris on the 26th of September ; and the Projet of an Act of Accession by the Prince Regent.

I have laid the same before the Prince Regent, and we have had a cabinet to consider what is fit to be done in consequence.

I forbear discussing the question of how far it might not have been more advisable, on every account, to prevent such a proceeding altogether. The work is done ; and it is one thing to wish it not to have been done, at least in such a manner, and another to refuse being a party to it after it is done.

It is quite impossible, however, to advise the Prince to sign the Act of Accession which has been transmitted to him. Such a step would be inconsistent with all the forms and principles of our government and would subject those who advised it to a very serious responsibility.

[A Treaty is an act of State, and the King or Regent of Great Britain can only be a party to an act of State through the instrumentality of others, who are responsible for it. Neither can he accede to a Treaty personally ; he must authorise a plenipotentiary to accede to it in his name and on his part, and it would be an incongruity for the Sovereign or Regent of Great Britain to accede to a Treaty through a plenipotentiary which the other Sovereigns had signed personally. The best course for the Prince to adopt is to write an autographical letter to the three Sovereigns according to the enclosed draft. This will obviate all these objections as well as those which would arise by the Prince refusing to be a party in any way to the act. By this letter, he gives his full sanction to all the principles which the other Sovereigns are desirous of consecrating. In transmitting the letters, the reason for the necessity of this course to be fully explained.]

DRAFT LETTER FROM THE PRINCE REGENT TO THE EMPERORS OF AUSTRIA AND RUSSIA AND THE KING OF PRUSSIA.

I have had the honour of receiving your Imperial Majesty's letter, together with the copy of the Treaty signed by your Majesty and your august Allies, at Paris, on the 26th of September.

As the forms of the British Constitution, which I am called upon to administer in the name and on the behalf of His Majesty my father, preclude me from acceding formally to this Treaty in the shape in which it has been presented to

[1] CCXXVIII.

E2

me, I adopt this course of conveying to the august Sovereigns who have signed it my entire concurrence in the principles which they have laid down, and in the declaration which they have set forth of making the Divine precepts of the Christian religion the invariable rule of their conduct in all their relations, social and political, and of cementing the union which ought ever to subsist between all Christian nations ; and it will be always my earnest endeavour to regulate my conduct in the station in which Divine Providence has vouchsafed to place me by these sacred maxims, and to co-operate with my august Allies in all measures which may be likely to contribute to the peace and happiness of mankind.

CCXXX.   [F. O. Cont. 29.]
CASTLEREAGH TO LIVERPOOL.   (No. 80.)

Paris, October 15th, 1815.

I have before apprized your Lordship that it was in contemplation before the Allies separated, to contract fresh engagements with each other, in the spirit of the Treaty of Chaumont, but applying the same to the existing state of affairs.

The Emperor of Russia expressed particular approbation of this measure as suggested in outline in the Memorandum which was transmitted home by Lord Stewart and His Imperial Majesty subsequently directed that the enclosed Projet marked No. 1[1] of such a treaty to be communicated to me.

However satisfactory it was to observe the Emperor enter with so much cordiality into the support of the Bourbons, and of the established order of things in France, it appeared to me that the proposed draft of a treaty was open to very considerable objections : 1st.   As not being sufficiently definite in the scope and nature of its stipulations.   2ndly.   As bearing on the face of it too strong and undisguised a complexion of interference, on the part of the Allied Sovereigns in the internal concerns of France, without sufficiently connecting such interference with the policy which a due attention to the immediate security of their own dominions prescribed.   3rd.   That it appeared to make the Allies too much umpires in all constitutional struggles in France by professing a determination to support *with all their efforts* both the monarch and the charter.   4thly.   That it gave the King too direct and unqualified a power over the Allied force stationed in France and thereby exposed the Allies to be improvidently compromised on questions of internal policy ; and 5thly.   That it presented but an indiscreet view of the extent of means, with which the Allies

[1] F. O. Cont. 29.   Besides the points enumerated by Castlereagh it is to be noted that this Projet limited future meetings of the Powers to the question of the execution of the Treaty of November 20th, 1815.

were prepared to support their engagements as well as of the particular objects to which these means were to be directed.

I therefore thought it necessary to deliver in, for the Emperor's consideration, the enclosed counter-projet No. 2[1], in which I have endeavoured to confine, where the engagement is explicit, the casus foederis as far as possible to known and defined obligations already resting upon other Treaties, leaving all future convulsions in France, which assume a character distinct from those already pronounced upon by Treaty, to be dealt with upon a principle of concert, and with reference to the particular circumstances of the case. It is impossible upon such unforeseen events to adopt an universal proposition, to stipulate too cautiously would weaken the King—to contract a prior too boldly in his support would involve us too deeply in the contention of France, certainly embarrass us in Parliament, and might encourage the Royalist party to presume very indiscreetly upon our support.

As the Treaty is now framed, especially in the exclusion of the family of Buonaparte, I think it will give a very powerful appui to the King, coupled with the article of the Treaty with France which limits the claim of retrocession of the fortresses to the regular succession.

It will also make the Jacobins feel, in truth the whole nation for they all require this admonition, that they cannot break loose again or escape from the fulfilment of the Treaty now made, without being committed with all Europe, and bringing down again a million of armed men upon their country.

I have endeavoured to keep the internal affairs of France in the background, and to make the colour of our political attitude and of our contingent interference as European as possible. I have at the same time, in order to soften the aspect of a Treaty which is necessarily directed against France, recognized sufficiently the principles of concert with the legitimate sovereign, so as to mark, that it is not against the government or the nation, but against an eventual faction in France, that our precautions are directed.

I am not aware that any further elucidation of this question is necessary. I forward the Projet and counter-projet by a special messenger, in the hope that I may have the advantage of receiving the sentiments of His Royal Highness' servants upon this subject before I am called upon to carry the measure into execution.

---

[1] This is practically the same as the Treaty subsequently signed. Castlereagh substituted a new form of words for Article VI., which extended the future reunions of the Sovereigns or their ministers to any matter which they might care to discuss. It is thus the British minister who is the real author of the " Congress-System."

I feel a strong persuasion that nothing can keep France quiet and within bounds but the strong hand of European power, and that a Treaty of this nature signed by the four great Powers (which happily at present implies the military power of all Europe extra France) will be more operative to that purpose, even than the instrument which we shall sign with the French Government itself.   It is the fear of our union that will keep France down, and the knowledge that the Duke of Wellington commands only the advanced guard of the force against which they will have to contend, if they again involve themselves in war.

Such a Treaty is the more desirable in as much as it will be signed with I believe a most sincere and earnest desire on the part of all the four cabinets to preserve their union, and to fulfil the purposes of the concert.   It may be right that I should take this occasion of stating to your Lordship what has occurred as to the mode to be observed in regulating the conduct of the allied troops to be left in France.   It is proposed to give the Duke of Wellington a full discretion under such instructions as can be previously agreed upon, to act as he deems best, without waiting orders from the respective courts : that the ministers of the four Powers resident at Paris should constitute a commission for the purpose of jointly corresponding with him, and keeping him informed, not only of the events passing, but of their sentiments upon them, and that whatever wishes or representations the French Government may have to convey to the Duke should pass through this channel,— the King and government being distinctly informed, that whilst he may implicitly rely on the most cordial support, whilst he preserves good faith with the nation, which we doubt not it is His Majesty's sincere intention to do, that he must not expect the aid of the Allied armies, if he is hurried, as has happened in Spain, into indiscreet and intemperate measures, and thereby involves his government in intestine warfare.

APPENDIX I

Official Communication made to the Russian Ambassador at London, on the 19th January, 1805, explanatory of the views which His Majesty and the Emperor of Russia formed for the deliverance and security of Europe.[1]

This document was the result of the mission of Novossiltzoff to London in 1804 with proposals for an alliance. In discussions with him and Count Vorontzoff the Russian Ambassador Pitt went over the whole ground of European politics which had been opened up by Russia. The suggestion of the special Guarantee came originally from Russia, as Professor Alison Phillips has pointed out. The final result was the treaty between Russia and Great Britain of April 11th, 1805, where the principle of Guarantee was recognized, though only in the most vague and general terms.[2]

The result of the communications which have been made by Prince Czartoriski to His Majesty's Ambassador at St. Petersburgh, and of the confidential explanations which have been received from your Excellency, has been laid before the King ; and His Majesty has seen with inexpressible satisfaction, the wise, dignified, and generous policy, which the Emperor of Russia is disposed to adopt, under the present calamitous situation of Europe. His Majesty is also happy to perceive, that the views and sentiments of the Emperor respecting the deliverance of Europe, and providing for its future tranquillity and safety, correspond so entirely with his own. He is therefore desirous of entering into the most explicit and unreserved explanations on every point connected with this great object, and of forming the closest union of councils, and concert of measures, with his Imperial Majesty, in order, by their joint influence and exertions, to insure the co-operation and assistance of other Powers of the Continent, on a scale adequate to the magnitude and importance of an undertaking, on the success of which the future safety of Europe must depend.

For this purpose, the first step must be, to fix as precisely as possible, the distinct objects to which such a concert is to be directed.

These, according to the explanation given of the sentiments of the Emperor, in which His Majesty entirely concurs, appear to be three :—

[1] This dispatch has generally been quoted by historians from Alison's translation (*History of Europe,* vol. V., chap. XXXIX.) of a French translation of the document in Hansard, vol. XXXI., 178. But this document which was laid before Parliament of May 5th, 1815, was only an extract from the original. The passages there omitted are here given in Italics with the exception of folios 49-73 which deal only with the plan of the ensuing campaign and the measures necessary to induce Prussia to join the alliance. The Document is endorsed " Draft to Count Woronzow, January 19, 1805. In Lord Mulgrave's No. 1 to Lord Gower," and is bound in a separate volume, F.O. Russia 60.

[2] See Alison Phillips, *The Confederation of Europe*, Part I., Chap. 3 ; Holland Rose, *Napoleonic Studies. Pitt's plans for the Settlement of Europe ;* Holland Rose, *Select Despatches . . . relating to the Third Coalition against France.*

1. To rescue from the dominion of France those countries which it has subjugated since the beginning of the Revolution, and to reduce France within its former limits, as they stood before that time.

2. To make such an arrangement with respect to the territories recovered from France, as may provide for their security and happiness, and may at the same time constitute a more effectual barrier in future against encroachments on the part of France.

3. To form, at the restoration of peace, a general agreement and Guarantee for the mutual protection and security of different Powers, and for re-establishing a general system of public law in Europe.

The first and second objects are stated generally, and in their broadest extent ; but neither of them can be properly considered in detail without reference to the nature and extent of the means by which they may be accomplished. The first is certainly that to which, without any modification or exception, his Majesty's wishes, as well as those of the Emperor, would be preferably directed, and nothing short of it can *completely*[1] satisfy the views which both Sovereigns form for the deliverance and security of Europe. Should it be possible to unite in concert with Great Britain and Russia, the two other great military Powers of the Continent, there seems little doubt that such a union of force would enable them to accomplish all that is proposed. But if (as there is too much reason to imagine may be the case) it should be found impossible to engage Prussia in the Confederacy, it may be doubted whether such operations could be carried on in all the quarters of Europe, as would be necessary for the success of the whole of this project.

The chief points, however, to which His Majesty considers this doubt as applicable, relate to the question of the entire recovery of the Netherlands and the countries occupied by France on the left bank of the Rhine. His Majesty considers it essential even on this supposition to include nothing less than the evacuation of the North of Germany and Italy, the re-establishment of the independence of the United Provinces and of Switzerland, the Restoration of the dominions of the King of Sardinia and security of Naples ; but on the side of the Netherlands it might perhaps be more prudent in this case to confine the views of the Allies to obtaining some moderate acquisitions for the United Provinces calculated (according to the principle specified under the second head) to form an additional barrier for that country. His Majesty, however, by no means intends to imply if very brilliant and decisive success should be obtained, and the power of France broken and overcome by operations in other quarters, the Allies might not in such a case, extend their views to the recovery of the whole or the greater part of these territories, but, as in the first instance it does not appear possible that they can be reconquered by the operations of the war without the aid of Prussia, His Majesty is inclined to think that this object ought in any Treaty of Concert to be described in such terms as would admit of the modifications here stated.

The second point of itself involves in it many important considerations. The views and sentiments by which His Majesty and the Emperor of Russia are equally animated in endeavouring to establish this concert, are pure and disinterested.

The insular situation and extensive resources of Great Britain, aided by its military exertions and naval superiority ; and the immense power, the established Continental ascendency and remote distance of Russia already give to the territories of the two Sovereigns a security against the attacks of France—even after all her acquisitions of influence, power and dominion—which cannot be the lot of any other country. They have therefore no separate objects of their own in the arrangements which are in question, no personal interest to consult in this Concert but that which grows out of the general interest and security of Europe, and is inseparably connected with it. Their first view, therefore, with respect to any of the countries which may be recovered from France, must be to restore, as far as possible, their ancient rights, and provide for the internal happiness of their inhabitants ;

---

[1] In Italics in Hansard.

but in looking at this object, they must not lose sight of the general security of Europe, on which even that separate object must principally depend.

Pursuant to this principle, there can be no question that, whenever any of these countries are capable of being restored to their former independence, and of being placed in a situation in which they can protect it, such an arrangement must be most congenial to the policy and the feelings on which this system is founded : but there will be found to be other countries among those now under the dominion of France, to which these considerations cannot apply, where either the ancient relations of the country are so completely destroyed that they cannot be restored, or where independence would be merely nominal and alike inconsistent with the security for the country itself, or for Europe : happily, the larger number is of the first description. Should the arms of the Allies be successful to the full extent of expelling France from all the dominions she has acquired since the Revolution, it would certainly be the first object, as has already been stated, to re-establish the republics of the United Provinces and Switzerland, the territories of the King of Sardinia, Tuscany, Modena, (under the protection of Austria), and Naples. But the territories of Genoa, of the Italian Republic, including the three Legations, Parma, and Placentia ; and on the other side of Europe, the Austrian Netherlands, and the States which have been detached from the German Empire on the left bank of the Rhine, evidently belong to the second class. With respect to the territories enumerated in Italy, experience has shown how little disposition existed in some, and how little means in any, to resist the aggression or influence of France. The King of Spain was certainly too much a party to the system of which so large a part of Europe has been a victim, to entitle the former interests of his family in Italy to any consideration ; nor does the past conduct of Genoa, or any of the other States, give them any claim, either of justice or liberality. It is also obvious that these separate petty sovereignties would never again have any solid existence in themselves, and would only serve to weaken and impair the force which ought to be, as much as possible, concentrated in the hands of the chief Powers of Italy.

It is needless to dwell particularly on the state of the Netherlands. Events have put out of the question the restoration of them to the House of Austria ; they are therefore necessarily open to new arrangements, and evidently can never exist separate and independent. Nearly the same considerations apply to the Ecclesiastical Electorates, and the other territories on the left bank of the Rhine, after their being once detached from the Empire, and the former possessors of them indemnified, There appears, therefore, to be no possible objection, on the strictest principles of justice and public morality, to making such a disposition with respect to any of these territories as may be most conducive to the general interests ; and there is evidently no other mode of accomplishing the great and beneficent object of re-establishing (after so much misery and bloodshed) the safety and repose of Europe on a solid and permanent basis. It is fortunate too that such a plan of arrangement as is itself essential to the end proposed, is also likely to contribute, in the greatest degree, to secure the means by which that great end can best be promoted.

It is evidently of the utmost importance, if not absolutely indispensable for this purpose, to secure the vigorous and effectual co-operation both of Austria and Prussia ; but there is little reason to hope that either of these Powers will be brought to embark in the common cause, without the prospect of obtaining some important acquisition to compensate for its exertions. On the grounds which have been already stated, his Majesty conceives that nothing could so much contribute to the general security as giving to Austria fresh means of resisting the views of France on the side of Italy, and placing Prussia in a similar situation with respect to the Low Countries ; and the relative situations of the two Powers would naturally make those the quarters to which their views would respectively be directed.

In Italy, sound policy would require, that the power and influence of the King of Sardinia should be augmented, and that Austria should be replaced in a situation which may enable her to afford an immediate and effectual support to his dominions, in case of their being attacked. His Majesty sees with satisfaction, from the secret and confidential communications recently received through your Excellency, that the views of the Court of Vienna are perfectly conformable to this general principle, and that the extension at which she aims, might not only safely be admitted, but might even be increased, with advantage to the general interest. In other respects His Majesty entirely concurs in the outline of the arrangement which he understands the Emperor of Russia to be desirous of seeing effected in this quarter. His Majesty considers it as absolutely necessary for the general security, that Italy should be completely rescued both from the occupation and influence of France, and that no Powers should be left within it, who are not likely to enter into a general system of defence for maintaining its independence. For this purpose, it is essential that the countries now composing what is called the Italian Republic, should be transferred to other Powers. In distributing these territories, an increase of wealth and power should undoubtedly be given to the King of Sardinia ; and it seems material that his possessions, as well as the Duchy of Tuscany (which it is proposed to restore to the Grand Duke), should be brought into immediate contact, or ready communication with those of Austria. On this principle *the part of the Milanese to the South West of the Adda, and* the whole of the territories which now compose the Ligurian Republic, *as well as perhaps Parma and Placentia*, might, it is conceived, be annexed to Piedmont.

The Three Legations might in His Majesty's opinion be annexed to the territories of Austria, and the addition which may be made to the acquisitions proposed for that Power, with advantage to the common cause. And the Duchy of Modena, placed as it would be between the new acquisitions of Sardinia and the Duchy of Tuscany (which may be considered under this arrangement as virtually Austrian) might safely be restored to its former possessors.

The observations which have been stated respecting the situation of Sardinia in Italy seem, in a great measure, to apply to that of Holland and Prussia, in relation to the Low Countries ; with this difference, however, that the Piedmontese dominions, affording in themselves considerable means of defence, they may be perhaps sufficiently secure in the possession of the King of Sardinia, supported by Austria, whereas the Netherlands being more open and exposed seem scarcely capable of being secured unless by annexing a considerable part of them to Prussia, and placing Holland in a second line of defence. With this view (supposing France to be reduced within its ancient limits) it might be proposed to annex to the United Provinces, as an additional Barrier, the part of Flanders lying within a military line to be drawn from Antwerp to the Meuse at Maestricht, and the remainder of the Netherlands, together with the Duchies of Luxembourg and Juliers, and the other territories between the Meuse and the Moselle to Prussia.

His Majesty indeed feels so strongly the importance both of augmenting the inducements to Prussia to take part and of rendering it a powerful and effectual Barrier for the defence not only of Holland but of the North of Germany against France, that he should even consider it as adviseable in addition to what has been already proposed, to put into possession of that Power the territories which may be recovered from France on the left bank of the Rhine, eastward of the Moselle, and His Majesty entertains a strong conviction that this arrangement (if it not in other respects be thought liable to insuperable objections) would be infinitely more effective for the protection of the North of Europe than any other that can be devised.

His Majesty is, however, aware that great difficulties may arise in regulating the proportionate acquisitions of Austria and Prussia, in such a way as to prevent their being the source of mutual jealousy, and this consideration it is which, amongst others, has operated as a great additional inducement of acquisition for Austria on the side of Italy.

He thinks it also important to remark that the acquisition to be held out to Prussia ought not to be measured merely by what would be in itself desirable but by the consideration of what may be necessary to outweigh the temptations which

France will not fail to offer to that Power, to secure its co-operation. These will probably be on an extensive scale, and in a quarter much more calculated to produce effects injurious to the interests of Austria and of Russia herself while, on the other hand, if the ambition of Prussia can be gratified in the manner proposed at the expense of France, it will be diverted from the views which it will otherwise form towards the North, the accomplishment of which would tend to increase, to an alarming degree, its influence both in Germany and over the secondary Powers of the Baltic. But, if notwithstanding these powerful considerations, it should still be thought by His Imperial Majesty that the augmentation here proposed to the territories of Prussia is greater than ought to be admitted, His Majesty will, (though not without reluctance) concur in any other arrangement that may be thought preferable by which a larger portion of the Netherlands may be allotted to the United Provinces, and the acquisitions of Prussia confined within narrower limits ; but he trusts that at any rate, it will not be necessary to reduce them to anything less than the territories on the left bank of the Rhine between the Meuse and the Moselle, and it will in this case, require much consideration, in what hands the territories on the left bank of the Rhine, east of the Moselle can best be placed or whether they may be safely left in the possession of France.

In the event of Prussia not being prevailed upon to enter into the concert, I have already stated His Majesty's conviction, that the views of the Allies on this side of Europe must be more limited ; and in that case probably nothing more can be expected than to obtain the complete evacuation of the North of Germany, and the re-establishment of the independence of Holland, together with the Barrier here stated within the line drawn from Antwerp to Maestricht, leaving the other territories on the left bank of the Rhine in the possession of France.

[A detailed description follows (folios 49-73) of the plan of campaign and the amount of force necessary to obtain the objects stated above. If Prussia joins the Alliance it is estimated that 500,000 men may be put into the field ; if, as is more likely, she abstains, 400,000. Details of the Plan of campaign are given. Russia is urged to do her utmost to induce Prussia to co-operate and especially is asked to notify her immediately that she will not agree to the acquisition of Hanover by Prussia.]

Supposing the efforts of the Allies to have been completely successful, and the two objects already discussed to have been fully obtained, His Majesty would nevertheless consider this salutary work as still imperfect, if the restoration of peace were not accompanied by the most effectual measures for giving solidity and permanence to the system which shall thus have been established. Much will undoubtedly be effected for the future repose of Europe by these territorial arrangements, which will furnish a more effectual barrier than has before existed against the ambition of France. But in order to render this security as complete as possible, it seems necessary, at the period of a general pacification, to form a Treaty to which all the principal Powers of Europe should be parties, by which their respective rights and possessions, as they then have been established, shall be fixed and recognized ; and they should all bind themselves mutually to protect and support each other, against any attempt to infringe them :—It should re-establish a general and comprehensive system of public law in Europe, and provide, as far as possible, for repressing future attempts to disturb the general tranquillity ; and above all, for restraining any projects of aggrandizement and ambition similar to those which have produced all the calamities inflicted on Europe since the disastrous æra of the French Revolution.

This Treaty should be put under the special Guarantee of Great Britain and Russia, and the two Powers should by a separate engagement, bind themselves to each other jointly to take an active part in preventing its being infringed. Such a Treaty might also be accompanied by more particular and specific provisions, by which the several Powers of Italy might be united in a closer alliance for their own defence. How far any similar system could be adopted for giving additional security for the Germanic Body is well deserving of consideration. Their present state is certainly very unsatisfactory with a view either to their own immediate interests, or to the safety of Europe. At the same time it appears to His Majesty very doubtful whether from local circumstances and other causes, it would ever be possible to consolidate them into any effectual system. Should this be found to be the case, the evils to be apprehended from their weak and exposed state might (as far as relates to the danger from France) perhaps be remedied by adopting a system (but on a larger scale) similar to that formerly established by the Barrier Treaty for the protection of the Netherlands. It might not be difficult to settle some general plan for maintaining at the joint expense of the different Powers of the Empire, fortresses of sufficient strength, and properly garrisoned, along the course of the Rhine from Basle to Ehrenbreiten, commanding the principal approaches from France to the most exposed parts of Germany, and the military custody of these fortresses (without infringing in other respects on the territorial rights of the Power in whose dominions they might be placed) might be confided to the two great Powers of Germany, according to their respective means of occupying them.

It seems also desirable, in order to give further security to the United Provinces (under any of the arrangements which have already been discussed) that they should be called upon to enter into an engagement jointly with Great Britain and Russia to maintain at all times their army on such a footing as may be thought necessary to provide for their defence against sudden attacks. In addition to this stipulation His Majesty in his Electoral capacity, might perhaps be induced to keep a considerable force (in consequence of arrangements with the British Government) ready to be employed on the first alarm for the defence of the United Provinces ; and His Majesty would also be ready to enter into a Concert with other Powers for defraying the expense of maintaining at all times an adequate and effective garrison to consist of German troops for garrisoning any fortresses now existing, or hereafter to be established, on whatever may be the line ultimately fixed as the Dutch frontier.

Having thus stated what more immediately relates to the specific objects of the Concert and of the means to be employed to give effect, there still remains one great and important question for consideration, and that is how far, either now or hereafter, the views of the Allies ought to be directed towards the re-establishment of monarchy in France, and the restoration of the Bourbon Family on the throne. His Majesty agrees entirely with the Emperor of Russia in thinking that such a settlement is in itself highly desirable for the future both of France and Europe, and that no fair occasion ought to be neglected of promoting it. But he at the same time thinks, that it ought to be considered only a secondary object in the Concert now to be established and one which could in no case justify the prolongation of the war if a Peace could be obtained on the principles which have been stated. It is one with a view to which no active or decided measures can be taken, unless a series of great and signal successes shall previously have been obtained by the Allies, and a strong and prevailing disposition for the return of the Monarch, shall then manifest itself in the interior of France. In the meantime in order to afford every reasonable chance for the attainment of this object, His Majesty entirely agrees with the Emperor of Russia, that it is highly important that in the conduct of the war, and in the public declarations and language of the Allied Courts, the greatest care should be taken to prevent any apprehension in the minds of any part of the French nation of any design either to dictate to them by force any particular form of government, or to attempt to dismember the ancient territories of France.

Such are the sentiments and observations which His Majesty is desirous of offering to the consideration of the Emperor on the great outlines of the important system which they are equally anxious to establish.

His Majesty will receive with the utmost attention and satisfaction, every fresh communication of the opinion of His Imperial Majesty on all the details connected with so extensive a subject. In the meanwhile from an anxiety to lose no time in laying the foundation of this great work, His Majesty has directed a project to be prepared of a Provisional Treaty conformable to the sentiments which appear to be entertained both by the Emperor and himself : and which, if it should meet with His Imperial Majesty's concurrence, he is ready immediately to conclude.

APPENDIX II

(i.).—Extracts from a Speech of Castlereagh in the House of Commons, March 20th, 1815.[1]

. . . If I were to lead the House to suppose that, in the arduous transactions in which I have been engaged, I had at any time suffered the machine of Congress to stand still, in order to screen my conduct and determination under the cover of previous instructions from my government, when the public interests might suffer from delay, or that I had withheld that impulse which the influence of Great Britain, when applied with decision, was calculated to give, I should think that I had grossly betrayed the trust reposed in me . . . If it shall appear, as the honourable member has, on this night and on many others, contended, that the honour of the Crown has been sullied, that the good faith of the country has been disregarded, and her character degraded in the eyes of Europe, I desire to be considered as alone responsible ; I am ready alone to meet the attack and to repel the charge.

[Castlereagh then proceeded to explain the state of the negotiations relative to the abolition of the Slave Trade—a point for which he had been particularly instructed to press the representatives of other Powers, even with offers of territorial cessions and pecuniary sacrifices : he argued—]

If foreign Powers have withstood those temptations held out for their conditional acceptance, whilst our exertions should be continued without relaxation to bring them to a more favourable decision, it is but fair and just for Parliament to conclude that there were serious difficulties in the way of those governments immediately lending themselves to our wishes, and that we are bound to make allowance for the motives which induced them not to embark in what they held to be to them a dangerous experiment. With a view to the success of the object itself, we ought not to disgust them by our inconsiderate reproaches.

Though the Slave Trade is not actually abolished, yet I have the satisfaction to announce that a great step has been made towards its suppression. The eight Powers who were parties to the Treaty of Paris have published a solemn declaration that it was fit that this detestable traffic should be swept from the face of the earth. The claim which particular Powers, who still traffic in slaves, make for themselves, is that so much time shall be allowed for its discontinuance as is necessary for the welfare, security, and internal tranquillity of their respective dominions, and more particularly their colonies ; and they pledge themselves to the world then to put an end to this nefarious trade. I am happy in being able to congratulate the House on this important result. It will be obvious that no small step has been gained, by inducing every Power in Europe not only to pronounce against the general principle of the traffic in human beings, but to pronounce in favour of its actual, final, and early extinction . . . Spain and Portugal, who have hitherto made the least progress towards the final accomplishment of the object, have declared eight years to be the utmost interval before it is abolished by them, and I do not despair that even this period may yet be reduced. With respect to France, although I have not yet been able to persuade the French Government to depart from their original determination, yet, from all the intercourse I have had with the minister

---

[1] This version, corrected by Castlereagh himself, is given in the *Castlereagh Correspondence I.*, p. 24 ff. It was made in reply to a hot attack by Whitbread. The news of Napoleon's return had already been received, but the full extent of his success was not yet known. I have omitted some of the passages concerning Genoa and Holland which went into details of the negotiations, but most of the other gaps are in the version given in the Correspondence.

of his Most Christian Majesty, my belief is that they are sincerely desirous to put the earliest termination to this trade that they can reconcile to the general opinion and the prevailing prejudices of their own nation.

I should not have satisfied Parliament, or indeed my own sense of public duty, if I had not made every effort to procure a partial abolition of the Slave Trade, particularly North of the Line. But I do not myself consider this important question as yet terminated at Vienna ; for some of the plenipotentiaries, for instance, that of Portugal, had not time to receive sufficient instructions on the subject from their government, and therefore did not deem themselves authorized to determine upon it. Measures have, in consequence, been taken to adjourn the Congress, as far as the Slave Trade is concerned, and to establish a commission, composed of accredited agents, in London or Paris, to continue the negotiations upon the subject.

[Having disposed of the question of the Slave Trade, Lord Castlereagh passed to the consideration of the proceedings of the Congress of Vienna, in regard to European States.].

Every gentleman in the House must be aware that the Congress was assembled for the purpose of carrying into effect the peace of Paris, a peace which received the approbation of even the honourable gentleman : not that I mean to imply that he is bound to applaud any proceedings that have been since founded upon it, if he thinks them not deserving of applause. The fair question then is, whether, taking the Treaty of Paris as the basis upon which the late deliberations at Vienna were established, and upon the general principles of which those deliberations were to be pursued, whatever declarations might at other times have been issued—whether, I say, under all the circumstances of the case, those who were engaged in this great undertaking have fairly and honourably executed the task imposed upon them, and what judgment the House and the world at large, for whom they acted, ought to pronounce upon their conduct.

I am prepared to meet the honourable gentleman upon that issue : I will, at the proper moment, disguise none of the circumstances of the case ; I will then disclose every particle of intelligence upon every single point ; I will, at the proper time, avow them openly ; and if, on the present occasion, I am accused of withholding any portion of these transactions, it is only because it is not possible for me, with a due regard for the interests of the public service, to lay them all open to the view of the world. But, on every part of this complicated question, I will be prepared to meet the honourable gentleman : I will be prepared to vindicate it against the foul calumnies with which, no doubt from misapprehension and misinformation, he has thought fit to impugn the councils of his country, and to bring charges of the most nefarious character against other governments that have been parties to those transactions, without the slightest foundation for his accusations, and, as I will take leave to say, with great prejudice to the general interests and welfare of Europe. In the commencement, the House will allow me to protest against the principle which the honourable gentleman has attempted to lay down for the sovereigns of Europe. If, as he contends, they had issued a Declaration, under the construction of which all the ancient governments of Europe which Time had swept away were to be re-created ; that those rude and shapeless fabrics, which had long been thrown down, and had long ceased to exist in any tangible form, were to be reconstructed without any consideration of the real tendency of such a reconstruction ; that those scattered fragments were again to be put together, without reflecting upon the probable consequences—upon the corruptions that had grown up under the shade of those antiquated and ruinous institutions—without recollecting how far those very governments had tended to produce the calamities by which Europe had been so long and so severely visited, and which might in time have the very effect of re-creating the dangers which we have just escaped—I say, if the Declarations of the sovereigns were to be so construed and understood, I should have felt ashamed that my country had belonged to a confederacy founded upon such a principle of imbecility.

The true question is—and I think the honourable gentleman is too much of a statesman and too manly in his understanding not to meet me upon that issue —whether the deliberations and decisions of Congress were guided by an ascertained and worthy principle ; whether the basis of a solid and lasting pacification was or was not in itself unsound ; and whether, for the sake of the attainment of any partial or selfish views, any of the parties, but more especially this country, had betrayed the trust reposed in them by the confidence of Europe.   It is upon these grounds, and these only, that I mean to argue the question, and to refute the assertions and positions of the honourable member . . .

I apprehend that, in the whole course of the negotiations lately held for the attainment of a general peace, it was perfectly understood that the purpose of the sovereigns of Europe, after the contests they had endured, was to establish and reorganize the two great monarchies of Europe, that had been almost annihilated as monarchies, to accomplish the designs of the late ruler of France —I mean, Austria and Prussia.

The object, as all gentlemen must be aware, was to gain and permanently secure greater safety on both flanks of the two States which were to form the immediate bulwarks of Europe, to give adequate power by means of the additional strength which they should supply to that State of North Germany which would be charged with the preservation of that portion of the Continent.   It was also desirable that a strong barrier should be interposed between the States of Italy and France, to prevent them also from arraying themselves against each other.   It was further wished that Switzerland should be re-established in her influence and independence, to keep up the chain of communication, and that Germany might be again confederated in the same system, to render it an impregnable bulwark between the great States in the East and West of Europe. The question is : Have these arrangements been calculated to produce such a state of things as all professed to be desirous of creating ; or have particular Powers been unjustly aggrandized, and have the Potentates acted at the Congress in the honest and faithful execution of the trust reposed in them, and of the general purpose which it was their interest to keep in view ?

And here I will beg leave to protest against another and, as I conceive, unfair mode in which the honourable member endeavoured to influence the House upon this subject.   He read a letter[1] written by the French minister, in reference to a particular question, in which the writer contends that the important point was not to be decided by throwing, as it were, the whole population of Europe into a general fund, and dealing it out in such quantities as might supply the wants of the various sovereigns whose power was to be augmented. I mean not to deny that the letter may have been written ; and, if so, it was done in general opposition to the allotment of the whole of Saxony to Prussia as a territorial aggrandizement.   If there were not powerfully operating circum-stances, I should be the first to admit that the principle of population ought not to prevail, if merely the morality of the question were at issue.   I hope it will not be denied that the importance of population, and of the wealth consequent upon it, is great, when we are arguing the question of a Balance of Power in Europe, and what shall be considered a just distribution of force between the sovereigns who are to be charged with maintaining the tranquillity of the Continent.   .   .   .

[Castlereagh then dealt at length with the question of Genoa.]   I set a high value, most assuredly, on the good opinion of the honourable gentleman ; I am always happy to meet with his approbation, and the more so because I seldom have that good fortune : but, whatever may be that value, and whatever the weight and deference due to his censure, it is not to prevent the kingdoms of Europe from taking measures for their own security and happiness.   I confess that I am not quite so fond of popularity as to wish for it at that expense ; but, when he asks me whether there were not secret articles in the Treaty of Paris, I answer that, if there were any which the parties to it were not ready at the

[1] Talleyrand to Metternich, Dec. 19, 1815, which had appeared in the Press and from which Whit-bread had quoted several passages.   *Supra* p. 273.

time to declare and avow, I should be willing to allow Europe and its Sovereigns to incur that execration to which the honourable gentleman is so ready to consign them.

The House will be aware that, whatever those articles might be, their application was not finally and entirely decided ; and that was the reason why they were not proclaimed. I admit very willingly that there were circumstances understood between the Powers at Paris that did not form part of the ostensible Treaty ; and, so they acted up to those principles, it cannot be contended that any deception was employed, that any fraud was practised, upon the people of Europe. So far am I—and I should think most reasonable men would concur with me—from blaming the parties to the Treaty for entering into this understanding upon various topics, that I should have thought it very unwise and a great indiscretion not to have come to some sort of previous decision.

The Honourable gentleman asks me whether in the Treaty there was anything respecting Holland. I admit that there was ; and, if any reproach be due on that account, I desire that I may bear my full share of the blame, and the more so, because I believe I may say that it was principally owing to me that Holland was mentioned ; and I should have despaired of the cause of the country if I had not done so, and betrayed, as I think, a criminal confidence in the ministers of France, if I had not brought them to an understanding of the essential interests of this country with regard to Holland before I parted with the essential securities which still I retained in my hands. At the same time, I was not to deprive France of the situation in which I wished to place her. I wished to make her an important and deliberating party to the Treaty ; and the House will allow me to state here that no confidence, no faith, that I placed in the conduct of the French Government, either with respect to the Slave Trade, or to any other subject, has been abused. France has conducted herself throughout these proceedings—and I hope this fact will produce, in the mind of the honourable gentleman, a practical sense of the fitness and necessity of preserving that Government, if, by any efforts of this country not inconsistent with moral and national prudence, or with what we owe to another great people, we are able to support it—France, I say, has conducted herself in a manner that must give the utmost satisfaction to all parties, who, I am sure, will feel the propriety of aiding and supporting a Government that has given peace to the world, and, by the situation in which it has been placed among the nations of Europe, is able and willing to maintain it . . .

France adopted all the engagements and fundamental Treaties which the Allies had made among themselves, and which were not generally disseminated. She came to Congress, in no way fettered in her decisions, or influenced in her judgment, a free agent to deliberate upon the important topics to be there decided. She did not come, as the honourable gentleman supposed, to throw loose the bonds that united together the European Powers in interest and action ; but as a free and independent State, to partake in the deliberations and to form her own decision how far she should support the Treaty of the Allies, and how far its engagements were consistent with the general salvation of Europe and the particular re-establishment of France.

If we had not obtained that previous recognition on her part respecting the future plans of Congress, what would have been the consequence ? France would have come to the Congress as an inimical, not a friendly Power. If for no other, this was surely an adequate reason for obtaining those stipulations, and for not making them the subject of communication to Parliament. They were not withheld because there was in them any principle of which Europe or her negotiators need be ashamed, but because such a disclosure would have been attended with many evil consequences, and the House must be sensible that they were not in a shape to be properly made the subject of deliberation. [Further consideration of the case of Genoa at length.]

In one part of his speech, the honourable gentleman said, that he knew not why the noble lord went to Vienna, why he did not stay there, or why, having come away, and re-appeared in Parliament, he is not prepared to give a full communication to the House. Why I went to Vienna, I trust he will not expect me now to explain. I should imagine that it is well known why I went. I went to Vienna, because I was ordered by my Sovereign to go ; and I returned to my place in Parliament, because I received a similar direction for that purpose. Why the order for my return was given, perhaps, the honourable gentleman will not think it necessary that I should explain. At the time when I left Vienna, the arrangements were not absolutely concluded and put into a regular shape to be laid before Parliament ; yet they had arrived at such a point, and been put into such a shape, as would enable me at least to touch upon those transactions, and give explanations upon such parts as particularly required my presence in the execution . . . With the exception of that single branch which relates to the arrangements of Italy southward of the Po, I may say that all the other points are finished and decided ; and to such an extent are they decided, that the arrangements have been reduced into articles in the same form as they would have in the ultimate Treaty to be entered into by all the Powers. These articles have been signed by the different plenipotentiaries of the sovereigns, and are considered as binding and obligatory upon them, only requiring to be finally and formally executed.

The honourable member has asked whether France has been a consenting party to those arrangements. I have no hesitation in stating, if it can be any satisfaction to him, that she has been a consenting party to them, with no more difference of opinion than, I may say, ought to prevail upon questions of such extreme doubt and difficulty. It gives me pleasure to be able to declare that France has acted upon the same broad and liberal principles that have guided the other Powers. She has been an honest party to the Congress, doing her duty to Europe and herself. Her plenipotentiary acted with perfect fairness and openness during the deliberations ; and though he may have written some particular note at a time when discussions upon a certain point were not terminated, and may, in the warmth of some of these discussions, have found something upon which to express his reprobation with regard to the arrangement alluded to yet, neither on the part of France, nor on the part of any other State that I am aware of, could any fair complaint be made of improper proceeding in any one respect ; and I think that I cannot adduce to the House a stronger proof of the inconvenience resulting from discussions of this sort, than the partial and unjust use made of the document to which I refer. I think that I cannot lay before it a more striking instance of the danger, the desperate danger, of suffering transactions of this nature to be called in question piecemeal, to be discussed and debated upon every single paper that chances to fall into the hands of any honourable member, instead of waiting till the proper time arrives, and the subject can be freely, fairly, and fully canvassed, and a judgment formed becoming the wisdom of the British Parliament. Instead of that, subjects yet under discussion at Vienna were dragged into premature debate in this House, and most serious injury was often done, not only to our cause, but to that of Europe at large. The honourable member produces in the House a document, he knows not how procured ; he discusses it, follows it up, pursues the subject to the fullest extent that it will admit of, or that his ingenuity can devise, and then, after doing all the mischief that is possible, as on this occasion, he asks whether it is an official document, and whether there is any foundation for all that he has been saying, and any reason for all the mischief that he has been doing. Against such a mode of proceeding, I feel it necessary to enter my protest.

With respect to two most important features of the late negotiations, I mean the reconstruction of the Austrian and Prussian monarchies—I call them most important features, because every man must be sensible that, until they were restored to their former rank and importance, there would remain a great blank in Europe ; that, until they were re-established in adequate strength, there was no bulwark against any future encroachments by France ; that, until they were placed upon their original footing, Europe was not herself, and was deprived of the two main pillars of her security—I say, with respect to the Austrian and Prussian monarchies, I have the satisfaction to state, that they have now, by the decisions of the Allies, regained their former rank and weight in the scale of Europe, in a mode which discharges them from many calumnies that the honourable gentleman has endeavoured to throw upon them. I am aware, and he is now aware, I apprehend, that he made those accusations upon imperfect information ; but, until he had obtained better proof, I should have thought, the more regular, as well as the more judicious course, both for himself and for them, would have been to withhold his assertions that Austria and Prussia were endeavouring to seize and appropriate to themselves, as if by right of conquest, territories to which they have no right, upon any principles of moderation or of fair repartition. But I may say, with perfect confidence, in justification of those States, after all that I have seen, that they have neither done nor consented to any act which should call in question the general moderation of those States.

The principle laid down as the rule of conduct for their reconstruction, was the state of the possessions in the year 1805. The House will, I am sure, admit that, in fixing upon that period, Austria, at least, did not choose a time that was particularly marked by any spirited aggrandizement. By taking 1805, instead of 1792, the period of the Revolution, she placed out of the question her possessions in the Netherlands. It is true that, in 1805, she had possession of the States of Venice, but she was then two millions weaker in population than in 1792. The period which Prussia took was the time immediately preceding the spoliation of that kingdom by France.

On a general view of the present state of these two monarchies, it will be found that, notwithstanding the unreasonable exertions to obtain additional and supereminent power, which they have been charged with making, notwithstanding the ambitious and grasping spirit which they are alleged to have shown, in consequence of the decision of the Congress, neither of them has obtained any accession of the least importance, beyond what they could demand under the strict application of the principle of re-establishment which they had at first laid down.

Though some of the territorial possessions of Prussia may lie wider, and be upon a somewhat more extended scale than formerly, yet it will appear, by the most accurate calculations, that the utmost she has obtained beyond what she had in 1805 is about 50,000 souls ; while Austria, from the slight alterations in her territorial possessions, has not gained more than three or four hundred thousand new subjects. So much for the greedy spirit of aggrandizement which they have shown ; and, upon the whole, I assert most decidedly that nothing can be less true than the imputations cast upon the arrangements made for the two Powers of which I have been speaking.

The honourable gentleman has referred, in a very pointed manner, to two other important transactions which came under the decision of the Congress— I mean, with regard to Saxony and Poland. On these subjects, I have no objection to give him and the House all the information I can, consistently with that reservation which I feel compelled, by a sense of duty, to observe respecting transactions not yet finally closed. All I have to beg is, that the honourable gentleman and the House will suspend their judgment until more complete information than, under the circumstances, I am able to supply, shall be afforded.

The honourable gentleman has arraigned, in the severest terms, the conduct of the Congress, on account of the arrangement adopted in regard to Saxony : he has called it a base and intolerable purpose to annex Saxony to Prussia. I should perhaps agree with him in thinking that it would not be wise or fit to give the whole of Saxony to the Prussian King ; and, having never concealed or disguised my opinion on that subject, I have no hesitation to avow that I was one of the ministers of the Congress, who differed from the Prussian plenipotentiary and others upon this point ; and that I was one of the persons who felt entitled, at Vienna, to contend, in the strongest manner, against the incorporation of the whole of Saxony with the Prussian dominions. I should have felt, however, that more intolerable injustice might be done in other directions ; but so strong were the sentiments of the British Government upon this subject, and so serious the remonstrances made, that the settlement now existing in Saxony was ultimately obtained by a sacrifice, in some degree, of the interests of Holland and Hanover.

But let me not be misunderstood. I never was one of those who contested the point upon the principle assumed by the honourable gentleman, that it must, in any case, be inconsistent with the duties of the Powers of Europe assembled at Vienna, with the express leave of the nation itself, to annex even the whole of Saxony to Prussia. I never opposed it on the ground of mere abstract right ; and I broadly and avowedly deny any assertions that may have been made regarding my conduct in that respect. I contended that the right of conquest, under the qualifications which I shall presently state, was a right which gave the conqueror a perfect warrant to annex the whole of a subjugated country to another State. I deny that I had argued this matter on any other principle, and cannot suffer the honourable member to give me credit for a line of conduct which he may perhaps applaud, but which I did not think fit to follow in this particular transaction.

I take no pleasure in stating anything that may be injurious to the illustrious monarch, who is now, I apprehend, at the head of the Kingdom of Saxony ; I hope that he will long continue to reign over his subjects in happiness, after the painful scenes through which he has passed ; but I must be allowed to argue, and I do it with perfect confidence, that never was the principle of conquest more legitimately applicable, or more justifiably exercisable than in the case of Saxony. Her conduct furnished, as the House knows, an instance of former unwarrantable aggrandizement, and of the most persevering resistance to the allies. The King drew the consequences upon himself by his own acts. His great exertions against the common cause of the rest of the European Powers are known ; and, although it is known that opportunities were afforded to the King of Saxony to unite his interests with those of the Allies, he thought fit, on his own view of the subject, to employ his efforts in maintaining the power of France. He made this choice after he had been placed in circumstances where he might have withdrawn himself from among the supporters of Buonaparte, if he had not thought that perseverance in the cause of the man who had given him his crown was not the best mode of preserving his dominions.

Saxony was a conquered country, in the strictest sense of the word ; though it is true that the Saxon army, on the third day of the battle of Leipsic, did join the Allies, and perhaps decide the victory, yet the House must know that Saxony, until that moment, which did not depend upon the voice of the sovereign, had been a Power whose army and resources were devoted to the cause of the common enemy against whom we were fighting . . .

I put this case to the House, with regard to Saxony : Admitting and believing that the re-establishment of Prussia in the same state of strength and security that she held in 1805 is necessary to the general repose and safety of Europe, if no other mode of re-establishing and restoring that kingdom had existed, is there any man, who, in point of justice, would have thought fit to put the case of Saxony in competition with that of Prussia ? Suppose it was impossible for the two kingdoms to exist in the new form which Europe was to take, is there any man who would say that Saxony should be continued and Prussia abolished, and her name swept from the face of Europe ? But that was not the question before the Congress ; the question respecting Saxony, from first to last, was this, whether in truth Prussia would derive from the annexation of Saxony that advantage which she expected. As there was ground to presume that Prussia could be reinstated without the sacrifice at least of the whole of Saxony, I was strongly of opinion that to push the general principle to extremity against Saxony would be doing mischief to Prussia, instead of promoting her ultimate and permanent advantage.

I was persuaded that the public feeling not merely of the people of Germany, but of other countries, would have been wounded by so great and complete a sacrifice of an ancient family ; that the general opinion of mankind would have revolted at such a proceeding, and that Prussia would be prejudiced in the general estimation of Europe by the annexation.   Prussia, it was true, had made unexampled efforts in the general cause ; but I did not think that in the eyes of Europe she would be entitled to demand so great a sacrifice.   Such being the state of my mind upon this very important point, I conceived it to be my duty to resist, as far as possible, the incorporation at least of the whole of Saxony with Prussia . . .

Respecting Poland, I should wish the House to reserve its judgment until the whole subject can be disclosed.   Whatever may be the final decision of the Congress in regard to that country, the House, I am sure, will be gratified to learn that the situation of its brave people will be considerably ameliorated by the new arrangements.   There was undoubtedly a strong feeling in the country upon the subject of independence and a separate government : indeed there was, I believe, but one feeling, and, as far as I was able, I exerted myself to attain that object . . .   Whatever may be the particular arrangements resolved upon, or the form of government that shall in future be established, I may venture to say, that in the Congress there was but one feeling—that the whole should be governed under a different system, as Poland.   That portion which will form the duchy of Warsaw will be under the sceptre of a different prince ; and I have reason to believe that the principle of the government in general will be found far more congenial with the feelings and wishes of the Poles than when they were placed under the authority of different masters from those to whom they will in future be considered to belong.   The natives will be relieved from those local difficulties which attached even to their principal duties and avocations, and upon the whole will be ruled upon a system of liberality befitting the spirit of the times.   Whatever policy may have formerly prevailed with regard to Poland, a general determination has been taken by such Powers as are interested in the question to promote, by all means, the welfare of the people of this most unfortunate portion of Europe, and to establish in the country a system by which the Poles shall be governed as Poles, with the rights and privileges that ought to belong to them. . . .

I can assure the House that, on my part, there was not wanting any exertion that appeared to me conducive to this important object, and consistent with the general peace of Europe, and indeed with the welfare of the Poles themselves, which, I trust, has been duly consulted.   I know that it was the wish of a vast number of persons in this country, and, I believe, in Poland, that it should be erected into a separate State, to maintain its own rank and independence in Europe ; but such was not the wish of all.   It was found inconsistent with the views of several of the other great Powers of Europe ; and the House must be aware that such a plan could not be carried into effect without the complete and general concurrence of all the parties interested. . . .

In contemplating the late arrangements, I should have little satisfaction, if I could persuade myself that, in supporting the views and objects with which I was specially entrusted, I had felt that I was maintaining the separate interests of Great Britain . . .   I felt throughout that I was not supporting separate interests ; that in all points our Allies were equally concerned, and that, in truth, our own welfare and theirs were intimately connected and closely bound together . . .

Upon the whole view of the foreign relations of this country, as they have been settled at the Congress, I cannot help thinking that Parliament will contemplate with satisfaction those important arrangements.   By them, we have obtained many advantages, and not the least, in which we participate with all Europe, is that we are delivered from the danger which might arise from the predominating power of France.   The wise measures adopted for this purpose have not degraded France from the high station which she ought to hold among the nations, while they have given to others additional power and security . . .

Taking, therefore, into view the general state of our relations abroad, even separating our policy and interests from those of the rest of Europe, I trust that the House will see that they have been discussed and determined in a temper productive of the best consequences ; and that it will feel that there is nothing left for this country in good sense or reason to wish for but a continuance of the blessings of peace, and a perseverance in that system by which they have been procured.

The honourable member, before he sat down, called the attention of the House to what is passing in an adjacent country. Whatever steps Great Britain may take, upon the issue of the contest which has thus unexpectedly been forced upon us depend all those blessings of peace, and all those advantages of arrangement, of which I have been speaking. Where is the man who can lay his hand upon his heart and say that, if the power of Buonaparte is re-established in France, any of those blessings which Europe was about to enjoy can be realized ? Who will say, if he again rules the destinies of France, that Europe can be tranquil, secure, or independent ? I consider that in the question now at issue in France is involved the more vital question, whether the world can return to that moral system by which happiness and the interests of mankind were to be upheld, or whether we shall remain, as we have been during the last twenty years, under the necessity of maintaining a system of military policy ; whether Europe shall in future present the spectacle of an assemblage of pacific or of armed nations. Shall the nations of the world take up arms to destroy each other, or lay them down to promote each other's happiness ? These are the questions to be decided by the result of the present contest in France—questions of the deepest interest ; for if, indeed, the authority of Buonaparte be restored, who can doubt that with him will be restored also that destructive military power ?—If that military power be re-established in France, where, let me ask, must we look for peace and prosperity, unless we conquer it with our swords ?

If it shall be necessary for Britain to return to that system which we have been so long and so painfully pursuing—if we must, at the moment of expected ease, again submit to the toils of war, and re-establish a military force necessary for our security—it will, doubtless, as on former occasions, be tempered by the wholesome checks of the British constitution. In this country, the military force must always be comparatively subordinate to the civil power, and our military institutions must always be inferior to our civil establishments : but, if Buonaparte prove successful, we must look forward to becoming again a military people ; while that man keeps up in France his military resources, a condition of defence by military power also can alone give security to Europe.

Let this country then, let France herself, reflect that upon the result of this new struggle—upon the management of which, or the part which this nation must take, I say nothing at present—must depend all our happiness or all our calamities. Upon the success of the family of Bourbon—who in my judgment have done for France the greatest acts of favour that a people could conceive, but more especially that act of grace by which peace, so long banished, was restored to her—depends the important question for this country, whether we shall return to that natural and happy state of peace, or whether we shall continue the struggle against the military power of France, under the artificial system which such a contest has heretofore rendered, and would again render, necessary. Upon this great question there can be, I am sure, but one feeling ; and I trust that Providence, conducting us through the remainder of the task which we may have to perform, will ordain only one result.

Upon the whole, I am persuaded that the House will perceive that, in the deliberations of the Congress, a great deal has been accomplished : indeed, for my own part, I know that nothing connected with the important and general interests of Europe has been omitted. With the pledge of mutual support which the Sovereigns will be prepared to give to each other, I know of nothing that can interrupt the general tranquillity of Europe, if Buonaparte be not allowed to infringe upon it. In conclusion, I feel satisfied that the House and the country will think with me, that never before was so much accomplished for Europe, and that we never had in our history a fairer prospect of bright days of continued happiness than at the present moment, if they be not clouded by new and unforeseen calamity.

(ii).—*Extracts from a Speech of Sir James Mackintosh on the Transfer of Genoa, April 27th, 1815.*[1]

. . I shall not presume to define on invariable principles, the limits of the right of conquest. It is founded, like every right of war, on a regard to security, the object of all just war. The modes in which national safety may be provided for, by reparation for insult, by compensation for injury, by cessions, and by indemnifications, vary in such important respects, according to the circumstances of various cases, that it is, perhaps, impossible to limit them by an universal principle. In the case of Norway, I did not pretend to argue the question upon the grounds so high as those which were taken by the writers on public law. These writers, who for two centuries have been quoted as authorities in all the controversies of Europe, with the moderate and pacific Grotius at their head, have all concurred in treating it as a fundamental principle, that a defeated sovereign may indeed cede part of his dominions to the conqueror : but that he thereby only abdicates his own sovereignty over the ceded dominion ; that the consent of the people is necessary to make them normally subject to the authority of the conqueror. Without renouncing this limitation of the right of conquest, founded on principles so generous, and so agreeable to the dignity of human nature, I was content to argue the cession of Norway, as I am content to argue the cession of Genoa, on lower and humbler but perhaps safer grounds. Let me waive the odious term " right,"—let me waive the necessity of any consent of a people, express or implied, to legitimate the cession of their territory. At least this will not be denied, that to unite a people by force to a nation against whom they entertain a strong antipathy, is the most probable means to render the community unhappy, to make the people discontented, and the sovereign tyrannical ; but there can be no right in any governor, whether he derives his power from conquest or from any other source, to make the governed unhappy. All the rights of all governors exist only to make the governed happy. It may be disputed among some, whether the rights of government be from the people ; but no man can doubt that they are for the people. Such a forcible union is an immoral and cruel exercise of the conqueror's power ; and as soon as that concession is made, it is not worth while to discuss whether it be within his right, in other words, whether he be forbidden by any law to make such a union ; but if every cession of a territory against the deliberate and manifest sense of its inhabitants be a harsh and reprehensible abuse of conquest, it is most of all culpable, it becomes altogether atrocious and inhuman, where the antipathy was not the feeling of the moment, or the prejudice of the day, but a profound sentiment of hereditary repugnance and aversion, which has descended from generation to generation, has mingled with every part of thought and action, and had become part of patriotism itself. Such is the repugnance of the Genoese to a union with Piedmont, and such is commonly the peculiar horror which high-minded nations feel for the yoke of their immediate neighbours,—Norway towards Sweden, Portugal towards Spain, in former and less happy times, Scotland towards England, are a few out of innumerable examples. There is nothing either unreasonable or unnatural in this state of national feelings. With neighbours there are most occasions of quarrel ; with them there have been most wars ; from them there has been most suffering ; of them there is most fear. The resentment of wrongs, and the remembrance of victories, strengthen our repugnance towards those who are most usually our enemies. It is not from illiberal prejudice, but from the constitution of human nature, that an Englishman animates his patriotic affections, and supports his national pride, but now looking back on victories over Frenchmen, on Cressy and Agincourt, on Blenheim and Minden, as our posterity will one day look back on Salamanca and Vittoria. The

---

[1] Hansard. *Parliamentary Debates*, vol. XXX. 918. Papers concerning Genoa had been laid before the House on April 7th, 1815 (Hansard XXX., 387). Mackintosh moved a long motion condemning the policy of the Government.

defensive principle ought to be the strongest where the danger is most likely frequently to arise. What, then, will the House decide concerning the morality of compelling Genoa to submit to the yoke of Piedmont,—a state which the Genoese have constantly dreaded and hated, and against whom their hatred was sharpened by continual apprehensions for their independence ? Whatever construction may be attempted of Lord William Bentinck's proclamations, whatever sophistry may be used successfully, to persuade you that Genoa was disposable as a conquered territory, will you affirm that the disposal of it to Piedmont was a just and humane exercise of your power as a conqueror ?

It is for this reason, among others, that I detest and execrate the modern doctrine of rounding territory and following natural boundaries, and melting down small states into masses, and substituting lines of defence, and right and left flanks, instead of justice and the law of nations, and ancient possessions and national feeling : the system of Louis XIV. and Napoleon, of the spoilers of Poland, and the spoilers of Norway and Genoa—the system which the noble Lord, when newly arrived from the Congress, and deeply imbued with its doctrines, had delivered, in his ample and elaborate invective against the memory and principles of ancient Europe, when he condensed the whole new system into two phrases so characteristic of his reverence for the rights of nations, and his tenderness for their feelings, that they ought not easily to be forgotten— when he told us, speaking of this very antipathy of Genoa to Piedmont, " that great questions are not to be influenced by popular impressions," and " that a people may be happy without independence." The principle article of the new system is the incorporation of neighbouring, and therefore hostile communities. The system of justice reverenced the union of men who had long been members of the same commonwealth, because they had been long fellow-citizens, and had all the attachments and antipathies which grow out of that fellowship. The system of rapine tears asunder those whom nature has joined, and compels those to unite whom the contests of ages had rendered irreconcileable. And if all this had been less evident, would no aggravation of this act have arisen from the peculiar nature of the general war of Europe against France ? It was a war in which not only the Italians, but every people in Europe were called by their Sovereigns to rise for the recovery of their independence. It was a revolt of the people against Napoleon. It owed its success to the spirit of popular insurrection. The principle of a war for the restoration of independence, was a pledge that each people were to be restored to their ancient territory. The nations of Europe accepted the pledge, and shook off the French yoke. But was it for a change of masters ? Was it that three foreign ministers at Paris might dispose of the Genoese territory ?—was it for this that the youth of Europe had risen in arms fom Moscow to the Rhine.

Ergo pari voto gessisti bella Juventus ?
Tu quoque pro Dominis et Pompeiana fuisti.
Non Romana Manus.[1]

The people of Europe were, it seems, roused to war, not to overthrow tyranny, but to shift it into new hands ; not to re-establish the independence and restore the ancient institutions of nations, but to strengthen the right flank of one great military Power, and to cover the left flank of another. This, at least, was not the war for the success of which I offered my most ardent prayers. I prayed for the deliverance of Europe, not for its transfer to other lords ; for the restoration of Europe, by which all men must have understood, at least, the re-establishment of that ancient system, and of those wise principles under which it had become great and prosperous. I expected the re-establishment of every people in those territories, of which the sovereignty had been lost by recent usurpation ; of every people who had been an ancient member of the family of Europe ; of every people who had reserved the spirit and feelings which constitute a nation ; and, above all, of every people who had lost their territory or their independence under the tyranny which the Allies had taken up arms to overthrow. I expected a reverence for ancient boundaries, a respect

---

[1] Lucan. IX. 256-8 I am indebted to my colleague, Professor Slater, for this reference.

for ancient institutions, certainly without excluding a prudent regard to the new interests and opinions which had taken so deep a root that they could not be torn up without incurring the guilt and the mischief of the most violent innovation. The very same reason, indeed, both of morality and policy (since I must comply so far with vulgar usage as to distinguish what cannot be separated), bound the Allied Sovereigns to respect the ancient institutions, and to regard the new opinions and interests of nations. The art of all government, not tyrannical, whatever may be its form, is to conduct mankind by their feelings. It is immoral to disregard the feelings of the governed, because it renders them miserable. It is, and it ought to be, dangerous to disregard those feelings, because bold and intelligent men will always consider it as a mere question of prudence, whether they ought to obey governments which counteract the only purpose for which government exists. The feelings of men are most generally wounded by violence to those ancient institutions under which these feelings have been formed, the national character has been moulded, and to which all the habits and expectations of life are adapted. It was well said by Mr. Fox, that as ancient institutions have been sanctioned by a far greater concurrence of human judgments than modern laws can be, they are, upon democratical principles, more respectable. But new opinions and new interests, a new arrangement of society which has given rise to other habits and hopes, also excite the strongest feelings, which, in proportion to their force and extent, claim the regard of all moral policy. As it was doubtless the policy of the Allies to consider the claims of ancient possessions as sacred, as far as the irrevocable changes of the political system would allow, the considerate part of mankind did, I believe, hope that they would hail the long-continued and recently-lost sovereignty of a territory as generally an inviolable right ; and that as they could not be supposed wanting in zeal for the sovereignty of ancient reigning families, so they would guard that re-establishment, and render it respectable in the eyes of the world, by the impartiality with which they re-established those ancient and legitimate governments of a republican form, which had fallen in the general slavery of nations. We remembered that republics and monarchies were alike called to join in the war against the French Revolution, not for forms of government, but for the social order. We hoped that Austria (to select a striking example) would not pollute her title to her ancient dominion of Lombardy, by blending it with the faithless and lawless seizure of Venice. So little republican territory was to be restored, that the act of justice was to be performed, and the character of impartiality gained at little expense, even if such expense be measured by the meanest calculations of the most vulgar politics. Vacant territory remained at the disposal of the Congress to satisfy the demands of policy. The sovereignty of the ecclesiastical territories might be fairly considered as lapsed. No reigning family could have any interest in it : no people could be attached to such a rule of nomination to supreme power. And, in fact, these principalities had lost all pride of independence and consciousness of national existence. Several other territories in Europe had been reduced to a like condition. Ceded, perhaps, at first questionably, they had been transferred so often from master to master ; they had been so long in a state of provincial degradation, that no violence could be offered to their feelings by new transfer or partition. They were, as it were, a sort of splinters thrown off from nations in the shocks of warfare, during two centuries ; and they lay like stakes on the board to be played for at the terrible game which had detached them, and to satisfy the exchanges and cessions by which it is usually closed. Perhaps such detached partitions of the social system are necessary in the European system ; but they are in themselves great evils. They are amputated and lifeless members, which, as soon as they lose the vital principle of national spirit, no longer contribute aught to the vigour and safety of the whole living system. From them is to be expected no struggle against invasion, no resistance to the designs of ambition, no defence of country. They have no independence: they have no country. They are individual men, but no longer a people. They are in themselves the defenceless part of the European commonwealth. They are the ready prey of every candidature for universal monarchy, who soon compels their passive inhabitants to fight for his ambition, as they would not fight against it, and to employ in enslaving other nations that courage which they had no noble interest to exert in defence of their own. Why should I seek examples of this truth in former times? What opened Europe to the first inroads of the French armies?—Not, I will venture to say, the mere smallness of the neighbouring states,—(for if every one had displayed as much national spirit in 1794, as the smallest states of Switzerland did in 1798, no French army could ever have left the territory of France),—but the unhappy course of events which had deprived Flanders and the Electorates and Lombardy of all national spirit. Extinguished by the form of government in some of these countries, crushed by a foreign yoke in others, without the pride of liberty, which bestows the highest national spirit on the smallest nations, or the pride of power, which sometimes supplies its place in mighty empires,—or the consciousness of not depending on another nation, without which there is no nationality,—they first became the prey of France, and afterwards they supplied the arms with which she almost conquered the world. To enlarge this dead part of Europe, to enrich it by the accession of countries renowned for their public feelings, to throw Genoa into the same grave with Poland, with Venice, with Finland, and with Norway, is not the policy of the preservers or restorers of the European commonwealth.

It is not the principle of the balance of power, but one precisely opposite. The system of preserving some equilibrium of power ; of preventing any state from becoming too great for her neighbours, is a system purely defensive, and directed towards the object of universal preservation. It is a system which provides for the security of all states, by balancing the force and opposing the interests of great states. The independence of nations is the end : the balance of power is only the means. To destroy independent nations in order to strengthen the balance of power, is the most extravagant sacrifice of the end to the means. This inversion of all the principles of the ancient and beautiful system of Europe, is the fundamental maxim of what the noble lord, enriching our language with foreign phrases as well as doctrines, calls " a repartition of power." In the new system small states are annihilated by a combination of great. In the old, small states were secured by the mutual jealousy of the great. The noble lord very consistently treats the re-establishment of small states as an absurdity. This single feature betrays the school where he has studied. Undoubtedly, small communities are an absurdity, or rather their permanent existence is an impossibility on his new system. They could have no existence in the continual conquests of Asia. They were soon destroyed amidst the turbulence of the Grecian confederacy. They must be sacrificed on the system of rapine established at Vienna. Nations powerful enough to defend themselves, may subsist securely in most tolerable conditions of society. But states too small to be safe by their own strength can exist only where they are guarded by the equilibrium of force, and the vigilance which watches over its preservation. When the noble lord represents small states as incapable of existence, he, in truth, avows that he is returned in triumph from the destruction of that system of the balance of power of which indeed great empires were the guardians, but of which the perfect action was indicated by the security of feebler commonwealths. Under this system, no great violation of national independence had occurred, from the first civilization of the European states, till the partition of Poland. The safety of the feeblest states, under the authority of justice, was so great, that there seemed little exaggeration in calling such a society the commonwealth of Europe. Principles, which stood in the stead of laws and magistrates, provided for the security of defenceless communities, as the safety of the humblest individual is maintained in a well-ordered commonwealth. Europe can no longer be called a commonwealth, when her members have no safety but in strength.

In truth, the Balancing System is itself only a secondary guard of national independence. The paramount principle, the moving power, without which all such machinery would be perfectly inert, is national spirit. The love of country, the attachment to laws and government, and even to soil and scenery ; the feelings of national glory in arms and arts, the remembrances of common triumph and common suffering, with the mitigated, but not obliterated recollection of common enmities, and the jealousy of dangerous neighbours, instruments employed (also by nature) to draw more closely the bands of affection to our country and to each other,—this is the only principle by which sovereigns could in the hour of danger rouse the minds of their subjects. Without this principle, the policy of the Balancing System would be impotent. To sacrifice a people actuated by this spirit, to overrule that repugnance to the yoke of a neighbour, which is one of the chief bulwarks of nations, is in the effect, and much more in the example, to erect a pretended balance of power by the destruction of that spirit, and of those sentiments, which alone render that balance effectual for its only useful purpose—the protection of independence.

The Congress of Vienna seems, indeed, to have adopted every part of the French system, except that they have transferred the dictatorship of Europe from an individual to a triumvirate. One of the grand and patent errors of the French Revolution, was the fatal opinion, that it was possible for human skill to make a government. It was an error too generally prevalent not to be excusable. The American Revolution had given it a fallacious semblance of support, though no event in history, more clearly showed its falsehood. The system of laws, and the frame of society in North America, remained after the Revolution, and remain to this day fundamentally the same as they ever were. The change in America, like the change in 1608, was made in defence of legal right, not in pursuit of political improvement, and it was limited by the necessity of the defence which produced it. The whole internal order remained, which had always been essentially republican. The somewhat slender tie which loosely joined these republics to a monarchy, was easily and without violence divided. But the error of the French revolutionists was, in 1789, the error of Europe. From that error, we have been long reclaimed by fatal experience. We know, or rather we have seen and felt, that a government is not like a machine, or a building, the work of man—that it is the work of nature, like the nobler productions of the vegetable and animal world, which man may improve, and corrupt, and even destroy, but which he cannot create. We have long learned to despise the ignorance or the hypocrisy of those who speak of giving a free constitution to a people, and to exclaim with a great living poet—

" A gift of that which never can be given,
        By all the blended powers of Earth and Heaven ! "

We have, perhaps, as usual, gone too near to the opposite error, and we do not make sufficient allowances for those dreadful cases which we must not call desperate, where, in long-enslaved countries, we must either humbly and cautiously labour to lay some foundations from which liberty may slowly rise, or acquiesce in the doom of perpetual bondage on ourselves and our children.

But though we no longer dream of making governments, the Confederacy of Kings seem to feel no doubt of their own power to make nations. Yet the only reason why it is impossible to make a government is, because it is impossible to make a nation. A government cannot be made, because its whole spirit and principles arise from the character of the nation. There would be no difficulty in framing a government, if the habits of a people could be changed by a lawgiver ; if he could obliterate their recollections, transfer their attachment and reverence, extinguish their animosities, and correct those sentiments which, being at variance with his opinions of public interest, he calls prejudices. Now this is precisely the power which our statesmen at Vienna have arrogated to themselves. They not only form nations, but they compose them of elements apparently the most irreconcileable. They make one nation of Norway and Sweden : they tried to make another of Prussia and Saxony. They have in the present case forced together Piedmont and Genoa to form a nation, which is to guard the avenues of Italy, and to be one of the main securities of Europe against universal monarchy.

It was not the pretension of the ancient system to form states, to divide territory according to speculations of military convenience, and to unite and dissolve nations better than the course of events had done before. It was owned to be still more difficult to give a new constitution to Europe, than to form a new constitution for a single state. The great statesmen of former times did not speak of their measures as the noble lord did, about the incorporation of Belgium with Holland (against which I say nothing), " as a great improvement in the system of Europe." That is the language only of those who revolutionize that system by a partition like that of Poland, by the establishment of the federation of the Rhine at Paris, or by the creation of new states at Vienna. The ancient principle was to preserve all those states which had been formed by time and nature, which were animated by national spirit, and distinguished by the diversity of character which gave scope to every variety of talent and virtue ; whose character was often preserved, and whose nationality was sometimes created by those very irregularities of frontier and inequalities of strength, of which a shallow policy complained, to preserve all these states, down to the smallest, first by their own national spirit, and secondly, by that mutual jealousy which made every great Power the opponent of the dangerous ambition of every other. It was to preserve nations, living bodies, produced by the hand of nature, not to form artificial dead machines, called states by the words and parchment of a diplomatic act. Under this ancient system, which secured the weak by the jealousy of the strong, provision was made alike for the permanency of civil institutions, the stability of government, the progressive reformation of laws and constitutions ; for combining the general quiet, with the highest activity and energy of the human mind ; for uniting the benefits both of rivalship and of friendship between nations ; for cultivating the moral sentiments of men by the noble spectacle of the long triumph of justice in the security of the defenceless ; and finally, for maintaining uniform civilization by the struggle as well as union of all the moral and intellectual combinations which compose that vast and various mass. It effected these noble purposes, not merely by securing Europe against one master, but against any union or conspiracy of sovereignty, which, as long as it lasts, is in no respect better than the domination of an individual. The object of the new system is to crush the weak by the combination of the strong ;—to subject Europe in the first place to an oligarchy of sovereigns, and ultimately to swallow it up in the gulp of universal monarchy ; where civilization has always perished, with freedom of thought, with controlled power, with national character and spirit, with patriotism and emulation, in a word, with all its characteristic attributes, and with all its guardian principles.

I am content, Sir, that these observations should be thought wholly unreasonable by those new masters of civil wisdom, who tell us, that the whole policy of Europe consists in strengthening the right flank of Prussia, and the left flank of Austria ; who see in that wise and venerable system long the boast and the safeguard of Europe, only the millions of souls to be given to one power, or the thousands of square miles to be given to another ; who consider the frontier of a river as a better protection for a country, than the love of its inhabitants ; and who provide for the safety of their states by wounding the pride and mortifying the patriotic affection of a people, in order to fortify a line of military posts. To such statesmen I will apply the words of the great philosophical orator, who so long vainly laboured to inculcate wisdom in this House : " All this I know well enough will sound wild, and chimerical to the profane herd of those vulgar and mechanical politicians who have no place among us ; a sort of people who think that nothing exists but what is gross and material ; and who, therefore, far from being qualified to be directors of the great movement of empire, are not fit to turn a wheel in the machine. But to men truly initiated and rightly taught, these ruling and master principles, which in the opinion of such men as I have mentioned have no substantial existence, are in truth everything, and all in all." [1] . . .

[1] Mr. Burke's Speech on Conciliation with America. New Parl. History, Vol. 18, p. 535.

CHELTENHAM PRESS, LTD.
SWINDON RD., CHELTENHAM